CHRIST-CENTERED PREACHING

CHRIST-CENTERED PREACHING

REDEEMING THE EXPOSITORY SERMON

BRYAN CHAPELL

Baker Books

A Division of Baker Book House Co
Grand Rapids, Michigan 49516

Published by Baker Books
a division of Baker Book House Company
P.O. Box 6287, Grand Rapids, MI 49516-6287

Sixth printing, January 1999

Printed in the United States of America

For information about academic books, resources for Christian leaders,
and all new releases available from Baker Book House, visit our web
site:

http://www.bakerbooks.com/

Library of Congress Cataloging-in-Publication Data

Chapell, Bryan
    Christ-centered preaching : redeeming the expository sermon : a
practical and theological guide for Bible preaching / by Brian Chapell.
    p. cm.
    Includes bibliographical references and index.
    ISBN 0-8010-2586-9
    1. Preaching. 2. Bible—Homiletical use. I. Title. II. Title: Expository
preaching.
    BV4211.2.C455   1994
    251—dc2093-46468

To my wife, Kathy,
for the love, family, home, and friendship
the Lord has graced us to share

CONTENTS

List of Figures

List of Tables

List of Charts

PREFACE

The two words about which the whole of this work could be wrapped are *authority* and *redemption*.

In our day two opposing forces challenge the effective exposition of the Word of God. The first well-documented foe of the gospel is the erosion of authority. The philosophies of subjectivism have joined hands with the skeptics of transcendent truth to create a cultural climate antagonistic toward any authority. Yet as the apostle Paul saw long ago this release from biblical standards inevitably makes persons slaves to their own passions and victims of each other's selfishness.

Our culture and the church are desperate for dependable truths that address the brokenness of the world this loss of authority accentuates. Not all answers that the church supplies through its preachers herald good news. Some simply have abandoned any hope of finding an authoritative source of truth. Others, sensing the culture's antipathy for anyone sounding as though they have definite, behavior-binding answers, avoid authority. If they retain a desire to heal, such pastors too often settle for a mere repackaging of counseling or management theories in religious-sounding words. By comforting with human answers, due to change with the next wave of best-selling books, such preaching masks rather than heals the pain in the soul.

Expository preaching that explains precisely what the Word of God says about the issues of our day, the concerns of our lives, and the destinies of our souls provides an alternative. Such preaching offers a voice of authority not of human origin, and promises answers not subject to cultural vagaries. As obvious as this solution may seem, its widespread adoption faces large challenges. Over the last two generations the expository sermon has been stigmatized (not always unfairly) as representing a style of preaching that degenerates into dry recitations of biblical trivia or arrogates into dogmatic defenses of doctrinal distinctives removed from ordinary life.

The time has come for redeeming the expository sermon—not only reclaiming its needed voice of authority, but also rescuing expository methods from practitioners unaware (or uncaring) of cultural forces, communication requirements, and biblical instruction that will make it an effective vehicle for the gospel. This book attempts to provide one approach to such a reclamation. Initially the text offers practical instruction that will bind the sermon to Scripture's truths while releasing it from tradition-bound attitudes and communication-naive practices that have needlessly burdened both pulpit and pew.

The second foe to the effective communication of the gospel that this work attempts to confront arises as an often unrecognized side effect of the first. Evangelical preachers reacting to the secularization of both church and culture can mistakenly make moral instruction or societal reform the *primary* focus of their messages. No one can blame these preachers for wanting to challenge the evils of the day. When sin closes in, faithful preachers have a right, a responsibility, and a desire to say, "Stop it!"

However, if these preachers' actual or perceived cure for sin's sickness is human character correction or cultural criticism, they inadvertently present a message contrary to the gospel. The Bible does not tell us how *we* can improve *ourselves* to gain God's acceptance. Fundamentally and pervasively the Scriptures teach the inadequacy of any purely human effort to secure divine approval. We are entirely dependent upon the mercy of God to be what he desires and to do what he requires. Grace rules!

However well intended and biblically rooted may be a sermon's instruction, if the message does not incorporate the motivation and enablement inherent in a proper apprehension of the work of Christ, the preacher proclaims mere Pharisaism. Preaching that is faithful to the whole of Scripture not only establishes God's requirements, but also highlights the redemptive truths that make holiness possible. The task may seem impossible. How can we make all Scripture center on Christ's work when vast portions make no mention of him? The answer lies in learning to see all of God's Word as a unified message of human need and divine provision.

By exploring how the gospel pervades all Scripture this book also establishes theological principles for redeeming the expository sermon from the well-intended but ill-conceived legalism that characterizes too much evangelical preaching. Christ-centered preaching replaces futile harangues for human striving with exhortations to obey God in dependence upon his work. True purity, spiritual confidence, and lasting joy flow from this precise and powerful form of biblical exposition.

ACKNOWLEDGMENTS

I write this book with deep appreciation for those whose contributions to my own thought and life have been significant.

Thanks are especially owed to Dr. Robert G. Rayburn, my homiletics professor, who settled for nothing less than excellence while consistently teaching that God's glory had to be the sole focus of the preaching task, and to Dr. John Sanderson, professor of biblical theology, who opened my eyes to the necessity of Christ-focus in all faithful exposition.

I am greatly indebted to the Rayburn family, especially Mrs. LaVerne Rayburn and her son, Dr. Robert S. Rayburn, for allowing me access to Dr. Robert G. Rayburn's unpublished writings and notes. Being entrusted with sharing some of Dr. Rayburn's insights is a great privilege.

Although the research and thought behind this work have spanned two decades, I have done most of the writing during a sabbatical provided by Covenant Theological Seminary. I want to express my thanks to the board of trustees for granting me this wonderful writing opportunity. Working at an institution governed by godly principles is a blessing for which I am daily thankful.

I am especially grateful to Covenant Seminary President Paul Kooistra, whose encouragement, ministry, and many hours of conversation along our jogging path about the role of grace in preaching have sharpened and strengthened my thought.

I am thankful for the ministry and friendship of the Rev. James Meek, associate dean for academics at Covenant Seminary, whose double duty during my sabbatical has allowed me to pursue this work.

As always, I owe more than words can express to the untiring and joyful service of Mrs. June Dare, whose secretarial skills always make me look better than I have any right to expect.

PART 1

PRINCIPLES FOR EXPOSITORY PREACHING

CONTENTS OF CHAPTER 1

GOALS OF CHAPTER 1

*To communicate how important preaching is
and what is really important in preaching*

1

WORD AND WITNESS

The Nobility of Preaching

English preacher Ian Tait quips that those who study the Bible only to gain more information may believe their minds are expanding when, in fact, only their heads are swelling. Knowledge purely for knowledge's sake "puffeth up" (1 Cor. 8:1). The riches of God's Word are no one's private treasure, and when we share its wealth we participate in its highest purposes. That is why, for more than a quarter-century, Robert G. Rayburn taught seminary students, "Christ is the only King of your studies, but homiletics is the queen."[1] Whether your studies are in a seminary, a Bible college, or a program of personal reading, they will be more rewarding when you realize how each element prepares you to preach with accuracy and authority. Every biblical discipline reaches a pinnacle purpose when we use it not merely to expand our minds but to extend the gospel.

Elevating preaching to such a lofty pedestal can intimidate even the most committed student of Scripture. Probably no conscientious preacher has failed to question whether the task is greater than the servant. When we face real people with eternal souls balanced between heaven and hell, the nobility of preaching awes us even as it underscores our inadequacies. We know our skills are insufficient for an activity with such vast consequences. We recognize our hearts are not pure enough to lead others to holiness. Honest evaluation of our expertise inevitably causes us to conclude that we do not have the eloquence or wisdom that will turn people from death to life. Such a realization can

1. Robert G. Rayburn was the founding president of Covenant Theological Seminary and its primary homiletics professor from 1956–1984. The quotation is from his unpublished class notes.

17

cause young preachers to run from their first preaching assignment and experienced pastors to despair in their pulpits.

THE POWER IN THE WORD

What we need in the face of doubts of personal effectiveness in an age that increasingly questions the validity of preaching[2] is a reminder of God's design for spiritual transformation. Ultimately preaching accomplishes its spiritual purposes not because of the skills of the preacher, but because of the power of the Scripture proclaimed. Preachers will minister with greater zeal, confidence, and freedom when they realize God has taken from their backs the monkey of spiritual manipulation. God is not relying on our craft to accomplish his purposes. God certainly can use eloquence and desires efforts befitting the importance of our subject matter, but his Word itself fulfills his agenda of salvation and sanctification. The human efforts of the greatest preachers are still too weak and sin-tainted to be responsible for others' eternal destinies. For this reason God infuses his Word with spiritual power. The efficacy of the message rather than any virtue in the messenger transforms hearts.

The Power of God Inherent in the Word

Precisely how God's truth converts souls and changes lives we cannot say, but we must sense the dynamics that give us hope in our own preaching. The Bible makes it clear that the Word is not merely powerful; it is without peer. The Word of God

creates: "God said, 'Let there be light,' and there was light" (Gen. 1:3). "For he spoke, and it came to be; he commanded, and it stood firm" (Ps. 33: 9).

controls: "He sends his command to the earth; his word runs swiftly. He spreads the snow like wool and scatters the frost like ashes. He hurls down his hail like pebbles. . . . He sends his word and melts them. . . ." (Ps. 147:15–18).

2. David L. Larsen, *The Anatomy of Preaching: Identifying the Issues in Preaching Today* (Grand Rapids: Baker, 1989), 11–12; Byron Val Johnson, "A Media Selection Model for Use with a Homiletical Taxonomy" (Ph.D. diss., Southern Illinois University at Carbondale, 1982), 215.

persuades: "[L]et the one who has my word speak it faithfully . . ." declares the Lord. "Is not my word like fire," declares the Lord, "and like a hammer that breaks a rock in pieces?" (Jer. 23:28–29).

performs his purposes: "As the rain and the snow come down from heaven and do not return to it without watering the earth, . . . so is my word that goes out from my mouth: It will not return to me empty, but will accomplish what I desire and achieve the purpose for which I sent it" (Isa. 55:10–11).

overrides human motives: While in prison the apostle Paul rejoices that when others preach the Word with "false motives or true" the work of God still moves forward (Phil. 1:18).

Scripture's portrayal of its own potency challenges us always to remember that the Word preached rather than the *preaching* of the Word accomplishes heaven's purposes. Preaching that is true to Scripture converts, convicts, and conforms the spirits of men and women because it presents the instrument of divine compulsion, not because preachers have any transforming power in themselves.

The Power of the Word Manifested in Christ

God fully manifests the dynamic power of his Word in the New Testament where he identifies his Son as the divine *Logos*, or Word (John 1:1). By identifying his Son as his Word, God reveals that his message and his person are inseparable. The Word embodies him. This is not to say that the letters and the paper of a Bible are divine, but that the truths Scripture holds are God's vehicle of his own spiritual activity.

God's Word is powerful because he chooses to be present in it and to operate through it. Through Jesus "all things were made" (John 1:3), and he continues "sustaining all things by his powerful word" (Heb. 1:3). The Word uses his word to carry out all his purposes.

Christ's redemptive power and the power of his Word coalesce in the New Testament with *Logos* (the incarnation of God) and *logos* (the message about God) becoming terms so reflexive as to form a conceptual identity. As the work of creation comes through the spoken Word of God, so the work of new creation (i.e., redemption) comes through the living Word of God. James says, "He [i.e., the Father] chose to give us birth through the word of truth, . . . "(James 1:18). The phrase *word of truth* serves as a pun reflecting the message about salvation and the One who gives the new birth. The same play on words is used by Peter: "For you have been born again, not of perishable seed, but of imperishable, through the living and enduring word of God" (1 Pet. 1:23). In these passages the message about Jesus and Christ himself unify. Both are the "living and enduring [W]ord of God" by which we have been born again.

Thus, it is not merely prosaic to insist that the preacher should serve the text,[3] for if the Word is the mediate presence of Christ, service is due. Paul rightly instructs the young pastor Timothy to be a workman "who correctly handles the word of truth" (2 Tim. 2:15) because the Word of God is "living and active" (Heb. 4:12a). Scriptural truth is not a passive object for our examination and presentation. The Word examines us. "It judges the thoughts and attitudes of the heart" (4:12c). Christ remains active in his Word performing divine tasks that one presenting the Word has no right or ability personally to assume.

These perspectives on the Word of God culminate in the ministry of the apostle Paul. The bookish missionary who was not known for his pulpit expertise nonetheless wrote, "I am not ashamed of the gospel because it is the power of God . . . for everyone who believes" (Rom. 1:16). As students of elementary Greek soon learn, the word for *power* in this verse is *dunamis*, from which we get our English word *dynamite*. The gospel's force lies beyond the power of the preacher. Paul preaches without shame in his delivery skills because the Word he speaks shatters the hardness of the human heart in ways no stage technique can rival.

In some ways the whole process seems ridiculous. To think that eternal destinies will change simply because we voice thoughts from an ancient text more than challenges common sense. When Paul commends the foolishness of preaching—not foolish preaching—he acknowledges the apparent senselessness of trying to transform attitudes, lifestyles, philosophical perspectives, and faith commitments with mere words (see 1 Cor. 1:21). Yet, preaching endures and the gospel spreads because God empowers puny human efforts with the force of his own Word.

Each year I recount for new seminary students a time when the reality of the Word's power struck me with exceptional force. The Lord's work overwhelmed me when I walked into a new members' class of our church. Sitting together on the front row were three young women—all cousins. Though they had promised to come to the class, the reality of their being there still shook me.

In the previous year each of these women had approached our church for help with serious problems. I got acquainted with the first after she

3. Herbert H. Farmer, *The Servant of the Word* (New York: Scribner, 1942), 16–17.

left her husband because of frustration with his alcoholism. As an Easter-only member of our church he had previously expressed little use for "religion," but he came seeking help when she left. He said he was willing to do anything to get her to return. They came together for counseling. He dealt with his drinking. They reunited, and now she wanted to become part of our faith family.

The second cousin also had fled her marriage before she came for help at the first cousin's suggestion. She was the victim of spousal abuse, and had sought solace with another man. Although we reached neither man, our ministry to this woman warmed her heart toward God. Even after her husband turned to other women, she left her lover and submitted her life to God's will.

The last cousin was also married, but she worked as a traveling salesperson and was living with several men as though each were her husband. An accident that injured her nephew brought our church into her life. As she witnessed the care of Christians for the child and for her (despite her initial hostility toward us), she found a love that her sexual encounters had not supplied. Now she, too, came to be a part of the family of God.

The presence of these three cousins in a church membership class was a miracle. How foolish it would be to think that mere words I had said—some consonants and vowels pushed out of the mouth by a little burst of air—could account for their decisions. No amount of human convincing could have turned them from selfish, pleasure-seeking, or self-destructive lifestyles to an eternal commitment to God. Hearts hostile to his Word now wanted fellowship with him.

God plucked three souls from a hellish swirl of family confusion, spousal betrayal, and personal sin. Yet, as unlikely as these events seem, they are readily explained. The Lord used his truth to change their hearts. In the terms of Scripture they "turned to God from idols to serve the living and true God, and to wait for his Son from heaven" not because of any preacher's skills but because of the Word's own power (1 Thess. 1:9–10).

When preachers perceive the power the Word holds, confidence in their calling grows even as pride in their performance withers. We need not fear our ineffectiveness when we speak truths God has empowered to perform his purposes. At the same time, to act as though our talents are responsible for spiritual change is like a messenger claiming credit for ending a war because he delivers the peace documents. The messenger has a noble task to perform, but he will jeopardize his mission and belittle the true victor with claims of personal achievement. Credit, honor, and glory for preaching's effects belong to Christ alone because his Word alone causes spiritual renewal.

THE POWER OF THE WORD APPLIED IN PREACHING

Expository Preaching Presents the Power of the Word

The fact that the power for spiritual change resides in God's Word argues the case for *expository* preaching. Expository preaching attempts to present and apply the truths of a specific biblical passage.[4] Other types of preaching that proclaim biblical truth are certainly valid and valuable, but for the beginning preacher and for a regular congregational diet no preaching type is more important.

Biblical exposition binds the preacher and the people to the only source of true spiritual change. Because hearts are transformed when people are confronted with the Word of God, expository preachers are committed to saying what God says.[5] We are not concerned to convey our opinions, others' philosophies, or speculative meditations. Truths of God proclaimed in such a way that people can see that the concepts derive from Scripture and apply to their lives preoccupy the expository preacher's efforts. Such preaching puts people in immediate contact with the power of the Word.

Expository Preaching Presents the Authority of the Word

Preaching in its essence addresses the perpetual human quest for authority and meaning. Though we live in an age hostile to authority, everyday struggles for significance, security, and acceptance force every individual to ask, "Who has the right to tell me what to do?" This question typically posed as a challenge is really a plea for help. Without an ultimate authority for truth all human striving has no ultimate value and life itself becomes futile. Modern trends in preaching that deny the authority of the Word[6] in the name of intellectual sophistication lead to a despairing subjectivism in which people do what is right in their own eyes—a state whose futility Scripture has already clearly articulated (Judg. 21:21).

---

4. Haddon Robinson, *Biblical Preaching: The Development and Delivery of Expository Messages* (Grand Rapids: Baker, 1980), 20. We will refine the definition later.

5. Sidney Greidanus, *The Modern Preacher and the Ancient Text: Interpreting and Preaching Biblical Literature* (Grand Rapids: Eerdmans, 1988), 15.

6. David Buttrick, *Homiletic: Moves and Structures* (Philadelphia: Fortress, 1987), 408.

The answer to the radical relativism of our culture with its accompanying uncertainties is the Bible's claim of authority. Paul commended the Thessalonian Christians because they accepted his message "not as the word of men, but as it actually is, the word of God, which is at work in you who believe" (1 Thess. 2:13). The claim of Scripture and the premise of expository preaching is that God has spoken. Our task is to communicate what he has committed to Scripture. Such efforts are not blind adherence to fundamentalist dogma but are a commitment to what both faith and reason confirm are the only basis of human hope.

Without the authority of the Word preaching becomes an endless search for topics, therapies, and techniques that will win approval, promote acceptance, advance a cause, or soothe worry. Human reason, social agendas, popular consensus, and personal moral convictions become the resources of preaching that lacks "the historic conviction that what Scripture says, God says."[7] The opinions and emotions that formulate the content of preaching without biblical authority are the same forces that can deny the validity of those concepts in a changed culture, a subsequent generation, or a rebellious heart.

When preachers approach the Bible as God's very Word, questions about what we have a right to say vanish. God can tell his people what they should believe and do, and he has. Scripture obligates preachers to make sure others understand what God says. We have no biblical authority to say anything else. It is true that our expressions are culturally conditioned, but the transcendence of his truth and the divine image-bearing privileges of our nature make it possible for us to receive and communicate his Word.

Only preachers committed to proclaiming what God says have the Bible's imprimatur on their preaching. Thus, expository preaching endeavors to discover and convey the precise meaning of the Word. Scripture rules over what expositors preach because they unfold what it says. *The meaning of the passage is the message of the sermon.* The text governs the preacher. Expository preachers do not expect others to honor their opinions. Such ministers adhere to Scripture's truths and expect their listeners to heed the same.

Expository Preaching Presents the Work of the Spirit

The expectations of expository preachers are themselves based on the truths of the Bible. If no amount of eloquence and oratory can account

---

7. J. I. Packer, *God Speaks to Man: Revelation and the Bible* (Philadelphia: Westminster, 1965), 18.

for spiritual transformation, who alone can change hearts? The Reformers answered, "The Holy Spirit working by and with the Word in our hearts."[8] The Word of God is the sword of the Spirit (Eph. 6:17; cf. Acts 10:44, Eph. 1:13). The extraordinary but normal means by which God transforms lives is his accompanying his Word with the regenerating and convicting power of his Spirit.

When we proclaim the Word we bring the work of the Holy Spirit to bear on others' lives. No truth grants greater encouragement in our preaching and gives us more cause to expect results from our efforts. The work of the Spirit is as inextricably linked to preaching as heat is to the light a bulb emits. When we present the light of God's Word, his Spirit performs God's purposes of warming, melting, and conforming hearts to his will.

The Holy Spirit uses our words, but his work, not ours, affects the hidden recesses of the human will. Paul wrote, "God . . . made his light shine in our hearts to give us the knowledge of the glory of God in the face of Christ. But we have this knowledge in jars of clay to show that this all-surpassing power is from God and not from us" (2 Cor. 4:6–7). The glory of preaching is that God accomplishes his will through it, but we are always humbled and occasionally comforted with the knowledge that he works beyond our human limitations.

These truths challenge all preachers to approach their task with a deep sense of dependence on the Spirit of God. Effective public ministry requires devoted private prayer. We should not expect our words to acquaint others with the power of the Spirit if we have not met with him. Faithful preachers plead for God to work as well as proclaim his Word. Success in the pulpit can be the force that leads a preacher from prayerful dependence on the Spirit. Congregational accolades for pulpit excellence may tempt one to put too much confidence in personal gifts, acquired skills, or a particular method of preaching. Succumbing to such a temptation is evidenced not so much by a change in belief as it is by a change in practice. Neglect of prayer signals serious deficiencies in a ministry even if other signs of success have not diminished. We must always remember that popular acclaim is not necessarily the same as spiritual effectiveness.

The spiritual dimensions of preaching undercut much of what you may be tempted to believe about this book: that is, if you learn to speak well enough you can be a great preacher. Not true! Please do not let the necessary emphases of this book, the comments of others, or the desires

8. *Westminster Confession of Faith*, 1.5.

of your own heart mislead you. Great gifts do not necessarily make for great preaching. The technical excellence of a message may rest on your skills, but the spiritual efficacy of your message resides with God.

THE EFFECTIVENESS OF TESTIMONY

Faith in the working of God's Word and Spirit does not mean you are without responsibility. Early-American pastor John Shaw once preached at an ordination sermon,

> It's true as one observes, God can work by what means He will; by a scandalous, domineering, self-seeking preacher, but it is not His usual way. Foxes and wolves are not nature's instrument to generate sheep. Whoever knew much good done to souls by any pastors but such as preached and lived in the power of love, working by a clear, convincing light, and both managed by a holy, lively seriousness? You must bring fire to kindle fire.[9]

There is no need to presume upon the goodness of God. Although the power inherent in the Word can work past our weaknesses, there is no reason intentionally to put hurdles in its path. Good preaching in one sense involves getting out of the way so that the Word can do its work. Shaw's comments remind us what clearing the path usually means: preaching and living in such a way as to make the Word plain and credible.

CLASSICAL DISTINCTIONS

Although they certainly are not inspired, Aristotle's classic rhetorical distinctions can help preachers consider their basic responsibilities and the attention each deserves. For while the apostle Paul taught us of the inherent efficacy of the Word, he also related his personal resolve to put no "stumbling block" to the gospel in anyone's path (2 Cor. 6:3).

In classical rhetoric three elements compose every persuasive message:

Logos—the verbal content of the message including its craft and logic.

9. John Shaw, "The Character of a Pastor According to God's Heart," sermon reprint (Ligonier, Penn.: Soli Deo Gloria, 1992), 3–4.

Pathos—the emotive features of a message including the passion, fervor, and feeling that the speaker conveys and the listeners experience.

Ethos—the perceived character of the speaker; determined most significantly by the concern expressed for the listeners' welfare. Aristotle believed ethos was the most powerful component of persuasion.

Listeners automatically evaluate each of these features in a message in order to weigh the truths that the preacher presents. This realization advises preachers who want to create clear access to the Word that changes hearts to strive to make each aspect of their message a door and not a barrier.

Paul reflects the importance of each of these components in his first letter to the Thessalonians (see fig. 1.1). Although his terms are not Aristotle's they echo features of the classic rhetor's categories and remind us that craft is not enough to make a message powerful if one's heart and character do not validate its truths. Paul makes it clear that though the Holy Spirit forges the path of the gospel, listeners advance to confrontation with the Word through doors the preacher opens with the message. Significantly, Paul cites his own life as affecting the reception of the message, thus giving scriptural credence to the notion that ethos is a powerful force in the ordinary process of spiritual persuasion.

FIGURE 1.1

Components of a Gospel Message

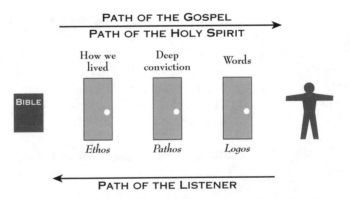

"Our gospel came to you not simply with **words** [*Logos*], but also **with power and with deep conviction** [*Pathos*]. You **know how we lived** [*Ethos*] among you for your sake" (1 Thess. 1:5).

Paul cites his conduct and his compassion not only as evidences of his "deep conviction," but also as integral sources of his message's "power." Although this book of homiletical method necessarily focuses on the elements of logos and pathos in preaching, the Bible's own emphases remind us that pastoral character remains the foundation of ministry. Preaching's glory may be eloquence but its heartbeat is faithfulness.

Phillips Brooks' oft-cited observation that preaching is "truth poured through personality" reflects biblical principle as well as common sense. Our fathers taught, "Your actions speak so loudly I can't hear what you say." Today's young people tell us, "Don't talk the talk, if you don't walk the walk." Each maxim merely reflects a higher wisdom that urges Christian leaders to "conduct [themselves] in a manner worthy of the gospel" (cf. Phil. 1:27). Our preaching should reflect the uniqueness of our personalities, but our persons should reflect Christ-likeness in order for his message to spread unhindered.

SCRIPTURAL CORROBORATION

There is no scarcity of Scriptures confirming the importance of ethos for the most effective proclamation. Beginning here with the pre-eminent passages on pastoral theology, and with emphasis added, are texts that link the quality of preaching to the quality of the preacher's character and conduct:

1 Thessalonians 2:3–8 and 11–12

For the appeal we make does not spring from error or impure motives, nor are we trying to trick you. On the contrary, we speak as men approved by God to be entrusted with the gospel. We are not trying to please men but God, who tests our hearts. You know we never used flattery, nor did we put on a mask to cover up greed —God is our witness. We were not looking for praise from men, not from you or anyone else.

As apostles of Christ we could have been a burden to you, but we were gentle among you, like a mother caring for her little children. We loved you so much that *we were delighted to share with you not only the gospel of God but our lives as well*, because you had become so dear to us.

For you know that we dealt with each of you as a father deals with his own children, encouraging, comforting and urging you to live lives worthy of God, who calls you into his kingdom and glory.

2 Timothy 2:15–16 and 22–24

Do your best to present yourself to God as *one approved, a workman who does not need to be ashamed* and who correctly handles the word of truth. Avoid godless chatter, because those who indulge in it will become more and more ungodly.

Flee the evil desires of youth, and pursue righteousness, faith, love and peace, along with those who call on the Lord out of a pure heart. Don't have anything to do with foolish and stupid arguments, because you know they produce quarrels. And the Lord's servant must not quarrel; instead, he must be kind to everyone, able to teach, not resentful.

Titus 2:7–8

In everything set them an *example* by doing what is good. In your teaching show integrity, seriousness and soundness of speech that cannot be condemned, ...

2 Corinthians 6:3–4

We put no stumbling block in anyone's path, so that our ministry will not be discredited. Rather, as servants of God *we commend ourselves in every way*: . . .

James 1:26–27

If anyone considers himself religious and yet does not keep a tight rein on his tongue, he deceives himself and his religion is worthless. *Religion that God our Father accepts* as pure and faultless is this: to look after orphans and widows in their distress and to keep oneself from being polluted by the world.

James 3:13

Who is wise and understanding among you? *Let him show it* by his good life, by deeds done in the humility that comes from wisdom.

ETHOS IMPLICATIONS

Guard Your Character

The influence of the preacher's testimony on the acceptance of the sermon requires us to put our lives under the rule of Scripture. With unblinking candor John Wesley once explained to a struggling protégé why his ministry lacked power: "Your temper is uneven; you lack love for your neighbors. You grow angry too easily; your tongue is too sharp—thus, the people will not hear you."[10] Wesley's honesty reflects Scripture's admonition and challenges each of us to guard our character if we desire effectiveness with the Word.

True character cannot be hidden, although it can be temporarily masked. Character oozes out of us in our messages. Just as people reveal themselves to us in conversation by their words and mannerisms, we constantly reveal ourselves to others in our preaching. Over time our word choices, topics, examples, and tone unveil our hearts regardless of how well we think we have cordoned off deeper truths from public display. The inside is always on view. People sense more than they can prove by the way we present ourselves in the most inadvertent ways.

With the insight of many years of preaching experience Haddon Robinson summarizes,

> As much as we might wish it otherwise, the preacher cannot be separated from the message. Who has not heard some devout brother pray in anticipation of a sermon, "Hide our pastor behind the cross so that we may see not him but Jesus only." We commend the spirit of such a prayer . . . Yet no place exists where a preacher may hide. Even a large pulpit cannot conceal him from view. . . . The man affects his message. He may be mouthing a scriptural idea yet remain as impersonal as a telephone recording, as superficial as a radio commercial, or as manipulative as a "con" man. The audience does not hear a sermon, they hear a man.[11]

No truth more loudly calls for pastoral holiness than the linkage of a preacher's character and the sermon's reception. I must recognize that if I were to return to churches I have pastored it is unlikely that people will remember many specifics I said. They may remember a particularly vivid illustration, the way a verse had a telling effect at some crisis moment in their lives, or the impression a particular message left on their minds. Yet, not one person will remember a dozen words of the thousands I have spoken through the years. The people will not remember what I said, they will remember *me* and whether my life gave credence to the message of Scripture.

So much does effective ministry rely upon the character of the minister that theologian John Sanderson advised students to play softball with pastoral candidates when their churches were interviewing new preachers. "Then on a close play at second base," would say Sanderson

10. As quoted in James L. Golden, Goodwin F. Berquist, and William Coleman, *The Rhetoric of Western Thought*, 3d ed. (Dubuque: Kendall-Hunt, 1978), 297.
11. Robinson, *Biblical Preaching*, 24.

with his tongue *mostly* in cheek, "call him out when he was really safe. Then, see what happens!"

Of course no one reflects Christ's character as purely as he desires. That is why God has not made the effects of his Word dependent on our actions. But as the eighteenth-century minister George Campbell said, "When our practice conforms to our theory, our effectiveness trebles."

Perhaps most of us have experienced the influence of pastoral character on sermons when we have visited a church at some friends' request to hear their preacher's "marvelous messages," but have heard mediocrity instead. Our friends' love and trust of their pastor generates their regard for the sermon and obscures its weaknesses. The character and compassion of the minister more determine the quality of the message heard than the characteristics of the message preached.

Love Grace

Emphasis upon the character of the preacher is futile and errant without underscoring the grace that conforms one's character and message to God's will. Human effort does not produce holiness. Selfless righteousness and sacrificial love are never self-induced. Attempts to conform our character to God's requirements by our actions are as arrogant as efforts to save souls by our talents. Powerful preachers must become well-acquainted with the grace their character requires.

No matter how great your skill you are unlikely to lead others closer to God if your heart does not reflect the continuing work of the Savior in your life. A grace-focused ministry recognizes the repentance our prayers must consistently express, confesses the divine aid that grants us the strength of our resolutions, obeys God in gratitude for the forgiveness Christ supplies, expresses the humility appropriate for a fellow sinner, exudes the joy of salvation by faith alone, and reflects the Love that claims our own souls and accepts our service without any merit of our own. Preaching without a grace focus concentrates on means of earning divine acceptance, proofs of personal righteousness, and contrasts with those less holy than we.

The necessity of grace in balanced preaching inevitably points both preacher and parishioner to the work of Christ as the only proper center of our sermons. Christ-centered preaching is not merely evangelistic, nor confined to a few gospel accounts. It perceives the whole of Scripture as revelatory of God's redemptive plan and preaches every passage within this context—a pattern Jesus himself introduced to us (Luke 24:27). Much more will be said about this later. What is critical at this point as we begin to consider the structural components of a sermon is to understand that the Bible requires us to construct our messages in such a way as to reveal the grace that is the ultimate focus of every text, the ultimate enablement for every instruction, and the only source of true holiness.

Without understanding our daily dependence upon grace we have little hope of reflecting the character that endorses the integrity of our messages. Discovering the redemptive context of every text allows us to use the whole Bible to discern the grace we need to preach and live so as to lead others to closer fellowship with our Lord. Joseph Ruggles Wilson, a nineteenth-century Presbyterian minister and the father of Woodrow Wilson, advised, "Become what you preach and then preach Christ in you."[12] His words remind us that the sanctifying Redeemer who conforms us to himself to endorse his message cannot be neglected in our sermons. Word and witness are inextricably linked in preaching worthy of Christ's gospel.

Without a redemptive focus we may believe we have exegeted Scripture when we have simply translated its parts and parsed its pieces without any reference to the role they have in God's eternal plan. John Calvin said, "God has ordained his Word as the instrument by which Jesus Christ, with all His graces, is dispensed to us."[13] No such process occurs when passages of the Word are ripped from their redemptive context as mere moral examples and behavioral guidelines. Grace keeps our character true to God and our messages true to Scripture. Reliance on this grace results in sermons empowered by God for he alone is responsible for the holiness and truth that fuel preaching's spiritual force.

Be a Great Preacher

Consciousness of God's enablement should encourage all preachers (including beginning preachers) to throw themselves wholeheartedly into their calling. Although the degree of homiletical skill will vary, God promises to perform his purposes through all who faithfully proclaim his truth. Even if your words barely crawl over the edge of the pulpit, love of God's Word, will, and people ensures an effective spiritual ministry. You may never hear the accolades of the world or pastor a church of thousands, but a life of godliness combined with clear expla-

---

12. Joseph Ruggles Wilson, "In What Sense Are Preachers to Preach Themselves," *Southern Presbyterian Review* 25 (1874): 360.

13. As quoted in Larsen, *The Anatomy of Preaching*. Compare John Calvin's *Institutes of the Christian Religion*, 2.9.1; 4.1.6.

nations of Scripture's saving and sanctifying graces engages the power of the Spirit for the glory of God.

If your goal is Christ's honor you *can* be a great preacher through faithfulness to him and his message. Paul offers this same encouragement to Timothy with promises that yet apply to you:

> Don't let anyone look down on you because you are young, but set an example for the believers in speech, in life, in love, in faith and in purity. Until I come, devote yourself to the public reading of Scripture, to preaching and to teaching.
>
> Be diligent in these matters; give yourself wholly to them, so that everyone may see your progress. Watch your life and doctrine closely. Persevere in them, because if you do, you will save both yourself and your hearers. [1 Tim. 4:12–13, 15–16]

QUESTIONS FOR REVIEW AND DISCUSSION

1. Why are expository preachers committed to making *the meaning of the passage the message of the sermon*?

2. Who or what alone has power to change hearts eternally?

3. What are *logos, pathos, and ethos*? Which most affects the persuasiveness of a message?

4. Why should every sermon have a redemptive focus?

5. On what does great preaching most depend?

EXERCISES

1. Locate and comment on biblical passages that confirm the inherent power of the Word.

2. Locate and comment on biblical passages that link the character of the messenger to the effects of the message.

CONTENTS OF CHAPTER 2

GOAL OF CHAPTER 2

*To identify the commitments a preacher assumes
in developing a well-constructed sermon*

2

OBLIGATIONS OF
THE SERMON

TRUTH IS NOT A SERMON

Why would a message organized around the following statements probably not go in the annals of preaching's greatest sermons?

1. The walls of Babylon were as much as 350 feet high and 80 feet wide.
2. The Gnostic heresy at Colosse contained elements of extreme hedonism and asceticism.
3. The Greek word for the "emptying" concept of Philippians 2:7 is *kenosis*.

The statements are clear, true, and biblical. Why do they not form a sermon?

First, the statements lack unity. No obvious thread holds these statements together. Without a unifying theme listeners simply have no means to grasp a sermon's many thoughts.

Second, the statements seem to have no purpose. They are simply disparate facts pried from the biblical moorings that communicate their cause and import. Without a clear purpose in view listeners have no reason to listen to a sermon.

Finally, the statements beacon no application. They have no apparent relevance to each other or to the lives of those addressed. Without application people have no incentive to heed a message. Why should they waste time giving attention to something that has nothing to do with them?

Statements of truth, even biblical truth, do not automatically make a message for the pulpit. Well-constructed sermons require unity, purpose, and application.

UNITY

Key concept: How many things is a sermon about? One!

Sermons of any significant length contain many theological concepts, illustrative materials, and corroborative facts. These many components, however, should not imply that a sermon is about many things. Each feature of a well-wrought message reflects, refines, and/or develops one major idea. This major idea, or theme, glues the message together and makes its features stick in the listener's mind. All the features of the entire sermon should support the concept that unifies the whole.

THE REASONS FOR UNITY

Constructing a message so that all its features support a main idea requires discipline. Boiling out extraneous thoughts and crystallizing ideas so that the entire message functions as a unit have tested many a preacher. Some yield to the pressure and dispense their ideas with the sequence, emphasis, and structure that most readily comes to mind. Others argue that they cannot say all they want about a text if they must relate particulars to a whole. So why strive for unity?

Speakers Need Focus

The words of an old hymn too often apply to our sermons as well as to our spiritual lives. We are "prone to wander." Preaching without the discipline of unity typically results in the preacher simply roaming from one stray thought to another. Such messages rarely communicate well. Listeners quickly tire of chasing ideas and anecdotes across the theological landscape in efforts to discover where their pastor is going.

We need unity in order to funnel the infinite exegetical possibilities into a manageable message. Quite literally hundreds if not thousands of pages of commentary and grammatical analysis could be written on any biblical text (and in many cases have been). The depth of the Word provides us with the inspiration for a lifetime of sermons even as it challenges us to find some means to keep our listeners and ourselves from drowning in its intricacies. Unity may seem binding at first but it actually frees preachers from entrapment in the labyrinth of language and explanation possibilities.

Listeners Need Focus

Sermons are for listeners, not readers. The degree of detail and excursus acceptable for an essay or a novel cannot be handled in an aural environment by listeners who cannot turn back a page, reread a paragraph, slow down, or ask the speaker to pause while they catch up. Listeners simply have less inclination and opportunity to decipher a sermon than readers do a textbook or a commentary. If the parts of a sermon do not obviously relate to a clear theme that gives the message's pieces form and purpose, then listeners are unlikely to focus their attention on the contents for long.

All good communication requires a theme. If the preacher does not provide a unifying concept for the message, listeners will. They instinctively will supply some thought peg on which to hang the preacher's ideas knowing that if they do not they will retain nothing. In the process of determining what thought peg to supply, the listeners can drop thoughts the preacher has already distributed. Neither is there any guarantee that the pegs listeners choose will support all the additional ideas the preacher wants to hang in their consciousness. When a wife asks her husband at Sunday lunch what the morning sermon was about, the answer *prayer* is too generic to have real-life consequence. As a result the response to the message will probably be more ho-hum than the preacher or the parishioner desired.

Listeners more readily grasp ideas that have been formed and pulled together. It is easier to catch a baseball than a handful of sand even if the two weigh about the same. The fact that a preacher's words are weighty does not mean listeners will respond to them when even the speaker has not managed to fit the ideas together.

The Nature of Unity

As we have already discovered, in expository preaching the meaning of the passage provides the theme of the message. This means that the unifying concept of the sermon should come from the text itself. Haddon Robinson asks us to determine the "Big Idea" of our messages by asking first, "What is the author [of the passage] talking about?" and then "What is he saying about what he is talking about?"[1] These are the foundation questions of an expository sermon. They force us to examine the various features of the passage and discern how the biblical

---

1. Haddon Robinson, *Biblical Preaching: The Development and Delivery of Expository Messages* (Grand Rapids: Baker, 1980), 41–44.

writer employs them for his own purpose(s).[2] Only in this way will we know how to unify the particulars of the text in accord with the perspectives and the priorities of the author.

In expository preaching unity occurs when the elements of a passage are demonstrated to support a single major idea that serves as the theme of the sermon. We want our theme to be the Bible's theme. This does not mean that only the *major* theme of a passage can serve as the theme of an expository sermon. A sermon on a minor theme of a passage may also be expository so long as the preacher demonstrates that there is sufficient exegetical material in the passage to support the theme presented *and* that this theme still accurately reflects the passage's truth in context.

The theme, purpose, or focus of the biblical writer must capture our messages and put them into its service for God's truth to rule our efforts. Our commitment to the sole efficacy of Scripture means that we want to be sure we are saying what the Bible says. Yet just as the features of a text develop its subject, so the features of our sermons must all contribute to its theme. Rarely do biblical writers simply dish out a smorgasbord of unrelated ideas (and when they do there is usually a larger purpose that the discerning interpreter can uncover). The components of a passage all contribute to the author's point. This is the way our sermons should function. Although many ideas and features compose a sermon, they should all contribute to one theme. A sermon is about one thing.

THE PROCESS OF UNITY

Once the preacher determines the importance of unity, the next question that arises is, How do I get it? The process is not complicated; only frequently ignored because it does take some work. But, the work will save the preacher much additional labor and his listeners much confusion. Follow these simple steps to obtain unity for your sermons:

I. Read and digest the passage to determine:
   A. The main idea the writer communicates through the text's features (i.e., discern what large concept the details support or develop); or,
   B. An idea in the passage that has sufficient material in the text to develop the main subject of a message.

2. Jay Adams, *Preaching with Purpose: A Comprehensive Textbook on Biblical Preaching* (Grand Rapids: Baker, 1982), 31–33.

II. Melt down this idea that the passage's features support and/or develop into one concise statement.

You will know you have unity when you can demonstrate that the elements of the passage support the idea that you will make into the theme of your message *and* you can state that idea in a form simple enough to pass the "3 A.M. Test."

The 3 A.M. Test requires you to imagine a spouse, a parent, or a parishioner awakening you from your deepest slumber with this simple question: "What's the sermon about today, Pastor?" If you cannot give a crisp answer, you know the sermon is probably half-baked. Thoughts you cannot gather at 3 A.M. are not likely to be caught by others at 11 A.M.

At 3 A.M. you know this will not work as a theme:

> When the sinful nation of Israel went into exile its messianic hope and vision were mistakenly and faithlessly diminished because pre-Ezran and pre-Nehemiahic proofs of God's sovereign plan, purpose, and intentions for his people were obscured in Babylonian circumstances of incarceration and oppression that would not be relieved until the Persian emancipation and further covenantal revelations in advancing redemptive history.

This will:

> God remains faithful to faithless people.

When we can crystallize the thought of a passage the focus, organization, and application of the message become clear for the preacher and the listener. Preachers who develop concise and accurate theme statements can speak with much greater detail without losing a congregation in a fog of specifics that has no compass concept.

THE GOAL OF UNITY

Unity strives for the communication of biblical truth, not merely for its discovery or statement. Unity organizes a message for a single thrust rather than a pouring out of disconnected thoughts. One sermon cannot be about the source of Samson's strength, how to determine God's will, and the proper mode of baptism. Seminarians often stumble in their early preaching attempts when they try to load everything they are learning into a single sermon. More experienced preachers recognize that they have this week, and the next, and the next to communicate

God's truths. Better for this day is one thought that can be held than a dozen that will slip from grasp.

With unity a sermon has the ability to focus on a subject in depth. The Scriptures fragment without unity and as a result their transforming force splinters. Preachers are particularly susceptible to following tangential thoughts and straying down so-called rabbit trails of incidental facts within the main points of a message because the outlines of our sermons are frequently more organized than are their developmental features.[3] Even subordinate ideas should contribute to the overall theme since the main points they support form the message's singular thrust.

A well-constructed message may have three points (or more, or less) but it is not about three things. A sermon whose main points allege (1) God is loving, (2) God is just, and (3) God is sovereign is not ready to be preached until the preacher determines the sermon's subject is not these three things but rather "The Nature of God." The single idea will hold the rest and, by illuminating their purpose, will deepen their impact.

A bearded maxim reminds us, "The main thing is to keep the main thing the main thing." The line is corny, but preachers whose messages make the greatest impact have taken it to heart.

PURPOSE

Key concept: The Fallen Condition Focus (FCF)

CONSIDERING THE FCF

Determining a sermon's subject remains only half-done when the preacher has discerned what the biblical writer was saying. We do not fully understand the subject until we have also determined its reason or cause. Consideration of a message's theme ultimately forces us to ask, "Why are these concerns addressed? What caused this account, these facts, or the recording of these ideas? What was the intent of the author? For what purpose did the Holy Spirit include these words in Scripture?"

Until we have determined a passage's purpose, we should not think we are ready to preach its truths. Yet, as obvious as this advice is, it is frequently neglected. Preachers often think that they are ready to preach

---

3. We will consider how to organize main points and subpoints in subsequent chapters.

when they see a subject in a passage, though they have not yet determined the text's purpose. For example, simply recognizing that a passage has features that support the doctrine of justification by faith alone does not adequately prepare a pastor to preach. A sermon is not just a systematics lesson. Why did the biblical writer bring up the subject of justification at this point? What were the struggles, concerns, or frailties of the persons to whom the text was originally addressed? Were the people claiming salvation based on their accomplishments, were they doubting the sufficiency of grace, or were they afraid of God's rejection because of some sin? We must determine the purpose of a passage before we really know the subject of our sermon.[4]

We do not have to guess that there is a purpose for the text. The Bible assures us there is a reason for every passage it contains, and it clearly tells us the basic nature of this purpose. The apostle Paul writes, "All Scripture is God-breathed and is useful for teaching, rebuking, correcting and training in righteousness, so that the man of God may be thoroughly equipped for every good work" (2 Tim. 3:16–17). Paul indicates that God intends for his Word to "complete" us.[5] That is why the translators of the King James Version interpreted verse 17 of the passage to read, "that the man of God may be *perfect*." God intends for every portion of his Word (i.e., "all Scripture") to make us more like himself.[6]

Since God designed the Bible to complete us, its contents necessarily indicate that in some sense we are incomplete. Our lack of wholeness is a consequence of the fallen condition in which we live. Aspects of this fallenness that are reflected in our own sinfulness and in our world's brokenness prompt Scripture's instruction and construction. Paul writes, "Everything that was written in the past was written to teach us, so that through endurance and the encouragement of the Scriptures, we might have hope" (Rom. 15:4). The corrupted state of our world and our being cry for God's aid. He responds with his Word, focusing on some facet of our need in every portion. Our hope resides in the assurance that all Scripture has a Fallen Condition Focus (FCF). God refuses to leave his

---

4. Adams, *Preaching with Purpose*, 27.
5. See the Greek term *artios* in verse 17.
6. Some exegetes understand the "man of God" in 2 Timothy 3:16 to refer to the Christian minister, in which case the "work" for which the Word equips refers to *ministry* rather than the *sanctification* of believers. This interpretation does *not* undermine the conclusion that God intends "all Scripture" to "complete" believers, since the minister's duties of "teaching, rebuking, correcting and training in righteousness" from "all Scripture" will convey God's perspective on the hearers' inherent need of the scope of biblical truth.

frail and sinful children without guide or defense in a world antagonistic to their spiritual wellbeing. No text was written merely for those long ago; God intends for each Scripture to give us the "endurance and the encouragement" that we need today. *The FCF is the mutual human condition that contemporary believers share with those to or for whom the text was written that requires the grace of the passage.*

Because an FCF beacons behind all Scripture, informed preaching strives to unveil this purpose for each passage. Obviously there may be more than one purpose for a text, but a sermon's unity requires the preacher to be selective and ordinarily concentrate on the Scripture portion's main purpose. The FCF determines the real subject of the message since it is the real purpose for the passage.[7] Ultimately, the one thing the sermon is about is how the text says today's Christians are to deal with the FCF. Various subdivisions and dimensions of the FCF may be developed as the sermon unfolds, but the main theme should remain clear. This agenda makes sense when we remember that the text's contents are God's response to an aspect of our fallenness. The FCF sets the tone, determines the approach, and organizes the information in the sermon.

DETERMINING THE FCF

Proper understanding of a passage and formation of a sermon require a clear FCF. Without determining an FCF of the text we do not really know what the Scripture is about even if we know many true facts about the passage.[8] The FCF reveals the Spirit's own purpose for the passage, and we should not presume to preach unless we have identified his will for his own Word. We must ask, "What is an FCF that required the writing of this text?" before we can accurately expound its meaning. The FCF enables us properly to interpret the passage, communicate its contents, and gives the congregation the Holy Spirit's own reason for listening.

The more specific the statement of the FCF early in the sermon, the more powerful and poignant will be the message. An FCF of "Not Being Faithful to God" is not nearly so riveting as "How Can I Maintain My Integrity When My Boss Has None?" Generic statements of the FCF give the preacher little guidance for the organization of the sermon, and the congregation little reason for listening. Specificity tends to breed

7. Sidney Greidanus, *The Modern Preacher and the Ancient Text: Interpreting and Preaching Biblical Literature* (Grand Rapids: Eerdmans, 1988), 128–29.
8. Ibid., 173.

interest and power by demonstrating that the Scriptures speak to real concerns.

Specific sins are frequently the FCF of a passage, but a sin does not always have to be the FCF of a sermon. Grief, illness, longing for the Lord's return, the need to know how to share the gospel, and the desire to be a better parent are not sins, but they are needs that our fallen condition imposes and that the Scriptures address. Just as greed, rebellion, lust, irresponsibility, poor stewardship, and pride are proper subjects of a sermon, so also are the desire to raise godly children, determining God's will, and understanding one's gifts. An FCF need not be something for which we are culpable. It simply needs to be an aspect of the human condition that requires the instruction, admonition, and/or comfort of Scripture.

The personality of the preacher, the circumstances of the congregation, and the emphases of a particular sermon can cause the statement of the FCF to vary greatly. A passage whose central focus is trusting in God's providence may equally well address the need to lean on God in hard times, the responsibility to teach others about God's abiding care, or the sin of doubting God's provision. There is not one proper way of formulating a passage's FCF for statement in a sermon. This is why preachers can preach remarkably different sermons on the same passage without any of their sermons being any less faithful to the text. A preacher must be able to demonstrate that the text addresses the FCF of the message, not that this sermon's FCF is the only one possible for this text.

Since the FCF can vary greatly from text to text, and can vary in sermons preached on the same text, preachers need to make sure the purpose of their sermons remains a purpose of the passage. Your FCF will remain faithful to the text and identify powerful purposes for your sermon if you ask three questions:

1. What does the text say?
2. What concern(s) did the text address (in its context)?
3. What do listeners share in common with those to (or about) whom it was written or the one by whom it was written?

By identifying our listeners' mutual condition with the biblical writer, subject, and/or audience we determine why the text was written, not just for biblical times, but also for our time. We should realize, however, that the Holy Spirit does not introduce an FCF simply to inform us of a problem. Paul told Timothy that God inspires all Scripture to equip us for his work (see 2 Tim. 3:16–17). God expects us to act on the problems that his Spirit reveals.

APPLICATION

Key concept: The "So what?!" of preaching.

No passage relates neutral commentary on our fallenness. No text communicates facts for information alone. The Bible itself tells us that its pages instruct, reprove, and correct. God expects scriptural truths to transform his people. Faithful preaching does the same. The preacher who identifies a passage's FCF for his congregation automatically gears them to consider the Bible's solutions and instructions for contemporary life. Therefore, biblical preaching that brings an FCF to the surface also recognizes the need for application.

Memorable in my own homiletics training was the air force colonel turned seminary professor who challenged students, no matter where they preached in future years, to imagine him sitting at the back of the sanctuary. With a benign scowl the professor growled, "In your mind's eye look at me whenever you have said your concluding word. My arms are folded, my face holds a frown, and this question hangs on my lips: 'So what? What do you want me to do?' If you cannot answer, you have not preached."

People have a right to ask, "Why did you tell me that? What am I supposed to do with that information? All right, I understand what you think—so what?" The healthiest preaching does not assume listeners will automatically see how to apply God's truths to their lives; it supplies the application people need.[9] If even the preacher cannot tell (or has not bothered to determine) how the sermon's truths relate to life, then people not only are unlikely to make the connection, but also will wonder why they bothered to listen.

THE NEED OF APPLICATION

The Bible's instruction and pattern indicate the importance of application in preaching. When Paul tells Titus, "You must teach what is in accord with sound doctrine" (Tit. 2:1), the Bible students of that day probably echoed the chorus of enthusiastic "Amens" today's seminarians voice at such a statement. But Paul did not by this direction mean

9. See chapter 8 for a full discussion of application in preaching.

that Titus was simply to teach theological propositions. In the next sentence the apostle begins to unfold what such "sound doctrine" involves:

> Teach the older men to be temperate, worthy of respect, self-controlled, and sound in faith, in love and in endurance.

> Likewise, teach the older women to be reverent in the way they live, not to be slanderers or addicted to much wine, but to teach what is good. Then they can train the younger women to love their husbands and children, to be self-controlled and pure, to be busy at home, to be kind, and to be subject to their husbands, so that no one will malign the word of God. Similarly, encourage the young men to be self-controlled. [Tit. 2:2–6]

Paul expects Titus' "doctrine" to give the people of his congregation specific guidance for their everyday lives. Such instruction does not merely characterize this one passage; it reflects the pattern of Paul's epistles. The apostle typically begins each letter with a greeting, moves to doctrinal instruction, and then applies the doctrine to a variety of circumstances. Paul refuses to leave biblical truth in the stratosphere of theological abstraction. He earths his message in the concerns of the people he addresses.[10] Our preaching has no higher purpose.

Biblical preaching moves from doctrinal exposition to life instruction. Such preaching exhorts as well as expounds because it recognizes that Scripture's own goal is not merely to share information about God but is to conform his people to the likeness of Jesus Christ. Preaching without application may serve the mind, but preaching with application requires service to Christ. Application makes Jesus the center of a sermon's exhortation as well as the focus of its explanation.

Clear articulation of an FCF drives a message's application and insures the Christ-centeredness of the sermon. The FCF marshals the sermon's features toward a specific purpose and therefore helps the preacher see how to apply the information in the text. At the same time the fact that the message is focused on an aspect of our fallenness precludes simplistic, human-centered solutions. If we could fix the problem with our own efforts in our own strength then we would not be truly fallen. Application that addresses an FCF necessarily directs people to the presence and power of the Savior as they seek to serve him.

Early statements of the FCF in the sermon may open the door to application in a number of ways. The preacher may open a spiritual or an

---

10. John R. W. Stott, *Between Two Worlds: The Art of Preaching in the Twentieth Century* (1982; reprint, Grand Rapids: Eerdmans, 1988), 140.

emotional wound in order to provide biblical healing; identify a grief in order to offer God's comfort; demonstrate a danger in order to warrant a scriptural command; or condemn a sin in order to offer cleansing to a sinner. In each case, the statement of the FCF creates a listener's longing for the Word by identifying the biblical needs that the passage addresses.[11] The surfacing of such needs compels the preacher to "do something" about them. This compulsion becomes the spiritual imperative that leads the preacher to discern the text's answers and instructions. When these crystallize, applications that are true to the text's purpose, focus, and context naturally develop.

CONSEQUENCES OF NONAPPLICATION

However well-selected is the meat of a sermon, the message remains precooked without thoughtful, true-to-the-text application. This rare meat is not at all rare in evangelical preaching, as Walter Liefeld attests:

> In earlier years (I hope no longer) I often did exegesis in the pulpit, in large measure because I was conscious of the deep and wide-spread hunger for teaching from God's Word. I finally realized that one can teach, but fail to feed or inspire. I think (and again hope) that my sermons today are no less informative but much more helpful.
>
> Expository preaching is not simply a running commentary. By this I mean a loosely connected string of thoughts, occasionally tied to the passage, which lacks homiletical structure or appropriate application. . . .
>
> Expository preaching is not a captioned survey of a passage. By this I mean the typical: "1. Saul's Contention, 2. Saul's Conversion, 3. Saul's Commission." (Acts 9: 1-19). In my own circles I think I have heard more sermons of this type than any other. They sound very biblical because they are based on a passage of Scripture. But their basic failure is that they tend to be descriptive rather than pastoral. They lack a clear goal or practical application. The congregation may be left without any true insights

---

11. Note: A "biblical need" may or may not be a "felt need." In recent years, much criticism has been offered of preaching that focuses on felt needs in order to make the gospel appealing (see Terry Muck, "The Danger of Preaching to Needs" [Jackson, Miss.: Reformed Theological Seminary ministries cass., 1986], responding to such works as Charles H. Kraft's *Communicating the Gospel God's Way* [Pasadena, Calif.: William Carey Library, 1979]). Such criticism rightly assumes that a steady diet of preaching focused on felt needs can make faith and worship purely matters of self-concern. At the same time, the gospel often helps people to see their biblical needs through felt needs (John 4:4–26; Acts 17:22–23). Preachers should not be afraid to help others see their biblical needs in order for such persons to discern their biblical obligations.

as to what the passage is really about, and without having received any clear teaching about God or themselves.[12]

A grammar lesson is not a sermon. A sermon is not a textual summary, a systematics discourse, or a history lecture. Mere lectures are *pre-sermons* because they dispense information without relevant application that focuses listeners on their obligations to Christ and his ministry to them.[13]

A message remains pre-sermon until the preacher organizes its ideas and the text's features to apply to a single, major FCF. We might represent the concept this way:

Textual Information (pre-sermon) —> Addressing an FCF + Relevant Application = SERMON.

A message that merely establishes "God is good" is not a sermon. However, when the same discourse deals with the doubt we may have that God is good when we face trial and demonstrates from the text how we handle our doubt with the truths of God's goodness, then the preacher has a sermon. A pre-sermon message merely describes the text. Such a "speech" may be accurate, biblically based, and erudite, but the congregation will know it falls short of a sermon even if the preacher does not.

A former student recently telephoned me for assistance because his congregation seemed to be growing less and less responsive to his preaching. "Last Sunday during the sermon," he said, "they just looked at me like they were lumps. I got no feedback whatsoever. What am I doing wrong?"

I asked him to describe his sermon to me. He responded by giving me the main points of his outline:

"Noah was wise."
"Noah was fearless."
"Noah was faithful."

"That sounds okay," I said. "Now, why did you tell them that?"

12. Walter L. Liefeld, *New Testament Exposition: From Text to Sermon* (Grand Rapids: Zondervan, 1984), 20–21.
13. Adams, *Preaching with Purpose*, 51; and, reiterated with even more force by the same author in *Truth Applied: Application in Preaching* (Grand Rapids: Zondervan, 1990), 33–39.

There was a long pause on the other end of the phone line. Then he groaned, "Oh yeah. I forgot!"

"Information without application yields frustration." The old adage rings true for preachers as well as parishioners. Preachers who cannot answer a "So what?" will preach to a "Who cares?" Only when we can demonstrate that the truths of Scripture were recorded for a purpose and have practical application to the lives of God's people do our sermons warrant a hearing. This is not simply because people have no reason to listen to what has no apparent relevance to their lives. Sermons that do not spell out the purposes and applications for which they were written also fail to fulfill God's stated will for his Word.

We are not simply ministers of information; we are ministers of Christ's transformation. He intends to restore his people with his Word and is not greatly served by preachers who have not discerned the transformation Scripture requires nor will communicate the means it offers. In future chapters we will discuss how the preacher remains true to the Scriptures and accomplishes these exegetical and communication tasks. Essential for the moment is the conclusion that unity, purpose, and application will help keep preachers faithful to their divine calling and to the Word's design.

QUESTIONS FOR REVIEW AND DISCUSSION

1. How many things is a sermon about? Why?

2. What is the Fallen Condition Focus (FCF) of a sermon?

3. Ultimately, what is the one thing a sermon is about?

4. What are three steps for determining an FCF of a sermon?

5. What are indications that a message is a "pre-sermon"?

EXERCISES

1. What are possible unifying themes for each of the following
   groups of main points?

God is good	Parents should discipline
God is faithful	Parents should sacrifice
God is sovereign	Parents should love

   Sin always contradicts God's will
   Sin sometimes veils God's will
   Sin never thwarts God's will

2. List five specific sins that might be the FCF of a sermon.

   List five specific "nonsins" that might be the FCF of a sermon.

CONTENTS OF CHAPTER 3

GOAL OF CHAPTER 3

*To explain basic tools and rules
for selecting and interpreting texts*

3

THE PRIORITY OF THE TEXT

BEGIN HERE

A nature trail that my family enjoys meanders through woods, parallels a stream, and circles a lake as it leads us to trees and rocks identified with placards that explain each landmark's significance. The explanations help us understand and enjoy features of the forest around us. But as interesting as the placards are, no trail sign is more important to us than the one at the outset where several identical-looking paths jut away from the parking lot into dense woods. The placard displays an arrow and these simple words: Begin Here. Knowing where to begin easily takes us to the explanations we need.

The same is true in preaching. Knowing the landmarks that characterize good preaching will not automatically guide us to excellence. We must first start down the right path. Expository preaching points preachers to the biblical text with the instruction *begin here*. This does not mean that preachers may not have thought about the trail before, or that they may have no idea what they want to see before they start down Scripture's path. We often will begin our sermon preparation by looking for what the Bible has to say about a particular concern or topic. Still, the text itself is the source of the truths we ultimately present. In the pulpit we are expositors, not authors. The sermon explains what the Bible says. This means that a preacher's first expository task is to choose a portion of Scripture from which to preach.

CONSIDERATIONS FOR SELECTING A PASSAGE

PASSAGE LENGTH

Although it may not be the first consideration of a pastor in selecting a passage, what you can cover in the time allotted for the sermon must affect the decision. When I was trained to preach, instructors liked using the terms *expository unit* for the Scripture portion an expository sermon covered.[1] The term has strengths and liabilities.

On the plus side, the concept of a unit encourages preachers to see scriptural passages as collections of unified thought packets rather than as arrays of disconnected verses.[2] The concept works especially well when we preach from didactic passages (epistles, biblical sermons, prophetic literature, etc.) that can be analyzed paragraph by paragraph. A paragraph of thought in such passages typically covers five to ten verses, contains a major idea with supporting concepts, and readily lends itself to expository development in a reasonably timed sermon.

The concept of an expository unit also has advantages over the idea of preaching paragraphs of Scripture because sometimes an expository sermon will cover passages much longer or much shorter than a paragraph. *Distilling* the essence of a long passage or *exploding* the implications of a single phrase are both legitimate homiletical tasks.

The unit concept encourages the preacher not to feel constrained by the paragraph or by the verse divisions of a particular translation. Most text divisions within the books of our modern Bibles have simply been added for readability, so the preacher does not need to address the passage in precisely the way translators have divided it if the thought that is being developed overlaps the translation's divisions. Prudence cautions preachers not to ignore completely the paragraph and verse divisions in our Bibles—scholars have usually advised editors to indicate the divisions on the basis of transitions of thought that they observe in the text. Still, the divisions are not divine and should not force the preacher to break down the passage precisely the way an editor has.

On the minus side, the terminology about expository units may limit the preacher's vision if it simply becomes synonymous with "a paragraph of thought." A few years ago I preached at the church of a friend who had attended seminary with me. I preached from one of the Gospel narratives that was many paragraphs long. Afterward my friend confided that he rarely preached from such narratives since we had been trained to preach only from expository units. By this he meant that he

---

1. See how Andrew Blackwood prepared for the terminology in *The Fine Art of Preaching* (1937; reprint, New York: Macmillan, 1943), 34–35; also Robert G. Rayburn in *Expository Preaching* (a textbook begun by Dr. Rayburn prior to his death).

2. Jay E. Adams, *Preaching with Purpose: A Comprehensive Textbook on Biblical Preaching* (Grand Rapids: Baker, 1982), 26.

almost exclusively preached a paragraph or two at a time. He missed the nuance of the term. An expository unit is a large or a small portion of Scripture from which the preacher can demonstrate a single spiritual truth with adequate supporting facts or concepts arising within the scope of the text.

Preachers can hardly communicate some important truths in narratives such as the flood or the prodigal son if they do not cover the entire account.[3] Messages from the poetic portions of Scripture must sometimes deal with themes that are echoed or developed many lines apart. A biblical writer may deal with a subject and lay it aside for parenthetical discussion before picking up the original thought again several sentences or even several chapters later. Some sermons must cover several chapters at once to relate a biblical concept; others should strive to capture the meaning of an entire book (e.g., Job or Ruth) or extract a truth running in the grain of a family of books (e.g., remnant or kingdom).[4] While beginning preachers are best advised to learn their expository craft by preaching from a paragraph or two of Scripture at a time, they are well advised to consider how they may ultimately expound passages of varying lengths since biblical truths are related through a great variety of literary means and lengths.[5]

SERMON LENGTH

The amount of time the preacher has to present the message affects the selection of the passage. I was raised in a tradition where the preaching started at about 9 A.M. on Sunday morning, broke for a noon meal, and then continued into the early afternoon. Needless to say, this practice left the preachers quite a bit of latitude in choosing their texts. However, rare as such preaching was in my youth, now it is almost impossible for most North American Christians to fathom. As we graze through the channels on our televisions with fingers poised on remote controls in order to relieve the slightest hint of boredom, the thought of listening to a sermon for hours practically paralyzes.

Cultural, ecclesiastical, and congregational differences still cause sermon lengths to vary greatly. In parts of Africa and the Caribbean a

---

3. Gordon D. Fee and Douglas Stuart, *How to Read the Bible for All Its Worth* (Grand Rapids: Zondervan, 1982), 77.

4. In the portion of chapter 9 on "Scripture" introductions, we will discuss how the preacher can present and expound lengthy portions of Scripture.

5. David L. Larsen, *The Anatomy of Preaching: Identifying the Issues in Preaching Today* (Grand Rapids: Baker, 1990), 90–91.

preacher who quits before an hour has passed has failed to fulfill his pastoral obligations. In many English and American churches where the authority of the Word has deteriorated, a ten-minute homily on a cultural topic has replaced even cursory explanations of "thus saith the Lord." At the same time proponents of the evangelical church growth movement in the United States often advocate eighteen-to-twenty-minute sermons as a means of reaching unchurched ears in our rapidly paced culture. Length of sermon is no automatic measure of orthodoxy, yet sermons long enough to explain what a passage means and short enough to keep interested persons listening will indicate much about the vitality of a congregation and the wisdom of the pastor.

For reasons both right and wrong the churches I have attended as an adult tend to expect sermons to be twenty-five to thirty minutes long.[6] This appears to be something of an evangelical norm in North America albeit there are many exceptions on both sides of the stopwatch. Well-schooled and biblically literate congregations can generally feast on the Word longer than others, but overfeeding is always possible and force-feeding remains the mark of either inexperienced or insensitive preachers. John Stott neatly sidesteps the issue of how long a sermon should be by saying "every sermon should 'seem like twenty minutes,' even if it is much longer."[7]

Whatever the norm of a particular congregation, however, the preacher still must have the wisdom to choose passages of such length and/or substance that they can be expounded within the allotted time. The occasion, the make-up of the congregation, a church's ministry and mission goals, worship-service parameters, and changes the church experiences in age, educational levels, or spiritual maturity can greatly affect appropriate passage and message length. Pastors should consider each of these factors in determining how long to preach and press expectations only with care and patience.

---

6. George Sweazey offers this neat synopsis: "In the circles with which I am most familiar, a fifteen-minute message seems miniature, twenty minutes is short, twenty-five minutes is usual, and thirty minutes is long" in *Preaching the Good News* (Englewood Cliffs, N.J.: Prentice-Hall, 1976), 145. However it is probably fair to say that in the time since Sweazey wrote those words the length of sermons in the mainline churches with which he is most familiar have continued to shorten. Stott does not debate Sweazey's basic analysis, writing, "No hard and fast rules can be laid down about the length of sermons, except perhaps that ten minutes are too short and forty minutes too long" in *Between Two Worlds: The Art of Preaching in the Twentieth Century* (1982; reprint, Grand Rapids: Eerdmans, 1988), 294.

7. Ibid.

There is always another verse that can be covered and another word that can be said, but ministers are best advised to select passages that allow them to quit before the congregation does. The well-prepared pastor always has more to say than time to say it. Part of the torture of sermon preparation is the discipline of setting aside for another occasion what there is not time to say in this message. We simply will say more that is heard if we preach less than all we know. In the pulpit, less can often mean more.

Perhaps the length of the passage and the corresponding length of the message are best determined when preachers remember the object of their sermons: enabling people to honor Christ. Messages should not be so short as to make God's Word seem incidental, nor so long as to make worship a burden. Either extreme robs Christ of the glory he deserves and the sweet prick his Word should provide the human conscience.

CONCERNS

Preaching on passages that are of particular meaning or interest to you is a great way to learn to expound texts. What excites or moves you is much more likely to elicit the passion from you that will excite and move others. Even experienced expositors will frequently choose texts because they address a particular personal concern.[8] Messages fired by a pastor's burning conviction tend to spark congregational interest as well as pastoral enthusiasm. However, preachers who choose texts to address their personal concerns need to be cautioned in at least two ways. First, make sure you do not impose your concern on the text. Solid exposition should demonstrate that the passage really speaks to the issue you want to address and that your passion to address a particular subject has not abused the original author's intent. Second, be aware that a ministry that only addresses the preacher's personal concerns can become too limited in perspective for the needs of a congregation. The pastor may end up riding hobby horses or unconsciously concentrating on personal struggles, thereby neglecting other important truths needed for a fully informed and mature congregation.

Congregational concerns should also influence what the pastor chooses to preach. A pastor will be regarded as out-of-touch and/or insensitive if he presses forward with a sermon program ignoring a community's employment dilemma, the death of a pillar in the church, a

8. Haddon Robinson calls this "topical exposition" in *Biblical Preaching: The Development and Delivery of Expository Messages* (Grand Rapids: Baker, 1980), 57.

local disaster, a building program, a young person's decision to enter the mission field, moral issues that the young encounter, health concerns that the elderly face, or a host of similar matters of significance to the life of the church. The world should not set the agenda for our preaching, but ministry that ignores the world that a congregation confronts is a sanctimonious sham.

Experienced preachers typically set aside a portion of each year to look backward and forward—backward at what the preaching has covered and what the congregation has encountered, and forward to what the preaching should cover in light of what the congregation needs to know or will likely experience. Efforts to educate and prepare a congregation for the scope of life's spiritual challenges will lead the pastor to a wide variety of topics and steer away from sermon ruts.

Many preachers try to use the slower summer months to plan the upcoming church year's preaching program knowing that the quality of each sermon will greatly increase if they know well ahead of time what passages and topics they will address. Planning ahead enables the preacher to establish a pre-sermon file that keeps sermon preparation from degenerating into the Friday-afternoon flurry or the Saturday-night fever whose results distress preachers and congregations alike.

A folder set aside for each upcoming sermon in the pre-sermon file will act as a magnet drawing ideas from your general reading and everyday experience. Flashes of insight, relevant quotes, newspaper clippings, exegetical discoveries, illustrations, and outlines can be dropped into the file over several weeks and will grant you vast resources for preparing the sermon the week that it will be preached.[9] Even if you do not use all the information in the file, its presence will take much of the pressure out of weekly sermon preparation because you will not have to spend precious hours scanning through books, magazines, and commentaries looking for that quote you read months ago that you know fits perfectly in this message—but that you cannot quite remember. Recognize that pastors without pre-sermon files typically fall back on clichés because they do not have time to find the insights that are memorable in the few hours each week they can devote to sermon preparation.

Many young pastors fear they will run out of preaching topics after a few months, but once they begin to know a congregation well enough to sense the depth and the number of its needs, doubts, griefs, sins, and

9. For additional ideas on preparing pre-sermon files see the author's *Using Illustrations to Preach with Power* (Grand Rapids: Zondervan, 1993), 178–86.

challenges concern quickly shifts to how so much can be addressed given the time allotted to preaching. Doctrinal principles that grant people the perspectives they need to handle a variety of problems as well as particular concerns that need direct instruction both need pulpit attention. At the same time we need to be careful that our ministries are not simply caught in the currents of congregational desires. A ministry can be as warped by lending too much of an ear to what people want to hear as it can by giving too much weight to what the preacher wants to preach (2 Tim. 4:3).

Different church traditions have used various means to round out the emphases of preaching in a local setting. Roman Catholic, Orthodox, Lutheran, and mainline churches in the United States often use a lectionary tied to the liturgical calendar which leads ministers to cover a variety of preselected texts each year. Reformed churches have typically resisted lectionary usage for a variety of reasons: the principle of *sola scriptura*, which dictates that Scripture alone should dictate what is preached; the practice of *lectio continua* as opposed to *lectio selecta*, that is, presenting texts in sequence (e.g., preaching through a book in a series; also known as "consecutive preaching")[10] instead of choosing diverse selections week to week, which was felt to lead to human emphases; the tradition of holding no day above another in reaction to Roman Catholic holy-day observances, which were seen as integral to sacramentalism; and the regard given to the autonomy of the local pulpit on the assumption that the Holy Spirit will grant the local preacher unction and insight for the task at hand.

Distance from the battles of the Reformation and a growing awareness of the need to speak directly to culture have made Reformed churches more willing to address seasonal matters, but not more willing to mandate a liturgical calendar. Baptist, charismatic, and many independent church traditions have taken similar courses in recent decades. All these traditions recognize that congregational health cannot be maintained without a ministerial commitment to preach "the whole counsel of God" (Acts 20:20, 27). Whether a lectionary, a personal agenda, a worship committee, a book sequence, or community pressures influence the texts you select, you must take care to prepare people for the matters they want you to address *and* those they would never choose to face. Congregational and pastoral appetites both may need to

10. John A. Broadus refers to this as "continuous exposition" in *On the Preparation and Delivery of Sermons*, ed. J. B. Weatherspoon (New York: Harper and Row, 1944), 146–47.

be curbed and refined somewhat in order to meet this goal lest a steady diet of what one considers to be chocolate cake malnourish everyone.

CATALYSTS

Series

What will help keep your text selection well-rounded? Honored practices and fresh approaches. Among the most honored practices is preaching text series. The *lectio continua* method provides significant benefits for the pastor preaching in sequence through a chapter or a book because

- matters in the text force the preacher to address a greater number of issues than readily spring to mind;
- sensitive matters can be addressed without the appearance of pointing a finger at persons or problems in the church (the matters simply appear next in the text sequence and avoiding them would even be more obvious);
- much cogitation and vacillation can be saved since the preacher does not have to go through the often time-consuming rigor of deciding what to preach on this week—the next section of the text is the obvious choice;
- much research time can be saved (especially for the young pastor) since each new sermon does not require completely new study of the book's or the passage's author, background, context, and cause;
- the congregation will learn to see the organizing themes and schemes of the Bible instead of perceiving it as an impenetrable mishmash of maxims, morals, and stories;
- the congregation and pastor can easily monitor the progress both of their journey through a book and of their exposure to important biblical and doctrinal topics. This last is especially important as pastor and congregation consider what matter future preaching should address.[11]

11. Stott advises a "partnership" between the pastor and parishioners in determining what and how matters should be addressed (*Between Two Worlds*, 198–200). By this he does not advocate that preachers abdicate their divine calling, but that they use committees and conversations with leaders and others in the church to take the temperature of the congregation to discern the type and dosage of scriptural medicine needing to be administered. A pastor who does not arrange to take the pulse of the congregation is a poor physician of souls.

Series preaching shows its greatest liabilities when preachers fail to make adequate or appropriate progress. Martin Lloyd-Jones may have preached on Romans for fourteen years, but without his exceptional abilities this extraordinary practice is likely to kill congregational interest and enthusiasm. The long-time practice of limiting Sunday school lessons to twelve-week sessions says much about the need people have for change. Recent studies that have convinced many publishers to package inductive Bible studies in seven-to-eight-week sessions say yet more about the tolerance even committed Christians in our culture have for the routine. Although master expositors make exceptions it is usually best to make sermon series last a few months at a maximum. People want to study their Bibles in depth, but like vacationers wanting more than one view of the Grand Canyon they generally like to move along. When the preacher announces for the fifth week in a row, "Turn with me in your Bibles for our continuing series on Ecclesiastes 2:15d," the snores may not be audible but the groans will be.

Series also cause problems if the preacher makes each sermon dependent on previous messages. Many times a topic or a passage will be better handled in a series of sermons, but each sermon should be decipherable without some code dispensed in previous messages. Too many references to "As we discovered last week . . ." or "Three weeks ago we saw that . . ." will make those who were present for the earlier messages sense failure if they cannot remember the reference, and will make those who were not present feel they cannot get the full impact of this message because they were not around for the preview. Those new to the congregation may feel they will never catch up or measure up to a series that has gone on for six months and promises to continue for three months more if the pastor does not take care to make most of each sermon stand on its own feet rather than on the shoulders of previous messages.

Series greatly aid a pastor's preparation and subject scope. Still, series generally work best when their duration is reasonable, their sermons are autonomous, and their subjects and/or approaches differ significantly from recent series. Preaching through Philippians will stimulate many fine expository messages. However, a series on the Christian family or the marks of a healthy church can lead the pastor to a sequence of texts in different books that can also be handled expositionally.

Contexts

If the sequence of a series does not signal the choice of a text, what else will help a pastor decide on what to preach? Following are some possibilities based on the preacher's life, church, or cultural contexts:

Personal abilities. Even though you want your knowledge and skills to grow there is no good reason to jump into an expository series on Ezekiel or Revelation if you do not yet have the background to handle accurately its contents. Tackle what you know best as you develop skills that will help you wrestle through more challenging passages.

The calendar. In most of our churches you can get away without talking about fathers on Father's Day, but woe to the preacher who does not mention mothers on Mother's Day. No mention of the resurrection on Easter will be a greater mystery than the empty tomb to those in the pew, and Christmas without the Christ child abuses most hearts.

The situation. At times the Scriptures act like a web capturing issues for us to consider as we travel through its corridors. Other times our situations force us to go on a safari through the Bible with our own concerns poised as nets to capture the text that will address our needs. Community concern over substance abuse in the local high school, a strike at a major employer, a tragedy, or a triumph all may prod the preacher to find relevant Scripture passages. Congregational concern about officer selection, vandalism, outreach, and a host of other issues also will stimulate selection of passages.

The most frequently addressed subjects should be those that reflect the everyday situations of the person in the pew. A pastor who lives among the people will know those struggling with a harsh boss, a prodigal son, guilt, depression, an unsaved relative, intolerant in-laws, an impossible spouse, irresponsible ambitions, unrestrained passions, and many similar concerns. Subjects such as these should be the FCFs addressed in many sermons and will serve as the compass to many suitable texts. These topics and texts should take precedence in preaching because only when people know how to live faithfully in ordinary moments will they be prepared to act faithfully in extraordinary situations.

Current events. Christian people need biblical guidance in order to address poverty, abortion, disasters, dissent, military crises, political issues, epidemics, economics, health care, and all the other issues of our day that they either do face or should confront. Evangelicals may not like it that the sage advice to prepare sermons with the Bible in one hand and a newspaper in the other came from Karl Barth,[12] but we can always

12. Arthur Michael Ramsey and Leon-Joseph Suenens, *The Future of the Christian Church* (SCM: London, 1971), 13–14.

comfort ourselves with the solace that Charles Spurgeon made the allusion first.[13]

Current events tend to get pastors in trouble when sermons begin to argue for specific political agendas, candidates, or programs. Although there are moments for exceptions, the preacher's commitments and expertise are usually best limited to relating the biblical principles Christians in responsible positions should employ as they bring God's Word to bear on their professional callings and ethical judgments. Of course, where there are clear biblical standards about an issue, preachers should speak with courage and clarity. We should recognize, however, a pastor who is perceived as a political animal is one who usually loses spiritual authority.

Hymnals. The hymnody of the church reveals much of what is dear to a congregation and a church's tradition. Both are ripe fields from which to harvest text suggestions.

Confessions, catechisms, and creeds. The doctrinal statements of a church need biblical explication in order for a congregation to know that its beliefs are more than traditional opinions. Pastors may find it hard to preach uplifting messages on their church's approach to baptism, biblical discipline, hell, the Trinity, or the inspiration of Scripture, but texts on these subjects need to be explored, thus fully informing and preparing a congregation for the spiritual challenges all face.

Others' messages. Sermons you hear and materials you read can be wonderful catalysts for your own sermons. Learn from past and present greats, glean from the novel, and use the significant thoughts of others to generate ideas for what you can or should say to your own congregation. Give credit if you borrow the work of others, but recognize that the greatest preachers always keep eyes and ears open to harvest ideas, quotations, illustrations, outlines, exegetical insights, memorable wording, and topics from fellow laborers in the gospel.[14] No preaching rubric should require you to be the originator of all the truth that parishioners receive. A file for storing articles of interest and ideas from others for future sermons is a must for most preachers.

The Holy Spirit. No catalyst for selecting a text is more important than sensitivity to the leading of God's Spirit. Prayer with godly concern for the good of others and the glory of Christ should lead you through the choices you must make among the catalysts for selecting a sermon's

13. Charles Haddon Spurgeon, *Lectures to My Students*, 3d series (1894; reprint, Grand Rapids, Zondervan, 1980), 54.
14. Stott, *Between Two Worlds*, 219.

focus. Preaching in the power of the Spirit is the culmination of a process that has been Spirit-led. The conviction that the Holy Spirit gave the Word should yield a commitment to seek his leading and the courage to speak more what he wants said than what we or our congregations fancy. In the heart where the Spirit burns glow the fires that refine questions about what texts we should preach and that light the way our thoughts should turn.

CAUTIONS

In my earliest years of ministry I most valued mining obscure texts. I thought the effort showed how serious I was about all of Scripture and believed that handling such passages well would show how qualified I was to preach. Preaching difficult and little-known texts was like showing my diploma. I later learned to love more shedding light on important texts or bringing new life to familiar texts. Concentration on the Bible's "fine print" gave people the impression they could not read their Bibles without me. The Bible became an opaque book because it was full of grammatical mazes and logical knots that I would untangle each week. Thus, by consistently choosing texts in the Bible's densest forest, I denied people the sunlight it more regularly offers and made them less willing to approach its paths. Some people may have thought much of my abilities to handle the Word, but more lost confidence in their ability to do the same.

We are obligated to handle the hard passages from time to time, but we also should remember the example of Christ's ministry. He preached about the familiar: David and the showbread, Jonah and the great fish, birds and flowers, the proverbs and prayer. The apostle Paul, while dealing with some complex subjects, was not ashamed to talk about Adam and Eve, the marketplace, a soldier's armor, and even how seeds grow. The importance of introducing people to reality of the Word in terms they know cautions us to remember basic guidelines in choosing texts for our sermons:

Do not avoid familiar texts. Biblical passages that are familiar typically are well known because they have been of great value to the church through the ages. Consistently to deny a congregation these passages is to deprive them of some of Scripture's richest treasure. Spurgeon, the prince of preachers, spoke over and over on Zacchaeus, Joshua, and the prodigal son. John Wesley loved to preach on Jesus Christ as our "wisdom, and righteousness, and sanctification, and redemption"

(1 Cor. 1:30). Paul simply said, "I have not hesitated to preach anything that would be helpful to you" (Acts 20:20).

Do not search for texts obscure in meaning. There is great warrant for expounding texts many misunderstand and for clarifying passages that unfold naturally in an expository series, but there is little value in explaining for the sake of explaining. Preaching should edify, not showcase erudition. Even if you know the meaning of "the baptism of the dead" and the names of all "the sons of Pahathmoab," consider whether there are more vital matters that sin-sick and life-battered people need this Sunday. Obscure texts occasionally preached may enable the preacher to highlight an issue made evident by the peculiar twists or the unusual features of such passages, but we should not confuse a congregation's enjoyment of an occasional taste of the exotic with a need for a diet of the same.

Do not purposely avoid any text. We should distinguish the discretion that wisely passes over some texts from the faithlessness that purposely avoids others. When Paul told the Ephesian elders, "I have not hesitated to proclaim to you the whole will of God" (Acts 20:27), his words imply the courage such proclamation has required. Wisdom and tact should guide our presentation of issues difficult for a particular congregation to face, but if the church never faces its faults and frailties the pastor has failed to preach everything it needs to hear.

Do not use spurious texts. Concern for what a congregation needs to hear should never lead the pastor to proclaim as authoritative texts that the Holy Spirit did not inspire. Scribal comments and errors that have mistakenly been included in some translations[15] should not be presented as the Word of God. Where there is the rare question about whether a particular passage is spurious, it is wise to see if the same truth can be preached from a more certain passage or briefly to provide the congregation with your reasons for using the text (since the marginal notes in most up-to-date translations will question the passage's authenticity).

Faith that the Holy Spirit knew what he was doing when he inspired the Word will keep us confident of Scripture's sufficiency without the spurious texts. We can keep the people to whom we preach confident of the Bible's authority by reminding them how rare such questions are when they do arise in the ordinary course of preaching. Scholars question the actual textual validity of less than one word in a thousand in

15. In the King James Version 1 John 5:7 is a prime example, and Mark 16:18 a sad one (given the way some groups have employed it as a test of spirituality).

our best translations. As a result we have little question of what statements appeared in the original manuscripts. The evangelical debate
with modern theologies concentrates not on what Scripture says, but on
whether to believe and obey what it says. The Holy Spirit's divine inspiration and providential preservation of Scripture is a continuing miracle
of God's spiritual care of our souls. A good study Bible prepared by scholars who accept the Bible's full authority will give preachers ample warning of a questionable text and will grant us the confidence that we are
preaching in accord with the Spirit's imprimatur.

TOOLS FOR INTERPRETING A PASSAGE

Once a passage is chosen (or as part of the selection process) we want
to be sure we are interpreting it properly. A host of good tools are available to help grant pastors confidence that they are preaching what the
Holy Spirit intends. None of these is a substitute for a solid biblical education, but even those with extensive training depend on study tools to
confirm, deepen, and brighten their interpretations. I list tools that
preachers commonly employ to help them interpret texts (the order of
this list indicates a sequence of tools that preachers frequently use when
preparing sermons).[16]

Study Bibles. No tool is more accessible and cost-effective than a
good study Bible. Many preachers may not even think of the Bible they
use as being a study tool since they use its resources so regularly and
instinctively. A good study Bible with verse cross-references, book syn-
opses, glossaries, concordances, explanatory notes, maps, Bible-charac-
ter summaries, charts, timelines, and other helps provides a succinct
library of information in the preacher's palm (see select examples in
table 1 in appendix 9). Other tools will cover a study Bible's details in
greater depth, but nothing is handier or more able to quickly inform the
preacher if an interpretation is on track or is heading for the briers.

16. Although many of its entries are now dated, Cyril J. Barber's *The Minister's
Library* (Grand Rapids: Baker, 1974, with its subsequent supplements) remains an excellent guide for determining the types of tools you need for scriptural research and pastoral
work. For excellent models of how to conduct exegetical research on a biblical passage see
Douglas Stuart's *Old Testament Exegesis: A Primer for Students and Pastors,* 2d ed. (Philadelphia: Westminster, 1984); the companion work, Gordon D. Fee, *New Testament Exegesis: A Handbook for Students and Pastors* (Philadelphia: Westminster, 1983); and
Walter Liefeld's *New Testament Exposition: From Text to Sermon* (Grand Rapids:
Zondervan, 1984).

Lexicons, grammatical and analytical aids. Preachers who are committed to translating passages (or their key portions) to determine precise meaning in the original languages keep lexicons close at hand. Lexicons explain the meanings of the original words behind our English translations. Complete lexicons provide definitions of an original word along with various uses of the word, its root meanings, examples of where it occurs, and possible guidance as to how its grammatical variations can affect its meaning (see select examples in table 2 in appendix 9).

Grammatical aids help the preacher see how a particular word's tense, case, number, usage, or context affects its meaning. Examples and explanations of each of the grammatical features with extensive indexes characterize the best grammars (see select examples in table 4 in appendix 9).

Exegetical (i.e., language analysis) aids help the preacher analyze a word's tense, case, and number so that its specific grammatical features can be identified or researched in a grammatical aid or lexicon. Seminary and Bible-college students in schools that encourage study in the original languages are familiar with the aids currently on the market (see select examples in tables 2 and 5 in appendix 9). Many are now incorporated into computer software at reasonable prices. Pastors who have grown distant from their original-languages training may well find that these tools can reacquaint them with this valuable line of study. In addition, a host of new print tools has found a home in the original-language study market. These computerized and print tools will parse the verbs in every verse for you, identify the number and case of every noun, and tell you the root of each word. We have come a long way from thumbing through massive grammars each time we could not remember a word or its grammatical ending. For advice on which tools will best suit your own purposes consult the guides to lexical aids listed in table 3 in appendix 9 of this book.

Concordances. Once you start working within a text you will often wonder how some of its words are used elsewhere in Scripture, or you will recall a text where a similar word or idea occurs that you could use to drive home a point, but you cannot remember its reference. Concordances help you find the reference by listing all the places where the word you are studying (or remembering) is found in the Bible (see select examples in table 5 in appendix 9). Modern concordances will also guide you to the original-language meanings and uses of the biblical words. A number of these tools now have numerical systems that cross-reference words to other reference sources. Some computerized concordances also have the capacity to provide exegetical information with references to where the Scriptures use the word.

Topical Bibles. Sometimes we use concordances simply to find where a topic is covered in the Bible by looking up references for key words relating to that subject. Topical Bibles shorten this process for you by listing the verses and/or passages pertaining to a topic under alphabetized topic headings.[17] Pastors who want to preach on a particular subject often use topical Bibles to scan passages quickly and decide which deals best with the topic as they want to address it.

Bible translations. Often preachers can discern nuances in the original text by comparing how the experts have variously translated the text.[18] One old saw says, "The King James Version is translated in the language of Pilgrim times, the New International Version is translated in the language of our times, and the New American Standard Bible is translated in the language of no time."—a line that is unfair because it fails to recognize the strengths of each version. We love the King James Version for the beauty of its language, but its scholars tended to translate passages that echo one another theologically or terminologically in such a way that the reverberations remain clear. The New International Version, which now sells more than any other, is the most accurate translation that strives for easy reading by translating original phrases into their "dynamic equivalent" in our idiom. The New American Standard Bible sacrifices readability for a more strictly equivalent translation which at times makes it sound more wooden, through it reads more accurately.

The Living Bible and other paraphrases will help you scan a large body of material in order to pick up its gist; the Amplified Bible and J. B. Phillips's translation concentrate more on communicating the nuances behind specific statements. There are strengths in most of the popular translations that are committed to the authority of Scripture, and they can be employed once you discern the purpose of particular translations.

Bible dictionaries, encyclopedias, and handbooks. Several major publishers offer reference works with definitions, explanations, backgrounds, timelines, and/or descriptions of key Bible characters, terms, concepts, places, or practices. Versions vary from single volumes to

---

17. *Nave's Topical Bible* is the best-known example.

18. Several works on the print and computer markets carry multiple translations so that the preacher can compare translations line by line in the normal sermon preparation process (e.g., *The Layman's Parallel Bible* and *Comparative Study Bible*, both published by Zondervan; and the various computer concordance programs listed at the end of this chapter that typically allow multiple-translation searches).

many tomes, but competition among these books, which can save a preacher many hours of numbing research, has driven the lesser-quality sources from the stores. Evaluate your pocketbook, your probable purposes, and buy a recent edition from a major evangelical publisher. You will have a quality work that will serve you for many years (see select examples in table 6 in appendix 9).

Commentaries. The best commentators have used all the tools already described plus more to help preachers see what a particular passage says. Commentaries usually are devoted to a single book of the Bible, but there are also good single-volume commentaries on the entire Bible whose abbreviated entries alert the preacher to most major concerns. Especially in the early stages of ministry, no well-prepared preacher considers sermon preparation to be complete without consultation of an up-to-date commentary.

Bible commentaries vary greatly in their length, quality, type, and price. Publishers frequently offer commentaries in large sets covering the entire Old or New Testament. The sets are often the most economical and convenient way of obtaining the resources you need to cover an entire Testament, but those with time for researching their purchases may want to consult resources that evaluate the quality of each volume in the set.[19] You can usually construct the highest quality commentary library by selecting the best volumes out of a variety of sets.

The expertise that commentaries bring to bear on a particular passage is at one moment their greatest benefit and danger. The mixed blessing is evident in the two types of pastors who will never make great preachers: The first is the one who will not listen to what others say, the other is the one who will only say what others say. The preacher who refuses to pay any attention to what gifted scholars have discovered are good and/or errant readings of a text mistakes personal arrogance for erudition. God does not give all his insights to any one person. At the same time, the preacher who says only what a commentator concludes is trying to preach by proxy.

You yourself must think through what the Scriptures say in order to be able to expound adequately and apply meaningfully what commen-

19. In addition to the works cited in table 3, appendix 9, by Tremper Longman, Gordon Fee, Frederick Danker, Brevard Childs, and David Scholer, consult Douglas Stuart's *A Guide to Selecting and Using Bible Commentaries* (Dallas: Word, 1990). A number of seminary faculties have also written guides to help their students build good personal-preaching libraries. I am aware of such guides at Covenant Theological Seminary, Dallas Theological Seminary, Trinity Evangelical Divinity School, and Westminster Theological Seminary.

tators say. No commentator has room to write down all the implications, insights, and truths given in a text. No distant educator or long-
dead scholar knows your situation or your congregation's concerns. It is
not wise habitually to run to a commentary as the first step of sermon
preparation lest your thoughts start running in a groove carved by one
not in touch with what you need to address.[20]

Commentaries are better used as a check rather than as a guide.[21]
Develop your exposition and tentative outline based on work with the
basic tools and then consult the commentaries to flesh out, refine, and
if necessary, revise your ideas. Try not to preach a dead or a distant person's sermon. Spurgeon advised, "The closet is the best study. The
commentators are good instructors but the author himself is far better. . . ."[22] God called *you* to this situation. He wanted no one else in
the universe to prepare this message for this moment other than you.
Joseph Ruggles Wilson reminded us of how unique is each preacher's
challenge:

> In other words, preaching is not an *imitative* exercise. Every preacher is
> to regard himself as an original exhibitor and enforcer of the terms of
> human salvation; a channel of gracious speech, markedly different from
> every other.
>
>   . . . Turn it which way we will, the conclusion is always before us, the
> preacher's preaching is just another form of *himself;* i.e., if he does *his own*
> thinking; exhibits no emotions that he does not actually *feel;* and presents
> divine truth, not as a bundle of opinions which orthodoxy has agreed
> upon, but as so much vital blood that has been made to course in *his* veins,
> and therefore takes the form of his own Christian *life.* It is these *live* men
> whom God supremely calls; men who have *eaten* the word, as a prophet
> did, and into whom it has passed to become a perpetual throb in their
> hearts; so that when if comes forth again, it will proceed upon its errand,
> bearing the warmth of their innermost experiences; those experiences
> wherein are traced the musings which continued until they could find
> vent only in fire; the fire that burns quickly into other souls, melts where
> it burns, and remoulds where it melts.[23]

20. Edward F. Marquart, *Quest for Better Preaching* (Minneapolis: Augsburg, 1985),
101, 106.
21. Arndt Halvorson, *Authentic Preaching* (Minneapolis: Augsburg, 1982), 52.
22. Cited by Helmut Thielicke, *Encounter with Spurgeon* (Grand Rapids: Baker,
1977), 116.
23. Joseph Ruggles Wilson, "In What Sense Are Preachers to Preach Themselves?"
Southern Presbyterian Review 25 (1874): 355–57.

Let the Holy Spirit work in your heart and mind to develop the message a commentator would approve, not design. Concern for precision should not so overwhelm you as to deny you or your listeners the insights God will grant you into his Word.

PRINCIPLES FOR INTERPRETING A PASSAGE

Concern to use good tools for interpreting biblical passages reflects our basic commitment to be true to the Bible. Expository preaching solemnly binds the preacher to represent the precise meaning of the text as intended by the original author or as illumined by another inspired source. As matter-of-fact as such a rubric may seem, homiletical history indicates how mutable is such a standard and how carefully it must be guarded. Early-church and medieval escapades into allegorical interpretation led ancient preachers to the conviction that the "literal interpretation" of the text was the least rewarding to preach.[24] Modern resurrections of the allegorical method regularly occur when preachers assume that the Holy Spirit will enable them to discern something more or different in the text than what was meant by the biblical writer or what we can demonstrate that the divine Author makes evident within the canon of Scripture.[25] Preachers' interpretations remain consistent with Scripture when they follow long-honored and proven interpretive procedures that expose the Bible's original intent.

Preachers must consider the context as part of any text. Context limits and imparts the author's intended meaning. We cannot maintain the integrity of any biblical statement without considering its surroundings. Our first task as expositors is to use the best tools available to interpret precisely what a biblical author's statements mean in their context.

24. Moisés Silva, *Has the Church Misread the Bible: The History of Interpretation in the Light of Current Issues*, vol. 1 of Foundations of Contemporary Interpretation, ed. Moisés Silva (Grand Rapids: Zondervan, 1987), 41; Bernard Ramm, *Protestant Biblical Interpretation*, 3d rev. ed. (Grand Rapids: Baker, 1970), 38.

25. Although the concept of the *sensus plenior* remains controversial in conservative circles, preachers regularly make interpretations based on matters such as how frequently a word is used throughout Scripture which would not always have been evident to the original writers. The Bible sometimes also demands we interpret texts on the basis of how a later biblical writer uses an earlier statement of Scripture with only loose connections to its original context meaning. The potential and limits of the *sensus plenior* concept need much fuller explication.

Use the Grammatical-Historical Method

Discovering the "literal meaning" does not mean that we disregard the figurative, poetic, colloquial, metaphorical, or spiritual ways in which the biblical writers sometimes communicate. Literal interpretation occurs when we explain what a biblical writer meant, not what his words may connote outside of their context. Original intent is sometimes called the "discourse meaning" of the text.[26] Such a designation helps us realize that we do not have to interpret a biblical reference to the sunrise as literally meaning the earth jumped from its orbit so that the sun could pass over it. We interpret the words in their linguistic context as we would if we were listening to someone talk today. Sometimes we use figurative, metaphorical, or colloquial terms to communicate, and so did the biblical writers.

Our task as preachers is to discern what the original writers meant by analyzing the background and grammatical features of what they said. Using grammar and history to discern a text's original meaning is called the grammatico-historical method.[27] This method allows the Scriptures to speak for themselves instead of letting the interpreter apply meaning to the text. Sometimes the latter does not seem dangerous when the preacher is committed to the historic truths of the faith. In such cases we may hardly blink when told that the water from Moses' rock represents the eternal water of Christ, or that the worm at which Jonah railed is the sin that eats at the believer's heart. Despite the absence of biblical statements confirming these interpretations they sound reasonable because they reflect biblical imagery and truths definitely appearing elsewhere. However, if anything in Scripture can mean whatever our imaginations suggest rather than what Scripture determines, then our opinions become as authoritative as the statements of God.

If we allow our imaginations to determine biblical meanings, then the water from the rock could represent baptism, the water from Christ's side, the water on which Peter walked by faith, the crystal sea on which the saved will gather, or the fountain that should go in the new sanctuary's foyer. If Scripture does not determine meaning, ultimately Scripture has no meaning.

26. Peter Cotterell and Max Turner, *Linguistics and Biblical Interpretation* (Downers Grove, Ill.: InterVarsity, 1989), 69.
27. See Walter C. Kaiser, Jr., *Toward an Exegetical Theology: Biblical Exegesis for Preaching and Teaching* (Grand Rapids: Baker, 1981), 87–88; and William J. Larkin, *Culture and Biblical Hermeneutics: Interpreting and Applying the Authoritative Word in a Relativistic Age* (Grand Rapids: Baker, 1988), 115.

Occasionally there may be a thin line between "it means" and "it may mean" but biblically bound preachers must recognize the difference. We may conjecture that the water and blood that flowed from Christ's side represents New Testament baptism and communion, but we had best not command such observances on such a basis. We should never bind scriptural obligations to personal speculations.

The Protestant Reformers used the principle of the "analogy of faith" (sometimes identified as "the analogy of Scripture") to guide their interpretations, and it should guide ours.[28] This standard requires preachers to use Scripture alone as the basis for their exhortations. Nothing but what we can establish Scripture itself attests should be the focus of our preaching. Expository preachers determine the biblical truths intended for the persons addressed by the text and then identify similarities in our present condition that require the application of precisely the same truths. This means applications may vary, but interpretations of a text's core ideas should not. For instance, Paul's command to "look not only to your own interests, but also to the interests of others" in Philippians 2:4 might be applied to concerns about little regard for the needs of others, divisive ambitions, or disrespect for the gifts of others, but the root idea of "selflessness based on Christ's example" must be maintained in preaching that is to be faithful to the original intent of the text.

Observe the Historical, Cultural, and Literary Context

Accurate interpretations require us not only to determine what particular words say, but also to see how they function in their broader contexts. The reason "every heretic has his verse" is because Scripture can be twisted to confirm almost anything if interpreters ignore contexts. Attention to historical and cultural context will help explain the "offense" of the cross (Gal. 5:11), and will indicate that healed lepers were not necessarily more thankful simply because they went to the temple before they went home (Luke 17:14). We determine literary contexts both by analyzing the concepts that surround a biblical statement *and* by identifying the type of literature in which the statement occurs.

Preachers should examine what chapters and verses surrounding a passage say in order to determine precisely what the biblical writer intends to communicate through particular words in the preaching portion. Without reading Romans 14 for the conceptual context you are likely to determine that those called "weak" in Romans 15 are precisely

28. Ramm, *Protestant Biblical Interpretation*, 55.

the opposite of what Paul intends. Although John and James often use the word *believe*, contexts indicate they are communicating quite different concepts by the term (cf. John 3:16 and James 2:19).

The temptation to lift verses from context is perhaps best evident in the way popular Christian culture uses Scripture with scant regard for original intent. A turn-of-the-century temperance hymn quotes "Touch not, taste not, handle not" (Col. 2:21, KJV) to condemn alcohol use. However, in context the apostle condemns those who use these words. In some wedding ceremonies beaming brides quote to grateful grooms, "Where you go I will go, and where you stay I will stay. Your people will be my people and your God my God" (Ruth 1:16), yet the words were originally said by a woman to her mother-in-law. Friendship rings, pendants, and refrigerator magnets warmly exude "May the LORD keep watch between you and me when we are away from each other" (Gen. 31:49), which in context was Laban's perpetual threat to harm Jacob if he ever returned to his uncle's territory—something akin to our endearment, "Cross this line and I'll cut your throat."

Study of a passage's context also requires preachers to identify the genre, or type of literature, in which a biblical statement occurs. Many an error has been made by interpreting proverbs as promises, prophecy as history, parables as facts, and poetry as science.

For example, proverbs are truisms, statements so tending to be true that the wise take them to heart. A modern proverb on child rearing says, "As the twig is bent so grows the branch." The ancient equivalent is "Train a child in the way he should go and when he is old he will not turn from it" (Prov. 22:6). Both statements tend to be true, but neither is always true . . . this is the nature of proverbs. Proverbs are prescriptive not predictive. God requires his people to heed his proverbs, but not to interpret them as promises. Great damage will be done to the intent of Scripture as well as the consciences of Christians if we confuse the distinctions.

By contrast, prophecies are predictive and need to be interpreted with this perspective in mind. If we do not indicate the future basis of Israel's "comfort" in Isaiah 40, we diminish Christ's ministry. Similar damage can be done if we use details intended only to give a parable form (such as the physical abyss between Lazarus and Dives in Luke 16) as the basis of a doctrinal formulation (such as heaven and hell being separated by physical barriers). Should we use poetic language describing the wings of God (Ps. 91:4) as a scriptural argument for God's actual form, our theology will quickly decay.

Determine the Redemptive Context

We determine the meaning of a passage by seeing not only how words are used in the context of a book or its passages, but also how the passage functions in the entire scope of Scripture. An accurate interpretation requires us to ask, "How does this text disclose the meaning or need of the redemption?" Failure to ask and to answer this question leads to preaching that is highly moralistic or legalistic because it focuses on the behaviors a particular passage teaches without disclosing how the biblical writer was relating those behaviors to the work of the Savior.[29]

Regard for context requires us to consider an immediate text in the light of its purpose in the redemptive message unfolding through all of Scripture. Consider how the instructions of the apostle Paul honored the Christ-centrality of the entire Word. Paul preached about marital relationships, child rearing, qualifications for church officers, stewardship, handling anger, on-the-job conduct, regard for government authorities, and many other practical concerns, and at the same time he wrote, "But we preach Christ crucified: a stumbling block to Jews and foolishness to Gentiles. . . . For I resolved to know nothing while I was with you except Jesus Christ and him crucified" (2 Cor. 1:23; 2:2).

Somehow, though Paul addressed many issues of daily living, he believed he was always preaching about the person and the work of Jesus. This must be the goal of expository preaching: the particulars of a passage need to be related to the overall purpose of Scripture.

In the latter portions of this book we will devote much time to discovering how expository preachers can mine the gospel gold from every biblical passage without adding matter to the text that is not already there, since preaching outside of redemptive contexts is a great weakness in current evangelical preaching. For the moment, it is sufficient to note that preachers need to interpret biblical portions in the light of Scripture's whole. This will inevitably force us to consider how a particular passage functions in revealing, preparing for, or reacting to the work of Christ that is the ultimate message of the scope of Scripture.

29. Reasons and means for determining the redemptive context are discussed much more fully in chapters 10 and 11 of this book.

QUESTIONS FOR REVIEW AND DISCUSSION

1. What are the benefits and the liabilities of selecting texts for preaching that address personal and/or congregational concerns?

2. What are benefits and cautions for preaching in series?

3. What cautions does a preacher need to observe when approaching spurious texts?

4. Why should a preacher be cautious about turning to a commentary as a first step in sermon preparation?

5. How does an allegorical method of interpretation differ from an expository method?

6. What ways can context affect the interpretation of a text?

EXERCISES

1. Use your research tools to determine what Greek word John and James use for *believe* in John 3:16 and James 2:19; indicate the various ways in which they use the word.

2. Use your understanding of a proverb to explain Proverbs 15:1 and Proverbs 26:4–5.

3. Use context to determine who the "weak" are in Romans 15.

CONTENTS OF CHAPTER 4

GOAL OF CHAPTER 4

To identify the historical, homiletical, and attitudinal components of expository messages

4

COMPONENTS OF EXPOSITION

THE GOAL

After the cruelty and selfishness of a thirty-seven-year-old man had forced his wife and children from his home, he called in desperation wanting my aid in getting them to return. I said I would try to help if he would agree to get counseling for his problems. He agreed and came to the church office several days later. He brought a Bible with him. I could not help but notice how strange it was to see this abusive man with a Bible under his arm. I had seen him many times before. He even attended our church occasionally, but I had never seen him with a Bible. Yet, here in the darkest hour of his life, he thought he would find wisdom and aid in a book written thousands of years ago. No doubt his thinking was colored with a desire to impress me, and he undoubtedly had little actual knowledge about how to discern what the Bible would actually require of him. Still, as do all expository preachers, I shared the man's instinctive faith that the Bible could address the deepest needs of his life.

Expository preachers and the people who sit before them each week are convinced that the Scriptures can be mined to extract God's wisdom and power for daily living. Poor preaching may cast some occasional doubt, but preaching that truly reveals what the Bible means has kept this conviction alive for a hundred generations. Our goal as expository preachers is to keep this faith alive by demonstrating week after week what the Word of God says about the daily concerns we and our listeners face.

This goal reminds us that most people do not want or need a lecture about Bible facts. They want and need a sermon that demonstrates how the information in the Bible applies to their lives. Expository preaching does not merely obligate preachers to explain what the Bible says, it obligates them to explain what the Bible means in the lives of people today. [1] Application is as necessary for sound exposition as is explication. In fact, the real meaning of a text remains hidden until we discern how its truths should govern our lives.[2] This means that full exposition cannot be limited to a presentation of biblical information. The preacher should frame every explanatory detail of the sermon so its impact on the lives of listeners is evident.

Such a perspective on the true nature of exposition challenges the notion some have of expository preaching. So much of the criticism expository preaching receives results from the assumption of some preachers that a sermon's primary goal is to expose listeners to information about the Bible. Sermons that mainly disseminate information seem out of touch, irrelevant, and even uncaring. Sermons that organize textual information and address immediate concerns also express congregational sensitivity while remaining as fully biblical.

If we were to think of the object of a sermon as a large stone to be moved, we would recognize that some think of an expository sermon as using all its resources and features as leverage to move information into the mind of the listener. Such a sermon model would look like figure 4.1.

FIGURE 4.1
An Information-Priority Message

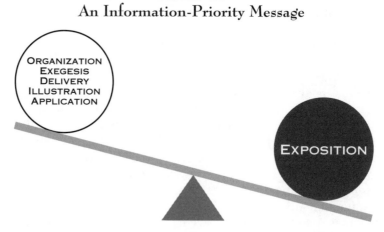

1. John Stott, *Between Two Worlds: The Art of Preaching in the Twentieth Century* (1982; reprint, Grand Rapids: Eerdmans, 1988), 141, 145–50.
2. D. Martyn Lloyd-Jones, *Darkness and Light: An Exposition of Ephesians 4:17– 5:17* (Grand Rapids: Baker, 1982), 200–201; see also John Frame, *Doctrine of the Knowledge of God* (Phillipsburg, N.J.: Presbyterian and Reformed, 1987), 93–98.

However, a true expository message uses all its resources to move application.[3] The sermon's features become the leverage to impel biblical understanding and action based on sound exposition into the life circumstances of listeners as well as information into their thoughts (see fig. 4.2).

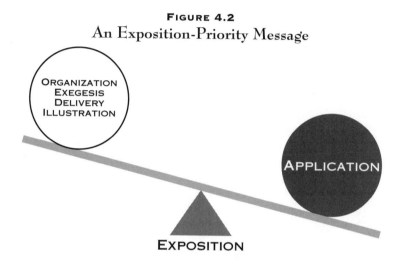

FIGURE 4.2

An Exposition-Priority Message

ORGANIZATION
EXEGESIS
DELIVERY
ILLUSTRATION

APPLICATION

EXPOSITION

Figure 4.2 is more in keeping with the understanding of John A. Broadus, the father of modern expository preaching. In his classic, *On the Preparation and Delivery of Sermons*, this master teacher and preacher concludes that in an expository sermon, "the application of the sermon is not merely an appendage to the discussion or a subordinate part of it, but is the main thing to be done."[4] Broadus's conclusion has ample biblical precedent. Exposition assumes the duty of exhorting the people of God to apply the truths revealed in Scripture not because of the opinion of experts but because of the instruction of God's Word.

THE PATTERN

Indications of our preaching obligations emerge in the Bible's descriptions of Christ's words as he accompanied the two disciples on the road

3. David L. Larsen, *The Anatomy of Preaching: Identifying the Issues in Preaching Today* (Grand Rapids: Baker, 1989), 96.
4. John A. Broadus, *On the Preparation and Delivery of Sermons*, ed. J. B. Weatherspoon (New York: Harper and Row, 1944), 210.

to Emmaus. Luke records, "And beginning with Moses and all the Prophets, he explained to them what was said in all the Scriptures concerning himself" (Luke 24:27). The word translated *explained* means to unfold the meaning of something, or to interpret.[5] Later the two disciples offer commentary on Christ's words saying, "Were not our hearts burning within us while he talked with us on the road and opened the Scriptures to us?" (Luke 24:32). This opening of the Scriptures expresses the concept of revealing the full implications of something (as in opening a door wide to show what is inside).[6]

Unfolding and opening the meaning of the Word of God characterize the expositor's task, not merely on the basis of Christ's example, but also on the basis of ancient biblical precedent, which further defines exposition's essentials. Probably the best description of ancient exposition occurs in Nehemiah's account of Israel's reacquaintance with the Word of God after the people return from exile in Babylon where they had forgotten God's law and the language in which it had been given:

> Ezra opened the book. All the people could see him because he was standing above them; and as he opened it, the people all stood up. Ezra praised the LORD, the great God; and all the people lifted their hands and responded, "Amen! Amen!" Then they bowed down and worshiped the LORD with their faces to the ground.
>
> The Levites—Jeshua, Bani, Sherebiah, Jamin, Akkub, Shabbethai, Hodiah, Maaseiah, Kelita, Azariah, Jozabad, Hanan and Pelaiah—instructed the people in the Law while the people were standing there.
>
> They read from the Book of the Law of God, making it clear and giving the meaning so that the people could understand what was being read. [Neh. 8:5–8]

Here the exposition of the Word involved three elements: presentation of the Word (it was read); explanation of the Word (making it clear and giving its meaning);[7] and exhortation based on the Word (the Hebrew terms indicate the priests caused the people to understand in such a way that they could use the information that was imparted).[8] The Word itself,

---

5. Gk. *diermenueo*.
6. Gk. *dianoigo*.
7. From *bin*: Hiph'il participle masc. plural = "causing to understand" (v. 7); and, from *parash*: Pual participle masc. singular = "made distinct or clear" (v. 8).
8. From *sekel* with the verb = "they gave the sense" (v. 8); and from *bin*: Consecutive with Qal imperfect, third person, masc. plural = "so that they understood" (v. 8). C. F. Keil comments, "It is more correct to suppose a paraphrastic exposition and application of the law . . . not a distinct recitation according to appointed rules" in *I and II Kings, I and II*

explanation of its content, and exhortation to apply its truths composed the pattern of proclamation.

These three elements in this Old Testament proclamation consistently reappear in New Testament practice.[9] Luke records that when Jesus first explained his ministry in the synagogue he read the Scripture (4:11–19), explained the import of what was read (4:21), and then made the implications clear—though it was not to his listeners' liking that the obvious application meant honoring Jesus (4:23–27).

Word presentation, explanation, and exhortation remain prominent in the pattern of New Testament proclamation. Although the elements do not always follow the same order, they remain present. Consider the way these Pauline instructions to a young preacher unfold:

1 Timothy 4:13

"[D]evote yourself to the . . . public reading of Scripture	**Word Presentation**
to preaching	**Word Exhortation**
(the actual term is *paraklesei*, meaning to exhort or entreat. It comes from the same root as *Paraclete*, the name Jesus gives the Spirit, who comes as our counselor, advocate, or comforter)	
and to teaching."	**Word Explanation**

2 Timothy 4:2

"Preach theWord . . . ;	**Word Presentation**
(here the word for "preach" is *kerusso*, which means to proclaim or publish)	
correct, rebuke and encourage with great patience	**Word Exhortation**
and careful instruction."	**Word Explanation**

Paul's practice was consistent with his instructions (see Acts 17:1–4).

Chronicles, Ezra, Nehemiah, Esther, vol. 3, trans. Sophia Taylor, from C. F. Keil and F. Delitzsch, *Commentary on the Old Testament,* 10 vols. (reprint; Grand Rapids: Eerdmans, 1976), 230.

9. After the exile (although some claim the essential form dated to Moses) these elements constitute the usual (but not exclusive) synagogue pattern for preaching, which in God's providence prepared the New Testament church to institutionalize this highly effective means of protecting and promulgating God's Word. Cf. Alfred Edersheim, *The Life and Times of Jesus the Messiah,* 3d ed. (Grand Rapids: Eerdmans, 1971), 443–46; and, W. White, Jr., "Synagogue," in vol. 5 of *The Zondervan Pictorial Encyclopedia of the Bible,* ed. Merrill C. Tenney, 5 vols. (Grand Rapids: Zondervan, 1975), 565–66.

At Thessolonica the apostle went into the synagogue and reasoned with the Jews "from the Scriptures." Paul first presented the Word to the people. Then Luke says that Paul was "explaining and proving" from the Word "that the Christ had to suffer and rise from the dead." With this explanation came at least an implied if not an overt exhortation to commitment; Luke next records, "Some of the Jews were persuaded and joined Paul and Silas, as did a large number of God-fearing Greeks and not a few prominent women."

I do not mean to suggest that these features of exposition form the only observable pattern in the biblical preaching record, nor that every feature is always equally evident. However, these features are consistent enough to challenge today's preachers to consider whether their exposition of Scripture faithfully reflects these biblical elements: presentation of some aspect of the Word itself; explanation of what that portion of the Word means; and an exhortation to act on the basis of what the explanation reveals. Not only does such a pattern of unfolding and opening the Word reflect a simple logic for preaching, it also conforms to Christ's instructions for our proclamation. Surely it is noteworthy that the parting words of our Lord in the Gospels command his messengers to proclaim his ministry in the expositional pattern of the prophets and apostles:

Matthew 28:19–20a

"Therefore go and make disciples of all nations . . .	
teaching them	**Word Explanation**
to obey	**Word Exhortation**
everything I have commanded you."	**Word Presentation**

Though a normative order does not appear in Scripture, the features of exposition occur together with enough frequency to suggest a common approach to expounding God's truth: present the Word; explain what it says; and exhort based on what it means. This is expository preaching.

THE COMPONENTS

Exposition does not merely involve the transmission of biblical information, but further demands establishment of the biblical basis for an action or a belief God requires of his people. Relating the tense of the verb, the tribe of the person, and the history of the battle does not adequately unfold the intended meaning of the text. Until people can see how the truths of the text would operate in their lives, the exposition remains incomplete. This is why explanation, illustration, and application act as the proof, the clarification, or the specification of the exhortation the preacher offers and the transformation God requires.[10]

This full-orbed understanding of exposition's content reduces the danger of an expository sermon merely degenerating into an exegetical paper, a systematics lecture, or a history lesson. Jerry Vines describes the danger:

> Some have understood an expository sermon to be a lifeless, meaningless, pointless, recounting of a Bible story. I can still remember a very fine man deliver such a sermon from John 10. He told us all the particular details about a sheepfold. We were given a complete explanation of the characteristics of sheep. We were informed about the methods of an Oriental shepherd. When the message ended we were still on the shepherd fields of Israel. We knew absolutely nothing about what John 10 had to say to the needs of our lives today. That is not expository preaching.[11]

Expository preaching aims to make the Bible useful as well as informative. Addressing a clear FCF as one researches and develops the sermon will keep the sermon on track biblically and practically. This practice keeps the goal of expository preachers and the intention of the writers of Scripture the same: to "take captive every thought to make it obedient to Christ" (2 Cor. 10:5). We want thought about God's Word to result in obedience to Christ.

Homileticians once divided sermons into three basic components: exposition (the explanations and arguments for what the text says); illustration (the demonstrations of what the text says); and application (the behavioral or attitudinal implications of what the text means).[12] These are helpful distinctions for teaching students to dissect others' sermons and to build their own. I will use these distinctions later in this book.[13] However, these traditional categories can damage expository preaching

---

10. Farris D. Whitesell, *Power in Expository Preaching* (Old Tappan, N.J.: Revell, 1963), xi; Jay E. Adams, *Truth Applied* (Grand Rapids: Zondervan, 1990), 42.

11. Jerry Vines, *A Practical Guide to Sermon Preparation* (Chicago: Moody, 1985), 5.

12. Cf. Broadus, *Preparation and Delivery of Sermons*, who divides exposition into the categories of explanation and argument separate from illustration and application, (144, 155); and Andrew Blackwood, *The Fine Art of Preaching* (1937; reprint, New York: Macmillan, 1943), 113.

13. Note, however, that I do not limit "exposition" to the details and the arguments of the text's explanation, but rather subsume explanation, illustration, and application under the larger heading of exposition. All are key in disclosing the meaning of a text.

if preachers do not see that explanation, illustration, and application are all essential components of opening and unfolding the meaning of the text. Explanation answers the question What does this text say? Illustration responds to Show me what the text says. Application answers What does the text mean to me? Ordinarily each component has a vital role in establishing listeners' full understanding of a text.[14]

We should not limit a sermon to technical explanations simply because it is expository. Biblical truths that the preacher cannot illustrate can hardly be considered apparent, and scriptural details that the preacher will not apply do not encourage obedience.[15] To expound Scripture fully means to unfold the meaning of a text in such a way that listeners can confront, understand, and act on its truths.[16] The more you preach, the more you will discover that this unfolding makes the components of exposition interdependent and, at times, indistinguishable. Illustration sometimes offers the best explanation; explanation focused on an FCF may sound much like application; and application may offer the opportunity for both illustration and explanation. As your expertise grows, the components of exposition will blend and bond to drive the truths of God's Word deep into the hearts of his people.[17]

In a traditional expository message each component of exposition occurs in every main point of the sermon because it makes no sense to explain something that can be neither demonstrated nor applied.[18] There are, however, good reasons to make exceptions to this traditional expectation: sometimes a sermon uses a series of explanations to build to an application or to veil implications for a later, more powerful impact. However, the beginning preacher will find that listeners usually pay closer attention to a message whose demonstrations and applications of truth occur regularly and frequently in the sermon. Today's cultural influences make it unreasonable for the preacher to expect a congregation to stay with a message for twenty-five minutes with the hope that something relevant will be said in the last five minutes. Congrega-

14. Broadus, *Preparation and Delivery of Sermons*, 155.

15. Larsen, *Anatomy of Preaching*, 96, 138–43.

16. Sidney Greidanus, *The Modern Preacher and the Ancient Text: Interpreting and Preachers Biblical Literature* (Grand Rapids: Eerdmans, 1988), 182–84.

17. Broadus, *Preparation and Delivery of Sermons*, 155; Ian Pitt-Watson, *A Primer for Preachers* (Grand Rapids: Baker, 1986), 101; Greidanus, *Modern Preacher and Ancient Text*, 182–84.

18. Broadus, *Preparation and Delivery of Sermons*, 211; Greidanus, *Modern Preacher and Ancient Text*, 182; D. Martyn Lloyd-Jones, *Preaching and Preachers* (Grand Rapids: Baker, 1971), 77; Vines, *Practical Guide to Sermon Preparation*, 133.

tional needs and capabilities make the old rule of including explanation, illustration, and application in every main point a reasonable guideline, even if one does not follow it every time.

THE BALANCE

A GENERIC APPROACH

The finest expository preachers prepare each message asking themselves this question while imagining that their listeners are present: What may I, with the authority of God's Word, require of you as a result of what we discern this text means? Recognition of listeners' spiritual need to discern personally a text's meaning for their lives, rather than simply accept the assertions or the dictates of the preacher, forces pastors to evaluate whether their messages are accessible as well as informative, applicable as well as erudite.

Concern for the needs of the listener as well as the information to be conveyed can affect the balance of the components in a message. As we have already seen, the pattern of exposition can vary. However, the most common order in which exposition's components appear is explanation, then illustration, then application.[19] This allows the preacher to establish a truth, then demonstrate and clarify its features before applying it. If each of these components were to be given equal time within the development of a message and/or its main points, then the form of the message would be a double helix (see fig. 4.3). There is something for everyone in roughly equal proportions.

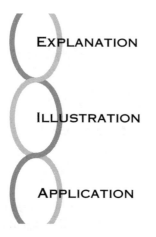

FIGURE 4.3
Balanced Exposition
Double Helix

EXPLANATION

ILLUSTRATION

APPLICATION

A CUSTOMIZED APPROACH

Fortunately, there are no generic congregations. Although it can be helpful for student preachers to prepare sermons that give equal attention to each of the sermon components so that they learn to use all the homiletical tools, differences

19. Later chapters will explain how and why this order should vary, but note for now this logical progression that is most common in expository preaching.

among congregations will require pastors to vary the proportions of the expositional components in their sermons.

Pastoral sensitivity and respect for the unique character of every group will determine whether the following descriptions are mere caricatures, but they do help demonstrate ways in which preachers may vary the composition of their messages.

Youth pastors typically swell the illustrative component of their sermons and drive application home behind a few well-chosen explanatory points (see fig. 4.4A). Blue-collar congregations often desire solid explanation whose relevance is more fully spelled out in down-to-earth application (see fig. 4.4B). When professionals and management types dominate a congregation the pastor may want to hit application more lightly since these persons are often most motivated by what they determine to do and are not accustomed to having someone else make decisions for them. In such a congregation it may be important to package the explanation in such a way that application becomes largely self-evident (see fig. 4.4C).

FIGURE 4.4

Exposition Component Variations

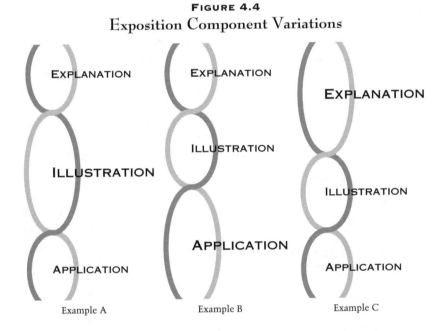

Each characterization is almost sinfully stereotypical and should not rule over common sense. My own experience has been that sermons that provide a healthy combination of all the expositional components can be preached with impact almost anywhere with only minor adjustments. This is not simply because congregations typically have a mix of people in them, but because we are each a mix of persons. Our minds need explanations of what the Bible says so that we know we have grasped the thoughts and standards of our God. Our hearts need the illustrations that so often touch our emotions or fire our imaginations to convince us that our God is not a cold collection of abstract ideas. We need application so that we have either the confidence that we are acting in accord with the will of God, or, that we gain the conviction that we must adjust our ways.

A HEALTHY APPROACH

Even though the relationships are not exclusive of one another it is often helpful to think that explanations prepare the mind, illustrations prepare the heart, and applications prepare the will to obey God. This approach cautions preachers to avoid messages that do not offer proportional servings of explanation, illustration, and explanation. For example, a sermon that is three-quarters explanation, one-quarter illustration, and one sentence of application (the classic seminary sermon); or, has one sentence of explanation, is three-quarters illustration, and is one-quarter application (the popular media message) is unbalanced. A balanced expositional meal carries each component in sufficient proportion to nourish the whole person.

No strict rules will determine what proportion these components should take in any specific sermon. The text, the topic, the purpose, the gifts of the preacher, the target audience, the situation, the makeup of the congregation, the time that may be required to express an idea, the persuasive or the structural advantages of placing one component over another at various stages of the message, and the relative strengths of individual components of exposition in a particular sermon all have a role in determining how the preacher should distribute explanation, illustration, and application.

This does not mean that the composition of every sermon is completely up for grabs. I have observed a consensus—maybe more a spiritual instinct Christians share than a standard of orthodoxy—that at least guides me as I consider how to communicate Scripture. Balanced Christians disdain messages whose illustrations dominate to the point of entertainment, whose applications extend to the level of diatribes, or whose explanations enlarge to ponderous displays of academic erudition. Each extreme reveals a preacher preoccupied with special or personal interests over congregational health. Preachers once posted this reduction of the preaching task in their studies:

> Preach
> reach
> each

Such a reduction still has great value.[20] It advises us to resist the emphases of our academic training, popular preaching, or a congregation's extremists who tempt us to preach without the balance that will nourish all the people at various levels of their being. Congregations need to hear what most preachers want to hear: solid explanation vividly illustrated and powerfully applied.

THE ATTITUDES

A DIVINE AUTHORITY

The way in which divine authority is expressed in the pulpit needs to be discussed before we examine, in subsequent chapters, how to use each component of exposition. Already we have examined why the expository sermon enables us to preach with authority. When we say what God says we have his authority. This realization should caution us against peppering our sermons with expressions such as "I believe this means . . . ," "I feel we should understand . . . ," or even, "I think. . . ." Quite frankly, except for peripheral matters, biblically astute congregations are not interested in what the preacher thinks. Larsen chides us, "There is no place in the pulpit for a preacher who stutters, 'Everyone outside of Christ is going to hell, I think."[21] People sit in the pews to hear what God attests in his Word. If you cannot say, "The Bible says . . ." about the core truths of the message then the congregation owes no more regard to your conclusions than it does to any philosopher's speculations.

In obedience to biblical imperatives an expositor must preach "as one speaking the very words of God" (1 Pet. 4:11). Preaching that lacks authority leaves a congregation longing for the divine voice. Lives sick-

---

20. Robert G. Rayburn's lecture notes indicate that he taught this reduction with its simple poignancy for more than twenty-five years at Covenant Theological Seminary.
21. Larsen, *Anatomy of Preaching*, 81.

ened by sin, confused by culture, and crushed by tragedy desire no "uncertain sound." Still, we need to understand that this authority resides in the truth of the Word rather than in a particular tone we bring to our messages. We need to distinguish carefully between preaching with authority and merely sounding authoritarian.

A pastor confident of the Bible's truth is able to preach with great force or with great gentleness and still speak with authority. Preaching with authority relates more to the confidence and integrity with which the preacher expresses God's truth rather than to a specific tone or posture the preacher assumes. The authority of the Word enables us to say the most challenging things to any person without apology, but that same authority lets us speak tenderly without compromising strength. Too often expository preachers get stuck in one gear, seeming to believe that to preach with authority they must project a certain hardness into their sermons. They sound as though they are trying by their efforts to make the Word authoritative rather than trusting its innate power to touch the soul.

A BIBLICAL MANNER

The same principles of exposition that require us to reflect the intent of the biblical author should direct us to speak in a manner appropriate for the truth being presented and the situation being addressed. The great variety of terms in the original languages that relate to preachers and their tasks confirm how manifold our expressions may need to be (see tables 4.1 and 4.2).

TABLE 4.1
Key Old Testament Terms

Term	Meaning	Reference (example)
parash	to distinguish or specify clearly (possibly, to translate)	Neh. 8:7–8
sekel	to give the sense or meaning	Neh. 8:7–8
bin	to cause to understand (to separate mentally for use)	Neh. 8:7–8
nabi	one who pours forth or announces under the divine impulse (a prophet)	Deut. 13:1; 18:20; Jer. 23:21; cf. Num. 11:25–29

hozeh	one who glows or grows warm (a seer or a prophet)	Amos 7:12
roeh	one who sees (a prophet)	1 Chron. 29:29; Isa. 30:10
qohelet	a caller or a preacher	Eccles. 1:1
qara	to call out	Isa. 61:1
basar	to announce glad tidings	Isa. 61:1; Ps. 40:9 (40:10 Heb.)
natap	to drip, to pour out words	Ezek 20:46 (21:2 Heb); Amos 7:16; Mic. 2:6, 11

TABLE 4.2

Key New Testament Terms

Term	Meaning	Reference (example)
kerusso	to proclaim as a herald concerning a king or his decrees	Rom. 10:14–15; 1 Cor. 1:21–23; 2 Tim 4:2 (more than 70 times in all)
euangelizo	to announce joyful news	Luke 4:18; cf. Acts 8:4 (more than 40 times)
diermeneuo	to unfold the meaning of, to expound	Luke 24:27–32
dianoigo	to open up, to thoroughly disclose	Luke 24:27–32
dialegomai	to reason, to discuss, to converse	Acts 17:2–3
paratithemi	to allege, to place alongside (used to describe Jesus' use of parables)	Matt. 13:31
logos	a word or a saying	Matt. 13:19–23
rhema	a word or a message	Rom. 10:17; 1 Pet. 1:25
diangello	to declare	Luke 9:60
katangello	to proclaim	Acts 4:2; 13:5

Note: these first two very common terms are used primarily, but not exclusively, of evangelistic activity directed to non-Christians

parresiazo-mai	to preach, to speak boldly	Acts 9:27–29
elencho	to expose, to correct, to convict, to reprove	2 Tim. 4:2; Titus 1:9; 2:15
epitimao	to rebuke or warn seriously	2 Tim. 4:2
parakaleo	to encourage, to comfort, to defend; lit., to call to one's side as an advocate	2 Tim. 4:2; cf. Acts 14:22
paramuthia	comfort, cheer, consolation	1 Cor. 14:3
martureo	to give a witness	Acts 20:21; cf. 1 John 4:14
homologeo	lit., to say the same thing, to agree with; to profess or to confess the truth of	1 Tim. 6:12
homileo	to converse or to talk with (to engage in conversation); this is the Greek word from which we derive the term *homiletics* for the study of preaching	Acts 20:11
laleo	to speak	Mark 2:2; cf. 1 Cor. 2:6–7
didasko	to teach	Acts 5:42
epilusis	unloosing or untying; an explanation of what is obscure or hard to understand	2 Pet. 1:20
suzeteo	to examine together, to discuss, to dispute	Acts 9:29
apologia	a verbal defense	Acts 22:1; 1 Pet. 3:15; Phil 1:7, 16; 2 Tim. 4:16
metadidomi	to share the gospel as a gift	1 Thess. 2:8; cf. Rom. 1:11; Eph. 4:28

These lists of the biblical terms related to preaching are not exhaustive, but they indicate the diverse tasks of God's spokesmen. Sometimes we must proclaim the joys of the gospel to the unsaved or simply converse with interested persons. Other times we must rebuke the regenerate, and still other times we must comfort the broken.

A Humble Boldness

As no one word captures all the dimensions of biblical preaching, no one style can reflect its many facets. This is all the more true because different personalities express authority differently. For some the most confident expression is spoken with an intense gaze and a level voice. Others use animated and forceful expressions to convey authority. Probably most of us vary the way we express authority based on the persons, circumstances, and issues present.

These observations seem to elude many expository preachers who take an authoritarian style to every occasion under the false impression that their tone will reflect their lack of biblical compromise. Unfortunately, a consistent authoritarian demeanor reflects a lack of biblical understanding:

> There is something inherently horrid about human beings who claim and attempt to wield personal authority they do not possess. It is particularly inappropriate in the pulpit. When a preacher pontificates like a tinpot demagogue, or boasts of his power and glory as Nebuchadnezzar did on the roof of his royal palace in Babylon (Dan. 4:28, 29), he deserves the judgement which fell on that dictator. . . .

> [T]he authority with which we preach inheres neither in us as individuals, nor primarily in our office as clergy or preachers, nor even in the church whose members and accredited pastors we may be, but supremely in the Word of God which we expound. . . .[22]

We do not need to pump our authority into the Word to make it effective. Confidence in God's authority over the whole of life will grant us the courage to speak his Word whenever and however it is appropriate. This holy boldness is not so much a particular manner as a commitment to speak the truth in love out of a conviction that God's Word provides wisdom for every challenge, issue, and need that humankind confronts (Eph. 4:15; 1 Pet. 3:15; 2 Pet. 1:3).

No one approach, attitude, or tone will suit all occasions. The same apostle who advised one young preacher to "rebuke with all authority" (Tit. 2: 15) advised another that "those who oppose him he must gently instruct, in the hope that God will grant them repentance . . ." (2 Tim. 2:25). In the passages where Paul commands both these young pastors

22. Stott, *Between Two Worlds*, 58.

to rebuke with authority, he also tells them to use the same authority to encourage (2 Tim. 4:2; Tit. 2:15). Our struggles to know which manner to assert in different situations make us no less qualified to preach the Word if our struggles make us more aware of the spiritual guidance we ourselves require. Writes Herbert Farmer,

> How may we have within ourselves that which shall impart to our preaching the right sort of authority, the conviction and confidence which lacks neither a proper respect for the hearer nor the humility of a sinful man, which is neither overridingly dogmatic nor weakly diffident? I suppose in the end the secret lies in the quality of our own spiritual life and the extent to which we are ourselves walking humbly with God in Christ.[23]

Our own relationship with Christ teaches us that we must treat people with compassion as well as confront them with the authority of the Word. As we need a stern hand in some moments and a loving embrace at others, so too do the people we face from the pulpit. The soul made sensitive by the recognition of its own sin, the awareness of God's sovereignty, and the miracle of the Savior's love is the one best suited to guide the tongue in the sanctuary as well as in the circumstances of life. Consistently aggressive or combative preachers ill disguise the spiritually resistant recesses of their own hearts.

Life is too complex, the obligations of preaching too myriad, and the message of Scripture too rich for preachers to impoverish their ministries with one style of sermonizing. Only in the worst caricatures do preachers speak with the same tone before a grieving family, wedding celebrants, a skeptical college crowd, a crisis-bound community, a rebellious congregation, a battered church, anxious leaders, or seeking sinners. Only the most limited preacher would try to comfort, convict, challenge, correct, encourage, and command with the same manner. Scripture's authority grants us the right to say what it says. Scripture's wisdom advises us to speak as prudently and diversely as it does. Our manner should reflect Scripture's content. Because we convey meaning not merely by what we say but also by how we speak, accurate exposition requires us to reflect a text's tone as well as define its terms. Sometimes this requires a voice reminiscent of the thunder on Sinai and other times the still small voice at Horeb.

23. Herbert H. Farmer, *The Servant of the Word* (Philadelphia: Fortress, 1942), 63.

A CHRIST-LIKENESS

The service that we render the text indicates that our tone should always resonate with the humility of one who speaks with authority because we realize we are under the authority of another (2 Tim. 4:2). Ultimately our awareness of the divine activity that empowers our words defines our preaching. As the Spirit of God uses our words to communicate his truth, we speak for God.[24] Despite the frailties and the foibles of our expressions, the Spirit burns away the dross of our preaching to refine Christ's very words in others' hearts. Martin Luther pictured this more vividly than we may find it comfortable to consider: "Now let me and everyone who speaks the word of Christ freely boast that *our mouths are the mouths of Christ.* I am certain indeed that my word is not mine, but the word of Christ. So must my mouth be the mouth of him who utters it."[25] This powerful image should caution us never to speak with a tone that compromises Christ's authority or contradicts his care. We represent him. Therefore we must consider how he would speak were he to address our listeners with the truths committed to our care. If the words we are saying came from Christ's mouth how would he say them? Our words must reflect his character as well as his truth if our preaching remains true to him.

---

24. *Westminster Shorter Catechism*, 89.

25. As cited by Edward Marquart in *Quest for Better Preaching* (Minneapolis: Augsburg, 1985), 83–84. Calvin wrote similarly in his *Institutes* (4.1.5): "Among the many excellent gifts with which God has adorned the human race, it is a singular privilege that he deigns to consecrate to himself the mouths and tongues of men in order that his voice may resound in them."

QUESTIONS FOR REVIEW AND DISCUSSION

1. What three elements of exposition consistently appear in examples of Old and New Testament preaching? What does the consistency of these elements say about the nature of exposition?

2. What three components of exposition usually occur in every main point? Why are all three important?

3. How may the proportion of the components of exposition vary according to the nature of the congregation? Why are all the components still important for all congregations?

4. What does the diversity of biblical terms related to preaching indicate about the tone and the manner of expository preaching? What, ultimately, should govern the tone of our sermons?

EXERCISES

1. Indicate how explanation, illustration, and application are used in Jesus' Sermon on the Mount (Matt. 5–7) and Stephen's speech to the Sanhedrin (Acts 7:2–53).

2. Determine how and why the tone of the gospel varies between Matthew 23 and Acts 17:16–31.

PART 2

PREPARATION OF EXPOSITORY SERMONS

CONTENTS OF CHAPTER 5

GOAL OF CHAPTER 5

*To explain how to prepare and present
the explanation component of a sermon*

5

THE PROCESS OF EXPLANATION

THE LABYRINTH

Our conviction that people are spiritually transformed only through personal confrontation with the truths of the Word of God complicates our preaching. We recognize that for most people in our culture the Bible is an opaque book with its truths hidden in an endless maze of hard words, unfamiliar history, unpronounceable names, and impenetrable mysticism. This situation and our calling obligate every expositor to lead people through this labyrinth so that they confront God's words for their lives. However, the best preachers guide in such a way that their listeners are able to discover that the labyrinth is a myth.

There are no dark passageways through twisted mazes of logic to biblical truth that require the expertise of the spiritually elite.[1] There is only a well-worn path that anyone can follow if the preacher will shed some ordinary light along the way. This is as good a definition of exposition as I can muster. Expository preaching sheds some ordinary light on the path that leads to understanding a text. An expositor not only must follow the path to shine this light personally, but also must learn when the light used to lead others glows too dimly, creates a blinding glare, or merely displays the preacher. The right amount of light expertly shined not only exposes the path but also helps those on the path to find their own way in the future. We will navigate this path first by outlining the steps a preacher follows in preparing an expository message, and then by describing how to shed light on that path while

1. John A. Broadus, *On the Preparation and Delivery of Sermons*, ed. J. B. Weatherspoon (New York: Harper and Row, 1944), 157.

presenting the message. Later chapters will concentrate on illustration and application; the remainder of this chapter will focus on the path that explanation follows.

THE PATH OF PREPARATION

SIX CRITICAL QUESTIONS

Before we begin to blaze the trail of exposition we have to determine where we are going. An expositor's course can be charted by determining what questions the pastor personally needs to answer in preparing the message. These questions provide a bird's-eye view of the expositor's path. Ultimately they determine what path our explanation will follow and the steps we should take to lead others along the way. At first glance the questions may appear so obvious and/or intuitive as to scarcely need identification, but significant questions on this list are unfortunately often left unasked or unanswered in sermon preparation.

This list is not meant to lock the preacher into a rigid pattern of preparation. The questions are listed in a logical order, but the mind may skip and jump along the way so that various questions blend together or change sequence. The greatest concern of the careful expositor is not the order in which the questions are asked, but the necessity that all be answered.

The first three questions relate to the preacher's research of the text's meaning:

1. What does the text mean?
2. How do I know what the text means?
3. What concerns caused the text to be written?

The reasoning for the first question is the most obvious: preachers need to do enough research to conclude what the scope and the particulars of the text mean. The second question begins to orient preachers toward their listeners. In a sense, this question forces the preachers to retrace the steps that led them to their conclusions of where the text was leading in order to identify significant landmarks that others will be able to follow. It is not at all uncommon for preachers to feel fairly confident about a text's meaning without being able to specify in their own minds what led to that conclusion. Solid explanations—and the second question—require the preacher to identify what establishes a text's meaning. The third question requires the preacher to determine the cause of the text. Although this question is related to the first two (and usually is integral to how they are answered), it is listed separately because its answer is vital to the ultimate development of the sermon and the answers to the expositor's remaining questions.

The next three questions determine how the preacher will relate the text's meaning:

4. What do we share in common with:
   a. Those to (or about) whom the text was written, and/or
   b. The one by whom the text was written?
5. How should people now respond to the truths of the text?
6. What is the most effective way I can communicate the meaning of the text?

Prior to answering these questions the preacher only has information about the text, not a sermon. Although many preachers may feel that when they have researched enough to determine a text's meaning they are ready to preach, they are mistaken. To this point they are only like "the little engine that could," chugging up the expositor's mountain saying, "I think I can preach. I think I can. . . ." Answering these remaining questions actually pushes the preacher over the crest of the mountain, converting a textual commentary or an exegetical lecture into a sermon.[2]

The fourth question takes us back to the principles of a Fallen Condition Focus (FCF).[3] By identifying what we share with the personages of Scripture we bring the truths of the text into immediate contact with the lives of our people. Not to do so simply steals from Scripture the impact God intends. I tried to demonstrate this to a student who once phrased a main point this way: "The Judaizers believed they could earn salvation with good works." The statement was true but was poorly designed for the main point of a sermon. It left listeners asking, "So what? What does that have to do with me?"

I asked the student to try to frame the main point in such a way that it would deal with what we have in common with the people in the text. He replied, "But, I don't have anything in common with those people. I don't believe my works will gain my salvation." "Oh!?" I replied, "I do. I don't believe in my head that my works will save me, but I sometimes

---

2. Jay E. Adams, *Preaching with Purpose: A Comprehensive Textbook on Biblical Preaching* (Grand Rapids: Baker, 1982), 51–52.
3. See chapter 2 for the development of the FCF concept.

feel and even behave that way. I am always tempted to believe that when I am good God will love me more. So is everyone else. We all have moments, or even years, when an aspect of us lives the Judaizers' theology." We all have vestiges of Babel with us—as a consequence of our fallen nature we are all trying to climb our ladders to heaven and claim responsibility for the grace that saves us. Our pride wars against the admission that there is no good in us. Our sinful condition forever struggles with our total dependence on grace. Only when we can identify the humanness that unites us with the struggles of those whom Paul had to warn about the Judaizers do we really know why he wrote and what we are to preach.

Preaching does not primarily point at what happened to others—it points to us. We are to look deep into our hearts and into the hearts of those about us to discover what the Scriptures are addressing at the level of our common humanity. Truth assumes living power when its meaning is discerned in the living contexts for which it was inscripturated. In some sense, we all share David's guilt, Thomas's doubt, and Peter's denial (1 Cor. 10:13). Therefore, a solid explanation of the text does not merely display the facts in a text or describe how they defend a doctrine. A full explanation of the text's meaning identifies how its FCF touches and characterizes our lives.

The fifth question of explanation may not appear to be part of the explanation at all. Determining how we should respond to the truths of Scripture may sound much more like application than explanation. However, this question must be asked as part of the explanation process or it is impossible to determine what we are explaining. Any text of Scripture has near limitless explanation avenues and possibilities. Only when we determine what the text requires as a consequence of the fallen condition that the sermon addresses do we know how to focus, phrase, and organize the explanation of the text. Determining for listeners what the text means for them is as central to the process of explanation as is the researching of grammar and history.

These last questions indicate that a sermon is not merely an outlined description of the text. It is an explanation of how the text indicates that contemporary people of God should respond to a mutual condition we share with the persons who were the original subjects and/or objects of the text. Since the sermon ultimately answers for the listener, What does this text mean to me? the explanation has to be framed in such a way that it maximizes meaning for the listener. Thus, adequate explanation requires accurate understanding of both the text and the audience. We must exegete our listeners as well as the text to construct a sermon that most powerfully and accurately explains what a text means. It is, after all, quite possible to say many true things about a text and yet communicate a highly inadequate or an entirely false meaning by not taking into consideration a congregation's background and situation.[4] What can be heard as well as what should be said demand attention as the preacher lays the path of explanation.

FOUR NECESSARY STEPS

Preachers provide answers to the critical questions that define the path of explanation by following four steps in their sermon preparation. Each step reflects a skill that preachers must exercise as they interpret a passage for a congregation's use. Preachers must learn to observe and interrogate the features of the text, as well as to relate and organize their conclusions about the text's meaning. These four steps are discussed in their logical order, but the sequence often varies and the steps frequently blend in the process of preparing an expository message.

Observe

The preacher uses the faculties of observation simply to determine what's here. The method is simple: read, read, and reread the text. Read broadly enough to see the context. Read closely enough to identify important or unique phrasing. Reread until the flow of thought begins to surface. Look up unknown words, names, and places so that you are sure you are reading with understanding. Make sure you become familiar with the features of the text even if you do not yet grasp its full meaning. Gazing deeply and carefully into the text is no cursory matter. As simplistic as it may sound to insist that the preacher must read the text carefully, the instruction cannot be overemphasized. Spurgeon's oft-quoted advice bears repeating, not because of its great insight but because of its frequent neglect: "Get saturated with the Gospel. I always find that I can preach best when I can manage to lie asoak in my text. I like to get a text, and find out its meanings and bearings, and so on, and then, after I have bathed in it, I delight to lie down in it, and let it soak into me."[5]

Listen to the text, absorb it, wrestle with it, digest it, immerse in it, breath it in as God's breath, pray over it. The greatest danger you will

---

4. Ian Pitt-Watson, *A Primer for Preachers* (Grand Rapids: Baker, 1986), 23–24.
5. Charles Haddon Spurgeon, *All Round Ministry* (reprint; Banner of Truth, 1960), 124.

face is that you will focus too narrowly or quickly on some features of the text and, by neglecting surrounding details, will misinterpret the whole. I confess that at times I have discovered in my own pulpit reading of Scripture only moments before preaching a sermon an aspect of the text that had eluded my attention (and undercut my conclusions) because I had focused too exclusively on the part of the text that interested me. I would love to spare you the horror of a similar realization in like circumstances.

Careful and complete reading of the text ordinarily leads to good conclusions about its meaning. Still, we must be careful to keep these initial impressions subject to the discoveries of further research. Our research should substantiate the validity of conclusions derived from a thorough reading of the text and usually will provide us with more details that broaden and deepen our insights. Occasionally, however, our research will indicate that our initial conclusions need revision. Exposition of depth and accuracy requires more preparation.

Interrogate

The expositor grows familiar with the text with a view to the task ahead. John Stott writes, "To expound a Scripture is to bring out of the text what is there and expose it to view. . . . The opposite of exposition is 'imposition', which is to impose on the text what is not there."[6] Your expository obligation requires you to do two things accurately and concisely in the pulpit: state what the text means; and show how you know. These obligations impose definite procedures during sermon preparation. In the reading stage, preachers primarily ask, What's here? However this question quickly leads to more penetrating questions: What does it mean? and Why is it here? Often these questions will lead to additional discoveries of what's here. Preachers interrogate the text this way knowing they must eventually discern what faith principles and exhortations the features of the text will support as well as knowing how to state the conclusions that are established by the information in the text.

Expository preachers prepare to explain a text by asking the questions their listeners would if they wanted to discover what it means. Most homiletics texts allude to the journalist's five Ws and an H that we intuitively use to get the facts: who, what, when, where, why, and how. Still, these questions describe what the preacher is trying to discover rather

---

6. John Stott, *Between Two Worlds: The Art of Preaching in the Twentieth Century* (1982; reprint, Grand Rapids: Eerdmans, 1988), 125–26.

than how to get there. The preparation of explanation leads the preacher down a well-worn path that he travels in stages that involve exegesis, outlining, backgrounding, and spotlighting. No stage is independent of any other and often one stage will shed more light on the discoveries of other stages (even those previously traversed). The nature of the passage, the purpose of the sermon, or the expertise of the preacher will also signal appropriate short-cuts or sequence variations in these stages. Still, although years of experience probably allow most preachers to ramble and roam unconsciously through these stages of preparation in ways best suited to their preparation styles, expository sermons require the insights of each stage.

Exegete the Passage (What Does It Say?)

In order to know what a passage means, we have to know what its words mean and how they are used. Exegesis is the process by which preachers discover the precise definitions and grammatical distinctions of the words in a text. Preachers with Greek and Hebrew expertise translate passages recognizing that even the best English translations of the Bible cannot fully communicate the nuances of the words in the original languages. Even pastors without the language skills or time to translate an entire passage can use the language tools described in chapter 3 of this book to conduct profitable "pinpoint exegesis."

With pinpoint exegesis the preacher looks up unknown words, or examines more fully words that, by their placement, tense, structural role, repetition, rarity, function, or relationships to other words in this (or related) passages demonstrate a key role in determining the text's meaning. For instance, many people refer to the fruits of the Spirit. It is significant that the passage from which this phrase is taken does not make the word *fruit* plural (Gal. 5:22–23). The grammar indicates that the Spirit brings to bear in some measure all the characteristics listed in these two verses. One cannot say, "I do not have to be kind because the kindness listed in this passage is not one of the fruits the Spirit has granted me." The Spirit only has one fruit, whose characteristics include kindness. Exegesis allows the preacher to require kindness of all who claim the presence of the Spirit.

Not always mentioned in discussions of exegesis is the importance of comparison. Comparing the number of times or the differing ways specific words are used (or are not used) in related verses, or comparing the way specific words are variously translated can indicate where preachers should focus their pinpoint exegesis or concentrate their translation efforts. Cross- and chain-reference Bibles, concordances, good commentaries, comparison versions of the Bible, and good observation skills will lead the preacher to significant interpretive insights on the basis of comparison exegesis.

The importance of original-language exegesis should not discourage preachers from using careful analysis of the text in English as a primary exegetical tool. One of the graces of the Spirit is the general clarity of Scripture.[7] While original-language study will add richness to our exposition, the Bible does not hide its truths in language mazes. Careful attention to grammar, syntax, word relationships, and logic development in a Bible version translated by scholars committed to biblical authority will provide you with the vast majority of your exegetical insights in terms that will be apparent to your listeners.[8] We do not want to convince our listeners or ourselves that it is not until we have twenty years of Greek and Hebrew that we can understand the Bible. God does not grant deep understanding of his Word only to persons with seminary degrees, and those who pretend otherwise feed their egos at the expense of those whose faith needs nourishment. Excellent preaching makes people confident that biblical truth lies within their reach, not beyond their grasp.

Outline the Passage (How Does It Fit Together?)

The thought of the biblical writer typically shines more clearly when the expositor outlines the passage. Outlines visually exegete the thought flow of the text and enable the preacher to see the chief features of its development. The length and nature of the passage under consideration determine what type of exegetical outline will best aid the pastor's study.[9]

Grammatical outlines (or diagrams) show the relationships of words in sentences. By identifying the subject, verb, object, and modifiers, complex thoughts can often be deciphered and misinterpretations avoided. A typical grammatical outline diagrams sentences according to standard grammatical conventions whether in an original language or in English (see chart 5.1).

---

7. *Westminster Confession of Faith*, 1.5.
8. See chapter 3 for a discussion of the strengths of various English versions.
9. These first two types of exegetical outlines receive helpful discussion and instruction in Haddon Robinson, *Biblical Preaching: The Development and Delivery of Expository Messages* (Grand Rapids: Baker, 1980), 68, 216; and J. Robertson McQuilkin, *Understanding and Applying the Bible* (Chicago: Moody, 1983), 108–21.

CHART 5.1
Examples of Grammatical Outlines

Grammatical Outline Example One:	Grammatical Outline Example Two:

Jesus | died
  \for
    \ungodly
    \the
	Lord | heard |cry
	  \the \my

By displaying the grammatical relationships of the words, a grammatical outline highlights the development of thought within a sentence and often helps clarify how specific words relate to each other.

Mechanical layouts help the preacher to see how whole phrases or sentences relate to each other. Whereas a grammatical outline diagrams word relationships within sentences, a mechanical layout attempts to diagram the relationships between sentences and phrases. A single mechanical outline can cover an entire passage or major portions of it.

Typically a mechanical layout identifies independent clauses (or main ideas) and then places dependent clauses (or developmental ideas) in subordinate positions under the independant clauses. There are no strict conventions to determine how to construct a mechanical layout. The idea is to place phrases and concepts in such a way that you are able to see how they correspond. Major ideas are usually listed to the left with subordinate phrases and conjunctions indented to indicate their relationships to the main clauses, but many variations will serve (see figs. 5.1, 5.2).

FIGURE 5.1
Traditional Mechanical Layout of 2 Timothy 4:1–2

(v. 1) In the presence of
      God
      and
      Christ Jesus
         who will judge
            the living
            and
            the dead
      and

> in view of his appearing
> I give you this charge:
> (v. 2) Preach the Word;
>   be prepared
>   in season
>   and
>   out of season
>   correct, rebuke, and encourage
>   with great patience
>   and
>   (with) careful instruction

FIGURE 5.2

Alternative Mechanical Layout of 2 Timothy 4:2

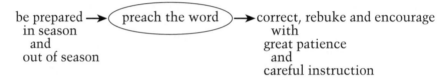

The mechanical layout often takes less linguistic expertise than a grammatical outline but still forces the preacher to ask questions about the structure of a passage and to determine the text's thought development. J. Robertson McQuilkin says that a mechanical layout "will keep [the interpreter] from assuming he understands the flow of thought before he has actually studied each part of the sentence and paragraph."[10]

There is no need to segregate the outlining alternatives. Often a preacher will apply a mechanical layout to a larger Scripture portion, but do a grammatical diagram of a particularly complex sentence within the passage. The mechanical layout can actually help spotlight areas that need closer grammatical examination. Mechanical layouts are applied to larger expository units and grammatical outlines aid the microscopic analysis of smaller portions. Neither alternative works well, however, when the expository unit becomes massive.

Conceptual outlines best serve the preparation of sermons covering many verses or even multiple chapters. When narratives or other Scripture portions require the preacher to analyze lengthy passages, an outline that captures the broad features of the text best serves sermon prep-

---

10. McQuilkin, *Understanding and Applying the Bible*, 116.

aration. Again there are multiple ways to construct such an outline. The goal remains to replace supporting thoughts in subordinate positions to main ideas. However, in a conceptual outline ideas (or the characters and events that represent them rather than precise phrases from the text) usually form the exegetical outline.[11] A statement listed in a conceptual outline may summarize many sentences:

2 Samuel 11–12:23

I. David Disobeyed
   A. Committed Adultery (11:1–5)
   B. Committed Murder (11:6–26)
II. God Convicted
   A. Sent a Prophetic Word (12:1–6)
   B. Identified the King's Sin (12:7–12)
   C. Specified the King's Punishment (12:11–12, 14)
III. David Repented
   A. Confessed Sin (12:13)
   B. Expressed Sorrow (12:15–17)
   C. Accepted Discipline (12:18–23)
   D. Renewed Obedience (12: 20)

Each of these three types of exegetical outlines has distinct advantages depending on the length of the passage and the nature of the pastor's questions about the text. The larger the expository unit the more advantageous are the latter styles of outlining. However, multiple approaches may well serve any single sermon preparation. Note also that outlines covering large portions of Scripture often paraphrase an author's thoughts rather than quote the text directly. In such cases outlining—in addition to describing the text's contents—requires the pastor to make interpretive decisions that will greatly aid the construction of the sermon.

Almost always it is important to use the space around an exegetical outline to make notes of textual insights that you discover in your study tools or that come to your mind as your sermon research advances. Write the insights near that portion of the outline representing the section of the text to which the insights apply. Keeping verse numbers visible in the outline makes this type of notation easier and helps preachers

---

11. A conceptual outline sometimes does work well using the precise phrases of an epistle where the paragraph nature of the writer's thought allows the preacher to identify major ideas and supporting concepts in the words of the text.

quickly find information in the exegetical outline when they later construct the sermon.

Careful reading, exegeting, and outlining of the text will automatically force the preacher to look up unfamiliar words, characters, quotations, events, references, or places, but the interrogation of the text is not complete until the preacher uncovers the background of the text. Backgrounding the text locates the passage in its historical, logical, and literary setting. The goal of this preparation step is simply to make sure that the preacher interprets the text in context. Since matters of context were discussed in chapter 3 I will not reiterate their importance here except to note that the preparation of explanation requires context research.

The preacher determines the *historical context* by reading and researching the culture, concerns, and events that surround and stimulate the writing of the text. Understanding the historical situation will cause the preacher to look at the chronology of events, the biography of the people, the details of the culture, and the time of the passage's writing. Reading broadly enough to see the development of the biblical writer's argument or concerns in this and other relevant Scriptures will reveal the *logical context* of the passage. Surrounding passages, the literary form (or genre) of the passage, the intended use of the text, the narrative voice, the role of this portion in the broader book or scope of Scripture, figures of speech, parallel passages, echoes and quotations of other references, or rhetorical patterns expose the *literary context* of the passage.[12]

Backgrounding cannot be isolated from the other preparation steps. Usually the preacher begins to collect background information when examining the context of the passage, and will gain much information about the role of the text in its setting when researching the passage's details. Study Bibles, commentaries, Bible handbooks, Bible dictionaries and encyclopedias, as well as the resources used in exegesis illuminate the background of the passage. Most preachers make notes of important background details at appropriate places in the exegetical outline or on other paper where it can be readily accessed for writing the sermon.

Relate

Simply collecting information about grammar, thought flow, and background does not prepare the pastor to preach on a text. Preachers

12. Leland Ryken, *Words of Life* (Grand Rapids: Baker, 1987), 21ff.

cannot really determine how to organize their explanations, or even how to state their discoveries meaningfully, until they consider the impact the information should have on the congregation. While researching the text, the best preachers are always asking themselves questions in their listeners' behalf. Questions such as, Who needs to hear this? What will make this sink in? What are we facing that is similar to this biblical situation? and How are we like these people in the Bible? will help preachers determine which features of their explanatory insights to highlight.

Although these questions may sound as if they are oriented more to the preparation of application than to explanation, sound exposition requires us to ask these questions at this stage in sermon preparation. Jerry Vines explains,

> I have found it very helpful to visualize certain members of my congregation as I study through a Scripture passage. I am constantly asking myself, What does this passage have to say to John Smith, Or Pam Jones? Or Billy Foster? Horne mentions a helpful practice followed by Alexander Maclaren. As Maclaren studied the Scriptures during his sermon preparation he placed across from his desk an empty chair. He imagined a person sitting in the chair as he prepared his sermons. He carried on a dialogue between himself and the imaginary person. Such a practice would be helpful at all times in keeping us aware at all times that we are preparing our message for real people.[13]

Note that these premier evangelical preachers do not wait until their Scripture research is done to start thinking about people. Explanation prepared in the abstract sounds irrelevant. When each word and every statement of the message are intimately related to the concerns of the people who must apply them to their lives, then the explanation assumes form and power.

The danger, of course, is that contemporary concerns will sway the preacher's interpretation. The preacher must remain aware of the temptation to soften or recast the passage's truths in light of a congregation's situation. Still, the greater danger of our aborting biblical truth by our speaking words and stating conclusions that do not breathe the air of the listeners must affect our sermon preparations.

Discerning the human background and the persuasive focus of the passage prepares pastors to relate the explanatory material to similar concerns faced by a present congregation and provides direction for the

13. Jerry Vines, *A Practical Guide to Sermon Preparation* (Chicago: Moody, 1985), 98.

message's organization. Without relating explanations of the text to the concerns of the congregation, there are really no fences to corral the thousands of explanatory alternatives, other than time constraints and the preacher's personal interests. Neither of these is more holy than the desire to explain matters in such a way that they can and will be heard.

Organize

Although the next chapter will cover the process of outlining the sermon in much greater detail, preachers need some general principles for organizing their research so that their preparation proceeds smoothly. An expositor's explanations must cover the entire text efficiently. This requirement obligates the preacher to sequence the explanatory material, exhaust the scope of the text, and subordinate incidental facts to critical information.

SEQUENCE AND ORDER

Putting textual information in some logical order is a common first step. It is also important to understand why the exegetical outline of the passage does not automatically determine the sequence in which the preacher makes explanations: (1) The exegetical outline describes the immediate text. It does not provide context and background information or indicate what emphasis of various components of the passage may be required for a particular congregation. (2) An exegetical outline does not necessarily include aspects of a biblical person's biography, the usage of a word in parallel texts, the previous argument of an apostle, or many other aspects of a passage—background, cause, or emphases. The preacher, by the way of explanation, must incorporate these into the sermon. Thus, insights from the exegetical outline, the passage's background, and present level of a congregation's knowledge about these matters must all funnel into the homiletical outline in order for a competent sermon to take shape. Although the two may echo one another closely, *the exegetical outline ordinarily is not the homiletical outline.* The exegetical outline establishes what the text says. The homiletical outline establishes how the text's meaning is best communicated to the congregation.

An expository sermon obligates the preacher to present the truths of a text, but not necessarily the pattern of the passage. The sequence of thought in the text may not allow the preacher to introduce background information efficiently or it may not make the truth of the text shine accurately and powerfully.[14] For example, a *writer* most often says significant things first and then develops them (e.g., Eph. 1; Heb. 1). However, listeners hear most clearly what a *speaker* says last. Therefore, in order for preachers to represent most accurately the truth that a biblical writer wants to emphasize, they may choose to say last what the author wrote first.

The text may also reflect a written pattern that for readers is understandable, but which is too complex for listeners.[15] For instance, some psalms are patterned after the Hebrew alphabet. The apostle Paul sometimes introduces a subject, then inserts a parenthetical thought before completing the original subject. In each of these cases preachers exercise sound judgment when they reorganize the information so that hearers can grasp the writer's thought. Robinson says,

> Sometimes the arrangement of ideas in the passage will have to be altered in the outline [i.e., the "sermon" outline]. Because of his readers, the biblical writer may follow an inductive order; but because of his hearers, an expositor may follow a deductive plan. Sermons from the epistles more easily fit into outlines than do poems, parables, or narratives. Unless a preacher remains flexible in the ways he communicates passages, he will find it impossible to accomplish the purposes of some passages with his audience.[16]

The advantages of following the pattern of the text are obvious: the pattern of the text tends to reflect the pattern of the biblical writer's thought; and listeners can more easily follow the structure of a sermon that they can see moves in a straightforward way through the text. Such straightforwardness can support the credibility and authority of the preacher's explanations, and gives listeners confidence that they can read the text easily. Still, these advantages of following the order of the text are overturned when the pattern of the text is too complex for listeners, the Scripture portion being expounded is only a piece of a larger pattern and to present it in straight order actually misrepresents its purpose, or the pattern may not effectively fulfill a homiletical need.

The more the pattern of a passage governs the truth that the biblical writer wants to convey, the higher is the obligation of the expositor to

14. Adams, *Preaching with Purpose*, 56–58.
15. Sidney Greidanus, *The Modern Preacher and the Ancient Text: Interpreting and Preaching Biblical Literature* (Grand Rapids: Eerdmans, 1988), 19.
16. Haddon Robinson, *Biblical Preaching: The Development and Delivery of Expository Messages* (Grand Rapids: Baker, 1980), 128–29.

make listeners aware of that pattern. Still, the preacher has a higher obligation to make sure the listeners understand and apply the truths of the passage than to guarantee that they will cover the passage in sentence or verse order.

EXHAUST AND COVER

Expositors do not need to cover a text in verse order, although they ordinarily do need to cover the scope of the text. An expository sermon obligates the preacher to base main points and subpoints of the sermon's explanation on the text, and not to skip important features of the passage.[17] A clear exegetical outline points to the material the preacher needs to mine in order to construct the homiletical outline and allows the preacher to see if the sermon inadvertently ignores significant aspects of the text.

When the preacher has mined each feature of the exegetical outline and has applied its truth to the homiletical outline then the text has been "exhausted." Exhausting the text is a distinction of expository preaching that obligates the preacher to deal with the entire passage.[18] This trait of expository preaching does not mean that the preacher must (or could) exhaust all the truth the passage contains, but rather indicates that the preacher has explained all the key sections of the text. Expository preachers implicitly say to their listeners, "Here, let me tell you what this text means." If they then fail to cover the textual territory they have not met their obligation to explain what lies there.[19]

Yet not everything has to be covered in equal detail. In order to cover the territory, the preacher will undoubtedly group some aspects of the text while minutely examining others. For example, a cursory comment may cover the content of three verses, or ten minutes may be spent on

17. David L. Larsen, *The Anatomy of Preaching: Identifying the Issues in Preaching Today* (Grand Rapids: Baker, 1990), 32. Robert G. Rayburn makes this distinction both in his personal lecture notes and in his unfinished volume on expository preaching.

18. Rayburn popularized this wording in his lectures on expository preaching. The terminology actually originates in Broadus, *On the Preparation and Delivery of Sermons* (114–15), though there the concept relates more to covering fully the subject proposed for the sermon rather than the passage itself.

19. A helpful way of checking to make sure you have covered the territory of the text is simply to see if you have referred to all the verses of the text in the sermon if the message expounds a didactic passage. Checking to see if you have mentioned the major characters or events that determine the conceptual development of a narrative passage will accomplish the same. Neither procedure will guarantee that the preacher has dealt with everything needed to explain the passage, but at least the preacher will not have skipped entire portions of the text.

one word. The FCF and the relative clarity of different portions of the passage will dictate how the preacher organizes the material. Still, the preacher must in some way deal with the entire text—taking special care *not* to neglect those features that pose problems or raise questions for the listeners. People should be able to walk away with a reasonable understanding of the entire passage.

Pastoral judgment, congregational sensitivity, and preaching experience will help the preacher develop a sense for what needs to be explained and what amount of explanation is required, but until these instincts develop, a good exegetical outline provides a healthy check for sermon preparation. The relationships of words and ideas in the exegetical outline brings to the surface major ideas and signals those portions of the text that need attention.

HIGHLIGHT AND SUBORDINATE

Because there is never enough time to cover every textual feature or every pastoral insight, the preacher must highlight certain ideas and subordinate others.[20] We make choices on the basis of what will best represent the text's instruction regarding the fallen condition focus of the sermon. Stott writes,

> [W]e have to be ruthless in discarding the irrelevant. This is easier said than done. During our hours of meditation numerous blessed thoughts and scintillating ideas may have occurred to us and been dutifully jotted down. It is tempting to drag them all in somehow. Resist the temptation! Irrelevant material will weaken the sermon's effect. It will come in handy some other time. We need the strength of mind to keep it till then.

> Positively, we have to subordinate our material to our theme in such a way as to illumine and enforce it.[21]

The homiletical outline will reflect the preacher's judgment of what takes a little explanation and what takes much. We must advance what addresses the FCF, elevate what reinforces our exhortation, eliminate what clouds the exposition, and rebut what challenges our explanations.

As a rule of thumb, expositors owe no more to explanation than what is necessary to make their points clear, but owe no less than what is necessary to prove their points. Crystallize your thought as much as possible. Divide what is too lengthy. Group what is too numerous. Make the

20. Arndt L. Halverson, *Authentic Preaching* (Minneapolis: Augsburg, 1982), 179.
21. Stott, *Between Two Worlds*, 228.

complex simple (and not vice versa). Clarify the obscure. Then, frame the whole in a structure that makes the scriptural basis of your exhortation as clear and memorable as possible.[22]

THE LIGHT OF PRESENTATION

Preparing explanations does not always equip the preacher to present them. Too much information and too much complexity can lead to confusion or paralysis. Although there are many valid approaches to presenting the material to a congregation, preachers are usually on sure ground when they follow these simple steps:

1. State the truth.
2. Place the truth.
3. Prove the truth.

These steps presume that the thought divisions of the explanation components form the principal outline of the message; that is, main point and subpoint statements summarize what the preacher believes the text means. Illustrations and applications develop these statements, but are not formal outline divisions.[23] By concluding what a text means (with a main point or subpoint statement), showing in the text where that truth originates, and establishing how the text backs the truth, preachers present the discoveries of their textual study in a highly comprehensible form.

The order of these steps can vary. Sometimes we may want to prove a truth before we state our conclusion. Other times it will be advantageous to delay pointing out where the text supports our conclusions. For the expositor the order of the steps is not as crucial as is the need to take each one. There are, of course, other valid ways of structuring sermons, but these "state, place, prove" patterns are the most natural way of constructing an expository message and typify the approach of most who are learning to preach.

22. Chapter 6 details outline structures and procedures.
23. In other words, an illustration may clarify a main point, "Prepare because Christ will come," but the main point is not the illustration itself. Cf. Hugh Litchfield, "Outlining the Sermon," in *Handbook of Contemporay Preaching*, ed. Michael Duduit (Nashville: Broadman, 1992), 173.

STATE AND PLACE

If you follow the most typical pattern of presentation, you will first state what the text means. This statement may be either a main point or a subpoint. Next, place (or locate) where in the text you derived that idea. If you are preaching on a didactic portion of Scripture (an epistle, a prophecy, a proverb, or a psalm), you will probably say, "The Bible makes this plain to us in verse six," or more simply, "Look where Paul says this in verse nine." Then read the verse (or the portion of it) that supports the statement you just made. Taking the eyes of the congregation to the biblical text grants authority to your words, assuring listeners that your statements directly reflect what God says and are not merely your opinion.

Sometimes your statement of the truth will be based on information from several verses (or from the context). In this case you must exercise good judgment about how you locate the textual evidence that supports your conclusion. It hardly makes sense to say, "Look at how sorrowful Jesus appears in verses nine through twelve and sixteen through thirty-six." In the few moments you can allow, no one can scan that much material to confirm what you said. Still, you can often summarize the content of a few verses, "Peter offers a doxology in verses two through four." Or, point out a feature that reappears in several verses, "Look how the word *joy* occurs three times in verse three and two more times in verse six."

When preaching on narrative passages we have less obligation to cite precise verses that support our statements. Since our conclusions are often based on events in the scriptural narrative that an earlier reading has firmly etched on the mind, the listener does not always need to see the verse that repeats what everyone already knows. We do not gain much by saying, "Verse forty-nine says Goliath fell down!" if everyone already knows he hit the ground. Still, where precise wording affects our interpretation we should continue to cite specific verses. The goal is to back our statements. Whether sight or memory of the text confirms our words, we meet that goal.

PROVE

Once you state a truth and locate where the text confirms that truth, it is still necessary to prove that the text means what you said it means. Homiletics texts at this point usually offer a myriad of formal proofs and forms of argument that preachers may employ to establish a biblical basis for their conclusions. However, before diving into these, I must remind us all that the Bible was originally written in the language of common folk and will be best interpreted when we remember that most of its meaning is in plain sight. If you listen closely to the best expositors, you will notice that, after they make a declarative statement of what the text means, they most often simply repeat or restate the portion of the text that supports their statement, which establishes its truth.

Restatement

If simply quoting the text or rewording it in a clearer form establishes the truth of your words, by all means conclude the explanation there. After all, what does it mean to "pray and not give up" (Luke 18:1), except that we should pray and not give up? We could say, "What this verse means is that we should pray and keep on praying." Yet, whether we repeat or reword the verse its meaning is clear without a great deal of further explanation because the verse itself is so clear. Again, I must reiterate that though homiletics texts spend much time discussing other forms of explanation, simple restatement of the text is the form of explanation expositors use most of the time. We make a declarative statement of what we believe the text means and then cite the scriptural portion that supports that statement as the obvious and sufficient proof.

Restatement uses the principles of focus and redundancy to make a point clear. Until the preacher restates (by quoting or rewording) the portion of the text that supports a declarative statement of meaning, the words of the text tend to blend together in the listeners' minds. By narrowing attention to a single phrase or verse, the preacher has made that portion of the passage jump out at the listener and its meaning becomes obvious. Because the highlighted portion of the verse is also a restatement of what the preacher just said, the repetition engraves more meaning on the minds of the listeners. This repetition would seem simplistic and redundant in a written document, but experienced preachers recognize that *repetition is one the most powerful oral communication tools.*[24] Since a listener (unlike a reader) cannot review what has preceded, repetition underlines what the preacher wants most to impress on others' minds. As a result, major ideas stated in crisp phrases often echo through a sermon like a refrain to signal the importance of key thoughts.[25]

---

24. Vines, *A Practical Guide to Sermon Preparation*, 78; Ralph Lewis with Gregg Lewis, *Inductive Preaching: Helping People Listen* (Westchester, Ill.: Crossway, 1983), 202.
25. Robinson, *Biblical Preaching*, 79–80; 138–39.

Narration

Retelling the story of what is happening in the passage is another way of explaining the meaning. This is really a broader form of restatement. Preachers may paint the background of the account, remind listeners of a biographical incident, recount a parable using more contemporary words or a modern situation, introduce dialogue from an event, create dialogue, or in general add interest and clarity to a passage by fleshing out the setting, the action, or the personalities involved.

A healthy imagination greatly aids the narration process. Portraying the facts of the passage with vividness, energy, and color makes the Bible interesting, clear, and real to listeners. A word of caution must be added, however. Preachers must be sure their narration explains what is in the account and does not add what the passage does not communicate. It is possible for story-telling to get too imaginative and too exuberant. If you end up basing a point of your sermon on an imaginary detail, then your narration is no longer exposition but imposition. Imposition occurs not only when we present as fact what the Bible does not, but also when we distract from the message of the Bible. Biblically minded congregations want clarity, not high drama. We must recognize the sometimes thin but always definite line between striving to create understanding of a passage and trying to dazzle listeners with our personal skills.

Description and Definition

Closely related to narration is description. With this form of explanation the preacher describes a word, a scene, a character, or a situation in such a way that listeners are better able to understand the text. For example, throughout the course of many sermons, the preacher could describe the passover service, an ephod, the geography of Palestine, a Roman coin, ancient fishing boats, the continuous action of the present tense in Greek, or a host of other unfamiliar biblical details, all of which can greatly aid a congregation's understanding of various biblical passages.

Frequently listeners need not description but definition. Our age, in which biblical literacy is low, obligates preachers to explain the words of a passage as well as to describe its features. The terms *justification, election, remnant, Sabbath, holiness,* and *sin* are so obvious to preachers that we forget that many people around us find the words mysterious or obtuse. The pastor who encourages parishioners to use the word *apologetics* when presenting their faith should not be surprised that most listeners will feel they have been encouraged to apologize for the gospel.

Definitions contained in a sermon are not usually of the same length or complexity as are the same definitions in the pages of textbooks. Definitions given in sermons need to be accurate but also should be clear and concise. This means we cannot usually provide a definition that will encompass every nuance of meaning to all people in all places. We are merely trying to define terms in such a way that they make sense for this sermon. Often we will contrast or compare a term with other terms to provide a meaning (e.g., *agape* v. *eros* v. *philia*). We may list synonyms for a term (e.g., *Sin* is any *wrongdoing* or *non-doing* of what God requires) or set it against common misconceptions (e.g., One doesn't have to be Hitler, Ghengis Khan, or Charles Manson to be guilty of sin). We want to provide people with handles that enable them to grasp enough meaning to understand the information in a particular sermon. Whether difficult words originate in the text itself or in our explanations of the text we must define our terms simply. Many volumes could be written on the meaning of *faith*, but in many messages Phillips Brooks' acronym *Forsaking All I Take Him* will well suffice. Excellence in preaching is more often displayed by this kind of sermon-specific clarity rather than by academic complexity.

Exegesis

Preachers who have the ability to study the Word of God in the original languages have a wonderful privilege of being able to plumb the depths of the Bible, and it is natural and appropriate to share the insights of our exegetical studies with our listeners. Most expository sermons make some reference to exegetical insights in order to expose the subsurface meaning of the text. Still, preachers must take care not to flaunt their education. Exegesis should help explain what a text means. It should not merely cloud meaning in a fog of Hebrew words, parsing notes, and grammatical terms unfamiliar to anyone without a seminary degree.[26] If no one will remember two seconds later that *metadidomi* means "share," why should we bother to mention the Greek term? If no one knows what *aorist* is, we should not pretend the mention of it clarifies the meaning of the text.

Preaching should never be an excuse to display our erudition at the expense of convincing our listeners that they can never really understand what the Scriptures say because they read only English. We are obligated to explain our exegetical insights in such a way that they

---

26. Edward Marquart, *Quest for Better Preaching* (Minneapolis: Augsburg, 1985), 105.

make the meaning of the text more obvious, not more remote. Robert G. Rayburn explains,

> Nothing is more wearisome to the average layperson than to hear a preacher explaining the cases of nouns and the tenses of verbs or the other grammatical matters in Greek or Hebrew. Well educated preachers are expected to know the languages of the Bible but the layman who has no knowledge of them is not impressed when grammatical observations are made using the original words in the text. He is interested only in knowing the true meaning of the text, not the mechanics of the method by which that meaning was determined.[27]

Young preachers often think that heaping exegetical intricacies on their explanations will expand their credibility when in fact this practice may damage it. Such academic excercises may demonstrate that the preacher does not know or does not care about the listeners' capacities. By all means use your translation tools and preach important exegetical insights, but do so in plain terms.[28] Share the fruit, not the sweat, of your exegetical labor.

Where your exegetical conclusions differ in some degree with the translation most of your listeners have in their laps, handle the differences carefully. A preacher who in essence asserts, "I know what your Bibles say, but I know better" may sound very arrogant. An even greater danger is that the preacher may convince people that their Bibles are untrustworthy. Translations by scholars committed to scriptural truth generally need the support of preachers who want their listeners to respect the authority of the Word. Usually it is far better to claim, "We gain an even richer understanding of the meaning of this verse by noting . . ." than to say, "The translators of the New International Version made a mistake here." Who can help wondering in the wake of such a statement where other "mistakes" are?

Argument

Presenting an argument that supports your explanation rarely justifies being argumentative. Nonetheless, we often need to present the

27. Robert G. Rayburn "Exposition," uncompleted ms., 7.
28. The Westminster divines admonished, "They that are called to labour in the ministry of the word, are to preach sound doctrine, diligently, in season and out of season; *plainly*, not in the enticing words of man's wisdom, but in the demonstration of the Spirit, and of power; faithfully, making known the whole counsel of God; wisely, *applying themselves to the necessities and capacities of the hearers*. . . ." (emphasis added; WLC, 159). John Calvin wrote, "I have always studied to be simple. . . ." (as quoted in Stott, *Between Two Worlds*, 128).

facts, the testimony of authorities, causal relationships, and logic that confirm the accuracy of our explanations. Sermons are usually prepared for a mixed group of people, including those who are informed and those not, those able to reason well and those not, those ready to accept the preacher's pronouncements and those who are not. Each of these factors must be considered as the preacher prepares to support, develop, and, where necessary, defend the exposition (1 Pet. 3:15).

It is beyond the scope of this book to give all the types of formal argument a preacher may use.[29] Yet, if preachers keep challenging themselves to prove their argument as they make declarative statements, then natural arguments tend to take shape in fairly good order. Still some cautions must be considered. First, not all things need to be proven—many are obvious. Second, few things need all the proofs you can muster—choose what is most powerful and most concise. Third, some things cannot be proven. Rayburn writes, "The preacher should never attempt to explain what he himself does not really understand nor should he ever attempt to explain a doctrine which is incomprehensible such as the doctrine of the Trinity. In an attempt to explain things which cannot be explained gross error will often be introduced."[30] Rayburn does not mean that we should abandon trying to gain an understanding of what is unclear to us or that we should avoid explaining what we do know about biblical truths that have incomprehensible aspects. Still, we should be ready to bow before the omniscience of our God when our understanding reaches its finite limits. There is no shame in our doing this or in teaching our listeners to do the same.

Whatever arguments we settle on, we must resolve to present them as interestingly and simply as possible. Many inexperienced preachers make the mistake of confusing complexity with seriousness, and tedium with orthodoxy. As a caution for this rather common error, homiletics instructors often present the so-called KISS principle (i.e., Keep It Simple Stupid). I find the principle misleading. Neither you nor your listeners are stupid. Your tools and your mind will provide you with wonderful proofs of the rich truths in God's Word. You should delight to proclaim truth as expansively and powerfully as God grants you the gifts to do so. All preachers simply need to make sure that what they preach will communicate and not complicate the truths of God. Doing this will require you to apply all the resources of your mind and heart. Although

29. For some traditional distinctions among the types of formal argumentation see Broadus, *On the Preparation and Delivery of Sermons*, 167–95.
30. Rayburn, "Exposition," 5.

it is relatively easy to express what you know in the jargon of theological textbooks and commentaries, the real challenge of preaching is to say the same things in the language of ordinary persons who are as intelligent as you, but are not as familiar with the Bible or the tools that explain it. For this reason keeping matters simple is *smart*. To say profound things obscurely or to say simple things cleverly requires relatively little thought, but to say profound things simply is the true mark of pastoral genius.

MORE LIGHT

By stating what a text means, placing that truth where it originates in the text, and proving how the text establishes that truth, you fulfill the fundamental obligations of an expositor: state what you know and show how you know. By meeting these obligations we illuminate a path to the text's meaning so that others can see the truth of Scripture, follow it to the source, and confirm its authority over their lives. This confirmation is critical because though we might at times wish our words alone would persuade others to act in a certain way, "it is a serious mistake to appeal for a response to an argument when the listener does not understand the Biblical basis for the truth that is at the heart of the appeal."[31] The church's greatest mistakes occur when the people of God honor what a leader says without examining that instruction in the light of Scripture.

In one of the key debates during the formulation of the Westminster Confession of Faith, one scholar spoke with great skill and persuasiveness for a position that would have mired the church in political debates for many years. As the man spoke, George Gillespie prepared a rebuttal in the same room. As they watched him write furiously on a tablet, all in the assembly knew the pressure on the young man to organize a response while the scholar delivered one telling argument after another. Yet, when Gillespie did rise, his words were filled with such power and scriptural persuasion that the haste of his preparation was not in the least discernable. Gillespie's message so impressed those assembled as the wisdom of God that the opposing scholar conceded that a lifetime of study had just been undone by the younger man's presentation. When the matter was decided, the friends of Gillespie snatched from his desk the tablet on which he had so hastily collected his thoughts. They expected to find a brilliant summary of the words so masterfully just

31. Ibid., 5.

delivered. Instead, they found only one phrase written over and over again: *Da lucem, Domine* (lit., Give light, O Lord).

Over and over Gillespie had prayed for more light from God. Instead of the genius of his own thought this valiant Reformer wanted more of the mind of God. His humble prayer for God to shed more light on the Word is the goal of every expositor. We pray that God will shed more light on his Word through us. We know that what we say must be biblically apparent, logically consistent, and unquestionably clear if we are to be the faithful guides God requires. It is not enough for our words to be true or our intentions to be good. To the extent that our words obscure his Word we fail in our task. To the degree that our words illuminate the pages of Scripture, God answers our and our listeners' prayers.

QUESTIONS FOR REVIEW AND DISCUSSION

1. What are the critical questions that preachers must answer in order to convert mere lectures to sermons?

2. Why is an exegetical outline by itself usually insufficient as a homiletical outline?

3. Why are preachers not necessarily obligated to present the pattern of the text as the structure of their sermons?

4. What advantages does an expositor have in following the "state, place, prove" steps? Do these advantages require these steps in this order?

5. How many proofs should a preacher present of any particular concept in a sermon? Which proofs of a particular concept should a preacher present?

6. What cautions should a preacher exercise in presenting exegetical insights in a sermon?

7. Why is profound truth in simple language a mark of pastoral genius?

EXERCISES

1. Create a mechanical layout of Philippians 4:4–7.

2. Create a conceptual outline of Matthew 14:22–32.

CONTENTS OF CHAPTER 6

GOAL OF CHAPTER 6

*To present the rationale for, the features of, and
an instructional system for good outlining*

6

OUTLINING AND STRUCTURE

OUTLINES FOR EXPOSITION

Why do biblical sermons on the same passages often sound so different? As architects using identical resources can create many different structures, so preachers handling truths developed in the preparation of a text's explanation may construct many different sermons. Design will vary with purpose. If preachers were interested only in describing the text, then messages on identical passages might sound very similar, since all could follow nearly identical *exegetical* outlines. However, preachers have greater obligations than simply reporting a text's features. In order to expound a passage a preacher must explain context, establish meaning, and demonstrate implications in a way that a specific group of listeners will find interesting, understandable, and applicable. To accomplish these goals an expositor designs a *homiletical* outline to create a sermon faithful to the truths of the text and relevant to the needs of a congregation. An exegetical outline displays a passage's thought flow; the homiletical outline organizes the preacher's entire thought development.

The first key to organizing a sermon is for preachers to determine the type of message they want to present.[1] In traditional homiletics, a *topical sermon* takes only its topic (i.e., the theme or the main subject) from the passage; the sermon is organized according to the subject's nature

---

1. Helpful discussions of the classifications of messages are offered in David L. Larsen, *The Anatomy of Preaching: Identifying the Issues in Preaching Today* (Grand Rapids: Baker, 1990), 32; Ian Pitt-Watson, *A Primer for Preachers* (Grand Rapids: Baker, 1986), 23; Edward Marquart, *Quest for Better Preaching* (Minneapolis: Augsburg, 1985), 103, 105; Sidney Greidanus, *The Modern Preacher and the Ancient Text: Interpreting and Preaching Biblical Literature* (Grand Rapids: Eerdmans, 1988), 15.

rather than according to the text's distinctions. In a *textual message,* preachers glean the topic of the sermon and its main points from ideas in the text. A textual message reflects some of the text's particulars in the statement of its main ideas, but the development of those main ideas comes from sources outside the immediate text.

Both topical and textual sermons have esteemed positions in history of the church and both have distinct advantages for certain situations and subjects. If a preacher wants to preach on a particular subject such as baptism, Christian responsibility in society, divorce, or perseverance, a topical or a textual approach often is best. Most of the sermons recorded in church history are topical or textual developments of a particular theme or doctrine. Settings wherein listeners are unlikely to have a Bible (e.g., weddings, funerals, community gatherings) call for messages of a textual or a topical nature.

An expository sermon takes its topic, main points, and subpoints from the text.[2] In an expository message the preacher makes a commitment to explain what *this* text means. The goal of such a sermon is simple: to have listeners personally understand what the passage under consideration means before they leave the service. References to other passages should occur only as the preacher attempts to confirm, corroborate, or elaborate matters that are evident in the immediate text. Merely because a thing is true, because it has a biblical foundation, or because it comes to the preacher's mind does not mean it has a place in an expository message. The main idea of an expository sermon (the topic), the divisions of that idea (the main points), and the development of those divisions (the subpoints) all come from truths the text itself contains. No significant portion of the text is ignored. In other words, expositors willingly stay within the boundaries of a text and do not leave until they have surveyed its entirety with their listeners.[3]

A sermon is not expository simply because it addresses a subject in the Bible. Neither does quoting numerous Scripture references in a sermon make a preacher an expositor. "It is one thing to quote a Bible passage. It is quite another to explain accurately what the passage really says, and what it actually means, especially in our contemporary circumstances."[4] A sermon that explores any biblical concept is in the

---

2. I am indebted to Robert G. Rayburn whose personal lecture notes contain the most articulate and refined statements of these distinctions that I have seen.

3. See the previous discussion on the expository sermon distinctive of exhausting the text in chapter 5.

4. Robert G. Rayburn, from the chapter on "Expository Preaching—A Method" in his uncompleted work on expository preaching, 4.

broadest sense "expository," but *the technical definition of an expository sermon* requires that it expound Scripture by deriving from a specific text main points and subpoints that disclose the thought of the author, cover the scope of the passage, and are applied to the lives of the listeners.[5]

During the past 150 years, expository preaching has gained prominence in conservative Western churches for at least two reasons: the evangelical search for a means to stem the erosion of commitment to biblical authority; and the nearly universal access to biblical material.[6] Evangelical pastors and scholars alike have responded to our culture's skepticism of all authority and to our society's loss of biblical knowledge by challenging parishioners to see the Bible for themselves.[7] These emphases and practices provide great benefits to the church: people in the pew become intelligent Bible readers; pastors become more confident proclaimers of God's requirements; people make decisions based on what God says rather than what humanity says; preachers are forced to speak about as great a variety of topics as the texts they use; the Bible's own authority remains center stage; the preacher's and people's loyalty to (and knowledge of) the precise statements of Scripture grows; Scripture becomes the judge of life and not vice versa.[8]

Yet, despite the wonderful benefits of expository preaching, large numbers of contemporary preachers have turned away from this disciplined approach to the text. Either because they do not understand how to prepare effective expository messages or because they have lost con-

5. Rayburn, "Expository Preaching," 6; Jerry Vines, *A Practical Guide to Sermon Preparation* (Chicago: Moody, 1985), 7; Haddon Robinson, *Biblical Preaching: The Development and Delivery of Expository Messages* (Grand Rapids: Baker, 1980), 20; Ilion T. Jones, *Principles and Practice of Preaching* (Nashville: Abingdon, 1956), 109; Andrew Blackwood, *Expository Preaching for Today* (Nashville: Abingdon, 1953), 13; John A. Broadus, *On the Preparation and Delivery of Sermons*, ed. J. B. Weatherspoon (New York: Harper and Row, 1944), 140–54.

6. Although Broadus argues for the antiquity of the expository method, his book, *On the Preparation and Delivery of Sermons*, first published in 1870, is the seminal volume for the codification and popularization of the expository method as we now know it (cf. Marquart, *Quest for Better Preaching*, 104). The erosion of scriptural commitments that would soon sweep this culture after the initial publication of Broadus's work indicates how critical was the timing of his methodology and why it was so widely adopted by evangelicals.

7. See John Stott's analysis of the antiauthority mood of our culture in *Between Two Worlds: The Art of Preaching in the Twentieth Century* (Grand Rapids: Eerdmans, 1982), 50–85.

8. David Waite Yohn, *The Contemporary Preacher and His Task* (Grand Rapids: Eerdmans, 1969), 152–53; Broadus, *Preparation and Delivery of Sermons*, 142.

fidence that a generation weaned on soundbites and remote controls can digest serious exposition, many evangelical pastors now question the continuing validity of expository preaching.[9]

This lack of confidence in so fundamental a form of preaching must be addressed. Our society shows no signs of vacating its antiauthority mood or of acquiring a more biblical worldview. Now may be the worst time to abandon a preaching method designed to address the spiritual weaknesses most apparent in our age. Thus, a key to the revival of effective exposition is teaching pastors to hone the structure of their messages so that the truth of Scripture can shine clearly through this long-trusted approach.[10]

OUTLINE PURPOSES

A well-planned sermon begins with a good outline—a logical path for the mind. If you had to instruct someone to go from New York to Los Angeles you would not advise them to "head that-a-way." You would provide a map identifying landmarks to keep them on course in each stage of their journey. The features of the preacher's outline serve a similar purpose, keeping listeners and speaker oriented throughout the message. The outline of the sermon is thus the mental map that all follow.

The advantages of clear outlines for listeners are obvious: good outlines clarify the parts and progress of the sermon in the listeners' minds and ears. Preachers may forget, however, that outlines are also important for the speaker's benefit.[11] Good outlines clarify the parts and progress of the sermon for the preacher's mind and eye. Creating an out-

9. E.g., Michael Rogness, "The Eyes and Ears of the Congregation," *Academy Accents* 8, 1 (Spring 1992): 1–2.

10. Although we should be thankful for the new forms of preaching that broaden the horizons and tools of the contemporary preacher (cf. the author's "Alternative Models: Old Friends in New Clothes," *Handbook of Contemporary Preaching*, ed. Michael Duduit [Nashville: Broadman, 1992], 117–131], I am also thankful for the wisdom of one of the deans of contemporary preaching, James Earl Massey, who writes: "Many voices are being raised advising that the old forms and approaches need to be adapted in the interest of greater variety and wider public appeal. There is much to be said for increased appeal and the need to move beyond stilted stereotypes . . . but when I hear discussions about some sermon form being outmoded I recall something musician Richard Wagner reportedly remarked upon hearing Johannes Brahms play his scintillating *Variations and Fugue on a Theme by Handel*. Although Wagner was not especially fond of Brahms, he was so moved by the composer's genius that he declared, 'That shows what still may be done with the old forms provided someone appears who knows how to use them'" [*Designing the Sermon* [Nashville, Abingdon, 1980], 24].

11. Robinson, *Biblical Preaching*, 128.

line for the message helps crystallize the order and proportion of ideas for the pastor. The preacher can thus evaluate at a glance whether the message's divisions all relate to a central unifying theme. At the same time the outline visually displays the proportions of the various parts of the message, while naturally indicating places for supporting ideas, applications, and illustrations.

No advantage for outlining weighs more heavily, however, than the credibility its organization grants the preacher. Organization not only promotes the communication of the message's content (*logos*), but it also is a vital indicator of the pastor's competence and character (*ethos*). "He's so disorganized" is a deadly assessment of any preacher's efforts. Such a characterization means the listeners have concluded that the preacher is either intellectually incapable of ordering thought or is too lazy to do so. The first conclusion frustrates listeners, the latter angers them, and either removes their reason for listening.

Despite recent debates over the necessity of presenting messages in outline form, there is no question that excellent preaching requires some structure.[12] As preachers mature they will discover that rhetorical "moves," homiletical "plots," concept-rich "images," thoughtful transitions, implied ideas, and other measures can often substitute for the formal statement of points in their outlines.[13] However, the importance of solid outlines for both student preachers and preachers whose messages have begun to unravel over the years should not be undermined. All well-communicated messages are at least *prepared* via an outline and require us to acquire outlining skills.[14]

---

12. David Buttrick, *Homiletic: Moves and Structures* (Philadelphia: Fortress, 1987), 23; Stott, *Between Two Worlds*, 228.

13. Buttrick (28ff.) uses the literary term *move* to argue for using language and images that turn thought (i.e., open, develop, and close a single idea) without stating outline points that he feels break the conscious engagement of the listener, create artificial separation between preacher and parishioner, and introduce complexity not palatable to contemporary audiences. Later portions of this chapter also offer suggestions for using key word structures and implied ideas as substitutes for the formal statements of outline points. Eugene Lowry, in *The Homiletical Plot: The Sermon as Narrative Art Form* (Atlanta: John Knox, 1980), suggests a five-step structure that makes the sermon mimic the dynamics of narrative to involve listeners psychologically and emotionally as well as cognitively in gospel discovery. See also "The Controlling Image: One Key to Sermon Unity," *Academy Accents* 7, 3 (Winter 1991): 1–2.

14. Hugh Litchfield, "Outlining the Sermon," in *Handbook of Contemporary Preaching*, ed. Michael Duduit (Nashville: Broadman, 1992), 174; James Cox, *Preaching* (San Francisco: Harper and Row, 1985), 137; George E. Sweazey, *Preaching the Good News* (Englewood Cliffs, N.J.: Prentice-Hall, 1976), 72.

Concerns that preaching from an outline can make the message sound too boxy or too segmented are legitimate. However, such worries are largely alleviated by using sound transitions, by employing techniques that reveal structure without exposing skeleton, and by remembering that good outlining makes sure listeners follow the sermon's thought but not reproduce the sermon's outline.[15] Sometimes the subject contains such complexity that the preacher must help the listeners by clearly marking each step of logic.[16] Other times the outline of the message has an aesthetic value that warrants its display. Usually, however, the preacher who pauses at each road sign on the sermonic journey only wearies those in the pews. Experience and judgment will guide preachers in making their sermonic landmarks clear enough to orient listeners, but not so plodding or patronizing as to frustrate them.[17] Since outlines can so greatly affect the quality of the sermon, we need to be sure we understand the principles of constructing them.

GENERAL OUTLINE PRINCIPLES

Sermons typically begin with an introduction that leads to a proposition that indicates what the body of the sermon will discuss. The body includes main points and subpoints that form the outline and that structure the sermon's explanation. Illustrations and applications act as supporting materials. A conclusion follows the body, summarizing the information in the message and usually containing the sermon's most powerful appeal. Despite modern challenges to this traditional structure, such messages still communicate well if preachers understand the principles to which key features of the outline must adhere.[18]

15. Stott, *Between Two Worlds*, 228–9. See also Sweazey, *Preaching the Good News*, 73.
16. Jay E. Adams, *Preaching with Purpose: A Comprehensive Textbook on Biblical Preaching* (Grand Rapids: Baker, 1982), 55–56; and, Broadus, *Preparation and Delivery of Sermons*, 113.
17. Broadus, *Preparation and Delivery of Sermons*, 111–13.
18. It should be noted that many of the modern challenges to traditional sermon structures result from modern redefinition of the preaching task. When the Bible loses its authority sermons are less concerned with communicating its specifics than with leaving religious impressions and making moral challenges. This change of focus necessarily calls for structures more compatible with eliciting human perceptions and less concerned with communicating biblical information. Note that most information-oriented communicators in our culture still use traditional communication structures. This is true whether the field is business, law, or education (cf. standard business and education seminars, and textbooks on making successful speeches or presentations). Many modern approaches to

UNITY

Good outlines display unity. Each feature relates to the one thing the sermon is about. This is usually accomplished by making sure that all main points support or develop the central theme statement or proposition, and all subpoints support or develop the main point to which they are subordinate. Eliminate everything that does not contribute directly to the focus of the sermon. Avoid all tangents. State each idea in such a way that it directly develops the overall purpose of the sermon or immediately supports a point that does.

BREVITY

State points as concisely as possible. Listeners do not have the opportunity to back up and reread what you just said. Get to the essence of each point and then use subsequent explanations to add proof, nuance, and appropriate qualifications. This does not mean that you want to state points in such a way that the first impression is inaccurate, but neither do you want to put every thought you have about an idea into what is essentially a summary statement of explanation. Use outline points as pegs upon which you can hang much additional information, remembering that pegs are not useful if they are nine yards long. For example:

NOT THIS: Because we are offered salvation in the name of Jesus Christ we must take great care not to live unholy lives lest our testimony damage the honor of Christ, the testimony of the church, and our Christian witness before those in the outside world and those in the family of faith.

BUT THIS: Live worthy of the name by which you are called—Christian.

Try to make each point of your outline pass the 3 A.M. Test.[19]

HARMONY

Main points should echo one another, and subpoints supporting a single main point should harmonize with one other. Usually this is accom-

---

preaching reflect more the communication standards of commercial advertisements, political speeches, or entertainment vehicles designed to make impressions rather than to provoke thought. Preachers must learn the value of many types of communication, but appropriate usage requires us to understand the underpinnings of each.

19. See chapter 2.

plished through *parallelism*. Nouns, verbs, and modifiers appear in the same order throughout the points, and the wording changes only as much as is necessary to indicate a major turn of thought. Bill Hogan writes, "It is usually helpful if the main words in each main point are the same form of speech: nouns corresponding with nouns, prepositions with prepositions, verbs with verbs, participles with participles."[20] Parallelism does more than simply give the impression of unity and form. The repetition of key terms in a consistent order is an audio cue that another major idea is being presented. Hundreds of sentences and sentence fragments whistle past listeners' ears during a sermon, so, when congregants hear something that orients their thought to earlier expressions, they have the landmarks they need to keep navigating the message.

Parallel terms keep the message pointing to the overall theme, cue the listeners to significant ideas, and highlight the central concept in each main point by drawing attention to the key words that do change.[21] Parallelism draws the attention of the ear, and focuses the mind on what differs among the points. Consider how you automatically know what each of these main points is about on the basis of the key word changes:

I. Pray, because prayer will reveal your heart.
II. Pray, because prayer will reach God's heart.
III. Pray, because prayer will conquer others' hearts.

What appears redundant in writing gives great power and clarity to speech because parallelism acts as an audio flag wave to say, "Hey, here's another main idea."

Skilled use of parallelism helps illuminate the outline of a message without forcing the preacher to enumerate main points or otherwise announce the outline. Some parallel portions of the main point may drift into a transition sentence between points, thus allowing key words to become central. In the preceding example, the second and third points could be introduced with the transition, "This passage indicates that you should pray because it reveals your heart, but why else should you pray?" The answers, "Because prayer reaches God's heart," and "Because prayer conquers others' hearts" then form the subsequent

---

20. William L. Hogan, "Sermons Have Structures," *The Expositor* 2, 1 (April 1988): 3.

21. Charles W. Koller, *Expository Preaching without Notes* (Grand Rapids: Baker, 1961), 52–53; Farris D. Whitesell, *Power in Expository Preaching* (Old Tappan, N.J.: Revell, 1963), 60.

main point statements. Preachers often divide sermons this way, indicating that the message will be about the reasons for some action, the marks of some characteristic, or the aspects of some truth. They then ask transitional questions that promote statements of the unfolding sermon's divisions in parallel terms. When they try to mimic experienced pastors who have imbedded the parallel wording in transitional statements, student preachers often mistake the statement of key words as the actual main point. The result is a message whose main points seem to cut the message apart rather than weave it together.

Although parallelism remains the most consistent means of harmonizing the points in a sermon, preachers have a number of other tools that help indicate divisions of thought. Main points and subpoints are almost always better grasped and retained if the preacher makes them correspond to each other in additional ways. Standard techniques include using key words that begin with the same letter (alliteration), sound similar (assonance, rhyme, rhythm), spur interest (created words, word play, contrasts, irony), and/or reflect a logical, a literary, or a pictorial pattern (ready, aim, fire; it was the best of times, it was the worst of times; chocolate sauce, whipped cream, and a cherry on top; bottom of the ninth, two out, one strike left). These "glow words" may seem frivolous, but even the most sincere preachers strive to use terms that sparkle for attention and shine in memory. Excellent preaching neither eschews such devices nor employs any one of them too frequently.[22] The psalmist was not too sophisticated to tie truth to a Hebrew acrostic and a pun was not beneath the dignity of Jesus. Expositors covet the words that make truth stick.

Still, as important as these verbal tools are for effective communication, nothing warrants bending the truth of Scripture to make it fit a word scheme. When Calvin bade farewell to the pastors in Geneva he said, "I have not corrupted one single passage of Scripture, nor twisted it as far as I know, and when I might well have brought in subtle meanings, if I had studied subtlety, I have trampled the whole lot underfoot, and I have always studied to be simple."[23] It is more important to be able to echo these words at the conclusions of our ministries than to make any sermon more interesting at the expense of biblical truth. Where the word choices for an outline will not work naturally, state the truth sim-

---

22. Most homiletics texts cite alliteration as the chief offender not only because its overuse has made it a virtual caricature of preaching, but also because preachers seem so often to warp the meaning of the text to fit their alliterative word schemes.
23. As quoted by Stott, *Between Two Worlds*, 128.

ply and let the Holy Spirit impress it on mind and heart. His truth will do more good than all our cleverness.

SYMMETRY

Each main point and its supporting features should occupy a roughly identical proportion of the message. If you have taken twenty-five minutes to explain your first main point and then say, "For my second main point . . . ," your listeners are likely to faint, even if you know the second division will only take five minutes.

The ear expects symmetry. If one point will be appreciably longer than the others, avoid making it last in the sermon. When length must vary, I think the longest main point should be the first with succeeding divisions getting progressively shorter. Other homileticians advise making the second point the longest in order to keep a congregation from judging the length of the entire message on the precedent of the first main point.[24] Still, all agree that approximate symmetry is the best approach and elongating the end is surefire disaster. As sermons approach their climax matters naturally accelerate. Thus, lengthy last points rob messages of powerful conclusions.

PROGRESSION

Listeners need to know their thought and understanding are advancing throughout the message. If any one point sounds too much like an idea that has already been covered, or if various points seem not to build to a higher purpose, ire grows and interest withers. No one wants to waste time listening to a sermon leading nowhere. Hence, preachers must maintain a sense of progression by keeping each point distinct and by making each point advance toward a culminating idea.

DISTINCTION

When a point sounds too much like a preceding point, homileticians say the two are "coexistent." A coexistent error makes listeners feel they are simply spinning their wheels over matters previously covered.[25] Rayburn writes, "Subpoints must never be coexistent with the main point. They must be distinct from it and still be a division of it. In the same way, the main points must not be coexistent with the proposition."[26] Points typically become coexistent when preachers become

24. Hogan, "Sermons Have Structures," 3.
25. Broadus, *Preparation and Delivery of Sermons*, 114–15.
26. Rayburn "Sermon Outlining," personal lecture notes, 2.

too involved in describing the text rather than in developing a message. As a result, an idea gets restated later in a sermon simply because it is reiterated later in a passage. When such restatement occurs *without apparent development of thought* listeners feel they have just taken an unnecessary U-turn.

For the same reason, main points must not appear to repeat one another in concept and/or terminology. If the first main point of a message is "Pray, because our prayers reveal God's purpose" and the third main point is "Pray, because prayer discloses God's purpose," listeners cannot help but feel that the latter point is redundant. Even if a distinction exists in the preacher's mind between the words *reveal* and *disclose*, listeners are unlikely to notice. A preacher will spare listeners much consternation by using words more obviously different from each other.

Nevertheless, distinctly different words will not remove a sense of redundancy if the concepts of two points are too similar (see fig. 6.1, p. 157). If the first main point remains as stated in the paragraph above, but the third is reworded as, "Pray because prayer discloses the divine will," listeners will think that they are destined for a rerun despite the vocabulary change. We must clearly distinguish all points. This standard also requires us to examine our subpoints to make sure the developmental ideas under one main point do not sound too much like the ideas already discussed under a previous main point.

CULMINATION

Points lead toward a climax when there is some apparent sequence to them. Some outlines proceed logically through an argument; others proceed chronologically or biographically; still others paint a picture by organizing the points of the outline around the description of a common experience, a captivating image, or a familiar allegory.[27] Logical, aes-

---

27. Barbara Hunter and Brenda Buckley Hunter list eleven separate organizational patterns in *Introductory Speech Communication: Overcoming Obstacles, Reaching Goals* (Dubuque: Kendall/Hunt, 1988), 31–32. More possibilities abound (cf. Larsen, *The Anatomy of Preaching*, 70). Standard structural alternatives include: problem/solution, proof of contention, cause to effect, effect to cause, explanation and application, story with moral, elimination of wrong alternatives (the so-called chase outline because the preacher chases down wrong leads to find a right answer), answers to a provocative question, and unfolding dimensions of a controlling image, story, or biographical sequence. As an example of these latter forms one of the best outlines I ever heard was prepared by a student who had been a crash investigator for the air force. By picturing the life of King Saul as a spiritual crash site the sermon led listeners through the steps of a disaster investigation to discover: point of impact; pilot or engine failure; prevention of recurrence.

thetic, and communication considerations all help determine the order of ideas: matters typically come first which explain others that follow; positives counterbalance negatives; abstracts precede concretes; a general principle may lead to particular applications; particular evidences may demonstrate a generic principle; causes render effects; actions imply motives; conclusions call for foundations; internal dynamics balance external forces; appeal follows instruction; imperatives warrant explanation. Each of these sequences (and many others like them including their inverses) naturally lead the listener down a recognizable path. Of course, at times the preacher will veil intentions in order to make an impact, but then the progression is into mystery or toward surprise that will also give the sermon a sense of purpose if the preacher builds suspense that drives home the ultimate concept.

Typically, progression stumbles when points become so compartmentalized that their relationships to the sermon's central purpose disappear. If the impact of the main points is simply "First we see God's wisdom," "In this other point we see God's providence," and "In this last point we gain insight into God's patience," listeners may well wonder what was the point of the whole discussion. In this example, these separate ideas do not appear to lead anywhere. They simply leave the listeners with a collection of impressions. If the purpose of each point does not become more and more evident as the sermon unfolds, a congregation rightly questions why the points were mentioned at all.

Progression also slows when the sermon contains too many divisions. If one main point has five subpoints and the next has seven subpoints, no one will remember the subpoints, and the sermon itself will get lost. Elaborate argumentation will tire and confuse rather than stimulate and clarify. Usually it is preferable to limit subdivisions to two or three ideas, and then use the discussion of those ideas to introduce more detailed analysis. A message that is all skeleton and no flesh holds little allure for most.[28]

SPECIFIC OUTLINE FEATURES

The general principles of outlining apply universally to the construction of expository messages. Excellent communicators may purposefully break the rules for a particular purpose, but the principles still

28. Rayburn, "The Discussion," personal lecture notes, 1.

guide if only by providing a benchmark by which to evaluate the exceptions. These general principles in turn hold implications for the specific features of sermon outlines.

The specifics introduced below reflect a particular method that I have found useful while training students in expository preaching. This method has strengths and weaknesses, as does any other. My desire in presenting these features is not to suggest that preachers should always structure sermons with every specific exactly so, but rather that they understand the reasoning behind these structures so that they can construct messages suitable for their own purposes. There is no one right way of shaping expository sermons and there are always exceptions regarding general principles as well as specific features. I have simply found it more helpful to lay a foundation on which students can build rather than point them to the vast homiletics horizon with the encouragement to preach as the spirit moves. Glean what best serves your preaching preferences while learning the foundational principles these specifics represent.

THE PROPOSITION

Definition and Development

Sermons are built on propositions. Classic homiletics describes a proposition as "a statement of the subject as the preacher proposes to develop it."[29] The proposition usually follows the introduction, summarizes its concerns, and indicates what the rest of the sermon will address. As a consequence, the proposition points both backward and forward—reflecting what has preceded and illuminating what will follow. The proposition is the germ of the entire sermon, and as a result its construction is crucial. In picturesque language homiletics instructors have virtually made canonical, Henry Jowett once wrote,

> I am of the conviction that no sermon is ready for preaching, nor ready for writing out, until we can express its theme in a short, pregnant sentence as clear as crystal. I find the getting of that sentence the hardest, the most exacting, and the most fruitful labor in my study. To compel oneself to fashion that sentence, to dismiss every word that is vague, ragged, ambiguous, to think oneself through to a form of words which defines the theme with scrupulous exactness—this is surely one of the most vital and essential factors in the making of a sermon: and I do not think any sermon

29. Broadus, *Preparation and Delivery of Sermons*, 54.

ought to be preached or even written, until that sentence has emerged, clear and lucid as a cloudless moon.[30]

By forming such a proposition the preacher isolates the message's dominant thought and, thus, orients the main points with the whole message, giving both definite direction and consistent unity. No matters are more vital for effective communication.

Most instructors advise preachers to form their propositions at the end of their sermon research.[31] At this point, study has probably yielded any number of notes, scribbles, and exegetical insights. Thus, the formation of a proposition forces the preacher to determine a central focus. Of course, one's mind does not always think sequentially and sometimes one sees main points before one has had a chance to determine a proposition that will include them all. Still, preachers need to form a proposition in order to give listeners direction as the message unfolds.[32] Every proposition should be stated broadly enough so that the main points are divisions (not additions) of its thought.

Balance

A simple statement such as "the effects of sin touch every life" might serve as an essay theme. A sermon proposition, however, is more than a theme. It establishes the concern that the message will address and sets the agenda for how it will be handled. Since an expository sermon applies biblical truth, the sermon proposition must also reflect the text's truth and what it requires. A proposition, then, is not merely a statement of a biblical truth, nor is it only an instruction based on a biblical principle. It is both.

A proposition is *the wedding of a universal truth based on the text with an application based on the universal truth.* A universal truth is the biblical principle derived from the sermon's dominant text.[33] The

30. J. H. Jowett, *The Preacher, His Life and Work* (New York: Doran, 1912), 133. Quoted in Hogan, "Sermons Have Structures," 2; Marquart, *Quest for Better Preaching,* 102; Stott, *Between Two Worlds,* 226; Donald E. Demaray, *An Introduction to Homiletics* (1974; reprint, Grand Rapids: Baker, 1978), 80; H. Grady Davis, *Design for Preaching* (Philadelphia: Fortress, 1958), 37; and, many others.

31. Davis, *Design for Preaching,* 37; Stott, *Between Two Worlds,* 228.

32. Fred B. Craddock, *As One Without Authority* (Nashville: Abingdon, 1971), 100; Ronald J. Allen and Thomas J. Herrin, "Moving from the Story to Our Story," in *Preaching the Story,* ed. E. Steimle, M. Niedenthal, and C. Rice (Philadelphia: Fortress, 1980), 158–59.

33. Rayburn, "Outlining," 1–2.

statement, "Jonah eventually went to Ninevah," is true, but it is not a universal truth because it does not provide a biblical principle that can be applied universally. Such a statement merely describes the text; it does not develop the message.[34] However, the Jonah narrative supports the principle, that "God's service requires obedience"—a universal truth applicable to all believers. When this truth is linked to an appropriate application such as, "Because God's service requires obedience, we must seek his will," a proposition emerges.

A truth without an apparent application or an instruction without biblical justification falls short of the requirements of *formal* propositions. Thomas F. Jones writes,

> Two common errors experienced by students of homiletics have to do with the failure to fashion a balance in the propositional statement between truth and human response. The faulty propositional statement often tells us only: 1) That something is true; or, 2) That something is required.

> An example of the statement which tells us only that something is true is given in the following: "Jesus Christ has provided the only hope of salvation through His death on the cross for sinners." This statement is true. The problem with such a statement however is that it leads us nowhere. . . . It may state a truth, but, as a propositional statement, it needs to do more. It needs to involve the hearer in the consequences of the truth. . . .

> The second type of weakness in propositions is the statement which tells us only that something is required . . . : "The believer in Christ must be diligent in the gospel in every way." This statement points us to a definite response to some truth, but it fails to tell us *what* truth. [35]

Propositions meet formal homiletical requirements when they will answer both why? and so what? The why question elicits the truth-principle component of the proposition. The so what compels the preacher to determine the application since ultimately that is what Scripture—and the sermon—requires.

---

34. Ibid., 2.
35. Thomas F. Jones, "Truth Has Consequences: or, Balancing the Proposition, " in *The Preparation and Delivery of Sermons*, Seminary Extension Training curriculum of Covenant Theological Seminary (1976; reprint, St. Louis: Multi-media Publications, 1992), 2.

Forms

There are a number of ways to phrase propositions to ensure that they wed principle and application. Two of the most basic are consequential and conditional statements.

A proposition in consequential form states something should be done as a consequence of a truth. The word *because* is used or implied:

Because Jesus died for the ungodly, we must present Christ to sinners.

A proposition in conditional form identifies a condition that warrants a response. The words "since" or "if" are typically used:

Since all have fallen short of the glory of God, we all must acknowledge our sin.

The phrase with the words *because, since,* or *if* does not have to begin the statement. The proposition will work just as well if the preacher says, "We must present Christ to sinners, because Jesus died for the ungodly." These forms work well because they naturally link, in a single statement that will reveal the sermon's overall content, a truth principle with an exhortation. This type of proposition allows preachers to *apply* biblical truth from the very outset of their messages, setting their biblical and pastoral obligations clearly in view in a very natural yet compelling fashion. Other grammatical formulas will work, but these forms consistently help preachers frame solid propositions.

Conditional or consequential forms allow you to test whether the proposition contains a universal truth. If the truth principle clause can stand on its own as a general statement of biblical truth, then the proposition has a solid foundation. For instance, "We must pray, because it is good" is a weak proposition because the principle statement ("it is good") cannot stand alone as a universal truth. There are exceptions in some cases wherein the application and principle clause together indicate a universal truth even when the principle clause cannot stand alone. In the statement that "We should pray earnestly, because Jesus commanded it," *Jesus commanded it* is not a universal truth—the antecedent of the word *it* is the preceding phrase: *We should pray earnestly.* Thus, both clauses supply the implied thought of the second phrase: Jesus commanded believers to pray earnestly—a universal truth. Similar dynamics occur when propositions begin with *In order to . . .* (e.g., *In order to honor God, we must obey his Word.*). Here again the universal truth emerges only by considering the proposition as a whole.

Note also that the application clause in each of the above examples is worded, *we should* or *we must*. Again, not too much should be made of these specific forms—the pronoun *you* may work better than *we* in some sermons.[36] Note also that a simple imperative verb sometimes works better than *we must* or *we should* statements.[37] For example, "Because God uses faithful prayer, pray!" includes truth and application as does "Because God uses faithful prayer, you should pray."

Many preachers like using *can* in the application clause as opposed to their using *must* or *should*. *Can* takes some of the imperative "bite" out of the application clause if a sermon needs a gentler tone. There is often wisdom in this word choice though it remains a bit dangerous because of the ambiguity of *can*. In colloquial English we use it as an encouragement to action: We can do it! Such usage works well in the exhortation clause of a proposition (e.g., Because God has freed Christians from the power of sin, we can serve him.). However, when *can* simply reflects the dictionary meaning—ability—then the proposition may deteriorate into a mere statement of fact rather than remain a wedded principle and exhortation (e.g., Because God grants forgiveness, he can set the conditions of our pardon.).

Perspective

Variations of and exceptions to these standard propositional forms go on *ad infinitum*. A list of such is not important. What is important is gaining a sense for what propositions should fundamentally accomplish. A proposition condenses a sermon's content. Since expository sermons answer What does the text mean? and So what? the propositions that encapsulate the message should also show *what is true* and *what to do*. This is accomplished formally by wedding a universal truth

---

36. I encourage students to ignore the senseless arguments over whether preachers should exhort with the words *we* or *you*. The arguments some preachers make for the exclusive use of one or the other are specious at best. The prophets obviously said, "You should . . ." at times (Exod. 20; Matt. 6:9). Yet it was also a prophet who said, "All *we* like sheep have gone astray, *we* have turned each to his own way . . ." (Isa. 53:6; cf. Rom. 15:4). Obviously, a preacher who never confronts others speaks without the authority Scripture grants, but a pastor who never identifies with sinners preaches with an arrogance even Jesus did not assume.

37. Some homileticians fear too much use of the imperative in sermons. These instructors wisely note that too much preaching simply degenerates into Bible- and head-thumping (see Stott, *Between Two Worlds*, 54–58; Larsen, *The Anatomy of Preaching*, 68). Yet preaching at its heart remains exhortation based on truth. For this cause preaching necessarily possesses an imperative character even when it adopts less strident tones (cf. Stott, *Between Two Worlds*, 156–57 and Adams, *Preaching with Purpose*, 51–52).

to an application. More informal alternatives abound than this chapter can contain. For this reason, we should reduce proposition foundations to this essential: *A proposition is a universal truth in a hortatory mode.* A proposition should reveal a truth from the text that forms the foundation for the pastor to exhort God's people to do what his Word requires.

With the perspective that propositions should reveal truth and lay the foundation for application preachers are able to develop propositions outside the standard forms that still provide listeners with adequate signals of the sermon's direction. The pastor may word a proposition in a nonuniversal form that nonetheless beacons a universal truth. For example: Jesus witnessed to sinners, meets none of the formal criteria for a proposition. But, if the preacher has prepared the introduction to communicate that Jesus' example is normative despite our reticence to follow him, then the proposition implies: *Since our God ministers to unlovely people, we must witness to sinners.* The formal proposition lies conceptually beneath the stated proposition.

Sometimes preachers use only one clause of the proposition early in the message and let the other emerge as the sermon develops. Sometimes a question indicates what the sermon seeks to answer and the actual proposition does not appear until the message's conclusion. A sermon may succeed without a proposition ever being stated if it is clearly implied. Consider how the following sermon introduction uses these principles to establish an unspoken proposition:

> A young woman came to my office some months ago with what she perceived as exciting news. "Pastor," she said, "I've just agreed to get married to the most wonderful man. He's kind, and considerate . . . he doesn't treat me like the other men I've dated who were so coarse and cruel. And, what's even better, after we are married I will be able to lead him to the Lord." What would you say to this young woman if you loved her enough to be completely honest with her? What does the Bible say?

Although no formal theme statement appears here, the proposition beacons clearly. The message will answer the question: What standards does the Bible give for Christian marriage? If we were to spell it out the proposition would be, *Because God sets standards for Christian marriage, we must marry as he instructs.* Here, however, the formal statement probably will never appear in the sermon because the pastor has found another way to beacon a universal truth in a hortatory mode. The proposition still appears, but not in traditional garb.

Homileticians get nervous talking about abbreviated and implied propositions because they recognize that some students will use the exceptions as an excuse not to discipline their thoughts. My approach has been to require students to state propositions formally during their early training, and then help them experiment with exceptions as their experience and expertise grows. Suffice it to say that a good sermon without a formal proposition does not owe its excellence to the fact that the preacher just could not come up with a proposition. Such a sermon more likely succeeds because the preacher had a proposition so clearly in mind that the entire sermon was framed to reflect its essence. Preachers build good sermons on solid propositions even if their formal statements do not appear in the actual messages.

MAIN POINTS

Main points are also universal truths in hortatory modes. Like propositions, main points may be reduced, abbreviated, and implied rather than formally stated. However, students will benefit from mastering the following foundational principles before experimenting with the infinite variations sound exposition ultimately encourages.

Formal Wording

Each main point is a division of the thought presented in the proposition. As a result, all the main points should develop or support the proposition in a similar fashion (i.e., they should be able to answer similar diagnostic questions about the proposition—who, how, when, where, why, why else).[38] Because main points are so closely related to the proposition, it is usually helpful if they reflect the proposition's structure. Thus, just as the main points should parallel each other (see the earlier discussion in this chapter), they should also parallel the proposition.

In the most formal wording of main points, one clause (principle or application) of the proposition is picked up by the main points and is repeated throughout the outline (see examples).[39] The main-point clause that is repeated is called the "anchor clause." If the anchor clause is the truth-principle clause, then the outline is "principle consistent." Each main point then answers: What should be done about this truth? If the

---

38. For instance, if the first two main points urge listeners to use Scripture to discover the standards for public worship, listeners will scratch their heads to discover the connection.

39. Haddon Robinson shows how to use this structure effectively in expository messages, *Biblical Preaching*, 129.

anchor clause is the application clause, then the outline is "application consistent" and the main points answer: Why should this be done?[40]

Principle Consistent Outline[41]

Proposition: *Because Jesus is the only hope of salvation,* we must preach Christ at every opportunity.

I. *Because Jesus is the only hope of salvation,* we must preach Christ in difficult situations.
II. *Because Jesus is the only hope of salvation,* we must preach Christ to difficult people.
III. *Because Jesus is the only hope of salvation,* we must preach Christ despite our difficulties.

Application Consistent Outline[42]

Proposition: Since Jesus alone provides salvation, *we must preach Christ at every opportunity.*

I. Since Jesus alone purchased salvation, *we must preach Christ at every opportunity.*
II. Since Jesus alone possesses salvation, *we must preach Christ at every opportunity.*
III. Since Jesus alone bestows salvation, *we must preach Christ at every opportunity.*

The clauses in the main points that do not remain consistent are the "magnet clauses." The magnet clauses naturally draw the explanatory elements of the main points to themselves because they contain the key word changes that attract the attention of listeners' ears. Thus, subpoints support or develop the magnet clauses since they contain the developmental features of the outline.

The universal truth found in the anchor clause should be developed either just before or just after the proposition (and/or early in the first

40. Note that the italicized anchor clauses indicate whether the outline is principle consistent or application consistent. tion of a third main point that urges them to prepare to die (cf. Broadus, *Preparation and Delivery of Sermons,* 115–17).

41. Note that I have structured this proposition and these main points in consequential form. The sentence structures in these examples are varied simply for demonstration purposes. Neither principle-consistent nor application-consistent outlines require conditional or consequential wording exclusively. Preachers use the form that best serves a particular outline's wording and purposes.

42. Note that I have structured this proposition and these main points in conditional form.

main point if necessary) since this premise is the foundation of the message. Usually this means that the anchor clause reflects a concept that requires little proof and is relatively obvious in the text.

Sound communication choices should go hand in glove with the main- and subpoint structures. Make antecedents clear—do not use pronouns to represent key thought in both anchor and magnet phrases.

NOT THIS: Because *he* loves *us, we* should worship *him.*
BUT THIS: Because *God* loves his *children, we* should worship *him.*

Experienced preachers also usually take passives and the nots out of main points. Application clauses worded with passive verbs do not exhort people to do anything, they simply state what happens to people—usually in the uninvolving third person (e.g., Because God delivers, believers are secure.). When too many main points concentrate on what *not* to do, people must guess what to do. Negative words in negative main points form negative messages that result in negative ministries. Keep the gospel the Good News. Make sure people know what the Bible intends as well as what it prohibits.

Advantages and Disadvantages

The advantages of constructing main points to reflect the structure of the proposition are many: the wording of each main point will keep the preacher true to the dual expository task of exposing and applying biblical truth; consistent parallelism in the anchor clause will give the message unity while signalling clearly the chief divisions of the message; parallelism will vividly highlight the key word changes in the magnet clauses, thus making the subject of each division distinct and the progress of each point clear.

The disadvantages of wording main points in this form should also be apparent. Chief is the length of each main point. Including principle and application in main points makes each a mouthful. The method gains some defense in the effects of its parallelism. Though formally worded main points are cumbersome, the repetition of the anchor clause acts as a verbal beacon signalling that vital information is at hand. Repeating the anchor clause is redundant for a reader, but with five to ten minutes of exposition between the statement of each main point the ear welcomes the tonal flag. The preacher does not expect listeners to redigest the anchor clause every time it appears. Anchor clauses provide orientation and are dismissed by the ear as it uses them to home in on magnet clauses.

Shorter Forms

I have indicated already that parallelism woven into transitions accommodates more abbreviated wording of main points (see pp. 134–35). With this in mind, preachers can readily convert formally worded main points to more concise statements by following these steps:

Step-by-Step Main Point Reduction Process

1. Note which element (principle clause or application clause) remains consistent in the outline; that is, identify the anchor clause.
2. Develop the concept of the consistent element in the sermon introduction (this element may also appear in the proposition statement).
3. Create an analytical question or implied question(s) based on the anchor clause: (e.g., who? what? when? where? why? how?)
4. Answer the question(s) with the developmental clauses (i.e., magnet clauses), which become the main points.

By using this step-by-step process the formal outlines presented above would melt into the following fundamental reductions:

Fundamental Reduction of Principle-Consistent Outline

Introduction: Develop idea that Christ is our only hope.
Proposition: Jesus is the only hope of salvation.[43]
Analytical Question: What are the consequences?

I. We must present Christ in difficult situations.
II. We must present Christ to difficult people.
III. We must present Christ despite our difficulties.

Fundamental Reduction of Application-Consistent Outline

Introduction: Develop need consistently to present Christ
Proposition: We must present Christ at every opportunity.
Analytical Question: Why?

I. Jesus alone purchased salvation.
II. Jesus alone possesses salvation.
III. Jesus alone bestows salvation.

43. Note that in these examples the anchor clause serves as the proposition. Complete propositions may also serve well even if the main points are reduced.

Although this process is not the only way to reduce main points, it is one fundamental reduction that keeps the principles of expository messages in the forefront. By beginning with main points that present both truth and application, preachers tend to maintain their expository obligations throughout a message. The formal wording sets the agenda, keeping both message and messenger on track. Even if preachers use only the key word changes of the developmental clauses as the eventual main-point statements of their sermons, the reduction process has still required them to consider what the meaning and requirements of the passage are—a healthy process for any preaching occasion.

The primary challenge in using the shorter main points is recalling that they also should promote the *goals* of formal expository outlines. Avoid the trap of making merely descriptive outlines[44]—main points should be hortatory in nature. Even if reduced main points do not contain an imperative clause, listeners should recognize that the ideas presented in the points provide conceptual leverage for the message's application. Main points should also remain as parallel, symmetrical, and progressive as possible.

Since we must state main points in complete sentences as we preach, many homiletics instructors advise always wording main points in complete sentences.[45] Although there are valid exceptions to this standard, the fact that it commonly aids completeness of thought in preparation and prevents grasping for words in presentation makes it sound advice. Making sure that all main points, even in abbreviated forms, are at least *based on* complete sentences will tend to keep the thought of the sermon well groomed.[46]

Remember the reduced forms of main points must promote unity— the very heart of sound sermon preparation. As the magnet clauses grow more distant from the formal statement of the anchor clause in a reduced outline, it is easy for the preacher to lose track of the central focus of the sermon. Even reduced main points should "sustain the same

---

44. Walter L. Liefeld, *New Testament Exposition: From Text to Sermon* (Grand Rapids: Zondervan, 1984), 20–21.

45. Paul Borden, "Expository Preaching," and Hugh Litchfield, "Outlining the Sermon," in *Handbook of Contemporary Preaching*, ed. Michael Duduit (Nashville: Broadman, 1992), 73, 173 respectively; see also Adams, *Preaching with Purpose*, 49; Larsen, *The Anatomy of Preaching*, 68.

46. Although some main points are only answers to questions, or mere sentence fragments, there must be an implied complete sentence behind what the preacher actually says in order for the listener to make sense of the point.

kind of relation to the subject."[47] This means that main points in all forms should develop, support, or prove the proposition. For example:

NOT THIS: Since Jesus is our Advocate . . .
    I. We should praise Him.
    II. We should pray to Him
    III. He died for the ungodly.

BUT THIS: Since Jesus is our Advocate . . .
    I. We should praise Him
    II. We should pray to Him
    III. We should serve Him.

In the second outline each main point will answer the diagnostic question: What should we do, since Jesus is our advocate? In the first outline, the third main point (even though it is grammatically correct and may reflect a truth in the text) will *not* answer a similar diagnostic question, and thus does not harmonize with the wording or the concepts developed in the other main points. Because diagnostic questions help harmonize the sermon, preachers often will ask such questions out loud during the message. Asking a strong diagnostic question after the proposition, for example, invites listeners to monitor the sermon development, makes the preacher keenly aware of the purpose of each main point, and gives the entire message a sense of unity.

Perspective

I would never contend that our discussion so far (regarding formally worded or reduced main points) exhausts the ways of organizing expository messages. These structures simply provide models that reflect sound homiletical principles and at the same time fulfill expository obligations. I emphasize these models for those wanting foundational guidance for organizing their thoughts because, though I know the Michael Jordans of preaching prefer 360° slam-dunks, most of us learn by beginning with straight jump shots.[48] By mastering the fundamentals you fill your future sermons with promise.

Once preachers grasp the principles that undergird outline construction, they tend to shorten main-point statements to a few key words, highlighting a truth that will drive the application. Sometimes formal

47. Rayburn, "The Discussion," 1.
48. For additional information on more novel structures for preaching see the author's "Alternative Models: Old Friends in New Clothes," 117–31.

wording works well—other times a single clause, or even a single word, works best. I tend to use reduced forms. However, if I find myself struggling to corral my thoughts, I typically go back to square one and use the discipline of the more formal structures.

Note also that I have used three main points in each of the outline examples but there is no need to put three divisions in every expository message. Homileticians enjoy debating why "three points and a poem" appears to be so standard in Western preaching, but most will agree that preachers should use the number of points that best serves the purpose of each specific sermon.[49] Three points generally indicate *developmental* thought: problem, plan, and effects; task, tools, and means; beginning, middle, and end; what, why, and how. Two-point messages are usually *balanced* tension: external and internal; spiritual and physical; divine and human; attitude and action. This tension typically holds the real point of the message (which explains why a two-point message with no conceptual counterbalance between the points feels incomplete). Outlines with more than three main points tend to use the divisions of the sermon as building blocks for a *cumulative* effect. Preachers listing "five biblical ways to love your spouse," or "seven marks of a godly man," use the points to build to a summary idea (these types of outlines are variously called catalogue, ladder, or diamond-facet forms).

SUBPOINTS

Guidelines

Subpoints are not universal truths in hortatory modes. In expository messages each subpoint is a summary of a biblical proof or feature that supports a precise aspect of the main point (specifically the magnet clause). This means that subpoints are thought pegs—usually concise sentences or sentence fragments—that introduce the biblical material that will support the main point. Subpoints point to an aspect of the text (remember that context is part of text) that will substantiate or develop the premise behind the main point. By using the state-place-prove formula of exposition preachers typically state the subpoint, cite *where* information in the text supports the statement,[50] and then explain *how*

---

49. Broadus, *Preparation and Delivery of Sermons*, 113; Stott, *Between Two Worlds*, 230; Adams, *Preaching with Purpose*, 56; Larsen, *The Anatomy of Preaching*, 68.

50. As has been stated earlier, preachers have a lesser obligation to read specific aspects of narratives familiar to all. Time constraints often make it wise to summarize the contents of long portions of the text that establish a subpoint rather than read lengthy quotations in the body of the message. See the state, place, prove process described in detail in chapter 5.

that information establishes the truth of the subpoint. When they have completed their outlines, expository preachers should be able to evaluate whether they have exhausted the text by looking to see if a subpoint (or main point) has dealt to some extent with every verse (or portion) of the text.

There is no standard number of subpoints. Simply because one main point has three subpoints does not mean the next main point must have the same, and not every main point needs subpoints. Where main points appear alone, proceed immediately to state-place-prove. Subpoints however should not appear alone, although subpoints are not required for each main point; where they do occur there must be more than one. Single subpoints confuse listeners because they sound like an idea competing with, rather than complementing, the main point. I advise using subpoints whenever the explanation of a main point exceeds a significant paragraph in length. Nothing so quickly loses listeners as mile upon mile of explanation without clear road signs (and the miles roll by quickly for the ear).

Subpoints organize and develop the thought of the main point. They should exhibit parallelism, proportion, and progression; each should relate to the main point in a similar fashion. Like main points, subpoints generally *develop the thought of the message,* not simply describe the features of the passage. For example, "Jesus went to Jerusalem" is a weak subpoint; the preacher is likely confusing the textual material with the subpoint itself ("Godliness requires sacrifice").

Experienced preachers do not usually announce subpoints.[51] Hearers understand subpoints by the way they are phrased (see the three mini outlines below). Where it is necessary to enumerate subpoints, preachers do not list subpoints alphabetically. We do not say, "Subpoint C is ..." but "Thirdly ...," or "Additionally. ..." Public-speaking experts advise that you number subpoints in your sermon notes so that you do not have to tumble through the mental gymnastics of converting letters to numbers while you are trying to talk.[52] Yet, this sound advice should not imply that all subpoints need enumeration. Although an outline is a logical path for the mind, it is not necessary for the listener to retain its every detail in order for the message to be effective. Great distress usually follows the preacher who worries at making sure the people get the outline. Be more concerned that listeners get the message.

51. Sweazey, *Preaching the Good News,* 74.
52. "Be Prepared to Speak," an instructional video prepared and distributed by Toastmasters International (San Francisco: Cantola-Skeie Productions, 1986).

Sermons sound like essays unless the preacher emphasizes the outline (which can create a stilted or artificial delivery). Listeners, who do not generally evaluate each separate thought of the sermon, want only to follow the preacher's flow of thought. No one leaves church saying, "My, didn't the pastor have a marvelous second subpoint under the third main point?" But if they say, "I can follow him," or "This preacher is easy to understand," then the preacher has organized and communicated the messages. Organization becomes an issue only when it is absent or belabored because on the best sermon highways listeners give little thought to the road surface. Only when the ride gets bumpy do they begin to pay attention to the details of the pavement. Keeping parishioner eyes on the sermon's goal rather than on its gravel requires pastors to forego homiletics jargon in sermons (e.g., "My first subpoint for this is . . ."). Subordinate ideas introduced with some of the techniques described below keeps subpoints from distracting listeners.

Types

Three types of subpoints occur regularly in expository messages. While these are not the only types of subpoints the frequency of their use and misuse warrants examination (see fig. 6.2, p. 158).

Analytical-question responses support or develop the main point by answering an overarching question: How do we know this is true? or, When should this apply in our lives? Preachers state the main point, then ask aloud an analytical question about it that prompts the subpoints. Each subpoint then introduces discussion about the answer it supplies in a standard state-place-prove pattern:

Using Analytical-Question Responses as Subpoints

Main Point: *Because Jesus is the only hope of salvation,* we must present Christ when it is difficult.

Analytical Question: In what types of difficulties must we present Christ?

Subpoints:
1. In circumstantial difficulties
2. In relational difficulties
3. In spiritual difficulties

Interrogatives are subpoints worded as questions. Each question (Who? What? When? How? How much? Why? etc.) functions as a subpoint by introducing an answer that develops (or supports) the main point.

Interrogative Subpoints

Main Point: *Because Jesus is the only hope of salvation,* we must
              present Christ when it is difficult.

Subpoints: 1. What types of difficulty may we face?
              2. What helps us face these difficulties?

Interrogative subpoints greatly aid communication because they force
preachers to ask questions listeners would ask if they were analyzing
the sermons. As a result, the preacher thinks as parishioners do and produces a much more listener-friendly message.

Preachers who use interrogatives as subpoints should *immediately*
give an answer with a concise statement that summarizes the truth
being established. Proceed with placing and proving the subpoint's
answer only after stating it. Occasionally a direct response can be
delayed, but if you wait until after the discussion of a subpoint to supply
a clear answer, listeners can grow frustrated with your apparent lack of
direction and disinterested in the explanation. An interrogative subpoint may have one answer (unified response) or multiple answers
(divided response). Remember, however, that no subpoint—even an
interrogative subpoint with a divided response—should appear alone
(fig. 6.2, p. 159).

Bullet statements are the most common form of subpointing that is
taught, though my own observation has been that the best communicators instinctively and more frequently use variations on the interrogative forms. Bullet statements encapsulate divisions in the explanation
of main points in short, crisp statements. These statements may be
declarative sentences or sentence fragments that make sense on the
basis of transitions and previous discussion.

Bullet Statement Subpoints

Main Point: *Because Jesus is the only hope of salvation,* we must present
              Christ when it is difficult.

Subpoints: 1. In the midst of busy-ness
              2. In the face of fear
              3. In the storm of anger

Bullet statements underscore the importance of concisely worded subpoints. If subpoints trail on, they detract from the thought of the main
point rather than develop it. A subpoint works as a verbal hammer

stroke that places a conceptual peg on which listeners can hang additional information.

Perspective

Subpoints divide the explanation of the main point into manageable thought packets. Typically they also provide the terms that will echo through that main point's illustrative and applicational features. Since the subpoint terminology is so significant to the structure of the main point, preachers can help listeners by using terms that have been drawn from the text (this applies to the wording of main points also). Such construction allows listeners to see in their own Bibles precisely where the preacher deduced the sermon's thought. Still, using textual terms in subpoints is not such an advantage that preachers should use phrases of the text that do not naturally express the truth of the passage as the sermon is developing it. The text will naturally be quoted as each point develops; thus, we need not worry that an outline fails to be expository simply because it does not recite the text in the point statements themselves.

Throughout this chapter I have presumed that subpoints *follow* the main point. I have found it useful for preachers to train this way, but excellent communication can occur when the subpoints lead to a main-point conclusion rather than prove a main-point premise. Much homiletical writing in recent years has revealed the great benefits of inductive preaching wherein particular ideas, illustrations, or instructions lead to more general principles (Jesus' most typical approach), as opposed to more traditional deductive sermons where general statements of principle begin each division of the message (Paul's common approach).[53] I find that inductive approaches facilitate applicational responses while deductive approaches facilitate argumentation. Each has its place not only in different sermons, but in different points of individual sermons.[54]

One note of caution: Listeners need a thought peg to anchor a main point's development at the outset of each division in the sermon. Almost any particular will do: a principle statement that will be proven, a specific instruction that will be justified, or an illustration whose significance will unfold. In ordinary conversation we sometimes say what

---

53. Ralph Lewis with Gregg Lewis, *Inductive Preaching: Helping People Listen* (Westchester, Ill.: Crossway, 1983), 61–66. See also the author's book *Using Illustration's to Preach with Power* (Grand Rapids: Zondervan, 1992), 25–30.

54. Greidanus, *Modern Preacher and the Ancient Text*, 184.

must be done before we say why, or we give an analogy before we make a point. In sermons, no canonical order exists for employing explanation, illustration, and application. However, main points should almost never begin with "bald explanation" of grammar, history, or contexts before the presentation of either a main point statement, an illustration, or an application that specifies a reason for the discussion. Do not leave your listeners questioning, "Why is the preacher telling us this?" Explanation needs some obvious warrant before we launch into discussion of "the origin of the pluperfect tense."

THE BASIC F-O-R-M

Although I have attempted to provide some perspective with which to conclude the discussion of each of these specific features of expository outlines, I recognize that the detailed instructions devoted to each can lead to a paint-by-the-numbers mindset. This danger is so apparent that most homiletics books state only the general principles for sermon structure that were presented earlier in this chapter. All professors, experienced preachers, and students recognize that attempts to enforce one style of sermonizing is something akin to saying that all artists must paint like Leonardo da Vinci or that all musicians must compose like Beethoven. The beauty, richness, and craft of noble expression cannot be confined to one form. Still, there are conventions—techniques, if you will allow such a term—that every craftsperson learns. In the hands of experts the techniques become tools that meld traditional practice and informed innovation into original masterpieces.

My hope is that students will learn techniques that will allow them to prepare sermons with knowledge and confidence. I do not intend that these specific techniques rule sermons, but rather that they contribute to rich and powerful messages crafted according to the insights, individual abilities, and informed choices of those led by the Spirit of God.

Although these guidelines may initially seem constraining, my intention is for them to free preachers from experiencing and causing confusion because they have never been introduced to specific standards for expository sermons. Sweazey offers compelling insights here:

> A sermon that is intelligently planned toward a purpose is not a limitation but a liberation because it enables the preacher to do what he most wants to do. . . . Liberty is not looseness. A kite that is released from its tether gets its looseness, but loses its liberty to be a kite. A "free balloon"

is the captive of every passing breeze. Jesus said that we discover real living not by wandering all over the map, but on the definite, narrow way. . . . A preacher does not find freedom by ignoring form and structure; these set him free to be a preacher. In the hours of working on a sermon, there is a kind of buoyancy in developing what is already outlined, but there is a wearisome feeling of heavy going in laboring out a sermon with no clear plan.[55]

In the classroom and in seminars around the country, I find that preachers have more questions about structure than they do about any other aspect of preaching. Candidly, I feel there are more important questions, but the frequency of these concerns indicates to me that the desire of homiletics instructors to give fair emphasis to the art of sermonizing has simply left many preachers overboard in a sea of structural possibilities. I have endeavored to be much more specific, recognizing that these standards are a starting point, not an end.

The bottom line for structure simply requires that all expository sermons have F-O-R-M. Every outline should be

> *F*aithful to the text,
> *O*bvious from the text,
> *R*elated to a Fallen Condition Focus, and
> *M*oving toward a climax

When preachers meet these criteria, sermons of many different shapes still represent Scripture and strike the heart with precision and authority.

FIGURE 6.1
Example of Outline with Coexistent Error

Proposition:
> *Because Jesus is the only hope of salvation,*
> we must preach Christ at every opportunity.
> I. *Because Jesus is the only hope of salvation,*
> we must preach Christ whenever there is an opportunity.
> II. *Because Jesus is the only hope of salvation,*
> we must preach Christ when it is not convenient.
> III. *Because Jesus is the only hope of salvation,*
> we must preach Christ when it is difficult.

55. Sweazey, *Preaching the Good News*, 71.

Subpointing

Proper Subpointing

Distinctions   Prop: *Because Jesus is the only hope of salvation, we must preach Christ at every opportunity.*

These bullet statements will answer similar *implied* questions; i.e., When, or What are these difficult situations?

I. *Because Jesus is the only hope of salvation, we must preach Christ in difficult situations (vv. 12–14).*
1. Facing circumstantial obstacles (v. 12)
2. Facing spiritual obstacles (vv. 13–14)

These interrogative sub-points *directly* ask similar questions. After the question a concise answer immediately follows. The answer may be unified or divided since the question (not the answer) is the subpoint.

II. *Because Jesus is the only hope of salvation, we must preach Christ to difficult people.*
1. Who are these people?
• Those who attack us (v. 16)
• Those who ignore us (v. 20)
2. How must we deal with them?
• We must be courageous (vv. 17, 21)

These analytical question subpoints respond to an overarching question asked about the main point.

III. *Because Jesus is the only hope of salvation, we must preach Christ despite our difficulties.*
When does this require us to preach?
1. In the face of present frustration (v. 15)
2. In the face of past failure (vv. 18–19)

Figure 6.2 (cont.)

Subpointing

Improper Subpointing

Problems

Prop: *Because Jesus is the only hope of salvation, we must preach Christ at every opportunity.*

Describing the text rather than outlining the message. Outline should indicate what a text means, not merely report what it says.

I. *Because Jesus is the only hope of salvation, we must preach Christ in difficult situations.*
    1. Peter ignored the authorities (v. 12)
    2. Peter spoke from jail (v. 13)

Subpoints are developing the anchor clause rather than the magnet clause.

II. *Because Jesus is the only hope of salvation, we must preach Christ to difficult people.*
    1. Jesus died to save the ungodly (vv. 16, 20)
    2. Jesus alone can save (vv. 17, 21)

Subpoints are not parallel and do not develop the main point in a similar way.

III. *Because Jesus is the only hope of salvation, we must preach Christ despite our difficulties.*
    1. Our preaching will bring hate (v. 15)
    2. Prayer overcomes opposition (v. 18)

Entire outline ignores vv. 14, 19

QUESTIONS FOR REVIEW AND DISCUSSION

1. Distinguish topical, textual, and expository sermons.

2. What are five general principles to observe in constructing homiletical outlines?

3. What two major components compose a formal proposition? What is a universal truth in a hortatory mode?

4. What are anchor clauses and magnet clauses? How do they function in formal main points?

5. What are advantages and disadvantages of using glow words in an expository outline?

6. Identify three main types of subpoints.

7. Why does prudent communication advise against beginning a main point with bald explanation? With what components may a main point begin?

8. How does the structure of an expository outline require craft and how does it reflect art?

Exercises

1. Prepare an example of a formally worded main point in conditional form; an example of a formally worded main point in consequential form.

2. Create a formally worded homiletical outline of 2 Timothy 4:1–5; or 2 Corinthians 6:14–7:1; or 1 Thessalonians 4:13–18.

3. Present the outline you created for exercise 2 above with the main points in a reduced form.

4. Perform a fundamental reduction on the following formal main points framed by Haddon Robinson[56] for Ephesians 1:4–14.

   I. We should praise God because he has elected us in Christ (Eph. 1:4–6).
   II. We should praise God because he has dealt with us according to his riches in grace (Eph. 1:5–12).
   III. We should praise God because he has sealed us with the Holy Spirit until we acquire full possession of our inheritance (Eph. 1:13–14).

5. Create formal main points reflecting these informal main points that Jerry Vines[57] framed for Colossians 2:8–23.

   1. Intellectualism[58] (vv. 8–10)
   2. Ritualism (vv. 11–17)
   3. Mysticism (vv. 18–19)
   4. Legalism (vv. 20–23)

---

56. From *Biblical Preaching* (Grand Rapids: Baker, 1980), 129.
57. From *A Practical Guide to Sermon Preparation* (Chicago: Moody, 1985), 121.
58. Note that this outline contains an interesting version of what Vines calls "backdoor alliteration"; i.e., the end of the key words correspond rather than the opening consonant.

CONTENTS OF CHAPTER 7

GOAL OF CHAPTER 7

*To explain the why and how of
illustrating expository sermons*

7

THE PATTERN
OF ILLUSTRATION

ORIENTATION AND DEFINITION

To this point we have chiefly examined the explanation component of expository preaching. After introducing the priorities and the parts of an expository sermon, we turned our attention to principles for choosing a text, interpreting what it says, explaining what it means, and organizing the explanation. To prepare for the next stage of sermon construction, we must return to a foundational understanding of what makes expository messages powerful. Merely dispensing biblical information in the form of description, proof, or argument may fulfill academic requirements for preaching, but scriptural priorities demand more.

The most powerful sermons bring truth to life by demonstrating and applying textual truths. Traditional expository messages fulfill these obligations when they include illustration and application along with explanation in every main point. We have represented the relationships of these three components of exposition in a main point with a double helix illustration (see chapter 4). Although the components of exposition need not always follow this particular order, we will continue to use this helix (see fig. 7.1) as a means of highlighting important instructional principles. We now need to see how the sermon progresses through illustration.[1]

FIGURE 7.1

Double Helix
Illustration
Perspective

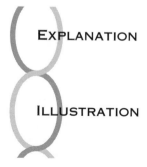

EXPLANATION

ILLUSTRATION

1. For a more extensive discussion of this subject see the author's *Using Illustrations to Preach with Power* (Grand Rapids: Zondervan, 1992).

Preachers typically think of illustrations as brief anecdotes that accompany a sermon's propositional statements of truth.[2] More technically, illustrations are stories whose details (whether explicitly told or imaginatively elicited) allow listeners to identify with an experience that elaborates, develops, and explains scriptural principles.[3] Through the details of the story, the listener imaginatively experiences a sermon's truths. The account does not have to be real or current, but the preacher must tell it in such a way that listeners can identify with the experience. The preacher tells the what, when, where, and why of an occurrence in order to give listeners personal access to the occasion. Along the way, he encourages each listener to see, feel, taste, or smell features of the event as though he or she were bodily present in the unfolding account. Then, along with these sensory details, the preacher also suggests the emotions, thought, or reactions that might typify the experience of one living through the situation.[4]

These sensory and emotional descriptions create the "lived-body" details that distinguish true illustration from figures of speech, allusions, or examples.[5] A quotation from an ancient sage or a statistic from a contemporary newspaper may add interest to a sermon, but neither has the descriptive characteristics that identify a full illustration.[6] In most quotations, allusions, and examples, the speaker *refers* to an account, whereas in an illustration the preacher *invites* the listener into the experience. The lived-body details flesh out the illustration in such a way that the listener can vicariously enter the narrative world of the illustration. Although the categories cannot be strictly drawn, for an example the preacher says, "I have observed. . . ." For an allusion the preacher says, "This reminds me of. . . ." For an illustration the preacher

　　　2. Ilion T. Jones, *Principles and Practice of Preaching* (New York: Abingdon, 1956), 141–42.
　　　3. Because he so fears that the term *illustration* will be confused with lesser forms of illustrative material, Jay Adams eschews the use of the word entirely and opts instead for the word *story* as the term that most accurately communicates the essentials of sermonic illustration (*Preaching with Purpose: A Comprehensive Textbook on Biblical Preaching* [Grand Rapids: Baker, 1982], 90–91). J. Daniel Baumann uses the life-situation designation for illustrations that create immediate applications for contemporary life (see *An Introduction to Contemporary Preaching* [Grand Rapids: Baker, 1972], 250).
　　　4. Adams, *Preaching with Purpose*, 86.
　　　5. The "lived-body" terminology is that of Maurice Merleau-Ponty whose *The Phenomenology of Perception*, trans. Colin Smith with revisions by Forrest Williams (1962; reprint, N.J.: Humanitas, 1981), xix, 122, 235–40, 274, 383, grants modern insight to the ancient illustrative practice of using the body's perceptions to further understanding.
　　　6. Robert G. Rayburn, "The Discussion," personal lecture notes, 2.

says, "I'll take you there. Live through this experience with me so that you will understand fully what this means." Whether an illustration is new to the listener or conjured from memory, the preacher verbally re-creates a slice of life to explain a sermonic idea.

WHY ILLUSTRATE

He did not want to offend me, but he wanted to be honest. He spoke with great hesitation because he did not want his emotions to get out of control, but it was obvious he felt deeply about what he wanted to say. "Dr. Chapell," he said, "I do not understand why you want us to put illustrations in our messages. I came to seminary to learn to explain to people what their Bibles mean. I didn't come here to learn to tell anecdotes. How can we communicate how seriously people must regard the truth of God if we have to tell them silly little stories?" I appreciated the honesty of the question; I know other students feel the same way.[7]

I know of no aspect of expository preaching that more troubles preaching students and conscientious pastors than illustration. We do not hesitate to offer explanations that require us to cite commentaries, grammars, and the church fathers, but illustrating a point with a story we concoct makes us question whether we are preachers or entertainers, pastors or baby-sitters. Students who are required to include illustrations in their messages complain of being forced to manipulate listeners. Pastors, who have discovered the necessity of telling a story to keep a congregation listening, shamefacedly confess the need of "little tales for little minds." Such confusing, even conflicting, notions require us to reset our bearings and determine what preachers should include in expository sermons.

Few question the pragmatic benefits of using illustrations to keep listeners awake, yet many preachers consider the stories they tell to be a necessary evil even though it undermines the seriousness, scholarship, and spiritual integrity of their messages. Such equivocation cannot be tolerated where souls are at stake. We must decide. Are illustrations

---

7. See *Using Illustrations to Preach with Power* (18), where I construct an illustration hierarchy demonstrating how illustration may be distinguished from allusion, example, analogy, and figures of speech based on the degree of lived-body detail in each. J. Daniel Baumann also offers a hierarchy calling illustrations in simplest form ejaculatory examples, in slightly more complex forms figures of speech and analogy, and in the most artistic forms parable, historical allusion and anecdotes (see Baumann, *An Introduction to Contemporary Preaching*, 173–74).

mere congregational pandering that godly preachers must avoid, or do illustrations have true value? History indicates that preachers have used sermon illustrations for more than two thousand years. Unless our sermons degenerate into "just telling stories," people do not complain about illustrations and, in fact, often cite them as the portion of the message they appreciate the most.[8] Have so many been so long misled, or are today's preachers too easily blinded by their academic training to the human factors that are as essential to excellent preaching as propositional proofs?

Beyond pragmatic concerns to maintain interest, I was not taught reasons for illustrating and I have not always defended the use of illustration in expository messages.[9] But I have changed. I discovered while pastoring that the mind yearns for, and needs, the concrete in order to anchor the abstract. This does not mean that illustrations should be merely a cognitive crutch or a supplement to sound exposition. Rather, illustrations exegete Scripture in terms of the human condition creating a whole-person understanding of God's Word. They are essential to effective exposition not merely because they easily stimulate interest, but also because they expand and deepen our understanding of the text.[10]

Illustrations will not allow mere intellectual knowledge. By grounding biblical truths in situations that people recognize, illustrations unite biblical truth with experience and, in so doing, make the Word accessible, understandable, and real in ways that mere propositional statements cannot.[11] We can misuse illustrations as much as we can

---

8. Byron Val Johnson, "A Media Selection Model for Use With a Homiletical Taxonomy" (Ph.D. diss., Southern Illinois University at Carbondale, 1982), 215; *The Directory for the Public Worship of God*, "Of the Preaching of the Word" (1645).

9. Chapell, *Using Illustrations*, 11–12.

10. Ibid., 67–86.

11. Walter R. Fisher, "Narration as Human Communication Paradigm: The Case of Public Moral Argument," *Communication Monographs* 51 (1984): 488; and the subsequent article "The Narrative Paradigm: An Elaboration," *Communication Monographs* 52 (1985): 347–67. Cf. Klaas Runia, "Experience in the Reformed Tradition," *Theological Forum* 15, 2 & 3 (April 1987): 7–13. Runia places in proper perspective much of the contemporary secular thought demonstrating how "experience does not precede the Word but rather follows after it." Encapsulating Calvin's thought, Runia explains, "Experience, however, is not the source of knowledge, in addition to Scripture. It is not an independent road to God, next to the revelation of Scripture." Experience "functions as a hermeneutical key for the understanding of Scripture," which Runia and the Reformers make quite clear is not rooted in, or limited by, human experience. Objective truth transcends human subjectivity, but full understanding of the Word of God, when opened by the Holy Spirit, is still contextualized for reflection and obedience by the experiential. See also Chapell, *Using Illustrations*, 49–66.

misuse any aspect of preaching, but potential abuse should not preclude appropriate use. In skilled hands, illustrations are among the most powerful preaching tools that preachers possess. In order to take full advantage of the power of this dynamic expository instrument, we must learn the functions it best serves and discern its misapplications.

Wrong Reasons to Illustrate

Preachers who illustrate primarily to entertain ultimately destroy the foundation of their messages. An entertainment ethic creates shallow congregations and hollow pulpits. People who attend such a church are implicitly taught that their own desires and sensations are to be the object of their worship. Such persons learn to evaluate the success of a sermon not by the conviction of spirit it brings but by the lightness of heart it offers. This shallow expectation is matched by the hollowness of purpose behind the pulpit: a message with no more solid an aim than personal acclaim. Such preaching inevitably fails. Congregations realize that no one always entertains well. They grow to resent the manipulation of their emotions in a world so in need of deep spiritual discernment. Over time, truth compromised for appeal loses its allure.

Ministers who justify their use of illustration on the basis of their congregations' lack of intellectual acumen or spiritual sophistication will also face bitter realities. There are times to use illustrations to simplify or clarify difficult truths, but preachers should not ordinarily preach in a way that cannot be understood without illustrations. If preachers are using illustrations merely to spoon-feed the so-called ignorant, then they are either overcomplicating their messages or are underestimating the intelligence of their congregations. Either alternative exposes an arrogant, patronizing attitude ill concealed by the pulpit, and not long tolerated by most congregations.

Even proponents of illustrations sometimes imply—and may state directly[12]—that illustrations entertain or spoon-feed. Yet, if the primary purpose of illustrations is not to keep people from nodding off or to explain what would otherwise be unclear, then why does expository preaching require illustrations? To answer we must delve into the ancient history of preaching as well as explore the insights of the most modern communication researchers.

---

12. W. E. Sangster, *The Craft of Sermon Illustration* (1946; reprint, London: Epworth, 1948), ix; Chapell, *Using Illustrations*, 21.

RIGHT REASONS TO ILLUSTRATE

The Crisis in Preaching

Widespread dissatisfaction with preaching has invaded our churches. The disenchantment began to surface almost a generation ago. Young and old alike complained of preaching that was lost in abstraction and buried in jargon, incapable of forging a clear path for an age in the midst of unprecedented change. Thoughts too lofty to touch the realities of life aroused criticism the like of which American preachers had not endured since battles over slavery eroded public confidence in the pulpit. Preachers scrambled to find answers. Experts studied, surveyed, and assessed. Their conclusions were not always based on biblical priorities, nor were they pleasant to hear, but they defined well the perceptions of the contemporary mind. Clyde Reid surveyed religious professionals and presented their conclusions:

> 1) Preachers tend to use complex, archaic language which the average person does not understand; 2) most sermons today are dull, boring, and uninteresting; 3) most preaching today is irrelevant; 4) preaching today is not courageous preaching; 5) preaching does not communicate; 6) preaching does not lead to change in persons; 7) preaching has been overemphasized.

Reuel Howe spoke to laypeople and catalogued similar complaints:

> 1) sermons often contain too many complex ideas; 2) sermons have too much analysis and too little answer; 3) sermons are too formal and too impersonal; 4) sermons use too much theological jargon; 5) sermons are too propositional, not enough illustrations; 6) too many sermons simply reach a dead end and give no guidance to commitment and action.[13]

These surveys and similar studies have triggered an explosion of works advocating novel approaches to preaching.[14] The proverbial baby and its bathwater seem often to have been flung out the back door together in this rush to develop new forms. Time will tell whether the new approaches have enduring value. What is now obvious is that few seem satisfied. The willingness of so many to experiment with so

13. Byron Val Johnson, "A Media Selection Model ," 215. See also Edward Marquart, "Criticisms of Preaching," chapter 2, *Quest for Better Preaching* (Minneapolis: Augsburg, 1985), 19–47.
14. Cf. Richard L. Eslinger, *A New Hearing: Living Options in Homiletic Method* (Nashville: Abingdon, 1987); Chapell, *Using Illustrations*, 25–30.

important a spiritual task highlights how desperate many consider their situation to be. Both pulpit and pew echo the concern that too many sermons have no direct link with real life. In order to reconnect our sermons with our people we must understand their situation.

The Currents of Culture

We are in the "age of visual literacy."[15] The average adult who spends fifty hours a year in a pew will also spend two thousand hours at home watching television. By the end of high school the average American school child will invest more hours in television (fifteen thousand hours) than in class (twelve thousand hours).[16] Some estimate that the average child will spend more time watching television before entering school than he will listen to his father during his entire lifetime. These same children will have watched 350,000 commercials by the time they are graduated from high school.[17] Add to these the influences of movies, video arcades, highway advertisements, grocery packaging, and overhead projectors, videotape, and analog computers. The conclusion is inescapable: "Ours is par excellence the Age of Illustration, an age when people are habituated to picture thinking."[18]

The average person in the pew does not depend on words alone for information. If the nation goes to war, anticipates election news, or craves information on a tragedy, printed words and expert analysts are not the primary informants. The modern mental palate lusts for visual images more than it wants statistical analysis. Crowds in the malls and airports will gather around television monitors waiting for the slightest glimpse of news while newspapers brimming with analyses lie in stacks at neighboring newsstands. Newspapers will not all go unread; a few persons will depend primarily on the newspaper or a news magazine, and many more will use the print sources to get more details. But even newspaper publishers know that only 4 or 5 percent of their audience will read beyond the first paragraph of the average story, and they know that readership will treble or quadruple with any story bearing a picture (the caption being the most read paragraph of the entire

15. Ralph L. Lewis with Gregg Lewis, *Inductive Preaching: Helping People Listen* (Westchester, Ill.: Crossway, 1983), 10.
16. David L. Larsen, *The Anatomy of Preaching: Identifying the Issues in Preaching Today* (Grand Rapids: Baker, 1989), 39.
17. Ibid., 133–34; David L. Larsen, "Volume of TV Viewing . . . ," *MetroVoice* (April 1993), 4.
18. Ian MacPherson, *The Art of Illustrating Sermons* (Nashville: Abingdon, 1964), 39.

account).[19] Audience interest and information consumption increase with sensory involvement even in these media.

Some believe these trends are the result of modern culture's audio-visual addictions. Television and stereo have become the sensory wall-paper of many an American's daily existence. Electronic sights and sounds accompany every waking moment. Computer-software companies and cassette-tape publishers bank on our need for sensory input by marketing interactive learning programs everywhere one turns. Whether these trends are actually a result of recent cultural developments, or are the exploitation of more basic human thought processes, remains to be seen. But there is no question that our culture trains us to reason and react experientially.[20]

Contemporary preachers must acknowledge these cultural challenges even if they are unsure how much to accommodate them. Although we should not too hastily abandon our rich preaching heritage, we must ask how we can best serve present needs.[21] Preaching practices that ignore the importance of experiential discovery indicate insensitivity to the typical parishioner's daily life and learning.

The Footsteps of Giants

These contemporary realities make the preacher's old admonition to "turn the ear into the eye" more important than ever. Yet, many preachers fear that by using multiple images in sermons they surrender to the vices and frailties of this age. A glimpse at the best preaching of all eras will put such fears to rest. With rare exceptions the most valued preaching throughout history has consistently relied on the inner eye.

Had not the apostles punctuated their words with images of the full armor of God, the race course, living stones, olive trees, or walking in the light, we would strain to remember their instruction. Had not Jonathan Edwards dangled sinful spiders over a pit of flame, no one would know "Sinners in the Hands of an Angry God." If William Jennings Bryan had not decried, "You shall not crucify mankind upon a cross of gold," his political "sermon" would have been forgotten the

---

19. *Principles of Advertising Design* (St. Louis: Delcom Seminars, 1978), 12, 35; *How to Write Advertising Copy* (St. Louis: Delcom Seminars, 1978), 22.

20. Neil Postman, *Amusing Ourselves to Death: Public Discourse in the Age of Show Business* (New York: Viking, 1985), 79–80.

21. James J. Murphy, *Medieval Rhetoric: A Select Bibliography* (Toronto: University of Toronto Press, 1971), 18; see also Murphy's *Rhetoric in the Middle Ages: A History of Rhetorical Theory from Saint Augustine to the Renaissance* (Berkeley: University of California Press, 1974).

next day. If Martin Luther King, Jr., had not lead us through a "dream" and onto a "mountaintop," would the march on Washington have been anything more than a ragged hike across a majestic mall? Books have extolled the sensory appeals of Charles Spurgeon, the images of Peter Marshall, the characterizations of Clovis Chappell, and the human dramas of Harry Emerson Fosdick. None of these men, of widely varying theological perspectives, preached in a time dominated by visual electronics, yet they dressed their sermons in strong illustrative images—with powerful results. Prior to this "age of visual literacy" these preaching giants tapped something deep and fundamental in the human understanding. We are just beginning to discover what this fundamental something is.

The Path to Perception

Our generation is witnessing a revolution in thought about the way people understand themselves and their world. Three centuries of relative consensus based on the Cartesian philosophical model of "I think, therefore I am" is being turned upside down. The contemporary model declares, "I am, therefore I think" or, more specifically, "I can, therefore I am."[22] Abstract thought is no longer seen as grounding our concept of who we are and our place in the world. Rather, it is claimed that our interaction with the world gives us our sense of being.[23] Our circumstances, the experiences that affect our physical beings, and situations that stimulate mental activity and emotive responses are the factors, theorists say, that create comprehension.[24] While such theories cannot fully explain spiritual understanding, they do help express how we ordinarily make sense of our world.

22. According to Jacques Derrida, as explained in Walter R. Fisher's "The Narrative Paradigm" (351), meaning is a matter of use rather than reference to people and things in the world. The notion is driven home with consideration of Maurice Merleau-Ponty's seminal work on the role of the body in perception that assaults compartmentalized theories of mental v. sensory perception and argues instead that the body itself is a primary structure of consciousness inseparable from mental perception (*Phenomenology of Perception*, 174, 235, 383).

23. Amadeo Giorgi, "The Body: Focal Point of 20th Century Cultural Contradictions," *South Africa Journal of Psychology* 13, 2 (1983): 40.

24. Merleau-Ponty in the *Phenomenology of Perception* (237) writes, "We are not, then reducing the significance of the word, or even of the precept, to a collection of 'bodily sensations' but we are saying that the body, insofar as it has 'behavioral patterns,' is that strange object which uses its own parts as a general system of symbols for the world, and through which we can consequently 'be at home in' that world, 'understand' it and find significance in it."

The need to promote understanding through experience echoes through the communication disciplines in an array of catch phrases. Advocates say we communicate best when we couch ideas in "human interest accounts,"[25] "life situations,"[26] "life stories,"[27] "experience-centered messages,"[28] "narrative paradigms"[29] "firsthand encounter,"[30] "piece-of life-illustrations,"[31] "lived-body experience,"[32] and even in "a story that participates in the stories of those who have lived, who live now, and who will live in the future."[33] The variety of terms grants rich expression to the power of personal experience.

We understand most fully what is real to us. Even as formal an expositor as Jay Adams argues that it is only when a truth touches us experientially or when we sense the impact it could have upon us that we can comprehend it fully.[34] Well-known preacher Steve Brown asserts even more boldly, "If you can't illustrate it, it's not true. We forget that doctrine isn't for doctrine's sake and theological propositions are not for theological proposition's sake. Those [illustrations] are ways by which we communicate the reality that we've discovered and that reality's a time-space thing [sic]."[35]

The union of knowing and doing—of understanding and experience—strengthens as the decades progress. In the early 1950s Edgar Dale dem-

25. The standard journalistic definition of human-interest accounts allows that they are stories in which persons recognize sensations or situations they have experienced or could experience. Such accounts picture ordinary or extraordinary persons in ordinary or extraordinary situations that evoke common sensations, emotions, or thoughts with which ordinary people can identify.

26. Lloyd M. Perry and Charles M. Sell provide an excellent discussion of the preachers and authors who use "life-situation" terminology in their book, *Speaking to Life's Problems* (Chicago: Moody, 1983), 15–18.

27. Edmund A. Steimle, Morris J. Niedenthal, and Charles Rice, eds., *Preaching the Story* (Philadelphia: Fortress, 1980), 12. See also Rolf von Eckartsberg, "The Eco-Psychology of Personal Culture Building: An Existential Hermeneutic Approach,"*Duquesne Studies in Phenomenological Psychology*, ed. Amadeo Giorgi, Richard Knowles, David L. Smith III (Atlantic Highlands, N.J.: Humanitas/Duquesne University Press, 1979), 233.

28. Lewis, *Inductive Preaching*, 41.

29. Fisher, "Narration as Human Communication Paradigm," 488. See also the subsequent article by Fisher, "The Narrative Paradigm," 347–67.

30. Webb B. Garrison, *Creative Imagination in Preaching* (Nashville: Abingdon, 1960), 95–96.

31. Louis Paul Lehman, *Put a Door on It* (Grand Rapids: Kregel, 1975), 27.

32. Merleau-Ponty, *Phenomenology of Perception*, 274, 235–38, 383.

33. Fisher, "Narration as Human Communication Paradigm," 6.

34. Adams, *Preaching with Purpose*, 86. See also Marquart, *Quest for Better Preaching*, 74.

35. Interview with Steve Brown, *Preaching* 8, 3 (November/December 1992): 4.

onstrated that learning occurs most effectively through direct, purposeful involvement. Teachers trained in the 1960s pondered the implications of a "learning pyramid" that showed we learn 10 percent of what we hear, 30 percent of what we see, but 60 percent of what we do. By the 1970s researchers could rank types of experiences that most effectively teach and, in doing so, discovered that people learn as much from "fully described" experiences as they do from actual experiences.[36]

By the 1980s and 1990s these discoveries were affecting every segment of our culture. Distaste for words divorced from experience typifies the contemporary intellect. More and more, schools are turning from lecture- to involvement-teaching because studies indicate that 70 percent of students of all ages are not analytic learners. Eight or nine out of every ten junior-high students engage in problem solving without linear reasoning. Six of ten high-school students learn better through exposure to concrete experiences rather than through abstract thought.[37] The case-study method, once typical only of law schools, now dominates many forms of professional training. Business professionals expect the weekend seminars they attend to involve them in the examination of numerous case studies, whether they are being taught how to sell tax-free bonds or negotiate a labor contract. Back at the office on Monday, these same professionals will instinctively evaluate the success of the seminar based on how realistic and down-to-earth the sample situations were. The accrediting agencies of our nation's major colleges and universities provide funding for training veteran teachers in all major disciplines to teach with case-study methods. The message is clear: Involve listeners or they will not learn. Preachers must hear this message.

The Guidance of Scripture

Listeners who experience concepts—even vicariously—actually learn more than those who must consider words and ideas in the abstract. What preachers have known instinctively for generations has a solid scientific foundation. Meaningful thought flourishes when tied to reality.[38] This discovery discloses the hidden value of illustrations. Listeners simply understand more deeply and more broadly when we exhibit biblical truths in identifiable experiences. The Scriptures themselves guide us to this understanding.

36. Johnson, "A Media Selection Model," 197.
37. Lewis, *Inductive Preaching*, 10.
38. Merleau-Ponty, *Phenomenology of Perception*, 235.

Although the gospel is logical, it is also spiritual, visceral, and impressionistic. The Word itself calls us to worship with our hearts and souls as well as with our minds (Deut. 6:5; Matt. 22:37). For this reason, illustrations involving the whole person in the understanding process operate in a manner consistent with the biblical concept of our complex nature. Wayne Oates, professor of behavioral psychology at the University of Louisville School of Medicine, writes,

> The Hebrew-Christian understanding of personality is a holistic one. Jesus states the commandment which is "first of all": "Hear, O Israel, the Lord our God, the Lord is one; and you shall love the Lord your God with all your heart, and with all your soul, and with all your strength." The Greek word, *"holes,"* is translated "all" and is repeated four times [in the passage]. My approach to understanding the human personality is to emphasize the oneness and totality rather than the division of personality into separate "faculties." When a person loves with all his or her mind, the whole being is involved, not just one part of the personality. Therefore, when you and I preach to the emotional needs of our audience, we are addressing them as total beings and not just as a "bundle of feelings."

Far from being unethical or unintellectual techniques, illustrations that engage the whole person in the experience of knowing by touching the heart and/or eliciting its responses are powerful, biblical instruments of learning and motivation. Because the Bible teaches that we are more than beings of pure mind, the best preaching never relies on intellectual appeals alone. If holiness were a matter only of mental agility, then computers would be sacred.

This analysis admonishes preachers not to consider illustrations an inane frill of popular preaching, but the inherent fabric of effective preaching. Illustrations do more than adorn thought. Because life experiences inform our souls, our psyches, and our thoughts, citations of such experiences function as primary tools of communication. Illustrations persuade, motivate, touch the heart, stir the will, and result in decisions.

When preachers ignore these real-life intermediaries that interpret and empower their words, they speak without efficient or managed effect. Communication of some sort will still occur, but the listeners will translate what they hear into their own experiences which may lead them on errant paths. Preacher-chosen experiential accounts are more likely to provide the intended interpretive contexts and biblical direction. The great preachers of our age know this. Billy Graham, Steve Brown, Charles Stanley, Chuck Colson, R. C. Sproul, John MacArthur, D. James Kennedy, John Stott, Chuck Swindoll, all know how to touch the heart with illustrations that spark biblical responses. Although they know that emotions that operate in isolation from considered thought are dangerous, they also know that rationality without the contexts of love, feeling, sensitivity, and even holy rage can be the antithesis of godliness.

The Way of the Master

If the Bible itself does not endorse the use of illustration in expository preaching, a pastor need not heed cultural currents, human precedents, learning theorists, or motivational guidance. Only that which God's Word indicates as valid tools for our preaching should we consider to be normative. We do not have to guess at what Scripture authorizes. The Bible says of Jesus, "He did not say anything to them without using a parable" (Mark 4:34).[39] Relating truth through illustrative narratives, parables, allegories, and images was Jesus' method of communicating. His was not an age of visual literacy par excellence (at least in terms of modern media) yet illustrative materials pervaded his expressions. If in Christ's time illustrations were necessary, how much more, given the contemporary influences, must today's preacher weigh the need for illustrative content.

Christ actually followed a long-established pattern. Not only was there the pre-Christian rabbinic tradition in the form of Haggadah (the way of story, as opposed to Halakah, the way of reasoned reflection on the Law),[40] but the Scriptures also are replete with symbols, images, and narratives that are the regular instruments of the communication of religious truths. Alister McGrath summarizes this point emphatically, *"Narrative is the main literary type found in Scripture."*[41] "Remove the narrative content from Scripture and only fragments remain,"[42] says Ralph Lewis. And Davis reiterates that this is not to say that propositional truths are not presented, but their proportion is diminutive compared to the experiential descriptions and narratives in the rest of the canon.[43]

---

39. Note that the passage goes on to indicate that until explanation accompanies the parable its truth remained unclear. Illustrations alone will not illuminate biblical truth. The genius of Scripture is its linkage of illustration and proposition in which both components of exposition expose and reinforce the truths of the other.

40. Beldon C. Lane, "Rabbinical Stories: A Primer on Theological Method," *The Christian Century* 98 (December 1981), 1306.

41. Alister E. McGrath, "The Biography of God," *Christianity Today*, 22 July 1991, 23.

42. Ralph Lewis, "The Triple Brain Test of a Sermon," *Preaching*, 1, 2 (1985): 10.

43. Henry Grady Davis, *Design for Preaching* (Philadelphia: Fortress, 1958), 157.

The Spirit that inspires the Scriptures reinforces the conclusion that people tend to seize images more readily than they do propositions, and if they take hold of enough images, then they grasp the principles.[44] Of course, propositional summary and explanation must still accompany the illustrative material. But the pattern of the Bible is to prepare, clarify, and epitomize truth through illustration, characterization, and example. The tree of life and the tree of the knowledge of good and evil symbolize the Adamic covenant (Gen. 2).[45] God pledged the Noahic covenant with the visual token of the rainbow (Gen. 9). He sealed the Abrahamic covenant both with a traditional contractual ceremony (Gen. 15) and with a foreshadowing sign of blood (Gen. 17). The Lord established the Mosaic covenant in signs and symbolic wonders (e.g., the burning bush, the staff turned into a serpent, water turned to blood, and the Red Sea parted), maintained it in symbol and ceremony (e.g., the ark of the covenant, the scapegoat, the Paschal lamb, the temple economy, the phylacteries and feasts), and characterized its truths in symbol-laden narratives (e.g., the provision of manna, the brazen serpent, wandering in the wilderness, and entry into Canaan).

The Old Testament history books are just what their designation indicates—narrative upon narrative that illuminates God's redemptive plan by characterizing his work among his covenant people. There is little propositionally stated systematic theology in the accounts of Joshua, Gideon, Samson, Samuel, Saul, and David. Instead, there is an unfolding pattern of God's dealings with mankind through the events that lead to the establishment of the Davidic covenant and Israel's subsequent history as it initially responds, then rebels, and finally is restored. In all its details and personalities the Bible illuminates the central truth, "The LORD, the LORD, the compassionate and gracious God, slow to anger, abounding in love and faithfulness, maintaining love to thousands, and forgiving wickedness, rebellion and sin. Yet he does not leave the guilty unpunished; . . ." (Exod. 34:6–7). The proposition is infrequently stated in full form but its truths are clearly explicated, easily understood, long remembered, and readily applied because of the stories that illustrate its essence.

Biblical truths often find their most profound expression in the Hebrew books of poetry. These wisdom books do not ordinarily contain

44. Macpherson, *The Art of Illustrating Sermons*, 40.

45. Note that these symbols are the shorthand of broader narratives. Jay Adams wisely notes that stories and story particles both represent illustrative tools preachers may biblically employ (90–91).

formal narratives (Job is a notable exception), but by their very nature employ metaphor, symbol, and image to bring experiences to mind that touch the heart deeply. Although the prophetic books contain high propositional content, their use of illustrative material remains significant. In Jeremiah 13, God commands the prophet to hide a linen belt and to retrieve it after many days. When Jeremiah retrieves the belt, it is ruined. The Lord says, "In the same way I will ruin the pride of Judah and the great pride of Jerusalem" (v. 9). In Ezekiel 12 the Lord tells the prophet to pack up his belongings in open view of the people of Israel in order to warn them that they will be forced to pack for exile if they do not repent. "Perhaps they will understand, though they are a rebellious house" (v. 3), says the Lord.

Similar episodes appear in the minor prophets. God requires Hosea to keep forgiving and receiving his wife, Gomer, though she turns to adultery with others. The Lord says, "Love her as the LORD loves the Israelites, though they turn to other gods. . . ." (Hos. 3:1). On a contrasting note God shows the prophet Amos a basket of ripe fruit because, "The time is ripe for my people Israel, I will spare them no longer" (Amos 8:2). The examples of illustrated truth as well as stated truth in the minor prophets are too numerous to mention individually. Suffice it to say that in all the prophetic books, as throughout the Old Testament, the use of illustrative tools remains consistent and is comprehensive. In *The Anatomy of Preaching*, Larsen summarizes the evidence: ". . . 75 percent of the Old Testament is narrative. What an explosive element for contemporary preaching."[46]

The New Testament does not abandon the Old Testament communication principles as is clearly evident in the Gospels. A. M. Hunter says that the parabolic element in Luke's Gospel amounts to 52 percent of the total.[47] Macpherson estimates that in the whole of Jesus' recorded teachings the illustrative ratio is actually more on the order of 75 percent.[48] The actual words of Jesus comprise 20 percent of the New Testament (the rough equivalent of twelve, thirty-minute sermons).[49] This means that a hefty portion of the Gospel material is illustrative, and that the Lord's own preaching methods and priorities leaned to the illustrative.

---

46. Larsen, *The Anatomy of Preaching*, 90.
47. Macpherson, *The Art of Illustrating Sermons*, 40.
48. Ibid., 40; Larsen put the proportion at 35 percent (154). No doubt varying definitions of "parable" skew the figures, but never so far as to deny the significance of illustrative content in Christ's messages.
49. Lewis, "Triple Brain Test," 11.

Ralph Lewis argues that it took three centuries for the church to abandon Christ's pattern of teaching and institutionalize the homiletical style of "universal abstractions" and "hortatory accent with fewer examples."[50] Even highly doctrine-oriented Paul sprinkles his epistolary messages with allusions to the narrative history of Israel, the arena, the sports field, the military, the marketplace, the temple, the home, and the school.[51] David Calhoun suggests that the chief differences among the four Pauline sermons to unbelievers in the Book of Acts are the allusions Paul chooses in relation to the four different cultures of those separate audiences.[52]

The biblical picture of illustration is not complete, of course, without reference to the incarnate Word as embodied truth. In a very real sense our knowledge and perceptions of God are a product of that most explicit illustration of his nature—Jesus Christ. The glory of God, who cannot be seen, was revealed in the Son, who "made known"[53] the Father (cf. John 1:14, 18). According to A. T. Robertson the wording translated "made known" traditionally means "to draw out in narrative."[54] In other words, the stories of Christ actually serve to illustrate the heavenly Father. Our comprehension of the spiritual involves the interaction of propositions and illustrations. With God's own Word as the endorsement and example, today's preachers have ample warrant to learn how to use illustrations for spiritual communication.

How to Illustrate

With the rest of the nation I listened hourly for the reports of the rescuers' progress as they fought rock, equipment failure, and time to rescue eighteen-month-old Jessica McClure from a well shaft in Midland, Texas. Left alone for a few minutes in her aunt's backyard on October 14, 1987, the little girl had playfully dangled her feet over an innocent-appearing, eight-inch opening in the ground. When she tried to stand up, she fell into the darkness. With one leg up and the other down, Jessica was wedged in the narrow shaft above the water but some twenty-two

50. Ibid., 11.
51. Liske, *Effective Preaching*, 185.
52. Dr. David Calhoun, professor of church history at Covenant Theological Seminary, personal discussion with the author in St. Louis, Mo., 24 April 1986.
53. First aorist (effective) middle indicative of *exegeomai*.
54. A. T. Robertson, *Word Pictures in the New Testament* (Nashville: Broadman, 1932), 18.

feet below the ground. Rescuers drilled a twenty-nine-foot vertical shaft parallel to the well and then bored a five-foot-long horizontal tunnel through solid rock to reach her. It took far more time than any had anticipated—fifty-eight hours. Medical personnel grew increasingly alarmed and warned that dehydration and shock were becoming greater dangers than the entrapment itself. Finally rescuers reached Jessica, but they could not pull her out. The way her body was wedged in the shaft foiled all their efforts. The health technicians conferred, checked the little girl's vital signs one more time, and then gave these awful orders: "Pull hard! She does not have more time. You may have to break her to save her."

When the rescuers pulled the last time Jessica came free without additional injury. But when I heard the instructions of the medical technicians to the rescuers I could not help but relate them to a sermon I was writing. I was explaining how God so much desires the salvation of his children that he will even allow them to experience hurt that will convince them of their need of him. As cruel as this providence may seem, it actually expresses a great love because God, who knows that no one's hours on this earth are unlimited, is willing to break us to save us. I believed deeply in what I was saying, but I recognized that the words seemed hollow—dry doctrine that might only communicate an uncaring attitude on my part for those who were actually experiencing such trials or for those with unsaved loved ones who might have to experience the same.

TAKE A SLICE OUT OF LIFE

The events in Midland came to my rescue. By isolating those events and relating key aspects to the truths I needed to communicate, I was able to tie a biblical principle to an experience that not only reflected real-life truth, but also allowed me to demonstrate doctrine in a context of compassion true to God's priorities and my own feelings. Just the snatch of a conversation out of an event lasting many days became the catalyst of a process that is always the first step in the craft of illustrating. We preachers isolate an aspect of some event, conversation, perception, or relationship in our experience, and associate it with the principle, the concept, or the proposition we wish to relate. In this way we provide an experience through which listeners are able to contextualize and interpret our thinking. An illustration thus becomes a snapshot from life. It captures a mood, a moment, or a memory in a narrative frame and displays that slice of life for the mind to see and the heart to know.

The process of isolation and association does not require a particular order. Sometimes preachers see in an experience something that reminds us of an associated concept (a child being rescued from a well's darkness reminded me of how God saves souls from sin's darkness). We may then file that isolated event (in memory or some catalogue system) until we preach on a passage whose explanation will benefit by such an association. Other times we will first formulate a concept or proposition and then try to isolate an associated experience that enables us to show others what we mean.

The preacher who wants to use illustrations well must cultivate the ability to isolate and associate experiences. To do this the preacher must learn to see everything as a passing parade of potential illustrations—every event, face, feature, and fantasy holds illustrative promise. The preacher is much like a photographer, constantly framing one moment, one event, one sequence after another. By doing this, what looks common to the ordinary eye becomes significant. Preachers should continually take those snapshots of life's grandeur and simplicity so as to relate both to the consistently awesome nature of God and to the too frequent tedium of their listeners' experience.

Nothing of life goes by us without notice. Preachers who illustrate well do not wait passively for the world to offer them something significant to note. Rather, we steal from the world the treasures others do not notice or do not have the opportunity to display. There is beauty in an oil slick, irony in a detergent ad, pageantry in a barn lot, and grief in an abandoned railroad track if the preacher will but see it. The psalmist saw in the nests of swallows his own heart's longing to be near the Lord (Ps. 84:3), and Jesus recognized faith in a mustard seed (Matt. 17:20). You too can see as much and show as much if you are committed to relating truth through the experiences that enable people to see beyond textbook propositions.

By showing truths in terms of experience with the world, you not only enable others to comprehend theological principles but also accustom them to seeing their world in a spiritual frame. These comments highlight the preeminent value of human-interest accounts, that is, life-situation illustrations.[55] D. W. Cleverley Ford writes,

> Admittedly, to quote from Dante, Dumas, Dostoievsky, and Dickens is impressive, but . . .[w]hat a congregation will most readily hear is references by the preacher to objects, events, and people's comments which he

55. Baumann, *An Introduction to Contemporary Preaching*, 175.

has seen and heard himself *in the recent past in the locality*. An illustration drawn from the derelict house in the next street, the aftermath of a recent storm, a local flower show, a current play at the theatre, is the kind that is most serviceable.[56]

This is not to devalue the use of historical examples, fictional allusions, parables, fables, allegories, and other forms of illustration; but to suggest that these, too, are used most effectively when they are infused with descriptions of familiar emotions, identifiable dilemmas, common traits, or situations to which listeners can immediately relate.[57]

If a historical event is used for illustration it should be presented as a slice of life with enough description of setting, drama, and persons that today's listener can find himself in that event. If you must refer to the Spanish Armada, take care to capture the event. Isolate its human features. Let the listeners see the cannons flash, feel the storm, and fear the shoals. No parishioner wants to endure another fourth-grade lecture on the history of England and Spain, hoping it may mean something now, even though it never did before.

TELL A STORY

To present illustrations well preachers need to learn the storytelling principles of the masters. While no set formula exists for presentation, by its very nature an illustration is a slice of life and has an implied beginning and end, background and development, and some point to make—in short, an illustration is a story.[58] Many of the components of the story may be implied rather than stated, or assumed rather than articulated. Jay Adams says that sermon illustrations appear in a variety of forms from fully fleshed out narratives to mere kernels of stories, but he insists these "stories" are what appeal to the senses and involve the audience.[59] Thus, we can agree with Dawson C. Bryan, who wrote decades earlier, "Practically every illustration should be as technically perfect in form as a short story." He was not merely advocating consci-

56. D. W. Cleverley Ford, *The Ministry of the Word* (Grand Rapids: Eerdmans, 1979), 204.

57. This advice also mitigates against the too-common tendency to use old preachers' tales, tired illustrations from steam-locomotive days, and anecdotes clipped from the latest illustration catalogue that have not been revised to reflect the immediate situation of persons present. Cf. Lehman, *Put a Door on It*, 27.

58. Adams, *Preaching with Purpose*, 90.

59. Ibid., 90–91.

entious preparation, but indicating the essential form that illustrations should take.[60]

Bryan wrote that good stories contain four chief components: a beginning; some action; a climax; and a conclusion.[61] Adam's list varies somewhat. He says there must be background (briefly sketched), a complication or a problem, suspense, a climax, and a conclusion.[62] Because the two authors reinforce each other, their lists can be combined to create a model for effective illustrations: An illustration will usually have an introduction, descriptive details, movement through crisis (i.e, creating suspense that leads to a climax), and a conclusion.

Introduce Artistically

The too-frequent form of illustrative introduction is the lame and unimaginative "Let me illustrate. . . ." Bryan provides variations on this theme, including: "Here we have an even more striking illustration of such spiritual understanding. . . ;" or, "Perhaps you will get this distinction best by a single illustration adapted from. . . ;" or, "Here is a roadside experience taken from the paper which gives vividness to what I mean. . . ."[63] Instead of involving the listener such beginnings seem to put a wall between the illustration and the truth it is supposed to illustrate. Of course, even these bearded techniques occasionally prove to be useful or necessary, but they should be used sparingly if the preacher really intends to involve the listeners in his thought. "Congregations can recognize illustrations without being told what they are."[64]

Transition statements announcing that we are about to illustrate may be necessary for readers but seem superfluous to listeners when the entire manner of the preacher indicates that an illustration is coming. In a very real sense an illustration is a demonstrative parenthesis coming before or after a passage of formal explanation. As such, illustrations are a change in the flow of things—not so much a break in the action as a shifting of gears. A simple way to introduce illustrations that is unobtrusive yet effective is simply to pause; to put in the clutch, as it were, in order to prepare for the gear shift.[65]

60. Dawson C. Bryan, *The Art of Illustrating Sermons* (Nashville: Cokesbury, 1938), 210.
61. Ibid., 220.
62. Adams, *Preaching with Purpose*, 93.
63. Bryan, *The Act of Illustrating Sermons*, 199.
64. Deane A. Kemper, *Effective Preaching* (Philadelphia: Westminster, 1985), 86.
65. Ibid., 86.

Next the preacher slices out the context of the illustration. Say when or where the event occurred. Separate the situation of the illustration from the immediate situation of the listeners. Jesus uses time separation to introduce the parable of the workers in the vineyard: "The kingdom of heaven is like a landowner who went out *early in the morning* to hire men to work in his vineyard" (Matt. 20:1, my emphasis). We demonstrate this as parents when we intuitively begin children's stories with "Once upon a time. . . ." The principle never ceases to operate. When the preacher begins with "It was five minutes to midnight and she still wasn't home . . . ," listeners move to a dimension of experience separate from where they are. Conceptual understanding can be built in this dimension as well as with illustration introductions that provide spatial separation as in the parable of the importunate widow, "*In a certain town* there was a judge . . ." (Luke 18:2, emphasis added).

Separation of time and space can be combined in a story's introduction. Hence we get "A long, long time ago in a galaxy far, far away . . ." at the beginning of the *Star Wars* dramas. The combination reminds us that experience is not limited to only one or two dimensions and, therefore, an illustration's introduction may not specifically indicate a separate time or space so much as a separate situation. The situation may be defined by the personalities involved (their relationships, accomplishments, or activities); by the event being recounted (its impact, import, or progress); or by the preacher's own reflection on his internal responses to an incident, an account, or a relationship. In the introduction to the parable of the sower Jesus simply says, "A farmer went out to sow his seed" (Matt. 13:3). No specific time or place is mentioned but nonetheless the Savior defines a particular situation—a life experience with which people can immediately identify.

The goal of the preacher mirrors that of a child's operating a box crane in a penny arcade. The child tries to lift a treasure from a mound of trinkets and place the prize where it can be claimed before time runs out on the machine. In an illustration the preacher attempts to lift listeners from their immediate situations and transport them to an experience that will claim their thought before their interest expires. The introduction of the illustration begins this transporting process by separating the listeners from their immediate experience and placing them in the context of another.

Care needs to be taken in these opening moments so as not to lose listeners. Remember: *the listener expects you to be illustrating the last thing you said before you began the illustration.* If you are going to illustrate something you said three minutes ago, or even three sentences ago, the matter needs to be summarized and restated before the illustration begins.

Second, recall that a sermon is not a research paper. Unless you are trying to make an impression that requires you to state the source of your illustration do not burden the listener with unnecessary documentation. Bryan writes, "[I]t is wise to begin at once with the example. The introduction of author, title, and chapter usually has a deadening effect, and, because of such, many an otherwise good illustration is brought forth stillborn."[66] This is more than a matter of artistic preference. By beginning with what the average listener could not read or has not read the preacher distances the listeners from the illustration. Not overburdening listeners with documentation does not mean you can take the credit for ideas not your own. Maintain pastoral integrity by using phrases such as, "The story is told of . . . ," or "I've heard it said that. . . ." Such phrases do no damage to the illustration but protect the pastor's reputation from the ravages of plagiarism.

Use Vivid Details

To keep listeners with us until the conclusion of an illustration, we must keep all its parts closely tied to experience by using concrete details to make it relate to the listener.[67] Webb Garrison explains why concreteness empowers illustrations and furthers understanding: "If I were to talk at length about my having been deeply moved by watching the setting of my son's broken arm, this would constitute a report of my feelings. But when I describe some factors that contributed to my mood, you are brought into the experience and feel with me. To re-create a moving situation is quite different from testifying to having been deeply moved.[68] Make the situation concrete to make the experience accessible and the message it communicates powerful.

The question is, How? How does the preacher make an experience concrete for his listeners? Answers Lenski, "Concrete objects, persons, actions, situations, etc., are *fully described*" (emphasis added).[69] When Jesus tells the parable of the prodigal son, he does not describe the reunion by saying, "The father expressed continued care for his wayward son." Jesus says,

66. Bryan, *The Art of Illustrating Sermons,* 199.
67. Davis, *Design for Preaching,* 256.
68. Garrison, *Creative Imagination in Preaching,* 95.
69. R. C. H. Lenski, *The Sermon: Its Homiletical Construction* (1927; reprint, Grand Rapids: Baker, 1968), 236.

> But while he [i.e., the son] was still a long way off, his father saw him and was filled with compassion for him; he ran to his son, threw his arms around him and kissed him. The son said to him, "Father, I have sinned against heaven and against you. I am no longer worthy to be called your son." But the father said to his servants, "Quick! Bring the best robe and put it on him. Put a ring on his finger and sandals on his feet. Bring the fattened calf and kill it. Let's have a feast and celebrate. For this son of mine was dead and is alive again; he was lost and is found." So, they began to celebrate. [Luke 15:20–24]

Jesus fleshes out the details that bring the illustrative experience to life. Christ describes perceptions, actions, dialogue, aphorisms, and scene changes—all to express one idea: The father still loved his son.

Details enable listeners to enter a situation they have not actually experienced.[70] Descriptions of sights, sounds, and sensations that the listeners would take in were they in such a context vicariously involve them in that experience. Thus, Lionel Fletcher once advised, "Don't hurry the telling of your illustrations. Tell them well. Build up the background, picture the whole scene, and make it live before the eyes of the congregation."[71] Garrison adds, "Words that name colors, shapes, sounds, odors, and other tangibles help create backgrounds that evoke moods. Anything that moves you can move your listeners—provided they are brought into firsthand encounter with stimuli that produced the emotion."[72]

Still, even though specifics are important, steer clear of details that are extraneous or extravagant. Preachers may fall in love with the artistry of detail to the extent that they remove the illustration from any identifiable experience. Lehman writes, "A certain amount of description becomes necessary to enable the listener to see the door and cross the threshold with you. This does not mean poetry—just description."[73] Unnecessary ornamentation, inefficient story descriptions, and extraneous detail may so flood the listener's mind with irrelevant thoughts that (although the speaker is admired for his erudition) no specific experience can be focused upon, lived through, and made meaningful. True eloquence requires the preacher to present vivid details in clear and concise terms. Dispense with the musing of philosophers, the

70. Eugene Lowry, *How to Preach a Parable* (Nashville: Abingdon, 1989), 106.
71. MacPherson, *The Art of Illustrating Sermons*, 214.
72. Garrison, *Creative Imagination in Preaching*, 95–96.
73. Lehman, *Put a Door on It*, 69.

jargon of psychologists, and the rambling of tale tellers in love with narrative embellishments.[74]

Spurgeon sums up the cautions regarding overdoing illustrative description:

> We are not sent into the world to build a Crystal Palace in which to set out works of art and elegancies of fashion; but as wise master-builders we are to edify the spiritual house for the divine inhabiting [sic]. Our building is intended to last, and is meant for everyday use, and hence it must not be all crystal and colour. We miss our way altogether, as gospel ministers, if we aim at flash and finery. . . . Some men seem never to have enough of metaphors: each one of their sentences must be a flower. They compass sea and land to find a fresh piece of coloured glass for their windows, and they break down the walls of their discourses to let in superfluous ornaments. . . . They are grievously in error if they think that thus they manifest their own wisdom, or benefit their hearers. . . . The best light comes in through the clearest glass: too much paint keeps out the sun.
>
> Our Lord's parables were as simple as tales for children, and as naturally beautiful as the lilies which sprang up in the valleys where he taught the people. . . . His parables were like himself and his surroundings; and were never strained, fantastic, pedantic, or artificial. Let us imitate him, for we shall never find a model more complete, or more suitable for the present age.[75]

Although Spurgeon's ornamental discussion may in some ways violate the principles he articulates, his point remains valid. Save the trumpets and the flowers for occasions when eternity does not hang in the balance.

Every detail of the account should serve the explanatory point being made.[76] To keep listeners on track, preachers not only must take care only to illustrate the last thing said, but also must tell the story of the illustration using the key terms by which they first explored that matter. The illustration should not merely reflect the concepts of the explanation: it should echo the terminology of the explanation as well. Ordinarily this means *we mine the wording of the subpoints* (or the key terms of the main point) for the terms we use to tell the illustration.

74. Ibid., 203.

75. Charles Haddon Spurgeon, *The Art of Illustration*, 3d series of *Lectures to My Students* (London: Marshall Brothers, 1922), 5, 6, 11, 12.

76. Bryan, *The Art of Illustrating Sermons*, 221. See also Thomas Fuller as quoted by John Stott in *Between Two Worlds: The Art of Preaching in the Twentieth Century* (Grand Rapids: Eerdmans, 1982), 240.

For example, if the explanation's subpoints indicate we should pray *fervently* and *consistently*, the illustration should tell a story using those terms. If, instead, the preacher tells of someone who petitions another devotedly, listeners may well wonder how the illustration relates to the explanation. In the preacher's mind "petitions another devotedly" may be synonymous with praying "fervently and consistently," but the listening ear longs for more consistent expression. The key terms of the subpoints were the listeners' signposts through the concepts in the explanation. Dispensing with these verbal trail guides in the illustration invites confusion and loses listeners. The key concepts *and* terminology of the explanation should beacon through the details of the illustration.

Create Crisis

An illustration's details should carry the narrative forward through its crisis. Narrative crisis does not have to be created by the threat of a tragedy. Crisis may be achieved by opening a door to scientific knowledge or by opening a new window from which to see the commonplace in a new light. At its heart, crisis is the tension of the not yet—not knowing the solution, not knowing the resolve, not knowing the punch line, or not knowing how the punch line will be delivered this time.

Crisis results from having sufficient, relevant facts to create a problem that the listeners have an interest in solving, and that forces them to journey through the narrative in order to discover the treasure found in the climax. If preachers do not bring the audience to the edge of wonder, grief, anger, confusion, fear, or discovery, then their words have no point—no hook on which to hang meaning. The internal tensions of illustrations hold the congregation because they spotlight the very types of experiences that bring people to hear the minister.

In the parable of the Pharisee and the publican, the incongruous prayer attitudes of two men who are apparently moral opposites create the tension. The outwardly moral Pharisee prays "with himself" (Luke 18:11). The despised publican, however, "would not even look up to heaven, but beat his breast and said, 'God, have mercy on me, a sinner'" (Luke 18:13). The crisis for Christ's audience is in determining proper prayer, and deciding what it reflects about dependence on God's grace rather than on self-righteousness. The complications in the details of the vignette create a tension between what these opposite men should be saying, and what they actually are saying. Without this crisis the story holds no impact.

Conclude Meaningfully

Following the advice of the adage, "Strike while the iron is hot," "strike" your illustration's conclusion while "heat" from the crisis is greatest. That is, place the climax of the account as close to the illustration's end as possible.[77] The crisis, then, stimulates interest and pulls listeners into an experience that the illustration typifies. Having drawn the listeners as much as possible into the experience, the preacher must make the point before interest, attention, and involvement diminish. Thus, illustrative conclusions have two elements: the story's end and the illustration's point.

The introduction isolates the experience; the narrative detail gives it form; crisis compels involvement; and the conclusion focuses meaning by relating the events in the illustration back to the explanatory point being made. There are a number of ways that this can be done, but normally the preacher states the relation in a crisp, verbal hammer stroke that drives the point home.[78] Lehman writes, "The bridge from the illustration itself to the interpretation must not be shaky or ill defined."[79] Such a bridge usually takes the form of a "grouping (or, interpreting) statement"; that is, a sentence or two in which the preacher reaches into the illustration for pertinent details, extracts them and, ties them to the idea being communicated.

Grouping statements demonstrate similarities between the illustration's details and the sermon's truths. The preacher might conclude an illustration with phrases such as "Even as so-and-so discovered this path we must . . ."; or, "In the same manner . . ."; or, "We too must . . ."; or, "We learn from this account that just as. . . ." An alternative is to cap the illustration with an application phrased in wording parallel to a key phrase or thought that occurred within the illustration. An illustration might end with the statement, "Without his guide, Joe could never have found his way back." The parallel grouping statement might then be: "Without our God, we can never find our way back." Parallel phrases remove the need for prefatory comments that indicate that the preacher is about to relate the illustration's details to the sermon's point because the parallelism automatically implies the relationship.

Donald Grey Barnhouse made many an illustration famous, but none more ably demonstrates how master preachers use interpreting state-

---

77. Bryan, *The Art of Illustrating Sermons*, 227–28.

78. Kemper, *Effective Preaching*, 86; Adams, *Preaching with Purpose*, 93; Sangster, *The Craft of Sermon Illustration*, 89; Bryan, *The Art of Illustrating Sermons*, 226.

79. Lehman, *Put a Door on It*, 89.

ments than this poignant illustration he told his children when their mother died:

> As he drove his children to his wife's funeral Barnhouse stopped at a traffic crossing. Ahead of them was a huge truck. The sun was at such an angle that it cast the truck's shadow across the snow-covered field beside it. Dr. Barnhouse pointed to the shadow and spoke to his children: "Look at the shadow of that truck on the field, children. If you had to be run over, would you rather be run over by the truck or by its shadow?
>
> The youngest child responded first, "The shadow. It couldn't hurt anybody."
>
> "That's right," said Barnhouse. "And remember, children, Jesus let the truck of death strike him, so that it could never destroy us. Mother lives with Jesus now—only the shadow of death passed over her."

I have used this illustration at more than one funeral. Not only does it speak movingly of deep biblical truth, but it also does all an illustration must with a great economy of words. Listeners focus their attention on the Barnhouses' situation, see what the children see, and even listen in on the dialogue. Even more crucial than a vicarious experiencing of the event, however, are the master preacher's final words to his children, which enable them to relate the details of the illustration to Christian death. The interpreting statement is short—two brief sentences. But by reaching into his illustration to grab key terms to weld the illustration and a theological concept together, Barnhouse's illustration provides comfort for us as it did for his children. No matter how well they are described, events generally do not interpret themselves, so such grouping statements at the conclusion of illustrations are crucial. Though a grouping statement can be implied as well as directly stated its essence must echo in the listener's mind for the illustration to remain faithful to the exposition's purpose.

CONCERNS REGARDING ILLUSTRATIONS

Illustrations that portray realism, integrity, and compassion magnify the persuasive power of a sermon. How we use illustrations and where we find them will largely determine their effectiveness.

ILLUSTRATION CAUTIONS

Use Illustrations Prudently

Remember that illustrations are a tool for exposition, not a substitute for sound explanation. The preacher who constructs sermons to serve illustration rather than solid biblical exposition inevitably drifts from pulpit to stage, from pastor to showman. Any trained public speaker can select a theme and gather a bundle of stories that will touch an audience emotionally, but this is not preaching. The proper focus of illustrations lies in presenting biblical truth in such a manner that it can be understood deeply and applied readily, rather than in providing popular enjoyment or pastoral acclaim.

Messages that are overloaded with illustrations damage the credibility of the preacher because hearers conclude, "All this one does is tell stories."[80] We achieve balance not through some ironclad standard for the number and placement of illustrations, but by a common sense assessment of how and where they will best serve the purposes of the message. Traditionally there is an illustration for each major division (i.e., main point) of a sermon.[81] Whether an illustration should follow each main points' subpoints or accompany a single subpoint whose explanation is particularly difficult, or serve as a transition showing the relationship between two points,[82] is better left to the discretion of the preacher, who has the best feel for what the message as a whole needs. For instance, if a powerful illustration drives the conclusion of a sermon *it may be wise to use the illustration of the final main point early* so that it does not impinge on the sermon's climax.[83] Mass-communication studies have indicated that it is often best to use an illustration immediately after the first statement of an expositional principle in a main point's development.[84] The technique intrigues while introducing a subject and thus allows the point to be made with a minimum of attention drop or listener argument.[85] This method is especially popular with broadcast preachers.[86]

All these alternatives indicate illustrations may properly appear at the beginning, in the middle, and at the end of a main point, as well as

80. Marquart, *Quest for Better Preaching*, 153.
81. Bryan, *The Art of Illustrating Sermons*, 172; Baumann, *An Introduction to Contemporary Preaching*, 180; Larsen, *The Anatomy of Preaching*, 66.
82. Bryan, *The Art of Illustrating Sermons*, 173–74.
83. More discussion of this in chapter 9.
84. Lewis, *Inductive Preaching*, 82.
85. Kemper, *Effective Preaching*, 81.
86. For additional information on the application of this principle to broadcast preaching see the author's chapter entitled "Alternative Models: Old Friends in New Clothes" in *A Handbook of Contemporary Preaching*, ed. Michael Duduit (Nashville: Broadman, 1992), 118–31.

in the transition between main points. Such a conclusion underscores the seductive nature of illustrations. Once a preacher discovers how powerfully good illustrations elicit audience response and then further realizes that they can surface almost anywhere in a sermon, the temptation is almost irresistible to use illustrations everywhere. We must resist the temptation. If we were to graph the emotional intensity of a sermon we would see that the peaks tend to rise around illustrations, especially if an application is made with the illustration. But if a sermon is all illustrative climaxes, no portion holds exceptional impact. Preachers who load illustration upon illustration in order to woo an audience find themselves in a classic hedonistic dilemma—people lose interest because of the commonness of the pleasure. Pastors lose credibility when their sermons do not possess adequate explanatory balance.[87]

The nature of the sermon, the nature of the illustrations, and the nature of the target audience all come to bear on the proper balance of expository components in a sermon. Popular today, in some circles, is the narrative sermon, which presents a biblical truth in a parable pattern[88]—an extended story (or a narrative structure) leading to a poignant moral or insight that constitutes the sermon. We should not condemn this method since it was often Jesus' manner of teaching. Such sermons can serve important purposes, and the proportion of illustrative content in them is necessarily large. Still, a balanced perspective will recall that Jesus used such an approach in contexts where he could assume his followers knew (or would become acquainted with) much additional biblical teaching (see Mark 4:10, 34). It is unlikely that Jesus believed a congregation would be fed adequately if this were its only diet.

Determine when and where to use illustrations by assessing what will make the message's application most effective. In some cases this will mean that illustrations must focus on clarifying the exposition to allow sufficient understanding to apply the text. In other instances it is better to use illustrations to create deep feeling about a matter that is so familiar that it no longer stimulates the response it should. Whether the leverage we provide is intellectual, attitudinal, or some combination of the two, illustrations work best when the preacher uses them to affect the will of the hearers. Such use ennobles illustrations by taking them

---

87. Spurgeon, *The Art of Illustration*, 4–5.

88. Cf. Edmund A. Steimle, Morris J. Niedenthal, and Charles Rice, eds. *Preaching the Story* (Philadelphia: Fortress, 1980); Eugene L. Lowry, *The Homiletical Plot: The Sermon as Narrative Art Form* (Atlanta: John Knox, 1980); Wayne Bradley Robinson, ed., *Journeys toward Narrative Preaching* (New York: Pilgrim, 1990); Chapell, "Alternative Models," 124–25.

from the realm of entertainment and placing them in a servant relationship to a sermon's expository purposes. People are simply more willing to attempt, or even to consider, what they believe to be possible.[89] When they see spiritual truth in scenes, incidents, and circumstances that form the common ground of human experience, acceptance of what the preacher says naturally grows.[90] Illustrations carry compelling evidential weight.

Use Illustrations Pastorally

Even if illustrations are not the focus of an expository message, they do focus congregational attention on the preacher's understanding of life and the Bible's relevance to it. Illustrations put pastoral integrity, competence, and compassion in full view. For this reason preachers must prepare illustrations with a keen awareness of their inherent pastoral implications.[91] Heeding these cautions will help keep illustrations from damaging your ministry:

Get the facts straight. Adept handling of facts instills listener confidence in a preacher. References to the "99 theses of Martin Luther," "the prison ministry of George Colson," "Einstein's discovery of x-rays," and "Churchill's warning that 'We have nothing to fear but fear itself'" do the opposite.

Beware of untrue or incredible illustrations. Resist the temptation to tell an account as though it were true if it is not. Do not say it happened to you if it did not. Even if the account is true, avoid it if it casts doubt on your veracity. You have lost much if you lose credibility.

Maintain balance. The illustrations of expository sermons rarely extend beyond a paragraph or two in a written manuscript. Be brief. Avoid stacking too many illustrations together. An illustration clarifying an illustration is a sure sign of danger.

Be real. Appreciate the epic in the immediate. If we too often illustrate with the great saints of yesteryear, we may hopelessly distance faith from the experience of most Christians today. Impressing everyone with the prayer life of E. M. Bounds, Charles Simeon, George Mueller, and Moses promotes a false perception of super spirituality. Illustrations that fly in the lofty clouds of spiritual

---

89. John Killinger, *Fundamentals of Preaching* (Philadelphia: Fortress, 1985), 30–31.
90. R. E. O. White, *A Guide to Preachers* (Grand Rapids: Eerdmans, 1973), 171.
91. Chapell, *Using Illustrations*, 156–75.

idealism ultimately destroy listeners' confidence that faith can be lived in real life.[92]

Do not carelessly expose, disclose, or embarrass. Be careful not to draw illustrations from sources that may inadvertently expose indulgence in or imply approval of entertainments or habits that may compromise your pastoral position (e.g., some congregations may approve references to popular adult movies, but in other settings parents may wonder why their pastor endorses what they forbid their teens to see.). Never disclose counseling confidences in such a way that individuals can be identified or even guessed about. Do not portray family, friends, or parishioners in embarrassing accounts unless you have secured their permission *and* indicate you have done so while telling the illustration.

Poke fun at no one but self. Ridicule of ethnic groups, dialects, political parties, gender, age, or any individual automatically calls into question your ability to communicate the grace of God even if people laugh at the joke. The only one you have a right to poke fun at from the pulpit is yourself. (Corollary: The only one you cannot pat on the back from the pulpit is yourself.)

Share the spotlight. Do not let yourself (your kids, your hobby, your dog, your vacation, your illness, your military service, your sports career) be the focus of too many illustrations. Never be the hero of your own illustrations. If good results give the credit to God.

Demonstrate taste and respect sensibilities. Birthing, blood and gore, bedrooms, and bathrooms do not merit graphic description from the pulpit. Where such references are needed, speak matter-of-factly and move along. Profanity or coarse language even of the mildest form can spark more anger from the pew than most preachers ever want to confront. Although people know the terms well, they do not come to church to hear them on their pastor's lips.

Finish what you begin. You cannot leave people hanging, wondering what happened to that little dog, or the boy in the hospital bed, or the neighbor who ran over the garbage can. Even if other aspects of the illustration make your point, unresolved aspects of a story

92. Baumann, *An Introduction to Contemporary Preaching*, 180. If you question the validity of this advice ask yourself which of the following grants you more hope for your own usefulness in God's service: the fact that Charles Haddon Spurgeon so struggled with depression that this "prince of preachers" was absent from his pulpit nearly a third of the time in his later life, or the story that he had such mastery of the pulpit that a workman was converted merely hearing Spurgeon quote John 3:16 while testing the acoustics in an auditorium.

may so dominate listeners' thoughts that they will hear little else you say.

ILLUSTRATION SOURCES

Preachers get illustrations from several basic sources: personal experiences (read about, heard from others, or personally lived), news accounts, historical accounts, literary materials, imagination, and the Bible. Seeing illustrations around you, keeping track of them as you read and study, and listening for accounts others tell is a constant challenge that becomes a lifestyle.[93] As the metamorphosis from parishioner who consumes sermons to pulpit servant who prepares sermons occurs, we all can naturally develop the skill of finding illustrations everywhere if we are convinced of the importance of doing so, and do not too early fall into the habit of only using the illustrations of others.[94]

Discovery Systems

Often illustrations will come to our minds as we prepare a message. If the point to be made is sharply defined, the impact of the truth will often throw mental sparks against a memory or recent experience, and the illustration immediately flames into light. However, most preachers will be seriously handicapped if they rely only on immediate inspiration for sermon illustrations. Most of us find that we must combine illustrations that we have stored with those that spring to mind when we prepare our messages.

A number of "systems" have been devised to help preachers save and retrieve the illustrations they discover, of which computer programs and subscription services are only recent innovations in a much-developed field. No illustration system is more important, or more basic, than knowing well ahead of time what your subject and/or text will be. Having that in hand some weeks prior to preaching a message is like having a powerful idea magnet. This does not mean that you should

93. Chapell, *Using Illustrations*, 179–86.
94. Unlike many other homiletics instructors I am not unalterably opposed to using illustration catalogues *so long as* preachers use the listed accounts as catalysts rather than as crutches. All preachers run into situations where we know we need an illustration but cannot think of something appropriate (especially in churches where the pastor must prepare messages four or five times a week). Having a reservoir of illustrations the preacher can revise, update, and personalize is valuable. However, preachers who habitually cut and paste others' illustrations will develop messages that are increasingly trite, staid, and impersonal.

have the entire sermon in hand weeks before it is preached. For most of us this is simply impossible, and even if it were not, such a practice might rob messages of their spontaneous fire. Still, by knowing generally what a sermon will be about, the preacher can begin to collect, sort, and evaluate illustrations long before they are actually needed.

Often preachers keep a letter-size file with a separate folder for each sermon planned for upcoming weeks or months. Then as an illustration comes to mind or you come across an article dealing with the subject, simply drop the material into the appropriate folder so that you have a healthy reservoir of ideas on hand for the week you must fully prepare the sermon. Not only will illustrations find their way into such a file, but potential outlines, exegetical discoveries, applicational thoughts, and expositional ideas will be drawn to the magnetic "pre-sermon file."[95] The preacher certainly does not have to use all the material collected in such a file. However, even if the pastor ends up using very little of the file for a particular message, over time such a system will undoubtedly put many more—and better—illustrative resources at the preacher's fingertips.

Retrieval Systems

When you come across an illustration write it down immediately. Be careful to write it down with sufficient detail so that you can remember what it is about. Most preachers who determine to "write it down more fully later" had best simply resign themselves to forgetting 90 percent of their potential illustrations. Many great communicators have disciplined themselves to carry a pocket notebook in order immediately to record illustrations and other thoughts pertinent to their messages. In recent years I have mimicked the practice of these experts by keeping a small tablet of stick-'em notes in my wallet. This way I always have paper to jot down an illustration. Later, I simply stick the note on a 3-by-5-inch card and file it in an appropriate pre-sermon, or other illustration, file.

My family has also long insisted that I be the last to read the daily paper, since when I do, sections tend to get savaged by my scissors. I read magazines with scissors in hand and books with a highlighter within reach. That which I cannot clip, I photocopy; or I jot down enough information in my wallet notes so that I can remember and retrieve the illustration when I need it. Then, I file the clipping, photocopy, or note with other illustrations. My illustration files may not be pretty, but then I am

95. See earlier discussion in chapter 3 of the pre-sermon file.

not trying to publish them. I am the only one who has to look at them and I know, if I make my work unnecessarily difficult, I am not likely to continue it.

What do you do with good illustrations that have no place in your pre-sermon file, or that you have used previously? File them.[96] As bother-some as it may be to set them up initially, illustration files will later save huge amounts of time and energy. Some preachers may prefer to develop their own topical system for cataloguing their illustrations, but you can save yourself much work by purchasing one of the good topical catalogs on the market today. Currently, I prefer to file my illustrations in a 3-by-5-inch card system marketed by a major publisher. The file readily accepts wallet notes, and I can easily change the topic categories by inserting or deleting tab cards. If I am undecided about which topic category an illustration best fits, or if I think it fits well in a number of categories, I simply make photocopies and file the illustration in each of the appropriate places.

Computer cataloguing systems are also adaptable, and some have high-powered topical search and cross-reference programs (often these can be updated monthly through various subscription services). Typi-cally, computer illustrations may be placed directly into a sermon manuscript using standard word-processing software. The only draw-back to computer cataloguing is the time needed to input illustrations that are not part of the original or the subscription packages. However, it is easier to file duplicate copies of the illustration in multiple topic and text categories using computer processing. If I did not depend so much on my wallet notes, I would probably prefer a computerized retrieval system. Evaluating one's own practices, needs, and budget will help each pastor determine which system will best serve individual needs and styles.

96. Topic and text files are both extremely beneficial. Excellent discussions of filing procedures are found in Haddon Robinson, *Biblical Preaching: The Development and Delivery of Expository Messages* (Grand Rapids: Baker, 1980), 154; and Leslie B. Flynn, *Come Alive with Illustrations: How to Find, Use, and File Good Stories for Sermons and Speeches* (Grand Rapids: Baker, 1987), 103–9.

QUESTIONS FOR REVIEW AND DISCUSSION

1. What distinguishes illustration from allusion or example?

2. What do listeners automatically assume the preacher is illustrating when the illustration begins?

3. How are the key words of the main point's explanation used in illustration?

4. What is a "grouping (or, interpreting) statement," and how is it used in illustration?

5. What matters help determine the proportion of illustration in a sermon?

6. What matters help determine the placement of an illustration in a main point? What are appropriate locations for an illustration? in a main point?

7. What are important cautions to remember when creating illustrations?

EXERCISES

1. Create an illustration for one of the main points you outlined in the exercises at the conclusion of chapter 6; or,

2. Create an illustration for the following main point: Because Jesus always intercedes for his church, we must pray consistently and fervently.

3. Choose a topic and create an illustration that uses at least three of the five senses.

CONTENTS OF CHAPTER 8

GOAL OF CHAPTER 8

To demonstrate how to apply the truths of expository sermons with relevance, realism, and authority

8

THE PRACTICE
OF APPLICATION

THE FUNCTIONS OF APPLICATION

Approximately one-third of American adults say they have had a born-again experience, and the figure has remained consistent for several years. However, surveys find little difference in the behavior of these born-again Christians before and after their conversion experiences. In fact, these surveys indicate that in each of three major categories—use of illegal drugs, driving while intoxicated, and marital infidelity—behavior actually deteriorates after a commitment to Christ. The incidence of drug use and illicit sex roughly doubles after conversion, and the incidence of drunken driving triples.[1]

Reasons for these troubling statistics vary widely, but they make clear the fact that faith can remain abstract idealism for too many. John Calvin's observation still rings true: "[I]f we leave it to men's choice to follow that that is taught them, they will never move one foot. Therefore the doctrine of itself can profit nothing at all."[2] Preachers make a fundamental mistake when they assume that by providing parishioners with biblical information the people will automatically make the connection between scriptural truth and their everyday lives.[3]

Application fulfills the obligations of exposition. Application is the present consequence of scriptural truth. Without application the preacher has no reason to preach because truth without application is

---

1. These Gallup Poll and Roper Organization survey are results in *National and International Religion Report* (October 1990), 8.
2. From Calvin's sermon on 2 Timothy 4:1–2, as translated in *Sermons on the Epistles to Timothy and Titus* (Edinburgh: Banner of Truth Trust, 1983), 945–57.
3. David Veerman, "Sermons: Apply Within," *Leadership* (Spring 1990): 121.

useless. This means that at its heart preaching is not merely the proclamation of truth, but is truth applied.[4] The Westminster divines understood this when they formulated the answer to the catechism question,
What do the Scriptures principally teach? The answer, what man is to
believe concerning God *and* what duty God requires of man (emphasis
added),[5] clearly specifies the dual task of the preacher who would unfold
the meaning of a biblical passage. The exposition of Scripture remains
incomplete until the preacher explains the duty God requires of man.

The duty that God requires in a passage is the "so what" of expository
preaching that causes application. I like David Veerman's summary,

> Simply stated, application is answering two questions: *So what?* and
> *Now what?* The first question asks, "Why is this passage important to
> *me?* The second asks, "What should I do about it today?"
> Application focuses the truth of God's Word on specific, life-related sit-
> uations. It helps people understand what to do or how to use what they
> have learned. Application persuades people to act. [6]

As helpful as these familiar distinctions are, a word of caution needs to
be added before summarizing the obligations of application. Too much
emphasis on duty, action, and What do you want me to do? can leave
the impression that application always requires the pastor to dictate
some behavior in a sermon.

Application may be attitudinal as well as behavioral. In fact, the frequent mark of immaturity among preachers is too much (or too early)
an emphasis on behaviors in the sermon. Mature preachers do not
ignore behaviors, but carefully build an attitudinal foundation for whatever actions they say God requires. This is more than a rhetorical tactic.
Its source is the biblical insight that out of the heart come the issues of
life (Prov. 4:23). Sermons that merely instruct, Don't drink, don't
smoke, don't chew, nor go with the folks that do, will lead to little spiritual maturity even if parishioners do all they are told. Many applications exhort action (e.g., share the gospel with a neighbor, turn from a
sinful practice, give to a worthy cause), but just as many should identity
an attitude needing change (e.g., prejudice, pride, or selfishness) or reinforce a faith commitment (e.g., grasping the freedom of forgiveness, taking comfort in the truths of the resurrection, or renewing hope on the

4. Jay E. Adams, *Truth Applied: Application in Preaching* (Grand Rapids: Zondervan,
1990), 39.
5. *Westminster Shorter Catechism*, question 3.
6. Veerman, "Sermons," 122.

basis of God's sovereignty). Transformation of heart and life are both legitimate aims of application.

Application justifies the exposition. If there is no apparent reason for listeners to absorb exegetical insights, historical facts, and biographical details, then the preacher cannot expect to hold their attention long. No doctor will have much success saying to patients, "Take these pills," without explaining why. Application explains why listeners should take the sermon's expositional pills. Through application the preacher implicitly encourages the parishioner to listen to the message's explanations because they establish the reasonableness and necessity of particular responses. Thus, "application is the main thing to be done."[7] The informed preacher uses every aspect of the sermon as leverage to move the message's application based on sound exposition (see fig. 8.1).

FIGURE 8.1
The Sermon as Application Leverage

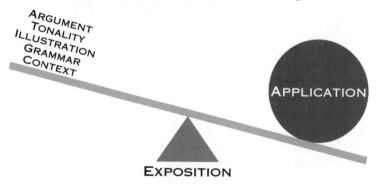

Application also focuses the exposition. Exegesis and explanation are bottomless pits of commentary possibilities if the preacher has no clear purpose in mind. Books containing entirely legitimate information could be written on almost any biblical passage.[8] But preachers have only a few minutes each week to expound what a passage means. How do we choose what to say? Application answers by forcing us to determine what information most strongly supports particular responses we say the passage requires of listeners in light of the Fallen Condition

7. John A. Broadus, *On the Preparation and Delivery of Sermons*, ed. J. B. Weatherspoon (New York: Harper and Row, 1944), 210. See also earlier comments in chapter 4 of this book.
8. See chapter 2.

Focus (FCF) of the message. The applications point to the FCF saying: This is what you must do about that problem, need, or fault on the basis of what this passage means. We select explanatory arguments and facts from the infinite possibilities on the basis of how readily they will support these applications. Application gives the exposition a target on which to focus (see fig. 8.2).

FIGURE 8.2

Application as Expositional Target

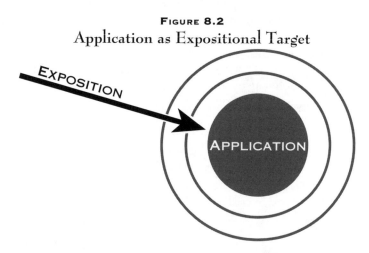

If the applications lose sight of the FCF, the message will degenerate into a handful of legalisms tacked onto randomly selected observations. Without building the exposition to support applications directed at an FCF, preachers simply choose to comment on what is most prominent in their own thought. In other words, by not identifying an FCF that the text addresses, preachers speak more what is on their minds than what is in the text at the precise moment they believe themselves to be doing the opposite.

Accurate exposition requires us to complete our sermon research by identifying appropriate applications that will focus the exposition according to the text's priorities. Therefore, though preachers determine application at the end of the sermon research stage (do not say what the text requires before determining what it means), they should have application in mind before beginning sermon construction. Do not start writing out the message before determining what the sermon seeks to accomplish. Application must precede final decisions about structure, wording, and even the tone of the message or else the preacher will be designing a highway without knowing its destination.

For my preaching students I have devised what I call "the left-field rule." The rule comes into effect when after writing the explanation and illustration of a main point, the preacher internally questions, "Hmmm. I wonder how I should apply this?" The question itself indicates that the preacher is in left field (that is, has become oblivious to chief obligations). If the preacher did not know what application the exposition was driving at, how was the route chosen? What determined the wording of the ideas, the choice of facts, and the framing of the illustrations if the preacher had no idea what response the text required? Without application the preacher was simply swinging blindly, hoping the ball of application would hit the bat of exposition. Home runs are more frequently hit when the batter sees the ball before swinging.

Although the precise details of the application may take shape only as the rest of the sermon itself takes form, decisions about the general thrust of the application of each stage of the message should precede the development of that portion of the message. Homiletics instructors vary as to how they express this, referring variously to the "aim," "big idea," "telic purpose," or "transformation" to which all aspects of the message drive. The richness of expression underscores the importance of one consistent principle: do not fire off information without having a target. Decide the response you intend before you craft the words.[9]

If this advice seems to devalue the importance of explanation in expository preaching, recognize that the chief purpose of application is not simply to give people something to do. *Application gives ultimate meaning to the exposition.* Even if the explanation of a sermon were to define every Greek and Hebrew word for prayer, were to quote at length from Calvin, Luther, and E. M. Bounds on prayer's meaning, were to cite fifty passages that refer to prayer, and were to describe the prayer practices of David, Jeremiah, Daniel, Paul, and Jesus, would listeners truly understand what prayer is? No. Until we engage in prayer we do not really understand it. Until we apply a truth understanding of it remains incomplete. This means that until a preacher provides application, exposition remains incomplete.[10]

No preacher really interprets what a text means at the human level by merely identifying its historical and grammatical roots. "God caused

9. Adams, *Truth Applied*, 41. The preacher should at least have the general instructional specificity in mind before constructing the message.

10. Sidney Greidanus, *Sola Scriptura: Problems and Principles in Preaching Historical Texts* (Toronto: Wedge, 1970), 157; John F. Bettler, "Application," in *The Preacher and Preaching*, ed. Samuel T. Logan (Phillipsburg, N.J.: Presbyterian and Reformed, 1986), 332.

the Word spoken in those days to be put in writing with a view to us and our salvation. . . . A respect for the true nature of the Bible opens the way for applied explanation in preaching"[11] (cf. Rom. 4:23–25; 1 Cor. 10:6–13). Preachers must translate what the text means. This is more than an exegetical task. We must make the meaning of the text concrete for contemporary people in contemporary situations. If we do not place the proclamation of gospel truth in a present world it will have no continuing meaning. Greidanus writes, "To put the issue succinctly: since the message was first addressed to the ancient church, it requires explication; since that message now needs to be addressed to a contemporary church, it requires application."[12] Traditional homiletical distinctions still have merit. Preachers do need to provide explanations of the text that demonstrate the validity of applications, and our listeners should ignore applications that have no clear biblical warrant. We simply must not let application become a tacked-on task. Application is the exposition that grants present meaning.[13] What we do as well as what we know enables our understanding of God's will for our lives (see Rom. 12:1–2).[14]

THE COMPONENTS OF APPLICATION

Expository messages require preachers to ensure that the applications they make will answer four key questions: What does God now require of me? Where does he require it of me? Why must I do what he requires? and, How can I do what God requires?

WHAT

Preachers answer the question, What does God now require of me? by providing instructions that reflect the biblical principles found in the text. This *instructional specificity* translates the text from ancient history to present guide. In order for the guidance accurately to reflect the Bible's intent, the preacher must discern the biblical principles reflected

11. C. Trimp, "The Relevance of Preaching," *Westminster Theological Journal* 36 (1973): 27.

12. Sidney Greidanus, *The Modern Preacher and the Ancient Text: Interpreting and Preaching Biblical Literature* (Grand Rapids: Eerdmans, 1988), 183.

13. D. Martyn Lloyd-Jones, *Darkness and Light: An Exposition of Ephesians 4:17–5:17* (Grand Rapids: Baker, 1982), 200–201. See also introductory discussions of the relationship of exposition and application in chapters 2 and 4 of this book.

14. John Frame, *Doctrine of the Knowledge of God* (Phillipsburg, N.J.: Presbyterian and Reformed, 1987), 93–98.

in the text that were directed to the people of that time and apply the same principles to the people of this time with instructions directed to their actions, attitudes, and/or beliefs.[15]

The need to base instructions on principles found in the text further justifies the prudence of phrasing main points as universal truths that the sermon's explanation will support. Since the preacher must acknowledge the discontinuity between an ancient people and the present congregation, mere description of the text will not support application. The application must be built on principles that the details of the text support.[16] The What should I now do? dimension of application will fail if the preacher does not explicate the text in terms of principle development.

Opinion, arbitrariness, or ignorance appear to dictate applications that are simply slapped onto the conclusion of a sermon that rehearses a text's details. The fact that Paul went to Jerusalem to deliver gifts no more supports an exhortation to tithe than the fact that Jesus wore sandals obligates us to use footwear.[17] Preachers must demonstrate that the facts of the text support application instructions because the instructions naturally follow from biblical principles that the explanation establishes.[18] The goal of the text's explanation should be to establish the validity of the principles on which the application must be based.

A simple and effective way of ensuring the cohesion of explanatory principles and sermonic applications is to use the key concepts and terminology of a main point's explanation to frame the application (see fig. 8.3). Word the instructions of the application with the key terms of the subpoints (or the main point itself). For example, use subpoints indicating that devoted prayer is consistent and fervent to frame and phrase the instruction that we should pray *consistently* and *fervently*. By phrasing the application's instruction with the key terms of the explanation, listeners not only understand why they were listening to all that explanation, but also immediately connect the instruction of the preacher with the authority of Scripture.[19] Listeners conclude: We must do this because it is what we have seen the Bible says.

15. Greidanus, *Modern Preacher*, 167; Veerman, "Sermons," 122–23.
16. Greidanus, *Modern Preacher*, 172–74.
17. Douglas Stuart, *Old Testament Exegesis* (Philadelphia: Westminster, 1980), 73.
18. Krister Stendahl, "Preaching from the Pauline Epistles, in *Biblical Preaching: An Expositor's Treasury*, ed. James W. Cox (Philadelphia: Westminster, 1983), 307–8.
19. Note how this procedure again underscores the necessity of having application in mind before settling on the phrasing and the form of the explanation.

WHERE

Instructional specificity uses biblical principles to establish what contemporary people should do, but if preachers never specify where in real life these principles apply, the instructions remain irrelevant abstractions. The mere exhortation that we should love our neighbors more hardly adds new challenge or insight to anyone's walk of faith even if the instruction accurately reflects a biblical principle. Who did not know this general teaching before sitting down in the pew? The instruction moves from generic principle to poignant application when the preacher identifies the contemporary situations that listeners face in which they should apply the biblical principle (loving the neighbor who supports a different political party, raises hateful children, laughs at your faith, or backs into your car and drives away without leaving a note).[20]

The aptness, relevance, and realism of this *situational specificity* is frequently a distinguishing mark of mature preaching.[21] The applications of beginning preachers often seem to fall into one of two categories: simple generalization (Go and do likewise) or instructional multiplication (e.g., Buy this book, pray in these phrases, associate with these people, give to this cause, perform this task, consider this suggestion, think this way, act this way, believe this way). The first error is lack of thought, the second error is undirected thought. The latter occurs when preachers think that they will seem to exhibit depth of thought by greatly multiplying the instructions a passage implies. Such a shotgun approach makes the preacher seem to be reaching for any possible idea rather that searching the depths of a text's meaning.[22] Seasoned preachers identify a biblical principle the text supports and then ask themselves, "Who among my listeners needs to hear this?" Such an approach enables them to discern applications that sink deep into individual experience rather than skim across the surface of life's possibilities. *Directing all applications toward different facets of a precise, poignant FCF will keep the entire sermon's application focused.*

By identifying to whom a biblical principle applies, the preacher naturally draws to mind the situations parishioners face and the guidance

20. Stuart, *Old Testament Exegesis*, 47.
21. David L. Larsen, *The Anatomy of Preaching: Identifying the Issues in Preaching Today* (Grand Rapids: Baker, 1989), 96; Herbert H. Farmer, *The Servant of the Word* (Philadelphia: Fortress, 1942), 84–97.
22. Adams, *Truth Applied*, 41.

this text offers.[23] To be fair, this frequently means that pastors who have the most experience in life have the greatest likelihood of developing powerful applications. Still, even beginning preachers can hone the craft of application by coveting the compliment, "Pastor, the Lord put on your heart just what I needed you to talk about. It seems as though you have read my mail."

Of course, offering application instructions in the context of situational specifics does not mean that preachers should pick on specific persons from the pulpit.[24] The goal of sound application is situational specificity, not personal identification. Think through the types of people—young parents, harassed clerks, lonely teens, new believers, tired saints—whose situations require scriptural guidance, comfort, and challenge. You cannot speak to all groups every week, but since we confront no temptation but such as is common to all, speaking to specifics will have some relevance for each person (1 Cor. 10:13). The extent to which you keep these specifics in touch with the more common concerns in your congregation the more your applications will speak to all.[25]

Prudence and judgment need to be applied to keep from inappropriately criticizing or exposing individuals from the pulpit. Still, the best applications are real enough to move beyond abstract instructions that are as easily dodged as they are acknowledged.[26] This application ethic derives from the old preaching rule that "the cure for dullness in the pulpit is not brilliance, but reality"; and its derivative, "generalization in the pulpit is the security of sin in the pew."

Applications that are true to the goals of expository preaching explain how believers today would have to live in specific situations to remain faithful to Scripture. This is no easy task. In fact, the strain of developing balanced, relevant, and fair situational specificity underscores why application is the most difficult task of expository preaching. The text contains the information for instructional specificity, but the experience, courage, care, and spirituality of the preacher provide the material for situational specificity (i.e., instructional specificity is supplied *to* you; situational specificity is supplied *by* you.).

23. Jerry Vines, *A Practical Guide to Sermon Preparation* (Chicago: Moody, 1985), 98; Edmund A. Steimle, Morris J. Niedenthal, and Charles Rice, eds., *Preaching the Story* (Philadelphia: Fortress, 1980), 108.

24. Veerman, "Sermons," 124.

25. See the author's "Old Friends in New Clothes," *A Handbook of Contemporary Preaching* (Nashville: Broadman, 1992).

26. Larsen, *The Anatomy of Preaching*, 97.

WHY

Applications must provide proper motivation as well as relevant instruction. We need only consider the example of the Pharisees to recall that it is more than possible to do all the right things for all the wrong reasons and be no more holy than those whose behavior is far less moral. A friend of mine is fond of saying, "There is a longing for heaven and a fearing of hell that is straight from Satan because it is nothing but sanctified selfishness." We must make sure our listeners know why they should heed our applications.

Because so much of part 3 of this book deals with proper motivation in preaching I will not belabor the point here except to highlight this basic precept: Make sure that you motivate believers by grace, not guilt. If God has freed his people from the guilt and power of sin, then preachers have no right to seek holiness by putting believers back under the weight Jesus bore.[27] For many preachers this is a particularly difficult imperative because they have been motivated by guilt so much in their own experience that they have no real concept of what else could motivate people to serve God. In fact, they fear that without guilt they will have no real leverage to induce obedience.

The alternative to guilt is its antidote: grace. Believers need to serve God out of gratitude and thanksgiving for the redemption he provides. All Scripture labors to put this grace before us (Luke 24:27; 1 Cor. 2:2), and informed expository preaching discloses the grace each passage contains.[28] This grace exposure is necessary not merely because God's mercy is the foundation of our faith, but because it is the only legitimate source of our service (Rom. 12:1). If we serve God because we believe he will love us less if we do not, punish us more if we do less, or bless us more if we do more, then we are not worshiping God with our actions; we are only pursuing our self-interests. In this case the goal of our lives is personal promotion or personal protection rather than the glory of God, and even our seemingly moral activities are a transgression of the first commandment.[29] Grace does not change the rules Scripture truly requires; rather it makes adherence to them true obedience.

Guilt drives the unrepentant to the cross, but grace must lead believers from there or we cannot serve God. Christ-centered preaching keeps the redemptive work of God as central to every sermon as it is to the

---

27. Cf. chapter 1 of the author's *In the Grip of Grace* (Grand Rapids: Baker, 1992).

28. Kenneth J. Howell, "How to Preach Christ from the Old Testament," *Presbyterian Journal*, 16 January 1985, 9.

29. Jay Adams, *Preaching with Purpose* (Grand Rapids: Baker, 1982), 152.

scope of Scripture on the premise that there is no more powerful a motivation to holiness than the love of God manifested in Christ's redemptive work.[30] When love motivates, then the Lord, his purposes, and his glory are our aim. Without this no application challenges the believer to serve any object greater than self. Whether the explanation component of a main point or the material immediately associated with the application supplies the grace motivation depends on the preacher's expositional choices. However, the application of an expository sermon is not complete until the pastor has disclosed the grace in the text that rightly stimulates the obedient response of believers.[31]

How

With motivation the expository preacher must supply means, or enablement. To placate constituents, elected officials have been known to pass bills that require sweeping changes and at the same time lack enablement clauses. As a result, plans that sound great are never implemented. Preachers must be careful not to fall into the same practice by telling people what they must do, and at the same time neglect to tell them how.

How can one who hates now love? How can an addict leave the drug? How can the negligent mature? How can one with no past discipline practice devotion? How can a life-long pursuit of self be transformed into a passion of selfless care? Simply saying so doesn't make it so. Complete application requires the preacher to spell out the practical steps and the spiritual resources that make the aims of the sermon attainable. An obvious but frequent example of failing to provide listeners with the instruction necessary for action occurs when preachers conclude sermons with a call to salvation although the sermon has never indicated what an unbeliever must do to repent of sin and commit to the Savior. Such preaching assumes listeners will know what to do despite the fact that those most needing to respond are the ones least likely to understand what God requires.

We must also be careful not to fall inadvertently into a self-help gospel in regard to application. When preachers tell their congregations to love their neighbors as themselves, but do not point to the Spirit who alone makes that this love possible, then people may assume that this

---

30. Ibid., 147; Greidanus, *Sola Scriptura*, 41, 135.
31. Remember that context is part of text. For additional discussion on finding and disclosing the grace inherent in every text see chapters 10 and 11.

love is something they can stimulate in themselves. Too many applications are simply human-centered exhortations to do better in the power of the flesh. Preachers may assume that people will not try to do as the Bible instructs without seeking God's enabling power, but this is a naive expectation. If preachers can neglect to mention divine dependence, why should they be surprised that the people forget to seek divine enablement?[32]

The power to do what God requires resides in God. Responsible preaching does not tell people their responsibilities without also informing them how to plug into this power. Jay Kesler, president of Taylor University, says that a sermon without enabling instruction is like shouting to a drowning person, "Swim! Swim!" The advice is correct but not helpful. It simply tells someone to do what in their situation they have no means to accomplish.[33]

Information regarding enablement may occur within the explanation that supports the application or in the application itself. Always in an expository sermon, however, the steps that the preacher indicates will help listeners apply the truths of the sermon must have some textual foundation. Exegete the Scripture with an eye not only for what act(s) of devotion and avenue(s) of discipline it advocates, but also for what means of dependence it suggests or supports that enable the application.[34] Remember it does no good for the application's principles to have biblical precedent if the preacher suggests purely human means to fulfill biblical commands. This fact again emphasizes the importance of determining application before finalizing the statements and the structure of

32. No evidence more confirms this for me than the dearth of discussion in the many homiletics texts on enablement addressing application researched for this text. Even the experts give rare thought to *how* people can do what God requires. It is so much easier to say what to do than to enable the doing.

33. Veerman, "Sermons," 121.

34. These three Ds (devotion, discipline, and dependence) summarize the aspects of biblical application traditionally associated with Christian enablement. All are valuable but the last is indispensable for Christ-centered preaching since without dependence the other two Ds can actually prompt unbiblical behavior disguised as means of soliciting God's aid. Prayer, for instance, rightly expressed is a confession of our weakness that seeks God's sovereign intervention (i.e., devotion and discipline with dependence); however, prayer can be used as a human attempt to leverage God (i.e., devotion and discipline without dependence). In the latter case the application's "how" ultimately resides in the degree, frequency, or fervency of a human effort. Means of enablement that reflect biblical priorities are not behaviors alone, but rather are acts of devotion and discipline grounded in faith concepts that direct, stimulate, and allow the human heart to rest, rely, and rejoice in God's work alone.

the explanation. More discussion of application's means will follow in the chapters on the theology of Christ-centered preaching.

The need to answer what, where, why, and how questions explains why preachers should dedicate a significant portion of expository messages to application. A sentence at the end of twenty minutes of survey will not do. Application that ignores any one of these four critical questions is not merely incomplete; it is unbiblical because in some dimension it fails to equip God's people for their service to him.

THE STRUCTURE OF APPLICATION

Understanding the components of application prepares us to consider how they fit into the structure of a standard expository message. Qualification offered in previous chapters needs to be reiterated here. There are many good ways of organizing expository messages. The structure detailed in this section exhibits certain instructional principles without intending to suggest that there are no other proper expository forms. At the same time, this structure is common enough to use as a standard without making its specifics normative.

If a main point unfolds according to the standard expository format described earlier, the exposition begins with a statement of the main point addressing the FCF. Explanation—usually in subpoints—then supports, clarifies, or proves the main point. If an illustration follows the subpoints then the subpoints first need to be summarized, since the ear expects the illustration to reflect the last thing said. This summary thus serves as the de facto introduction to the illustration. Because such a summary encapsulates the explanation of the main point it will likely sound very similar to the main-point statement that the subpoints all support. The illustration of that statement unfolds in a narrative that echoes key terms of the explanation. These key terms rain into the illustration to keep its concepts and terminology consistent with the explanation. The illustration then concludes with a grouping (or interpreting) statement that reaches into the narrative and pulls the key thoughts into another summary statement. Since this statement summarizes a story that itself unfolds from a summary statement of the explanation, it is likely that the illustration's summary statement will also echo the main point.[35] But more than merely concluding the illus-

---

35. For more discussion of this process as it relates to illustration see chapter 7. At this point it should also be evident that the two major strands of this expositional double helix are composed of the *concepts* and *terms* that ultimately develop and unify all the components of the main point.

FIGURE 8.3
Main Point Application Development

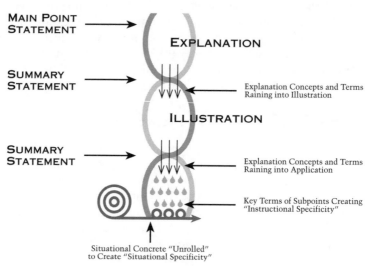

MAIN POINT
STATEMENT ———→

EXPLANATION

SUMMARY
STATEMENT ———→

Explanation Concepts and Terms
Raining into Illustration

ILLUSTRATION

SUMMARY
STATEMENT ———→

Explanation Concepts and Terms
Raining into Application

Key Terms of Subpoints Creating
"Instructional Specificity"

Situational Concrete "Unrolled"
to Create "Situational Specificity"

tration this grouping statement is also an introduction to the application (see this process displayed in fig. 8.3).

The illustration's summary statement acts as the introduction to the application and serves as, or sets up, a general statement of principle that begins the application.[36] Almost all preachers use these overarching statements of biblical principle to begin their application. We conclude our explanations with a generic statement such as, "You, too, should examine your heart to see if you love your neighbor as you ought," or "Pray with the fervor that indicates you are serious about the salvation of the lost." Far too many preachers also conclude their applications at this point. Having proven a biblical principle these preachers

36. Note that this structure assumes that each main point contains application according to the standards of a traditional expository method. I recognize, however, that preachers may choose to build to an application concentrated at the conclusion of the message as is characteristic of a "Puritan" sermon. We simply must question whether an approach that requires listeners to pay attention for twenty minutes (or more) before the preacher makes the message relevant will communicate well in our times. A modifying approach has the preacher offering general conclusions throughout the message that are made more particular in the conclusion or offering particular applications throughout the message that the conclusion gathers into a more generic and powerful thrust. Each approach has value. However, sound communication principles require preachers to avoid offering entirely new applications in sermon conclusions (see further discussion in chapter 9).

FIGURE 8.4
Application Magnified

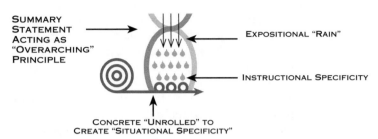

SUMMARY STATEMENT ACTING AS "OVERARCHING" PRINCIPLE

EXPOSITIONAL "RAIN"

INSTRUCTIONAL SPECIFICITY

CONCRETE "UNROLLED" TO CREATE "SITUATIONAL SPECIFICITY"

believe that they have fulfilled their expository obligations and that people will automatically translate the principles into their lives. For reasons already mentioned, this is too often a futile hope.

The overarching statement of principle is merely the beginning of sound application. A magnification of the graphic in figure 8.3 will help explain what should characterize well-developed application (see fig. 8.4):

The overarching principle statement needs real-life delineation. So, give specific instructions that reflect what people can (or should) do, believe, or affirm in order to apply the general principle to their lives. Word these instructions with the key terms of the explanation that have rained through the illustration and now flow through the application. This expositional rain keeps the instructions in contact with the earlier explanation calling to the listener's mind and ear the biblical authority that backs them. By providing this instructional specificity the preacher fulfills the obligation of answering the what question. Why and how questions are often answered at this stage also if they have not already been addressed in the explanation.

To answer the where question of the preacher must now identify concrete situations to which the general principle and the specific instruction(s) apply. First, draw the instructions down into a real-life situation (see fig.8.4). Typically the description of this concrete (that is, the real-life situation) involves some detailing of circumstances and a specific explanation of how the instructions would function (or what they would require) in such a situation. In essence, the preacher makes the biblical instruction drop into the life of the listeners. No single concrete, however, is likely to identify a situation all listeners confront. If the preacher simply stops here, the sermon may have arrived at a destination many find irrelevant. As a result, the preacher needs to unroll the concrete into further situational possibilities.

Rarely will the preacher have the time to discuss these additional possibilities in the same detail as the initial concrete. The goal is to expose listeners to a situation in which the biblical principles apply and then allow them to consider how the same principles function in parallel situations with which they can also identify. For instance, the preacher might describe the obligations of loving a next-door neighbor who has caused hurt in one's life as the concrete, and then remind listeners that these instructions also apply to neighbors at work, school, and even church. The initial concrete allows the preacher to shine the light of Scripture into some dark corner of life. The details in that corner allow the preacher to focus the beam realistically before directing it and the listeners' attention to other areas of their lives (see fig. 8.5).

FIGURE 8.5

Focusing Application with Situational Specificity

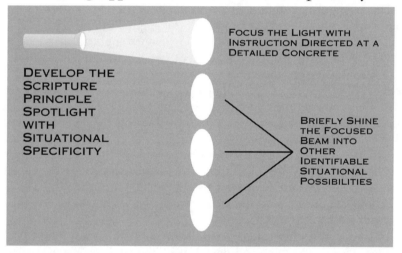

The greater the relevance and the realism of the initial concrete for the majority of listeners the more likely the application will apply to an entire congregation. Often the situational specifics that the pastor unrolls after the concrete are mentioned simply to include listeners who may not have been able to identify with the original concrete. Still, if in presenting the concrete preachers identify a dilemma, an emotion, or a stress common to the human condition, they should not be overly concerned that not everyone has faced precisely the same situation. In the loneliness we all have felt we can identify with the loneliness of an elderly widow whose family will not visit—even if not all of us have faced precisely this same set of circumstances. Even though a business may not have collapsed beneath us, we have all had enough of failure to identify with the man whose greatest efforts have come to naught (cf. 1 Cor. 10:13). By providing situational specificity preachers are far more likely to include and involve all listeners than by speaking only in terms broad enough to cover all possibilities. Norman Neaves writes of the embracing power of the specific:

> I'm tired of sermons that do not live where people live, that don't connect with the real stories and struggles by which their lives are shaped, that never touch the earth or breath the air that the congregation breathes. Maybe there are those who enjoy developing the universal sermon, the one that can be preached everywhere and anywhere, that has a quality of being timeless. But as far as I am concerned, everywhere and anywhere really means nowhere; and those who strive to be timeless, are usually, simply not very timely. . . . [T]he particular is higher than the universal.[37]

One need not agree with all the philosophical roots of Neaves's thinking to appreciate the pastoral wisdom in his words. His perspective not only echoes the situational specificity of Scripture, which states general principles in small proportion relative to personal accounts, but also reminds us how integrated expository components may become in mature preaching. An illustration may provide an application with realism and relevance. When the illustration of a main point also serves as the concrete of the application, I refer to it as a double-edged sword. Such illustrations both clarify the explanation and situate the application. Most of the time the applicational concrete is not a full illustration, but it does contain enough description to bring a definite circumstance, emotion, failing, feeling, challenge, or need to the listener's mind.

By combining a general principle of application with instructional specifics that apply in other identifiable situations the preacher provides truly usable biblical exposition.[38] Listeners gain an understanding of the principles they must heed when the sermon is removed from the realms of abstraction and irrelevance. Listeners comprehend and under-

---

37. Norman Neaves, in *Preaching the Story*, eds. Steimle, Niedenthal, and Rice, 108.

38. Adams comments, "When I say that preaching is truth applied, I mean that the truths of a passage are not merely expounded; they are so expounded (applied) as to effect change in the listener. . . . [C]reeds should lead to deeds. . . . [Y]ou ought to be proclaiming God's Word in order to accomplish the purpose for which He sent it," in *Truth Applied*, 42–44.

stand what underlies the advocated actions as well as the real-life consequences, thus producing mature, committed believers.

THE DIFFICULTY OF APPLICATION

IDENTIFYING THE BREAKING POINT

The specificity that makes application powerful also exposes why it is the most difficult aspect of expository preaching. The thought that is required to be specific strains our mental and spiritual resources. Although accurate explanation can hardly be called easy, at least the unmined raw material lies within the pages of Scripture. We derive application from far less obvious terrain. Sound explanation requires good scholarship. Solid application requires deep spirituality. A pastor who is keenly aware of the soul's struggles and who is intimately acquainted with scriptural remedies has what it takes to produce sound applications. Such a pastor knows not to harangue over obvious misbehaviors, not tritely to remind others to employ "the means of grace" (i.e., pray more, read the Bible more, go to church more), and not to rely on a habit-hewn appeal to come to Christ.

Application requires creativity and courage: *creativity* to imagine the battles of daily life fought with the truths of God, and *courage* to talk about this reality on a personal level. Apart from all the homiletical jargon about form, structure, and content, preachers know instinctively what makes application the most difficult part of preaching—the rejection we invite by being specific. J. Daniel Baumann writes,

> What is it that causes some sermons to be ineffective? One of the results of Ziegler's studies was that the sermons which contained applications to the daily lives of the congregation were the sermons that were unanimously rejected by the congregation. The frequency of rejection and the intensity of the rejection exactly paralleled the amount of daily application contained in the sermon. I would suggest that individuals are becoming more and more reluctant to accept that kind of application, religious or otherwise, to their daily lives. That kind of prescription implies that one person is in a position to tell others just what they should do with their daily lives.[39]

When listeners conclude that a pastor has "stopped preachin' and gone

---

39. J. Daniel Baumann, *An Introduction to Contemporary Preaching* (Grand Rapids: Baker, 1972), 250.

to meddlin,'" the sermon fails. Yet, insightful application seems almost to invite this accusation.

Throughout the explanation and illustration of a main point listeners can happily nod in agreement (or nod off) in security. But application requires commitment and action, not assent and neutrality. Sound application ventures out of hypothetical abstraction and elbows its way into business practices, family life, social relationships, societal attitudes, personal habits, and spiritual priorities. Application disrupts lives and as a result is the point at which listeners are most likely to tune out a sermon. Whether we like it or not, the breaking point of most sermons is application (see fig. 8.6).

FIGURE 8.6

The Application Breaking Point

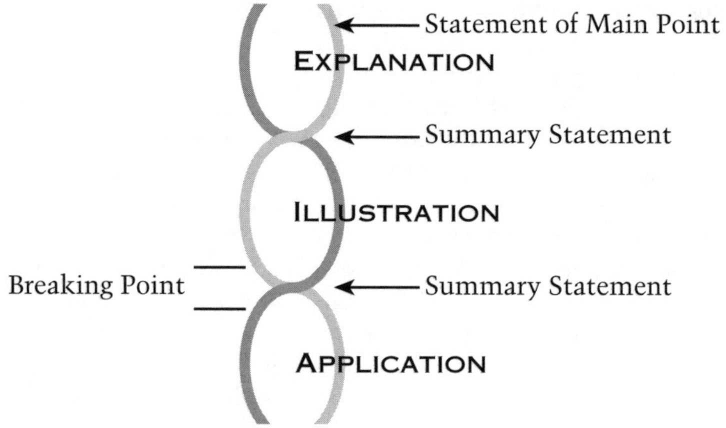

A denial of the breaking point will accomplish nothing. Blaming others for this human frailty only leads to frustration. Believing that mature congregations are guilty of no such fault only exposes naïveté. Should preachers avoid application to keep rejection at a minimum? No! The Bible will not allow such neglect of God's instructions. Our calling obligates us to put humanity's duty to God before his people in clearest terms. God does not charge us to dismiss the breaking point, but to overcome it.

OVERCOMING THE BREAKING POINT

Forewarned is forearmed. When preachers know that application will likely spark negative responses to their message, they have an advance opportunity to prepare the sermon so as to maximize its impact. We should not perceive such preparations as openings to soft-pedal God's requirements, but as means to gain them an optimum hearing. Sermons must sometimes offend to remain faithful to the gospel (Rom. 9:33), but we must make sure that the offense is in the truth itself, not in our failure to present it wisely and well (1 Cor. 10:32–33). We should grieve for the pastors who seem to believe that the mark of their orthodoxy is *their* offensiveness, and who forget that the origin of the offense should be God's message, not their manner (2 Cor. 6:3, 6–7). Believers in whom the Spirit has worked have the capacity to receive the most convicting truths with joy when they represent the compassion of God rather than a power play of a preacher (1 Thess. 1:6). The following are tools that preachers can use to overcome application's breaking point without abandoning the priorities of Scripture.

Conclusive arguments. The primary tool of preaching is truth. Preachers should apply that which they have logically demonstrated that God's Word requires. Unfortunately, a conclusive argument does not always persuade. The truth of the old maxim, "He who complies against his will / Is of his own opinion still," often exhibits itself in our churches. If preachers are unwilling to confess the truth of this line they have only to examine their own hearts. Why do we who have so much knowledge of God's requirements still sin? Because conclusive arguments (as indispensable as they are to biblical preaching) do not always persuade even us to obey God. For this cause we need additional tools to help us craft effective application.

Disarming illustrations. Deane Kemper writes, "One of the most important uses of stories and quotations is to short-circuit emotional reaction. When you are advancing ideas that may receive a less-than-receptive hearing or even be met with resistance, an illustration can provide an indirect lead-in that is more likely to gain a fair hearing than a more frontal, didactic approach."[40] The nature of the narrative can demonstrate the goodwill of the preacher. A story also has the ability to guide hearers along a narrative trail that leads to scriptural conclusions, which is better than immediately confronting listeners with arguments that raise their defenses.[41] Kemper also indicates that select quotations from respected experts may open listeners' minds to ideas they might not consider on the preacher's authority alone.

40. Deane Kemper, *Effective Preaching* (Philadelphia: Westminster, 1985), 87.
41. Bryan Chapell, *Using Illustrations to Preach with Power* (Grand Rapids: Zondervan, 1992), 155.

Common-sense proposals. Applications should be relevant, realistic, and achievable. Applications lacking in common sense destroy the credibility of the preacher and impede the acceptance of scriptural truth. Preachers use three common types of applications without common sense:

Pie-in-the-sky principles. "Smile more every hour," "Love every neighbor with all your heart," and "Resolve never to fear again," exemplify applications that live only in pastoral idealism and spiritual hyperbole. The instructions as stated are unattainable. As a result, they have no connection to real life and should not have been uttered. These applications either will convince listeners that they cannot do what Scripture requires or that their preacher lives in a make-believe world.

High hurdles. These applications are based on behaviors beyond the capacities of all but a few listeners. "You should learn Greek and Hebrew so that you can confirm the truth of my words," or "Everyone here should resolve to go to the Holy Land so that you can see the type of terrain Jesus faced." No one would deny that such goals would be nice to achieve, but the average person has no chance of doing what the preacher instructs.

Narrow focus. Applications that the preacher knows nearly no one will do even if they are able are not worth the breath and time. For example, too many preachers sell books from the pulpit. But unless the book obviously makes a dramatic impact on a large number of people, how many in the congregation will actually take the time that week to drive to the local bookstore, make the order, and plop down their money? One, two, any? How many will even remember the name of the book by Sunday dinner? Preachers who too often offer applications that few can apply lose the confidence of most.

Of course the likelihood of implementation should not determine whether the preacher will apply truths that people reject simply because of the hardness of their hearts. Courage, not common sense, is the issue in this case.

God does not excuse ministers from proclaiming his truth simply because people do not want to hear it, but neither does he want preachers to remove his Word from the reach of his people. Even proper applications can be presented at inopportune times or when people are not ready (or able) to hear. Those at the Jerusalem council who gave instructions to the church at large wrote, "It seems good to the Holy Spirit and to us not to burden you with anything beyond the following . . ." (Acts 15:28). And even Jesus said to his apostles, "I have much more to say to you, more than you can now bear" (John 16:12). Pastoral prudence as well as biblical prescription must govern application because patience and faithfulness are both scriptural mandates (Gal. 5:22).

Task sensitivity. The minister who raises his fist and angrily preaches, "The people in this church must love each other more for us to grow," probably makes an impact opposite to that intended. The tone must match the task. A preacher whose application compels love must speak in love. A preacher who says, "If we really understood the resurrection we would not struggle with grief," should realize the words will more likely condemn than comfort. Some applications require stern expression (Tit. 1:10–13); others need gentleness (2 Tim. 2:24–26). Jesus drove moneychangers out of the temple with a whip and yet the Scriptures say he would not break a "bruised reed" (Isa. 42:3). The authority that the Word of God grants its proclaimers does not mean we must always speak in rebuke. Our authority also grants us the right to encourage (Tit. 2:15).

Mature guidance. If only the preacher decides what parishioners should do, they will not grow. Nothing creates and perpetuates spiritual babies more than pastors who will not allow people to come to their own conclusions and take responsibility for their own actions. On occasion preachers must point to situational specifics and at the same time provide sufficient information and guidance for adults (and sometimes children) to make their own decisions. Even those with apostolic authority practiced this sort of participatory application in order to foster spiritual maturity (e.g., Acts 15; 2 Cor. 1:23–24; 2:9; 2 Tim. 2:24–26; Philem. 8–9, 14, 21). "We need both direct and indirect application"[42] in sermons. Such preaching can help listeners build up their own faith resources by giving them the information needed to make correct decisions, then confronting them with the decisions they must make.

Mandate clarity. Preachers who cannot *differentiate between a scriptural mandate and a good suggestion* drain biblical power from their ministries. You must make sure the Scriptures—not you—demand what your application requires. Preachers may suggest many things that help listeners fulfill God's demands, but we err greatly when we imply (or believe) that our suggestions are the Bible's requirements. A twenty-minute devotional every day is a good suggestion, as are reading the Bible as a family at meals, engaging in a small-group Bible study, and enrolling in a Scripture memory courses. However, the Bible requires none of these specific practices. When we take a good suggestion and

---

42. Larsen, *The Anatomy of Preaching,* 100.

make it a biblical mandate not only do we arrogate our own thoughts to the canon of Scripture, we inevitably preach a pharisaism that implies people can earn grace by meeting our standards. Practical suggestions for meeting a biblical requirement are often needed in application, but these suggestions are proffered, not commanded.

Respect for complexity. One of my favorite radio commentators says, "For every complex problem there is a simple answer 'that is wrong!'" A preacher's willingness to admit that a sermon will deal only with a narrow aspect of a large concern, or that more extensive answers must await later occasions and further reflection may do far more to bolster application than flip responses, quick solutions, and cliché condemnations. Young preachers often feel that they will damage their credibility if they confess, "I don't know," or "I will have to study more before I have a good answer." Yet such responses may best display the wisdom of the preacher. Thoughtful congregations know no one has all the answers to every concern. We preachers destroy our credibility when we pretend otherwise. We usually offer the worst applications when we preach outside our expertise (e.g., advising congregations on what a union contract should say, specifying how to politic for a particular legislative bill, dictating legal or medical procedures). Where clear biblical principles apply, preachers have warrant to address all of these issues. Unfortunately, preachers too often confuse the desire to say something with the right to say anything.

Respect for the complexity of life's concerns does not mean that all our applications have to be complex. We should not be afraid of simple applications spoken with sincerity and thoughtfulness that make them powerful.[43] Our applications should be true but not trite; apparent but not painfully obvious; and sufficiently plain yet poignant enough to get beneath the skin. No one wants to languish in a pew for thirty minutes listening to the proof for an application they knew to do before they sat down. Providing new (or fresh) motives, reasons, benefits, consequences, or means for commonly accepted duties remains every pastor's challenge.

At the same time preachers must be cautious not to make simplistic applications about controversial subjects without sufficient exposition to enable uninformed or nonagreeing listeners to handle the instruction. Keeping the FCF in view from the introduction through the conclusion will help keep application from dangerous steps off the path of your exposition.[44] A sermon dealing with the need for fidelity in mar-

43. Veerman, "Sermons," 121.
44. Larsen, *The Anatomy of Preaching*, 99; Adams, *Truth Applied*, 41, 69.

riage is probably not the best place for a thrown-in line such as, "And, similarly, faithfulness to God requires that we not participate in the lottery, abort the unborn because of their gender, or ignore the homeless." Applications are not always legitimate simply because somewhere a sermon will support what you say. If this sermon does not adequately support the application, think twice before offering it. You do not want to raise more snakes of controversy in a sermon than your exposition provides biblical sticks to kill.

Spiritual integrity. Application also requires personal trustworthiness. Why should people listen to a preacher tell them what they do not want to do, have not done, or will need to change? If the answer is not "Because they know the preacher loves them and the Lord too much to withhold truth they need," then the application will fall on deaf ears. Even when it hurts people listen to application when they perceive spiritual integrity in the preacher. Such trust does not rise from academic exegesis or homiletical structure but results as a pastor's life reflects the indwelling Spirit.

So many pastoral matters require prudence, judgment, and discernment. How do we know when to tackle an issue head-on? How do we know when to say precisely what to do and when to let others make their own decisions? When does gentleness become compromise, and when does forcefulness degenerate into arrogance? How do we know when to say, "I don't know"? No textbook can answer these questions. Our resources remain the Word *and* the Spirit. Only preachers whose minds and motives are conformed to God's will by the Spirit's daily work will reflect the wisdom and maturity of judgment that grants power over application's breaking point.

Our lives confirm the wisdom and the care behind the way we apply the Word (1 Thess. 1:8–12). Ultimately our sermons have power because the discretion and the compassion evident in our actions demonstrate the presence of the Spirit in our words. Applications are not a license for preachers to take potshots from behind the pulpit (e.g., "We need leaders in this church who will lead by example in giving"), or to preach their personal interests (e.g., respect my position, attend my prayer meeting, join my church). Preachers who employ such applications may believe that their brass indicates courage but thoughtful people eventually recognize those preachers who substitute personal polish for spiritual fire and heed them little. Ultimately, the Spirit alone can apply the truths of his Word, so sermonic application succeeds only when we preach for his purposes and in dependence on his work.

THE ATTITUDES OF APPLICATION

Application focuses the impact of the entire sermon on the transformation(s) God requires in his people. This is not the time to mince words or abandon care. Direct application *right between the eyes—with love.* From the pulpit, say exactly what you mean exactly as you would say it to a loved one. The spiritual welfare of others requires that you not obscure your meaning in abstract idealism, which disturbs no one and has no potential to get you in trouble. If the young people need to stop seeing violent or pornographic movies, tell them so. If the church will not heal until gossip stops, say so. If political differences are dividing believers, address the problem. Speak with tact. Speak with love. But do not fail to say what the situation requires and what the Bible demands.

In application preachers pour out their hearts. Without application preachers have difficulty preaching with fervor. After all, who can say with heartfelt conviction, "Paul went from Iconium to Lystra"? The need of the people of God to sense the impact of his Word draws feeling from our own hearts. Exposition not powered by application usually falls flat and robs the message of serious consideration. After all, there is something fundamentally irrational about paying attention to someone who says he has something important to say, but who speaks without the passion that signals its importance.

Passion comes naturally to our sermons when we speak as though we are addressing a real concern with a friend. If a friend were to come to our door one evening and confess that his teenage son is destroying his family, we would invite the friend to sit at our kitchen table and we would talk plainly. The hurt in our friend's eyes would dissuade us from pompous idealisms, the need to offer real help would make us turn to the Bible for practical aid, and our friendship would keep us speaking with love even if we had to say hard things. The best preaching offers no less. Application presented as though we are speaking to a friend across a kitchen table has more spiritual potential than a dozen sermons designed for delivery from Mount Sinai. When Jesus spoke, the Bible records, the common people delighted to hear him because he spoke so plainly about their concerns. Preaching that represents him should still speak as he did.

Our voices will quiet, however, if we do not maintain a final attitude in making application—forgiveness. A mark of naive or inexperienced preaching is the expectation that, because the preacher says the right thing, the people will do the right thing, right away. Some sins are corrected in a conversation and some require faithful preaching over a generation—or more. Preachers who cannot tell people what the Bible requires and still love them when they act as though the words were never spoken will ultimately fail to do God's will in the pulpit. Frustration, anger, and despair are the sure companions of the preacher who cannot forgive the regular failure of God's people to apply his Word. Application that remains strong and steady week after week arises from a mind fixed on God and from a heart that beats for broken people in a fallen world.

Questions for Review and Discussion

1. What is the main thing to be done in an expository sermon?

2. What are four basic questions that complete application must answer?

3. What distinguishes instructional specificity from situational specificity? Why are both important?

4. What is expositional rain?

5. What is a sermon's breaking point and how is it overcome?

6. Why and how should a preacher differentiate between a scriptural mandate and a good idea?

Exercises

1. Create two paragraphs of application for one of the main points you outlined in the exercises at the conclusion of chapter 6; or

2. Create two paragraphs of application for the following main point: Because Jesus always intercedes for his church, we must pray consistently and fervently.

3. Explain how the following verses bear on the attitude with which a preacher should express application:

   2 Timothy 2:24–26   Titus 1:10–13
   2 Timothy 4:2   Titus 2:15
   1 Thessalonians 2:7–12

CONTENTS OF CHAPTER 9

GOAL OF CHAPTER 9

To present principles for constructing effective introductions, conclusions, and transitions

9

INTRODUCTIONS, CONCLUSIONS, AND TRANSITIONS

NECESSARY PIECES

A good friend once began a wonderful sermon with this artful dodge:
"Two of the foods I most admire are products of childhood memories. I remember the delight I took in my Aunt Bessie's sour pickles. Using a secret recipe and cucumbers from her own garden Aunt Bessie made pickles so crisp they would snap like a firecracker when you crunched down on that first sour bite that puckered your lips before drenching your tongue in a sweet dill that made you ache for more. Those pickles always added some spark to the fall picnic in my home church, but they were only a prelude to the real treat. Between the morning and afternoon preaching the women gathered around great kettles over open fires lit behind People's Bible Church in rural Red Bank, Mississippi. There in those magic caldrons beneath the smoke that danced between the steeple and the woods cinnamon, sugar, sweet dough, and tart apples from local orchards somehow coalesced into fried apple pies so delicious that a large mouthful could almost make you swallow your tongue. All my adult life I have been in search of sour pickles like my Aunt Bessie's and fried apple pies like those cooked at People's Bible Church in Red Bank, Mississippi. But as with the search for an introduction to this sermon, I have yet to find anything that meets the requirements."

So began this supposedly introductionless sermon. Yet, whether the preacher intended it to be so or not, his denial of having an introduction was his message's introduction. Introductions, conclusions, and transi-

227

tions cannot be avoided. Regardless of our intentions or abilities our sermons will have introductions, conclusions, and transitions. The first words you say introduce your message, the last words you say conclude it, and the material that ties these two events together inevitably contains transitions. The real question is whether these necessary pieces will serve or burden the message. Knowing the purposes and structures that characterize the best of these components will help answer that question.

PURPOSES OF INTRODUCTIONS

TO AROUSE INTEREST IN THE MESSAGE[1]

To assume that one's listeners automatically share one's own interest in the sermon is a mark of an inexperienced preacher. Such a preacher reasons that because God's people *should be* interested in God's Word that they *will be* interested in a discussion of it. Only in a perfect world would such an expectation have merit.

The tiresomeness of so many sermons; the weekly assaults on the realities of faith from family, friend, and foe; the weariness prompted by work stress; the overdone Saturday-night fun; the competing influences of the entertainment media; the seeming irrelevance of prophets and apostles dead for at least two millennia; and the mere redundancy of a lifetime of Sunday-morning rituals combine to make congregational interest in any message a minor miracle that no minister should ever take for granted. Explains Bill Hogan:

> You must remember that you come to the pulpit having spent hours in the study poring over the passage on which you are to preach. You have been thinking over your subject for days, or weeks, perhaps even for years. But your people have probably not thought about it at all. Indeed, they may not even know what it is going to be before you stand up to speak. (Pray that they will know after you have finished.) The chasm separating their thoughts from biblical ideas may be vast. In the introduction you must enter their world and persuade them to go with you into the world of biblical truth, and specifically the truth that is the burden of the sermon.[2]

1. Haddon Robinson says introductions should "Command Attention," which—though not the classic terminology—could hardly be stated better (see *Biblical Preaching: The Development and Delivery of Expository Messages* [Grand Rapids: Baker, 1980], 160).
2. William L. Hogan, "It Is My Pleasure to Introduce . . . ," *The Expositor* 1, 3 (August 1987): 1.

Sermon introductions are never superfluous. The preacher who, after commanding, "Open your Bibles to . . . ," immediately launches into a discussion of the history and grammar of the text has not exegeted the nature and the circumstances of those who must listen and thereby forfeits a hearing.

Today's communication researchers say that audiences generally decide within the first thirty seconds of a presentation whether they are interested in what a speaker will say.[3] This modern reality underscores the importance of gaining attention in the opening moments of a sermon, but the insight is not new. The Roman orator Quintilian said that "a flawed introduction is like a scarred face"—you will not give its bearer more than a glance.[4] The introduction is so crucial to the likelihood of listeners hearing the rest of the sermon that preachers have long adopted the maxim, "Well begun is half done."[5] Only the conclusion rivals the introduction for determining whether listeners will digest the sermonic food. No matter how good the meat inside, if these surrounding "slices of bread" are moldy do not expect anyone to take a bite.

An introduction should present the listeners with an arresting thought that draws them away from apathy or competing interests and makes each person say, "Hey! I need to hear this." The introduction may pique curiosity, concern, mirth, or wonder, but no matter what avenue the preacher takes the task remains the same: Get their attention! Do not delay the effort. If the opening sentence will not stimulate interest when it stands alone, reject it. Make the opening words count.[6] You may not have a second chance to make that first impression that triggers eternal consequences.

The key to arousing interest is to involve your listeners.

3. Only a generation ago the time allowance for this judgment was sixty seconds (cf. D. W. Cleverley Ford, *The Ministry of the Word* [Grand Rapids: Eerdmans, 1979], 215). The media influences of our culture continue to compress our attention spans.

4. Quintilian 4.1.61.

5. To which John A. Broadus adds the quip, "Ill begun is apt to be wholly ruined," *On the Preparation and Delivery of Sermons*, ed. J. B. Weatherspoon (New York: Harper and Row, 1944), 103.

6. Michael J. Hostetler adds these important comments about opening sentences: "First, let the opening sentence *be* an opening sentence. Let silence separate it from all that precedes it, whether music, Scripture reading, or pulpit small talk ("Thank you, Mrs. Murphy, for that truly wonderful solo."). It takes discipline not to muddle or to mumble into the sermon. Good preachers are not afraid of the silence, especially that moment of quiet immediately before the sermon's opening sentence that sets the sermon apart from the preceding item in the liturgy." *Introducing the Sermon: The Art of Compelling Beginnings*, The Craft of Preaching Series (Grand Rapids: Zondervan, 1986), 30.

Involve their imaginations.
Involve their sense of wonder.
Involve their appreciation of the past.
Involve their fear of the future.
Involve their outrage.
Involve their compassion.

In some way make them need to go with you into the body of the message. What makes an introduction most interesting are features that indicate the message will have an impact on the listeners' lives.

To Introduce the Subject of the Message

The introduction must indicate what the message will be about. An introduction that arouses interest but does not focus attention on the subject actually gives listeners a false lead. Confusion and resentment can result. The all-too-common practice among after-dinner speakers, business-seminar instructors, and not a few preachers of beginning messages with humorous anecdotes that have nothing to do with their messages may elicit laughter but also creates distrust of the speaker. When it is obvious that the joke has nothing to do with the subject, listeners know they have been manipulated and they typically adjust their expectations toward more enjoyment while bracing against any persuasion from one so calculating.[7]

The preacher may begin with a thought-provoking question, a story, a quotation, an anecdote, or a host of other means, so long as when the introduction is over the central thought in the listeners' minds is the subject of the sermon. Adams writes, "The purpose of an introduction is to lead the congregation into the matter to be discussed. If it fails to do that, it fails."[8] The introduction may illustrate, demonstrate, state, imply, indicate by contrast, or in some other way signal what the preacher will address. However, by the conclusion of the introduction every listener should know that the message is about "Christian leadership," or "the path to marital happiness," or "means of sanctification," or "marks of a sound church," or "an answer to loneliness," because the introduction has aroused interest in this specific subject.

---

7. Cf. Ralph Lewis, *Speech for Persuasive Preaching* (Wilmore, Ken.: Asbury Seminary, 1968), 95; Donald E. Demaray, *An Introduction to Homiletics* (Grand Rapids: Baker, 1974, 1978), 68; Hogan, "It Is My Pleasure," 2; and Robinson, *Biblical Preaching*, 166.
8. Jay E. Adams, *Preaching with Purpose* (Grand Rapids: Baker, 1982), 59.

To Demonstrate Concern for the Hearers

The introduction is the preacher's handshake of good intent. With these opening words the preacher welcomes listeners into the sermon while assuring them that what they are about to hear is important to them and good for them. As was discussed in chapter 1, nothing is more important for the credibility of the speaker and the reception of the message than the listeners' perception of the preacher's concern for them. "Your job is to so describe the problems that people face and the solutions that Scripture gives that listening to God's Word becomes important—nothing less than an event."[9] No hearer has reason to progress beyond a sermon's introduction if it does not point to an obvious personal consequence.

In the introduction, the preacher indicates *why* listeners should listen to the message by identifying the Fallen Condition Focus (FCF) of the sermon.[10] The failure to do so is one of the most common and deadly omissions in evangelical preaching.[11] We preachers are almost universally adept at using introductions to indicate *what* our sermons will be about, but we seem equally unskilled at explaining why our hearers need to listen. We introduce subjects without reasons. Why is it important for our listeners to hear a sermon on justification, perseverance, or God's sovereignty? Until we identify a fallen condition that makes it important *and* helpful for our listeners to know the information in our message, we give the average person no more incentive to listen to us than to attend a lecture on quantum physics. Haddon Robinson explains,

> Early in the sermon, therefore, listeners should realize that the pastor is talking to them about them. He raises a question, probes a problem, identifies a need, opens up a vital issue to which the passage speaks. Application starts in the introduction not in the conclusion. Should a preacher of even limited ability bring to the surface people's questions, problems, hurts, and desires to deal with them from the Bible, he will be acclaimed a genius. More important than that, he will through his preaching bring the grace of God to bear on the agonizing worries and tensions of daily life.[12]

9. Jay E. Adams, *Truth Applied: Application in Preaching* (Grand Rapids: Zondervan, 1990), 72.
10. See discussion of the Fallen Condition Focus in chapter 2.
11. Cf. Robinson, *Biblical Preaching*, 107.
12. Robinson, *Biblical Preaching*, 164; see also Sidney Greidanus, *The Modern Preacher and the Ancient Text: Interpreting and Preaching Biblical Literature* (Grand Rapids: Eerdmans, 1988), 184.

The more specific, poignant, and personal the preacher makes the presentation of the FCF the more powerful will be the introduction (see fig. 9.1). There should be no question what the FCF of the message is by the end of the introduction. Normally the preacher states the precise FCF toward the end of the introduction in a concise sentence that acts as the obvious launching pad for the rest of the sermon. It is not enough to present the FCF in general terms—as though there is a problem out there somewhere that someone should be concerned about sometime. The preacher must frame the FCF in such a way as to make it immediately and personally apply to the listeners.[13] Statements such as these can capture the FCF that drives the development of the sermon: "When you cannot see God's purposes, God's promises can make you angry," or, "It is hard for us to raise teens in a culture where all values are relative," or, "When we know we are guilty, the gift of grace does not feel like it costs us enough."

Even if the preacher only implies the FCF, it should still be so clear that people feel compelled to listen. Almost every minister knows that there are three kinds of preachers: those to whom you cannot listen; those to whom you can listen; and those to whom you must listen. No factor more assures that you will be the last than your willingness consistently to launch your sermons from introductions that convince people they need to hear what follows. Lest this goal appear to be mere pandering to the desires of the day consider this ringing exhortation of John Knox: "In a word, if we as preachers are not speaking to the needs of the contemporary world, it is a fair guess that we have not really heard the gospel of the early church. . . . Only authentically biblical preaching can be really relevant; only vitally relevant preaching can be biblical."[14] Identifying the FCF in the introduction not only gives people some stake in the message, but also convinces them that their preacher is in touch with their world, wants to help, is open to their needs, and truly desires to make the Word of God an authentic instrument of healing in a broken world.[15]

13. Adams, *Preaching with Purpose*, p. 64; Hogan, "It Is My Pleasure," 3.

14. John Knox, *The Integrity of Preaching* (New York: Abingdon, 1957), 26–27. Ian Pitt-Watson echoes, "Every sermon is stretched like a bowstring between the text of the Bible on the one hand and the problems of contemporary human life on the other. If the string is insecurely tethered to either end, the bow is useless." John Stott cites this and similar statements attributed to Martyn Lloyd-Jones, Phillips Brooks, C. H. Spurgeon, Jonathan Edwards, Chrysostom, and others while making the same point in *Between Two Worlds: The Art of Preaching in the Twentieth Century* (1982; reprint, Grand Rapids: Eerdmans, 1988), 146–50.

15. Demaray, *An Introduction to Homiletics*, 68.

By framing the FCF in the introduction the whole message penetrates daily experience with an application thrust that begins with the preacher's first words.[16] This emphasis not only makes listeners expect and desire answers, but also gives preachers a weekly zeal for their messages. When we begin to see that our sermons have real answers to real problems and that people really want to listen, our calling reignites with each message. We have cause to preach! No preaching rationale provides greater purpose or joy.

To Prepare for the Proposition

Homiletics texts unanimously agree that the introduction prepares the listener for the body of the sermon.[17] Since this is an introductory text, however, more specific directions may prove helpful. In a formally constructed sermon the introduction prepares for the body of the message by leading to the proposition. Because the proposition is the theme of the overall message, an introduction that leads into the proposition automatically orients the listener to the body of the message. However, this orientation will go astray if the preacher does not recognize that the proposition is not a theme tacked onto the introduction. *The proposition is actually a summary of the introduction.*

If the listener feels unprepared for ideas stated in the proposition, then the introduction has not properly led into the proposition. This occurs if either the *concepts* stated in the proposition did not originate in the introduction, or if *terminology* used in the proposition does not originate in the introduction. For example, if the introduction is a story about a child lost without a guide, then listeners will scratch their heads in consternation at a proposition urging them to, "Tithe because God is gracious." The concepts are not related.

Listeners also become disoriented if the preacher uses inconsistent terminology. When the introduction repeatedly refers to a child who is lost, but the proposition speaks of sinners who do not know the Lord, the change of terms can confuse listeners even if the preacher has the same concept in mind. The listening ear waits for the proposition to use the terms that the introduction indicates are vital. If the proposition does not the listener feels like one given a map to a city whose main

---

16. Cf. David L. Larsen, *The Anatomy of Preaching: Identifying the Issues in Preaching Today* (Grand Rapids: Baker, 1989), 99; Greidanus, *The Modern Preacher*, 182; Adams, *Truth Applied*, 41, 73.

17. Robinson, *Biblical Preaching*, 164; Demaray, *The Anatomy of Preaching*, 69; Jerry Vines, *A Practical Guide to Sermon Preparation* (Chicago: Moody, 1985), 138.

FIGURE 9.1

The Introduction Chain

AROUSE INTEREST

INTRODUCE THE SUBJECT
Prepare for the Proposition's Concept
Prepare for the Proposition's Terms

MAKE IT PERSONAL
Identify the Reason for the Sermon
State the Fallen Condition Focus
Make Each One Need to Hear

BOND TO SCRIPTURE

ATTACH THE PROPOSITION

streets have been renamed. Therefore, the introduction should prepare for the proposition in concept and terminology. All *key* terms of the proposition should beacon in the introduction before they appear in the proposition.

Recognition that the introduction is an immediate preparation for the proposition warns preachers against separating the introduction from the body with a Scripture reading. Although occasionally there are good, creative reasons for such a sequence the preacher who separates the proposition from the sermon's introduction or body with a Bible reading ordinarily destroys the thought flow and cohesion that propositions are designed to facilitate.[18] Preachers who regularly introduce the sermon before reading their Scripture text are probably confusing a sermon introduction with a Scripture introduction (see this chapter's section on Scripture introduction). Reference to the Scripture does have a place in the introduction—not through a reading of the text but by an indication of how the text will address the FCF. After stating the FCF, the preacher usually grounds the sermon in Scripture by indicating how (or, at least that) this text addresses the subject.[19] This bonding of the

18. Broadus, *Preparation and Delivery of Sermons*, 102.
19. Hostetler, *Introducing the Sermon*, 50.

message's concepts to Scripture usually occurs in a brief sentence or two immediately preceding the proposition in order to establish hope for an FCF solution and authority for the proposition's assertions.[20]

The introduction chain (fig. 9.1) pictures the overall character and ordinary sequence of components in effective introductions. Observe how the links in this chain take actual form in an analysis of the following introduction adapted from an account by John Alexander[21] in *The Other Side* (table 9.1).

TABLE 9.1

A Sermon Introduction Analyzed

Arouse Attention	The stench was unbearable. It was a poor section of town even by Haiti's standards and as missionary
Introduce Subject: Dealing with overwhelming worldly misery.	leader John Alexander walked through the market he wanted to *close his eyes* to the *misery* around him.—Awful food being sold in a shantytown without sewers; the crowd so dense he could hardly move; and, kids with red hair. He knew that Caribbean children do not usually have red hair unless they are starving. The whole situation sickened him.
Note: *Key* (italicized) terms of the proposition echoing throughout the introduction.	He had *seen* it all before in other towns, in other countries, on other trips. But this time he wrote, "I couldn't stand it. I went home and took a nap. Sometimes I'd like to take a nap for the rest of my life. Not that I'm suicidal. But I'd sure like to *shut the truth out*, somehow."
Statement of FCF: Wanting to close one's eyes to misery. **Making It Personal:** Involving the listeners' own feelings and concerns.	I do not like these words any more than the one who wrote them, but I understand their cause. I know the feeling of wanting to *close my eyes* to the *misery* of the world because it seems that if I really look at it, the horror will suffocate me. You know the feeling, too. Whether it is because of *misery* in your own life, or in the lives of those you love, or those you pity, you know the near-overwhelming desire to just *shut your eyes* to the *despair* and take a nap. What we have no *might* to stop we have no desire to face.

20. Note that traditionally one of the primary purposes of introductions is to establish the authority of the speaker (see Demaray, *Introduction to Homiletics*, 69–70; Broadus, *Preparation and Delivery of Sermons*, 102).

21. Hostetler directly quotes the article, *Introducing the Sermon*, 60.

Bonding to Scripture   But neither resignation nor *despair* are biblical
                              responses to human suffering. The God who does not
Proposition   *shield his vision* from our hurt offers his *faithful*
                              more purpose and our world more hope than snoring
                              oblivion. Here in fourth chapter of Amos the prophet
                              phones in this wake-up call: *Open your eyes* to this
                              world's *misery*, because the *Almighty* God uses
                              faithful vision to overcome *despair*.

TYPES OF INTRODUCTIONS[22]

Human-interest account. The John Alexander account is an example of an introduction based on a human interest account—a brief story of someone's experience with which hearers can be made to identify. Because of their natural ability to involve listeners' thoughts and emotions, human-interest accounts are ordinarily the most dependable and effective way to introduce sermons.[23] Whether the account is serious or humorous, derives from history or the neighborhood, comes from something read or personally experienced; the unrivaled ability of such stories to capture attention and to direct toward biblical concerns makes them foundational forms of sermon introduction.

Simple assertion. When listeners are already primed to consider the subject of the sermon a simple assertion of intent may serve as an introduction. This is particularly true if the subject is so troublesome, pressing, tragic, or controversial that a human-interest account might seem to trivialize the matter. "Today, I want to talk to you about how gossip is hurting our church and what we should do about it," is an arresting opening that will perk interest. Note, however, that some of the most difficult issues in Scripture have been introduced with human-interest accounts (e.g., 2 Sam. 12:1–4; Matt. 21:28–32; Luke 15:1–2).

Startling statement. This brief form of introduction is designed to jolt the congregation to attention. Jay Adams offers this wonderful example:

22. Although Lloyd Perry lists thirty-six different types of "instruments or materials" for use in sermon introductions (*Biblical Sermon Guide* [Grand Rapids: Baker, 1970], 36–37), Michael Hostetler says they can all be boiled down into two categories: "what you have experienced or read" (p. 29). I attempt to list only some of the most basic forms of introduction here.

23. For further discussion of how and why human-interest accounts communicate so effectively see chapter 7.

There is a murderer sitting in this congregation today. . . . Yes I mean it. Just yesterday he murdered someone. He didn't think that anyone saw him, but he was wrong. I have a written statement from an eyewitness that I am going to read. Here is what it says, "Everybody who hates his brother is a murderer." [1 John 3:15]

These lines have also been used effectively:

"What this world needs is fewer churches . . . and more bodies of Christ."

"Your arms are too short to box with God."

"I hate him for what he did to me, and I hate me because I can't forgive him."

Two strong cautions must accompany startling statements. You cannot begin with a startling statement every week—only infrequent use of this tool makes it effective. Do not forget that the introduction requires more than jotting an opening line. Evan a startling statement must flow into a personalized FCF and a clear proposition. This second caution applies also to the other types of introductions listed here.

Provocative question. Asking a question that provokes thought or initiates an unvoiced discussion with the listener is often a strong way to begin a sermon. "Why does grass grow in my driveway and not in my lawn?" "What does God require when you no longer love the one you married?" Haddon Robinson offers this crisp series of questions sure to perk up ears: "Can a woman who works be a good mother? What do you say? What does the Bible say?"[24] Whether the question is complex or simple, a provocative question is an advantageous way to begin the sermon.

Catalogue. Grouping or listing items, ideas, or persons in such a way that they reveal the central concept of the sermon is a standard form of introduction. When the children in *The Sound of Music* sing, "Raindrops on roses and whiskers on kittens, bright copper kettles and warm woolen mittens . . . ," they engage in a catalogue song making the point that simple pleasures make life tolerable. A list of disasters at the beginning of a sermon may well make the counterpoint that the uncertainties of our existence make life without faith intolerable. Lewis Smedes offers this poignant combination of a catalogue introduction and a human-interest account while describing the participants in a church service whose everyday lives require a supernatural hope:

24. Robinson, *Biblical Preaching*, 163.

A man and woman, sitting board-straight, smiling on cue at every piece of funny piety, are hating each other for letting romance in their marriage collapse in a tiring treadmill of tasteless, but always tidy, tedium.

A widow, whispering her Amens to every promise of divine providence, is frightened to death because the unkillable beast of inflation is devouring her savings.

A father, the congregational model of parental firmness, is fuming in the suspicion of his own fatherly failure because he cannot stomach, much less understand, the furious antics of his slightly crazy son.

An attractive young woman in the front pew is absolutely paralyzed, sure she has breast cancer. . . .

A submissive wife of one of the elders is terrified because she is being pushed to face up to her closet alcoholism.

Ordinary people, all of them, and there are a lot more where they come from. What they all have in common is a sense that everything is all wrong where it matters to them most. What they desperately need is a miracle of faith to know that life at the center is all right.[25]

Other options. Interesting quotations, striking statistics, biblical accounts with contemporary descriptions, correspondence excerpts, parables, familiar or pithy poetry, object lessons, and a host of other creative options may also serve well as sermon introductions. Nothing works all the time; most work best only if they are used infrequently; almost all work better if the preacher will vary the introductory approach from week to week.

Chief offenders. Two of the most commonly used but ineffective types of sermon introductions are historical and literary (or logical) recapitulation. With these introductions preachers perform the vital expository task of establishing the context, background, and limits of the text. These concepts are important, but are misplaced if they occur in an introduction. Many people sit in our pews assuming that the ancient writings of Scripture have nothing to do with contemporary life and in the first two minutes of the sermon the preacher does nothing but convince them they are right. Bill Hogan writes,

25. Lewis B. Smedes, "Preaching to Ordinary People," *Leadership* 4, 4 (Fall 1983): 116.

What is the first unspoken, even unconscious, question in the average listener's mind? Probably it's this: *is it worth the effort to listen to what the preacher is going to say?* Listening, after all, is hard work. . . . But will those first two or three sentences make them want to keep listening? Imagine a sermon that begins as follows (and I have heard plenty that were almost as dull): "In this difficult passage the sacred writer refers to a long-forgotten custom of the Moabites." Difficult? Sacred writer? Long-forgotten? Moabites? Can you blame a listener who concludes that it is easier and more worthwhile to think about the starting lineup for today's game for the next half hour?[26]

Information about the text is absolutely crucial to its faithful exposition, but few (and perhaps none) will hear that information if the preacher makes little effort to assure that the listeners can hear, and that the introduction has not turned them off. Jay Adams offers this stark advice:

Do not begin with the text; begin with the congregation as Peter and Paul did. Turn to the passage of Scripture only when you have adequately oriented your congregation to what they will find there *and only when you have sufficiently stirred up in them a concern to know about it* [emphasis added].[27]

If you must begin by recapping forty years of Israel's history that precipitates this prophecy, the argument of Paul that precedes this problem text, or the events in David's life that punctuate this lament, at least paint the summary well. Comtemporize your comments with enough narrative details, current language, and modern parallels that people today can identify with the biblical situation. Give the recap a human-interest account feel that invites listener interest and causes personal concern while you are contextualizing.

CAUTIONS FOR INTRODUCTIONS

DISTINGUISH THE "SCRIPTURE" INTRODUCTION

Much confusion exists over what sermon introductions should accomplish because pastors have not been taught the ancient wisdom of

---

26. Hogan, "It Is My Pleasure," 1; cf. Jerry Vines, *A Practical Guide*, 139.
27. Adams, *Truth Applied*, 71. Cf. Stott, *Between Two Worlds*, 245; and Edward F. Markquart, *Quest for Better Preaching* (Minneapolis: Augsburg, 1985), 107.

preparing a Scripture introduction. Confusion begins at the moment that the preacher invites listeners to turn to the biblical passage the sermon will expound.[28] After the preacher has said, "Please turn with me in your Bibles to Romans 6:15–23 . . . ," what comes next? Does the preacher simply stand in an awkward silence while parishioners thumb through their Bibles to find the text? Does the preacher immediately commence reading with the hope that people will catch up when they find the passage? Neither.

After announcing the text, three obligations immediately fall on the preacher. The first of these obligations (although it may not come first in actual sequence) is to contextualize the text so that listeners will understand the reading. This may involve offering brief background comments (a sentence or two at most), providing definitions for unfamiliar words, and otherwise quickly orienting the listeners to the passage. As a second obligation the preacher must create a longing for the Word (see table 9.2). For many of our listeners the Bible is simply a fog too dense for navigation. Others will look at the Bible as a mountain of trite and tired truths they have scaled too often and from which they expect no new vistas. Those eager to read, those scared to read, and those calloused to reading all sit before the minister who must draw each within the confines of the Word.

TABLE 9.2

Example of a Scripture Introduction

Creation of Longing	Christians are rarely uncertain about Christ's commands to forgive—and they are often haunted by their own inability to forgive. If you know what it is to hate your own bitterness . . . if you want to know how to let the poison drain from your own soul, . . . then this passage is for you.
Brief Contextualization	You need not be ashamed that you need to listen because here in Matthew 18 Jesus tells his own disciples how to deal with their unforgiving hearts. If you are as human as they are, read with me what we all need to know. . . .

28. The following comments assume the practice of reading Scripture immediately before the sermon. However, even if someone reads the text for the sermon earlier in the service similar principles still apply for those who truly want parishioners to follow in their Bibles.

Homileticians identify the phase of the sermon prior to the Scripture reading as the ante-theme.[29] In these moments the preacher hints at issues the sermon will address to stimulate the congregation's interest in the passage as well as the message. The ante-theme quickly makes people sense enough promise and/or interest in the text to venture forward with the preacher, so if the Scripture introduction labors beyond four or five sentences it is usually too long. With the Scripture introduction, the preacher primarily prepares for the reading of the Word, not for the complexities of the entire sermon.

The argument over whether the traditional prayer for illumination should precede or follow the Scripture reading is less pivotal than whether the listeners follow the reading. If you use such a prayer (my preference) place it where it best serves the thought, flow, and purposes of the message. Many variations have good warrant (see fig. 9.2).

The final obligation of the Scripture introduction is easily met—and easily forgotten: Reannounce the text. Anticipate your listeners, doing what you do when you finally get to the chapter previously announced. You lean over to your neighbor and ask, "What verses did the preacher say?" The experienced preacher knows human nature well enough to anticipate and answer the question with a second (and even third) repetition of the reference.

FIGURE 9.2

A Common Pattern for Effective Sermon Beginning

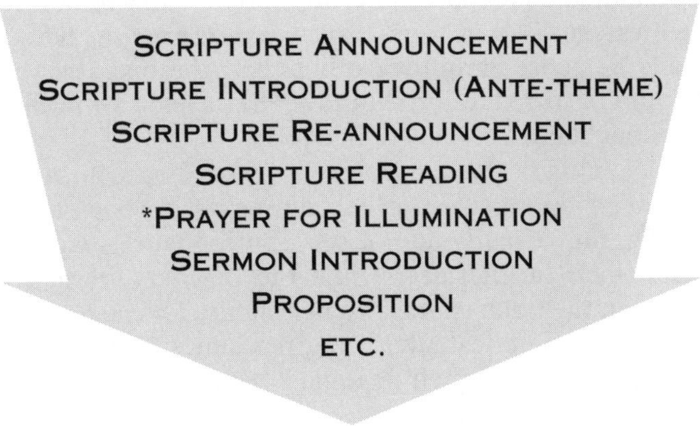

SCRIPTURE ANNOUNCEMENT

SCRIPTURE INTRODUCTION (ANTE-THEME)

SCRIPTURE RE-ANNOUNCEMENT

SCRIPTURE READING

*PRAYER FOR ILLUMINATION

SERMON INTRODUCTION

PROPOSITION

ETC.

*Also functions well prior to Scripture Introduction or the Scripture Reading

29. Thomas Chabham of Salisbury (fl. 1230) in his *Summa de arte praedicandi* offered pioneering guidance in the use of the pro- or ante-theme.

Scripture introductions can also relieve preachers of certain textual obligations. The preacher can use the ante-theme to summarize portions of a narrative so that the Scripture reading need not become too lengthy and listeners can focus on paragraphs key to the sermon's development. The preacher may also slice out purposes in the Scripture introduction, indicating that the sermon will be about only particular verses or particular subjects from the reading. In this way an expositor can put the larger context of a passage before a congregation without seeming to neglect or skip matters that are not the focus of the sermon. The preacher simply predefines the narrower territory that the message will cover.

HONE THE "SERMON" INTRODUCTION

Be brief. Sermon introductions that roam more than three or four standard-length paragraphs (two to three minutes) usually drift into danger. "He took so long setting the table that I lost my appetite for the meal," is an accusation variously applied to some historic preachers[30] and best avoided by contemporary ones. "If you can't strike oil in three minutes, you should quit boring."[31]

Be focused. The introduction is often called the porch of the sermon, and preachers are as frequently cautioned that listeners "do not want a porch on a porch."[32] Focus the introduction. Try not to make one story lead into another. Excise extraneous details and tangential comments. There should be no opportunity for listeners to wander from the focus of the message. This caution also advises against the tendency in introductions to quote Scriptures other than the text the sermon should expound. The introduction should act like a neon arrow directing all airborne thoughts to a single landing strip.

Be real. This is the age of conversational speech. Although highly impassioned or argumentative comments have a definite place in preaching, they usually do not serve introductions well. The preacher who starts off in high gear while the listeners are just getting their thoughts on the track is likely to race alone. Theologian Robert Dabney once gave this practical advice to preachers who might be tempted to slight the situation of their hearers:

30. Cf. Broadus, *Preparation and Delivery of Sermons*, 107; Robinson, *Biblical Preaching*, 165.

31. Vines, *A Practical Guide*, 139.

32. Broadus, *Preparation and Delivery of Sermons*, 105, 107; Vines, *A Practical Guide*, 139.

Just as you must lead their thoughts from where they are to where you want them, so you must lead their affections to higher levels. Be careful not to give vent to the full fervor of your emotion at the outset. One master teacher of homiletics has warned, "When he [the preacher] is all fire and they [the congregation] as yet are ice, a sudden contact between his mind and theirs will produce rather a shock and a revulsion than sympathetic harmony." His emotion is to their quietude extravagance. He must raise them first a part of the way toward his own level.[33]

Lay the kindling before starting a fire.

Be specific. Broad generalizations and obvious abstractions are immediate turn-offs. Who wants to listen to a sermon that begins with the so-called insight that goals are important in life? Our academic training habituates us to state the generic first and then work toward the particular. However, the best introductions start with specifics.[34] Instead of offering the obvious: Some people believe God is arbitrary, state the personal consequence: My friend says that because he sinned God gave his son cancer. Instead of opening a message with textbook principles: God saves us by faith alone, speak of the human concern: When will you be good enough for God?

Be professional. Because so much of the preacher's credibility, the congregation's interest, and the sermon's progress rides on these opening words, they must be well prepared.[35] The preacher is most vulnerable to grasping for words and to nervous error in these heart-racing moments, but simply reading a manuscript to avoid mistakes does not help in these times when good communication skills and eye contact are requisite for trustworthy speakers.

Write out the opening paragraphs so you are sure what to say, then commit the opening sentence(s) to memory so that listeners are sure of you. Although homileticians vary over the best time to write the introduction, most preachers begin to construct the introduction after they have roughed out the sermon's outline and then they continue to hone its elements as their preparation progresses.[36] Do not try to memorize the entire introduction. Beyond the opening sentence(s) memorize concepts, not words, so that your delivery has a natural, conversa-

33. Robert L. Dabney, *Lectures on Sacred Rhetoric* (1870; reprint, Carlisle, Penn.: Banner of Truth, 1979), 141.

34. Broadus, *Preparation and Delivery of Sermons*, 106.

35. Robinson, *Biblical Preaching*, 166–67.

36. Broadus, *Preparation and Delivery of Sermons*, 107; Hogan, "It Is My Pleasure," 2; Adams, *Preaching with Purpose*, 64; Demaray, *An Introduction to Homiletics*, 76–77.

tional flow. Still, know precisely what you intend to communicate and where the flow will lead. Nothing so manages nerves as well-planned words.

Introduce the message without spoken or implied apologies even if you feel unprepared. The outset is no time to prejudice a congregation against you, your message, or the potential of the Holy Spirit to work beyond human weakness.[37] You will better communicate your confidence and the strength of your intent with a healthy pause before your introduction: look directly at the congregation, square your shoulders, take a measured breath—then begin.[38]

Purposes of Conclusions

Were one to graph the conceptual and emotional intensity of a well-constructed sermon, the results would look like figure 9.3. The message that starts with a gripping introduction should end with an even more powerful conclusion.[39] Because listeners are more likely to remember the conclusion than any other portion of the message,[40] and because all the sermon's components should have prepared for this culmination, the conclusion is the climax of the message.

The last sixty seconds are the most dynamic moments in excellent sermons. With these final words, the preacher marshals the thought and emotion of the entire message into an exhortation that makes all that has preceded clear and compelling. The conclusion is the sermon's des-

---

37. Broadus, *Preparation and Delivery of Sermons*, 104; Hogan, "It Is My Pleasure," 2; cf. Demaray, *An Introduction to Homiletics*, 105.

38. Robinson, *Biblical Preaching*, 166.

39. Broadus, *Preparation and Delivery of Sermons*, 123.

40. With the exception of their perception of the speaker, which is what they most remember, what people are most likely to remember of a sermon can be seen in this "Sermon Component Retention Hierarchy":

> Concluding material
> Introductory material
> Illustrations (particularly of the conclusion and/or introduction)
> Specific applications (particularly if the listener strongly agrees or disagrees)
> Basic idea of the message
> An interesting thought in the message
> A main point statement
> An expositional concept

For a discussion of the implications of this hierarchy (which when properly analyzed argues for the importance of each component) see the author's *Using Illustrations to Preach with Power* (Grand Rapids: Zondervan, 1992), 151–52.

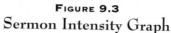

FIGURE 9.3
Sermon Intensity Graph

Note overall upward progression of the entire message.

tination. Its contents are alive—packed with tension, drama, energy, and emotion. Note well: This never means bombast and does not necessitate grandiloquence since deep feeling and powerful thought are often expressed in the most quiet, sincere terms. Masterful conclusions sometimes thunder and other times they crackle with an electricity barely audible to the ears, but the best endings always soundly register in the heart.

Good conclusions require careful craftsmanship. G. Campbell Morgan said, "Every conclusion must conclude, include, and preclude."[41] To conclude the conclusion must truly end the message. To do this well the conclusion must include what had been previously said and preclude the possibility that the implications and the consequences of the message will escape the listeners. In order to accomplish these purposes conclusions contain these components:

Recapitulation (i.e., concise summary). The preacher should briefly place before the listeners the key thoughts of the preceding exposition.[42] Most of the time the preacher can simply summarize the main ideas of the sermon by restating the key terms of the main points (not entire main-point statements) or by echoing these (or other) key terms in a final illustration. The preacher only reminds listeners what has preceded and does not preach the sermon again. A summary that goes over two or three sentences is much too long. One sentence of concise recap will serve. Concluding summaries should sound like hammer strokes, not sonatas.

---

41. G. Campbell Morgan, *Preaching* (1937; reprint, Grand Rapids: Baker, 1974), 87.
42. Robinson, *Biblical Preaching*, 168; Demaray, *An Introduction to Homelictics*, 95.

Exhortation (i.e., final application). Although we have already examined the contemporary inappropriateness of delaying the applications of a sermon until the conclusion, this does not mean that conclusions are devoid of application. In the conclusion the preacher summons previous thought and present emotions and exhorts the congregation to act in accord with the thrust of the message.[43] Usually, and for maximum impact, preachers incorporate this exhortation into the conclusion's last sentence or two.

> It is in the conclusion that the appeal to "believe," or "go" or "do" something or other is made. . . . The purpose of the conclusion, then, is not merely to bring the sermon to an end. It does that. But the principal function that it serves is to capsulize and capitalize on the sermon *telos* [i.e., purpose]. The listener goes away with the conclusion, which always calls for some change on his part, in mind. It must be powerful.[44]

In the conclusion the preacher exhorts people to act on what the sermon has already made clear.[45] Thus, the primary purpose of the conclusion is motivation. There should be no new exposition or application in the conclusion, but rather a determined effort to mobilize the will of the listeners to conform to previously specified imperatives. This means that the concluding exhortation is often broader than the applications in the main points. The final challenge urges listeners to consider all that has preceded and inspires them to do what has already been made clear. Now is not the time to reargue the case or newly prove any specifics. Bring horizons into view, melt hearts, and prod the will.[46] Sage preachers once taught, "If there is no summons, there is no sermon."[47] The advice may sound antique, but the minister who does not seek this pinnacle effect likely possesses little contemporary impact.

Elevation (i.e., climax). Thought and emotion should arrive at their greatest height and most personal statement in the conclusion, which indicates that all that the message has led to is significant, vital, and moving. If the content of the message and the manner of the messenger do not indicate import at the end, the sermon will probably fail. Broadus

43. Stott, *Between Two Worlds*, 246–53.
44. Adams, *Preaching with Purpose*, 69.
45. Cf. Broadus, *Preparation and Delivery of Sermons*, 125; Demaray, *An Introduction to Homiletics*, 95; Larsen, *The Anatomy of Preaching*, 124–25; Robinson, *Biblical Preaching*, 167.
46. Stott, *Between Two Worlds*, 247–48.
47. Broadus, *Preparation and Delivery of Sermons*, 210.

writes, "Weakness in manner, thought, or words draws the nails instead of driving them deeper. Deep passion, thoughts that burn, strong words are the instruments required, whether the conclusion be a direct drive on the will or an appeal to the heart."[48] If you are not moved, do not expect anyone else to be. To exhaust oneself prior to the conclusion so that the sermon ends weakly may seem noble, but it will strike the listeners as indicative of little forethought or, worse, little courage.

Termination (i.e., a definite end). Like the first sentence of a sermon, the last should also make a significant impression.[49] Its structure should indicate professionalism and fully prepared thought. Its content should hold the entire sermon in nugget form. Its wording should be able to echo in the mind of the listeners throughout the week. These expectations require the preacher to plan for a definite, purposed, pointed end. Sangster admonishes:

> Having come to the end, stop. Do not cruise about looking for a spot to land, like some weary swimmer coming in from the sea and splashing about until he can find a shelving beach up which to walk. Come right in, and land at once. If the last phrase can have some quality of crisp memorableness, all the better, but do not grope even for that. Let your sermon have the quality that Charles Wesley coveted for his whole life: let the work and the course end together.[50]

Sangster's advice reminds us that even if conclusions do not meet other homiletical ideals they are still improved if they end crisply.

TYPES OF CONCLUSIONS

Although as many resources can be used for conclusions as for introductions[51] two types predominate: grand style and human-interest account. In a grand-style conclusion the preacher heightens the manner of expression and the choice of words to indicate that the message has come to its climax. Summary, final exhortation, and end are stated in elevated language with an intensified delivery that communicates the import of the thought. This style allows the preacher to state the mes-

---

48. Ibid., 126.

49. Demaray, *An Introduction to Homiletics*, 101; Broadus, *Preparation and Delivery of Sermons*, 107, 126.

50. W. E. Sangster, *The Craft of Sermon Construction* (1951; reprint, Grand Rapids: Baker, 1972), 150.

51. See "Other Options" above in the discussion of "Types of Introductions." Cf. Larsen, *The Anatomy of Preaching*, 123–27.

sage's point directly while depending on vocabulary choices and delivery skills to express the intensity that effective conclusions require. Student preachers may find this direct approach appealing, but they frequently lack the oratorical polish to make it succeed. Experience will cultivate the instincts and the skills to use grand style effectively, but the sense of climax needed for effective conclusions is consistently available at an early stage of training through human-interest accounts.[52]

For all the reasons stated earlier in this chapter and in chapter 7 human-interest accounts involve listeners as few other sermon components can. If the account chosen for the conclusion is both personally gripping and apt for the sermon's subject, the preacher has the opportunity to rally both the hearts and minds of the listeners and motivate their wills. Manipulation of emotions with a story that does not drive home the principles that have been developed in the message ranks among the worst abuses of preaching. But, failing to engage the heart, stimulate the will, excite the mind, and elevate the soul concerning eternal truths at this most crucial stage is nearly as great a crime.[53] Preachers who ethically use a human-interest account to elicit honest emotions, stir genuine feelings, and provoke appropriate convictions are following biblical injunctions to urge, persuade, and encourage.[54] Conclusions should neither contrive emotions nor avoid them.

CAUTIONS (HINTS) FOR CONCLUSIONS

Poems and quotations. The stereotypical three-points-and-a-poem sermon holds little promise for persuasive power in this age of low literary appreciation. The modern mental palate has little appreciation for difficult words, remote references, and high-blown speech.[55] Not only does the preacher give the final word to someone else when concluding with a poem (or hymn) quotation,[56] but also the citation of flowery expression turns off many contemporary hearers. Unless the poem says precisely what you intend, says it better than you could, and touches a deeper chord than you can reach, frame your own final words. But, if you do use an appropriate quotation, use as brief a portion as possible, signal the significance of the lines before you cite them, and vocally emphasize

52. Demaray, *An Introduction to Homiletics,* 97.
53. Ibid., 103.
54. Adams, *Preaching with Purpose,* 69.
55. Ibid., 66–67.
56. Larsen, *The Anatomy of Preaching,* 127; David Buttrick, *Homiletic: Moves and Structures* (Philadelphia: Fortress, 1987), 105.

the key ideas. Remember also it is a crime at the sermon's most convicting moments to break eye contact, bury your head in a manuscript, and flatly read obscure words. Conclusions need to be largely committed to memory and movingly spoken from the heart.

High notes. Try to end on a high note. Even the most darkly convicting messages need to end with a ray of hope—a light at the end of the tunnel. If Scripture requires you to take people to the mat, do so. But do not abandon them there. The preacher who leaves a congregation depressed, despairing, and pessimistic about their sin or situation has failed to preach.[57] Remember the gospel is the "Good News." Conclusions should challenge and lift the heart. Clovis Chappell rightly asserted, "No man has a right so to preach as to send his hearers away on flat tires. Every discouraging sermon is a wicked sermon. . . . A discouraged man is not an asset but a liability."[58]

Anticlimax. Sustain the climax by avoiding common causes of anticlimax. When the preacher seems to have raised the emotions, hammered home the point of the message, called the hearers to action and then launches anew into more oratory, listeners despair or grow angry. William Jennings Bryan's own mother once scolded him, "You missed several good opportunities to sit down."[59] Conclusions work best if there is only one per message.

One way of avoiding an apparent dual ending is to move the illustration of the final main point early into that point's exposition (especially if the conclusion is a human-interest account). In this way the dynamics of the final point's illustration will not too closely impinge on the thoughts and emotions of the conclusion. Phillips Brooks consistently used the third main point of his messages as the conclusion in order to avoid this conflict.

Extending the sermon long beyond its climax is an anticlimax that will rob the entire message of power. By contrast, ending a message prior to a climax will make it seem to have ended abruptly or simply to have been ill prepared.[60] Although a sudden stop can have a beneficial arresting effect, simply running out of words does not justify its use.[61]

The sermon also dodges anticlimactic tendencies if the summary of the message is placed before the conclusion's climax rather than after

57. Larsen, *The Anatomy of Preaching*, 129.
58. As quoted in Demaray, *An Introduction to Homiletics*, 100.
59. As quoted in Vines, *A Practical Guide*, 145.
60. Demaray, *An Introduction to Homiletics*, 99.
61. Robinson, *Biblical Preaching*, 171.

it.[62] If the summary comes after the climax make the recap extremely brief. Forcing new arguments into the conclusion or preaching a point in the prayer following the conclusion because you forgot it during the message are also sure-fire ways of blunting a sermon's ending.[63]

Rhetorical questions. Preachers often end sermons by using questions as launching pads for listener reflection. Unfortunately, questions at the end of sermons have a tendency to make the entire matter dissolve into space. When preachers conclude with rhetorical questions, they intend listeners personally to consider the matters discussed in the sermon. Instead, the matters are often so generally posed as to drain off the power the message might have (e.g., "And, what do you think?"). Students wisely avoid rhetorical questions in homiletical training. If you use such questions, be very specific about what you actually summon the listener to consider.[64] Too often rhetorical questions simply demonstrate that the preacher did not get around to thinking of a more fitting conclusion and this is the best that momentary reflection and extemporaneous expression can provide.

Wraparounds. A highly professional way of concluding is to hearken back to material mentioned in the sermon's introduction (or other earlier portions of the message).[65] Complete a story, echo an earlier thought, refer to character or story specifics in a previous illustration, resolve a tension, repeat a striking phrase, refer to the opening problem, or in some other way end where you began. This wrapping up of the sermon[66] gives the message a sense of being packaged and thus communicates craft, thoughtfulness, and conscientious preparation.

Professional preparation. Professionalism radiates from conclusions that are relatively brief (not more than two or three significant paragraphs), focused, and end poignantly. Conclusions do not always need impassioned speech but they do need telling words.[67] The last sentence of the conclusion needs special preparation. A powerful phrase—per-

---

62. Broadus, *On the Preparation and Delivery of Sermons*, 127.

63. Demaray, *An Introduction to Homiletics*, 99; Robinson, *Biblical Preaching*, 169–70.

64. I recognize that formal rhetoric would not categorize these as rhetorical but rather as maeutic questions; i.e., questions whose answers have already been supplied. True rhetorical questions have no answers. Jay Adams suggests modifying rhetorical questions with "cluster-question" endings (multiple questions grouped together to refine a point) that leave no question what the conclusion specifically requires (see *Preaching with Purpose*, 68).

65. Larsen, *The Anatomy of Preaching*, 127.

66. "Circular closure" is a common artistic device in literature, rhetoric, and music.

67. Broadus, *On the Preparation and Delivery of Sermons*, 128.

haps one that echoes from an earlier point in the message, a verse of Scripture movingly quoted, or a simple, clear sentence—mark quality preaching.[68] Each requires previous, careful preparation.

Homiletics experts differ on when preachers should prepare conclusions.[69] Idealists argue that the conclusion should be the first component prepared so that the sermon has a definite destination. Realists want the conclusion prepared after the sermon has taken shape so that it definitely embraces the evolved message. Practitioners understand that the conclusion sometimes jumps onto the field of preparation and declares its presence before any other sermonic team members arrive, and other times you have to drag it from bed and pummel it into shape long after the other members have assumed their positions. Probably the most balanced approach lies in generating a basic plan for the conclusion in the sermon's embryonic stages, but modifying the conclusion to conform to the message's specifics as it develops.

Whatever the timing of their preparation, however, all master preachers agree that conclusions take time. We cannot too strongly emphasize the need for preparation since too many preachers delay constructing a conclusion until they are worn out from preparing the meat of the sermon. As a result, these preachers are tempted to extemporize (rationalized as letting the Holy Spirit inspire) that portion of the sermon that holds the potential for greatest impact. Larsen recommends that his students spend two-thirds of their time on the last one-third of the message.[70] You may not agree with this time allotment, but you should at least acknowledge that it makes no sense to spend the least amount of preparation on that aspect of the sermon that holds greatest spiritual potential.

Finally. It is best not to announce the conclusion.[71] Let your manner and thought indicate the culmination. If you say, "Finally . . ." or "In conclusion, . . ." in this culture you have tacitly told everyone to stop looking at you and to glance at their watches. Of course, if the sermon has lulled listeners into oblivion, an announcment can serve as a final, desperate effort to raise the eyelids of those who have abandoned hope

---

68. Brian L. Harbour, "Concluding the Sermon," in *Handbook of Contemporary Preaching*, ed. Michael Duduit (Nashville: Broadman, 1992), 221–22.

69. Cf. Broadus, *Preparation and Delivery of Sermons*, 123; Stott, *Between Two Worlds*, 243.

70. Larsen, *The Anatomy of Preaching*, 121.

71. Vines, *A Practical Guide*, 144; Demaray, *An Introduction to Homiletics*, 100; Robinson, *Biblical Preaching*, 171.

for an end. If you do say, "Finally, . . ." mean it. Nothing so frustrates listeners as an announced conclusion that never arrives. White chides:

> An apostle may say "Finally, brethren . . ." and go on for two more chapters: but not you. A troubled English vicar asked a farm-labourer why he came to church only when the assistant preached. "Well sir," said the labourer, "young Mr. Smith, he says 'in conclusion' and he do conclude. But you say 'lastly' and you *do* last."[72]

PURPOSES OF TRANSITIONS

Introductions charge into the message. Explanations, illustrations, and applications burble in the body. Conclusions cap the whole. Each component performs separate, vital functions but if the pieces remain too segregated the sermon will feel like patchwork and the prominence of the seams will obscure the overall design. Something must sew the components together. Transitions do this.

Although they contain little raw information, transitions greatly contribute to the thought of the message—aiding its flow, progress, and beauty. Skilled transitions often are the distinguishing mark between mundane messages and excellent sermons.[73] With transitions, the preacher demonstrates the relationships of the introduction to the body of the sermon, the parts of the body to each other, and the conclusion to all that has preceded.[74] These relationships are most frequently logical connections, but transitions are also psychological, emotional, and aesthetic links. Good transitions harmonize the conceptual and emotional rhythms that run through a sermon.

Transitions not only tie the components of the sermon together, but also signal progress and direction to the listener. But the job of transitions is not merely to point forward. They must also relate present matters to previous discussion. Consistent tie backs to the sermon's major concept(s) at significant junctures in the message indicate that preachers are aware of congregation and communication needs. Since listeners cannot see your outline, transitions cue the listener as to which thoughts are major, which are minor, and how they relate.

72. R. E. O. White, *A Guide to Preachers* (Grand Rapids: Eerdmans, 1973), 111; cf. Robinson, *Biblical Preaching*, 171.

73. Broadus, *Preparation and Delivery of Sermons*, 120.

74. Robinson, *Biblical Preaching*, 131.

Sometimes preachers insert transitions into the sermon simply to distinguish ideas. When the preacher states a subpoint in the next sentence after a main point (or states the first main point on the heels of the proposition) listeners often cannot discern which was the major idea. They may wonder if the second statement is really a new thought or if it is merely a refined version of the first statement acting like an apositive. Although preachers can do a great deal with voice and gesture to limit confusion, simply separating the statement of a major idea from subordinate ideas with a sentence or two of preparatory transition often helps avoid problems.

My wife once said of a pastor, "Everything he said was true; he just didn't seem to have a clue how to pull it all together." Such a characterization will not apply to preachers who remember they must use transitions to review where we have gone; preview where we are going; secure an immediate matter to the larger theme; and/or remove questions about how varying ideas relate to each other.

TYPES OF TRANSITIONS

Knitting statements. The phrase *Not only . . . , but also . . . ,* is the foundational form of transition. The words reach back into previous comments, point toward upcoming discussion, and pull the two together.

The essence of this transition is manifested in many different forms. The statements, "If this is true, then these are the implications. . . ." "Our understanding is not complete until we also consider . . ." and many similar variations capture the significance of the not-only-but-also concept. Parallel wording that picks up key terms summarizing earlier thought and then repeats them in a slightly different form to signal upcoming thought accomplishes similar purposes.[75]

Not-only-but-also variations come in many different lengths. Even the simple word *next* reminds the listener that something has preceded and something more will follow. Other connector words (e.g., however, therefore, consequently, yet, etc.) can also provide this service.[76] A short series of sentences can stimulate similar dynamics. Consider how this brief paragraph glues what is ahead to what is behind:

75. See examples of parallel wording in the "Grouping Statement" discussion of chapter 7; e.g., "Just as we cannot turn to God without faith, we will not turn to another without trust."

76. George E. Sweazey, *Preaching the Good News* (Englewood Cliffs, N.J.: Prentice-Hall, 1976), 78.

We have seen how this text demonstrates God's love. But knowing that God means well is not enough warrant to offer him our trust. Good intentions do not make everything work out all right. That is why the Apostle Paul continues his argument with proof of God's sovereignty. God does not just desire what is good for us; he accomplishes it. Because God is sovereign we can trust his love.

Statements like these that knit together strands of previous and following thought accomplish transitions' most fundamental purpose.[77]

Dialogical questions. The preacher can also signal progress by asking questions that stimulate further discussion. The preacher whose inner ear hears the questions playing on listeners' minds and then asks those questions for them *out loud* employs a powerful rhetorical tool. The dialogue the preacher initiates in the listeners' behalf not only convinces them that the preacher respects their thought, but also invites them to continue progressing through the message on a course that promises to satisfy their concerns.[78]

Examples of questions that involve listeners while orienting them to its progress are: If this approach won't work, what will? What plan does God offer for this? and, What must come next? Make listeners dive into an explanation with you by asking, "What in the world does this verse mean?" or, better yet, "How do we know what this verse means?" You can introduce an illustration with, "How can we see this more clearly in our own experience?" Listeners will never tire of the question: How can we apply this truth in our lives?

Loading the sermon with questions that move the listener into and through the sermon stimulates interest in the message so long as the answers are clear. Following the proposition with a strong overarching question that you design the main points to answer can effectively begin many messages.[79] But the dialogue should not cease in the sermon's opening moments. Even the most apathetic listener wants to know answers to questions such as these: What else do you do when all else fails? Did God forget that he was a sinner . . . then, why would God

77. Recall also that the nodes between the expositional components act as transitions if the preacher properly uses the summary of one component as the de facto introduction to the next component (see discussion in chapters 7 and 8).

78. Larsen asserts that Jesus' recorded teachings include one hundred questions, *The Anatomy of Preaching*, 154.

79. A good diagnostic question that establishes the subject of the overall sermon can also substitute for the proposition. See further discussion of the uses of diagnostic questions to set up the main points in chapter 6.

FIGURE 9.3
Double Helix Transition Perspective

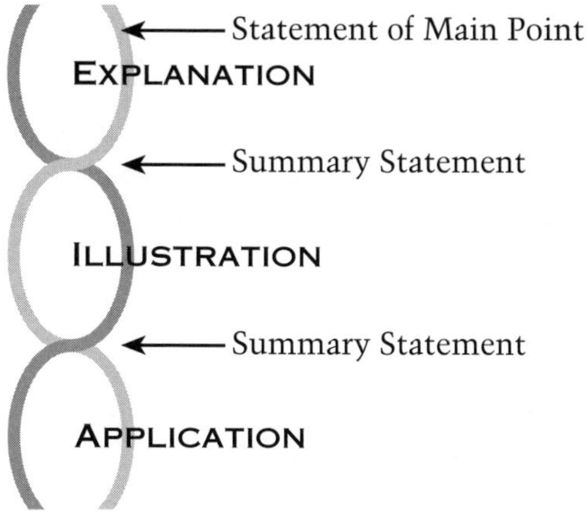

choose him? How can you face loneliness in the eyes of one you love? Using such questions to frame and set up subpoints as we discussed earlier [80] can take advantage of this dynamic and energize the entire message.

Numbering and listing. There is little artistry in simply numbering ideas, but the preacher who lists ideas as first, second, third, readily orients the listeners to specific stages of the sermon's thought. Preachers who make such encyclopedic references to their ideas need to remember, however, that hearers are not reading the sermon's outline. Listing subpoints as *A*, *B*, and *C* shows rhetorical insensitivity. Saying, "first," or "second" for each main point *and* each subsequent subpoint causes great confusion for hearers who will struggle to categorize the third, fourth, and fifth mention of "first" through the course of the sermon. Also be careful not to say, "In the third place, . . ." if you have not previously announced (and usually reviewed) what came first and second.[81]

As a final caution, remember that simply numbering one's way through a sermon is a fairly dry and pedantic way to proceed. Unless the ideas require exceptional clarity other forms of transition are usually more stimulating.

---

80. See the discussion of subpointing in chapter 6.
81. Cf. Sweazey, *Preaching the Good News*, 78.

Picture painting. When a controlling image[82] forms the basis of the sermon's outline, the preacher can often make transitions by referring to other aspects of that image. A reference to "The flip side of the coin is . . . ," draws an image to mind that alerts the listeners that the preacher is about to contrast thoughts. Of course, sermons can be built on much more complex images that the preacher can progressively "paint" in order to indicate progression of thought (e.g., "Since God is the architect of our salvation he does not merely plan his love for us, he designs our love for him. Next we need to see what characterizes that design."). A separate illustration can also act as a transition with images or relationships within the story indicating how ideas in the sermon connect.

Billboards and branches. An important but often neglected area of transition arises between the introduction and the body of the message. Here skilled preachers often telegraph how they will handle issues raised in the introduction by use of a billboard. Billboards are crystallized statements of the main points (typically using only key words) in the order they will appear (e.g., "In order to have an assurance of your relationship with God you must believe that the love of Jesus is greater than sin, circumstances, and Satan.").

Sermon billboards usually occur just before or just after the proposition (and are occasionally incorporated into the proposition) to indicate the direction and organization of the message. Billboards quickly orient listeners to the sermon's plan and solemnly bind the preacher to follow the path that the billboard indicates lies ahead. Failure to follow the path signalled will confuse and frustrate listeners. Reiterating key features of the billboard through the course of the message keeps listeners on track, and can be a very efficient way of summarizing the entire message in the conclusion.

Mini billboards may appear throughout the message as preachers preview subpoints in specific main points or signal the development of other subordinate ideas. One automatic way of doing this is to use conjunctions in main-point statements. The preacher who says, "Since God commands love without partiality, we must love the lovely and the unlovely," has already implied, "First I will talk about love for the lovely and, next, I will discuss love for the unlovely." Conjunctions in main-point statements indicate branches in the preacher's thought. If you do not intend to follow these branches eliminate the conjunctions from the main-point statements.

---

82. See chapter 6 for a discussion of types of outlines.

Billboards and branches help preachers efficiently meet the first and last obligations of this traditional rhetorical instruction:

1. Say what you will say.
2. Say it.
3. Say what you said.

Despite the antiquity of this maxim, homileticians in the past and in the present have questioned the wisdom of announcing a sermon's divisions ahead of time.[83] Legitimate concerns about making the message too boxy, linear, time-conscious, and anticlimactic need to be weighed when deciding to use billboards. Certainly, if the preacher intends to build some suspense or arrange an ironic twist, then preannouncing points serves no good purpose. However, where the train of thought is complex, the discourse lengthy, interest difficult to stimulate or maintain, and where clarity will be promoted by a bird's-eye perspective on the relation of the points to one another, then some form of billboarding may well serve the sermon.

ULTIMATE MEASURES

This chapter cannot exhaust all the possible functions and forms that introductions, conclusions, and transitions assume. I have tried to indicate principles and principal alternatives. Appropriate exceptions abound and many variations are needed. Specific purposes will supersede all rules for the preacher who taps the wisdom of the refrain, "Never do anything always."

Remember also that no amount of homiletical skill will substitute for the Spirit's work. The ultimate measure of a sermon's success is not whether it had a great introduction, a powerful conclusion, or smooth transitions, but whether it communicates transforming truths. Sermons succeed when the Holy Spirit works beyond human craft to perform his purposes. However, only the most arrogant servant will impose on the Master's goodness by anticipating blessing for shoddy work. We serve best when we not only depend on the Holy Spirit to empower our words, but also craft them so as to honor him.

---

83. Cf. Broadus, *Preparation and Delivery of Sermons*, 118; Buttrick, *Homiletic*, 85; Sweazey, *Preaching the Good News*, 73–74, 78.

Questions for Review and Discussion

1. What are four major purposes of sermon introductions?

2. What are five major types of sermon introductions? What are two common but *ineffective* types of introductions?

3. What is the difference between a sermon introduction and a Scripture introduction?

4. In what two ways should the sermon introduction prepare for the proposition?

5. What are four major purposes of sermon conclusions?

6. What are two major types of sermon conclusions?

7. What is the most basic form of transition?

EXERCISES

1. Create a sermon introduction for the message you previously outlined from 2 Timothy 4:1–5; or 2 Corinthians 6:14–7:1; or
   1 Thessalonians 4:13–18; or create a sermon introduction for an
   alternative message. (Attach the proposition to make sure it flows
   from the introduction.)

2. Identify the following components in the introduction you created for exercise 1: interest arousal; introduction of the subject;
   statement of FCF; making it personal; bonding to Scripture; and
   terminological preparation for the proposition (see example following figure 9.1).

3. Create a conclusion for the message you previously outlined from
   2 Timothy 4:1–5; or 2 Corinthians 6:14–7:1; or 1 Thessalonians
   4:13–18; or create a conclusion for an alternative message. Identify the concise summary, climax, final exhortation, and definite
   end in this conclusion.

Part 3

A THEOLOGY OF CHRIST-CENTERED MESSAGES

CONTENTS OF CHAPTER 10

GOAL OF CHAPTER 10

*To present the overarching theological concern for
constructing sermons as indicated in previous chapters*

10

A REDEMPTIVE APPROACH TO PREACHING

REVIEWING THE FALLEN CONDITION FOCUS

Why does the development of expository sermons depend on the clear identification of a Fallen Condition Focus?[1] To this point the most obvious answer relates to homiletical structure. A clear FCF provides the sermon with a distinct aim so that the preacher can organize the entire message to address a unified purpose. The FCF not only targets the information in the sermon, but also directs the preacher to relevant application supported by the text itself. Beyond these standard homiletical goals, however, there are theological reasons for germinating sermons from a passage's FCF.

GROUNDING THE FALLEN CONDITION FOCUS

The theological ground for designing messages with an FCF base derives from the principle evident in 2 Timothy 3:16, a touchstone verse for all biblical preaching. As we have already observed (see chapter 2), the fact that "All Scripture is inspired by God . . . in order that the man of God might be complete" necessarily implies that even the most gifted persons remain spiritually incomplete apart from God's revelation. God uses his Word to make us what we could not be on our own. In this sense, God's Word acts as an instrument of his redeeming work. Scripture continually aims to restore some aspect of our brokenness to spiritual wholeness. Our condition as fallen creatures in a fallen world requires this redemptive work not merely for our salvation, but for our

---

1. See the earlier discussion and definition of the Fallen Condition Focus in chapter 2.

continuing sanctification. Thus, all Scripture—and by corollary all expository preaching that unfolds its meaning—focuses on some aspect of our being that needs completion. Preaching that remains true to the purpose Scripture sets for itself addresses an FCF.

We have already discussed how to determine an FCF for an expository message (see table 10.1). Expository preachers are ready to prepare a sermon only after they identify a mutual condition shared by those in the biblical context and those in the contemporary context. This premise is derived from the understanding that God intended the text to serve both an original purpose and a present use.[2] These are not separate purposes. The original intent reveals proper present use by highlighting some common aspect of the human condition addressed by the scriptural truths displayed in the text.

TABLE 10.1

How to Determine the Fallen Condition Focus (Review)

Three-Step Process: (Ask these questions.)

1. What does the text say?
2. What concern(s) did the text address (in its context)?
3. What do listeners share in common with those to (or about) whom it was written?
   and/or
   the one by whom it was written?

Scripture itself teaches us that in an original FCF resides meaning for present biblical purposes. Paul writes to the Corinthians,

> [I]t is written in the Law of Moses: "Do not muzzle an ox while it is treading out the grain." Is it about oxen that God is concerned? Surely *he says this for us*, doesn't he? Yes, *this was written for us*, because when the plowman plows and the thresher threshes, they ought to do so in the hope of sharing in the harvest. If we have sown spiritual seed among you, is it too much if we reap a material harvest from you? [1 Cor. 9:8–12, emphasis added]

Moses wrote for his own situation, but Paul recognized proper understanding of original intent (i.e., if even oxen should expect to share in

---

2. Sidney Greidanus, *The Modern Preacher and the Ancient Text: Interpreting and Preaching Biblical Literature* (Grand Rapids: Eerdmans, 1988), 166.

the fruit of their labor, so should people) had present implications for God's people facing similar concerns.

Over and over again the apostle uses the Old Testament in this way. In the next chapter of the same letter to the Corinthians he alludes to the devastations that came on ancient Israel when it yielded to temptation to command certain behaviors of New Testament believers who were similarly tempted:

> Now these things occurred as examples to keep us from setting our hearts on evil things as they did. Do not be idolaters, as some of them were. . . . We should not commit sexual immorality, as some of them did . . . . We should not test the Lord, as some of them did. . . . And do not grumble, as some of them did. . . . These things happened to them as examples and were written down as warnings for us. . . . [1 Cor. 10:6–11]

Initial intent of a previous millenium had definite implications for present practices in the apostle's mind and in the Spirit's plan.

But original purposes did not merely provide behavioral guidance. They were signposts to faith. For those people who might be tempted to believe that their salvation depended on their works Paul wrote, "The words 'it was credited to him' [i.e., Abraham] were written not for him alone, but also for us, to whom God will credit righteousness—for us who believe in him who raised Jesus our Lord from the dead" (Rom. 4:23–24). Paul recognized that identifying the concern that a passage originally addressed was the key to applying its truths to present needs.

Facing the fact that every passage was written to address a fallen condition in its original context and in our present situation underscores truths that we previously discussed:

1. Until we have determined its FCF we do not really know what a text is about even if we know many true facts about the passage.
2. We should never preach on a passage until we have determined an FCF the Holy Spirit intended this Scripture to address.

As expository preachers we must ask, "What is an FCF behind the inspiration of this text?" before we can accurately expound its meaning. We must determine the target the Holy Spirit intended in order to aim our exposition of the text accurately. Thus, identifying current biblical need our listeners share with those in the biblical situation that required the inspired writing is prerequisite for every expository sermon.

Incorporating the Fallen Condition Focus

The approaches to expository preaching proposed in this book have already (although perhaps without your conscious recognition) prepared you to incorporate an FCF into your exposition. We have developed each element of the sermon to support the principles of FCF. The unifying theme of the sermon—the one thing that the message is about—is how the truths of the passage address an FCF. The introduction of the message identifies this FCF by bringing to the surface the reason the truths of the passage were inspired in the biblical context and the reason they are needed in the present situation. The introduction also prepares for the proposition that formally states how the preacher will present the truths of the passage in light of this FCF.

The structure of the proposition, whether it is stated formally or appears in an abbreviated form, further supports development based on an FCF. By making sure that the proposition indicates how the truths of the passage will be applied, the preacher ensures an understanding that something must be done as a consequence of the text's instruction. This understanding makes listener response—rather than the static acquisition of information—the goal of the message. Such a goal indicates that human brokenness has to be addressed in active terms. Our fallenness is not merely an abstract principle—not a theological phantasm for philosophical consideration—it is rather the daily reality that corrodes without the balm and the correction of Scripture.

The body of the sermon indicates how the scriptural balm should be applied to our lives and what regimens God requires for our spiritual health. Main points formulated to reflect and to support the principles of the proposition provide the information that acts as biblical leverage for the preacher's exhortations. Explanation and illustration unfold and demonstrate meanings that supply the reasoning and the reality that make the sermon's applications acceptable and accessible. The conclusion drives the matter home, marshaling the forces of heart and mind for a final exhortation that calls the listeners to respond to their fallen condition with the biblical guidance that the sermon has disclosed.

DECIPHERING THE REDEMPTIVE SIGNALS

Thus far we have focused on the negative—centering the development of the sermon on the mutual problem that both original and present targets of the text share. There is, however, a necessary and welcome reverse. Why does all Scripture focus on some aspect of our fallen condition? The clear answer is: to supply the warrant and to define the character of the redemptive elements in Scripture that we can, in turn, apply to our fallenness. The Bible's ultimate aim is beautifully positive. Scripture addresses features of our incompleteness only because such a focus concurrently signals the work of God that makes us whole. The goal of expository preaching is to decipher these redemptive signals so that our listeners understand a text's full meaning in the context of its gospel intent.

SUB-CHRISTIAN MESSAGES IN PREACHING

Unless we identify the redemptive purposes in a text it is possible to say all the right words and yet send all the wrong signals. I witness this miscommunication almost daily on the top-rated radio station in our city that broadcasts a morning "meditation." Each morning the preacher addresses some topic with a Bible verse or two. The subjects run the gamut from procrastination, to parenting, to honesty on the job. The station turns up the reverberation whenever this preacher speaks so that it sounds as though the words come direct from Mount Sinai. Not to pay attention seems like a sin. I would guess that few even question the content of the man's words. As he reminds us from the Bible to practice punctuality, good parenting, and business propriety, I realize a hundred thousand motorists are nodding their heads and saying in unison, "That's right . . . that's how we should live."

I have even played tapes of this preacher's meditations to seminary classes and asked if anyone can discern error in what he says. Rarely does anyone spot a problem. The preacher quotes his text accurately, he advocates moral causes, and he encourages loving behaviors. The problem that I point out to students and that is carefully hidden from the broadcast audience is that the radio preacher is not a Christian. He represents a large cult headquartered in our region.

How can this be? How can so many Christians (even those well-informed) so readily grant assent to one whose commitments are radically anti-Christian? Some answer that their lack of protest results from the radio preacher's care to avoid saying anything controversial. They contend that he hides his heresy beneath a veil of right-sounding orthodoxy. Such defenses miss the point even as his proponents have missed the problem. The radio preacher has not hidden his heresy; he exposes it every time he speaks in what he fails to say. The real problem is that evangelical preachers inadvertently and so frequently present such similar messages that Christians fail to hear the difference between a message that purports to be biblical and one that actually is.

A message that merely advocates morality and compassion remains sub-Christian even if the preacher can prove that the Bible demands such behaviors. By ignoring the sinfulness of man that makes even our best works tainted before God and by neglecting the grace of God that makes obedience possible and acceptable, such messages necessarily subvert the Christian message. Christian preachers often do not recognize this impact of their words because they are simply recounting a behavior clearly specified in the text in front of them. But a message that even inadvertently teaches others that their works win God's acceptance inevitably leads people away from the gospel.

Moral maxims and advocacy of ethical conduct fall short of the requirements of biblical preaching. Jay Adams explains with impassioned eloquence:

> If you preach a sermon that would be acceptable to the member to a Jewish synagogue or to a Unitarian congregation, there is something radically wrong with it. Preaching, when truly Christian, is *distinctive*. And what makes it distinctive is the all-pervading presence of a saving and sanctifying Christ. Jesus Christ must be at the heart of every sermon you preach. That is just as true of edificational preaching as it is of evangelistic preaching.
>
> . . . [E]dificational preaching must always be evangelical; that is what makes it moral rather than moralistic, and what causes it to be unacceptable in a synagogue, mosque, or to a Unitarian congregation. By evangelical, I mean that the import of Christ's death and resurrection—His substitutionary, penal death and bodily resurrection—on the subject under consideration is made clear in the sermon. You must not exhort your congregation to do whatever the Bible requires of them as though they could fulfil those requirements on their own, but only as a consequence of the saving power of the cross and the indwelling, sanctifying power and presence of Christ in the person of the Holy Spirit. All edificational preaching, to be Christian must fully take into consideration God's grace in salvation and in sanctification.[3]

A textually accurate discussion of biblical commands does not guarantee Christian orthodoxy. Exhortations for moral behavior apart from the work of the Savior degenerate into mere pharisaism even if preachers advocate the actions with biblical evidence and good intent. Spirituality

3. Jay Adams, *Preaching with Purpose* (Grand Rapids: Baker, 1982), 147.

based on personal conduct cannot escape its human-centered orbit though it aspires to lift one to divine heights.

A BIBLICAL THEOLOGY FOR PREACHING

But how do expository preachers infuse the redemptive essentials into every sermon without superimposing ideas foreign to many texts? Many Old Testament passages make no explicit reference to Christ's "substitutionary, penal death and bodily resurrection." New Testament texts abound that commend moral behaviors with no mention of the cross, the Holy Spirit, or enabling grace. Can we really be expositors and bring out of the text what it does not itself mention? The answer lies in an axiom mentioned earlier: Context is part of text.

No text exists in isolation from other texts or from the overarching biblical message. Just as historico-grammatical exegesis requires a preacher to consider a text's terms in context, correct theological interpretation requires the expositor to discern how any text's ideas function in the wider biblical message. Some meanings we discern by taking out our exegetical magnifying glasses and studying a text's particulars in close detail. Other meanings we discern by examining a text with a theological fish-eye lens to see how it relates to the texts, messages, history, and developments around it. Accurate expositors use both lenses, knowing that a magnifying glass can unravel mysteries in a raindrop but fail to expose a storm gathering on the horizon.

The branch of biblical study devoted to examining Scripture in the light of the overarching themes that unite all its particulars is called biblical theology. The insights of biblical theology are critical for preachers who want to expound a text so as to stay true to the passage and consistent with the gospel. Geerhardus Vos outlined the keys that will keep our preaching on track in the introduction to his seminal volume on biblical theology. He began with the simple observation that "revelation is a noun of action relating to divine activity."[4] All scriptural revelation discloses God. Every verse in the Bible in some sense points to him. Yet, because God is God, no single verse, no single passage, no single book contains all we need to know about him. In fact, had God totally revealed himself to our earliest faith ancestors they would not have had the theological background or biblical preparation to take in all that God has since disclosed to humankind about himself. For this reason God's revelation through biblical history was progressive. This

---

4. Geerhardus Vos, *Biblical Theology* (1948; reprint, Grand Rapids: Eerdmans, 1975), 5.

does not mean that early revelation differs from or in any sense contradicts what God ultimately reveals. Says Vos, "The progressive process is organic: revelation may be in seed form which yields later full growth accounting for diversity but not true difference because the earlier aspects of the truth are indispensable for understanding the true meanings of the later forms and vice versa."[5] Each verse, each recorded event, and each passing epoch of biblical history God uses to build a single, comprehensive understanding of who he is.

Our understanding of who God is, however, remains inextricably bound to what he has done. Writes Vos, "Revelation is inseparably linked to the activity of redemption. . . . Revelation is the interpretation of redemption."[6] This means that in order for us to expound biblical revelation from any passage we must relate our explanation to the redeeming work of God there present. The redemptive dimension of a particular Scripture may not seem to dominate the text's landscape because the redemptive features of a passage sometimes appear only in seed form, just as revelation does. Still, to expose the revelation properly we must see its redemptive content and context. We must relate even seed-form aspects of the text to the mature message they signal, or for which they prepare us, in order fully and rightly to interpret what the passage means. You do not explain what an acorn is, even if you say many true things about it (e.g., it is brown, has a cap, is found on the ground, is gathered by squirrels) if you do not in some way relate it to an oak tree. In a similar sense, preachers cannot properly explain biblical revelation, even if they say many true things about it, until they have related it to the redeeming work of God that all Scripture ultimately purposes to disclose.[7]

A BIBLICAL FOCUS FOR PREACHING

By recognizing that all Scripture is redemptive revelation inspired to

5. Ibid., 7.
6. Ibid., 5, 6.
7. It cannot be denied that the Scripture writers (or, at least, the divine Author) intended for particular passages to be viewed from multiple perspectives to provide opportunities variously to *emphasize* moral obligation, doctrinal articulation, historical sequence, character development, or worship instruction. Still, expositors must not forget the One who is the Yes and Amen of all God's promises, the Alpha and Omega of all God's purposes, the Beginning and the End of all holy endeavor, the first and the last means of performing all scriptural duty (2 Cor. 1:20; Rev. 22:13). Preachers should become well aware of the various perspectival purposes and layers individual texts may contain, but the absence of grace from whatever instruction the preacher ultimately offers will automatically identify a focus grown too narrow for Christian purposes (cf. John 5:39, 46).

address humanity's fallen condition (or incompleteness), preachers uncover the positive focus in all Christ-centered preaching. The text's FCF defines God's mercy as it reveals human need. The revelation that points out our need of God's redemption activity demonstrates, by that very need, the corresponding dimensions of the Redeemer's person and work that are required to fill that aspect of our incompleteness.

When I was a child my mother spent an afternoon making a special chocolate pudding for our family of eight. When she brought the fabulous dessert to the dinner table, however, the impact was marred by the deep imprint of a child's finger smack in the middle of the bowl. Someone had sneaked an early taste. My mother asked, "Who?" No one "fessed up," but that did not faze my mother's investigation. She simply began matching the index fingers of the six children to the hole in the top of the pudding until she found the finger that fit (it wasn't mine). The impression revealed not only the pudding's incompleteness, but also identified the features of the one who would fill the hole. So God's imprinting of our incompleteness on a passage of Scripture does not merely demonstrate an aspect of our fallenness; it also reveals the nature and character of him who must make us whole.

Although every biblical passage addresses an FCF, no text tells us what we must do to complete ourselves or to make ourselves acceptable to God (by our actions) for then we would not be truly fallen. No passage tells us what we can do or should do to make ourselves holy (as though we could lift ourselves by our own bootstraps to divine approval). The Bible is not a self-help book. The Scriptures present one, consistent, organic message. They tell us how we must seek Christ who alone is our Savior and source of strength to be and do what God requires. To preach these "musts" of what people should be and do, and yet not mention he who enables their accomplishment warps the biblical message. God's redemptive work is integral to every biblical passage's proper exposition. Thomas F. Jones writes,

> True Christian preaching must center on the cross of Jesus Christ. The cross is the central doctrine of the holy scriptures. All other revealed truths either find their fulfillment in the cross or are necessarily founded upon it. Therefore, no doctrine of Scripture may faithfully be set before men unless it is displayed in its relationship to the cross. The one who is called to preach, therefore, must preach Christ because there is no other message from God.[8]

8. Thomas F. Jones, "Preaching the Cross of Christ," unpublished essay presented in 1976–77 homiletics lectures at Covenant Theological Seminary, 1.

These words are not hyperbole, but rather reflect the ethic of the apostle Paul who wrote to the Corinthians, "[A]s I proclaimed to you the testimony about God . . . I resolved to know nothing while I was with you except Jesus Christ and him crucified" (1 Cor. 2:1–2).

Paul's commitment to make his ministry reflect "nothing but Jesus Christ and him crucified" may strike us as not only not feasible, but also as not genuine. After all, we could reason that Paul addressed church worship standards, biblical discipline, stewardship, family relationships, governmental responsibilities, and the history of Israel, and even quoted Greek poets. Does not all this prove the apostle did more than talk about Jesus and his crucifixion? Apparently not to Paul. In Paul's mind every subject, every address, and every epistle had a focus. Everything he did centered on making the cross and its implications evident. Although the apostle addressed many topics and drew on many sources, the panorama only displayed the Redeemer's work in richer detail.

This apostolic ethic reflected the principles of exposition the Savior had himself revealed. Jesus propositionally stated the redemptive focus of all Scripture when he walked with the two disciples on the road to Emmaus. There, "beginning with Moses and all the Prophets, he explained to them what was said in all the Scriptures concerning himself" (Luke 24:27; cf. John 5:39, 46). Jesus said that all the Scriptures were about him, and what he verbally stated on the road to Emmaus, he visually demonstrated on the mount of transfiguration. When the archetypal representatives of the Old Testament law and prophets, Moses and Elijah, appear with Jesus near the culmination of his earthly ministry (Matt. 17) they testify that all preceding Scripture directs the believer's gaze to this One. Thus, the circle of Scripture closes about Jesus.[9] The law and the prophets that precede and the apostolic ministry that follows the work of the cross make Jesus their center. Prophets, apostles, and the Savior all testify that all the Scriptures ultimately focus on the Redeemer. How then can we rightly expound them and not speak of him? Expository preaching is Christ-centered preaching.

EXPOUNDING THE REDEMPTIVE MESSAGE

Assenting to the redemptive focus of Scripture is often far easier than disclosing it. How one gets redemptive truth out of the text and into the

9. John Calvin, *Institutes of the Christian Religion*, 2.6.3.

sermon can stretch both our exegetical and our preaching skills. Commitment to the insights of biblical theology requires a homiletical methodology that grants preachers and listeners access to the redemptive truths each passage contains. The next chapter deals with this methodology in greater detail, but it is appropriate at this juncture to identify some errant paths and to point in the directions that lead to faithful exposition of the text.

TOPICAL AND TEXTUAL APPROACHES

A topical sermon may creatively add redemptive truth to the message since the preacher is not bound to disclose the precise meaning of a specific text in such a message. The much repeated characterization of Spurgeon that "no matter where he began in Scripture, he always took a shortcut to the cross," exemplifies a method that bypasses the direct statements in the text. This is not to say that a topical sermon necessarily leads to unbiblical conclusions or to inappropriate redemptive connections. Such an approach simply progresses without clear biblical authority.

The same authority vacuum exists for textual sermons that include redemptive truth through analogy, illustration, or addition. In an analogy or an illustration the preacher may find material that brings to mind some aspect of the redeeming work of God, which gives entry to a redemptive focus. Unfortunately, the redemptive focus results from the preacher's words rather than from the Word. Including a redemptive focus by adding material that the preacher has not developed from the immediate text also requires homiletical moves without clear biblical warrant. Several years ago I heard a well-known preacher deliver a sermon on the subject of procrastination. In each phase of the message he told us why the Bible requires us to "make the best use of the Lord's time." The message then ended with an altar call. No mention of the redeeming work of Christ, no development of the necessity of the atonement, no scriptural instruction on the need of salvation preceded the call to come forward. In the call itself the preacher explained the essence of the gospel, but this explanation had no origin in the text before us. The redemptive truths were simply added to the message—not developed out of the text.

EXPOSITORY APPROACHES

Expository preaching will not allow the preacher to add material to the text in order to derive a redemptive focus. An expositor develops the message of the sermon out of the material in the text. How, then, can expositors always uncover a redemptive focus that remains fair to the text?

Text Disclosure

A text may make a direct reference to Christ or to an aspect of his messianic work. Specific mention of Jesus or his saving activity may occur in a Gospel account, a messianic psalm, an epistle's explanation, a prophetic utterance. In such cases the task of the expositor is plain: Explain the reference in terms of the redemptive activity it reveals. A preacher who does not see redemptive work in an account of Christ's exorcism of a demon, a scene from the crucifixion, or a prophecy of the Savior's domination over evil cannot properly expound the text. When features of God's plan or power to defeat Satan and restore spiritual wholeness reside on the plain face of the text, a preacher places the passage in proper context simply by presenting its contents accurately. But, though many biblical passages specifically mention Christ's person and work, many more do not. What other alternatives may an expositor pursue to stay Christ-centered?

Type Disclosure

God's redemptive work in Christ may also be evident in Old Testament types. Typology as it relates to Christ's person and work is the study of the correspondences between persons, events, and things that first appear in the Old Testament to preview, prepare, or more fully express New Testament salvation truths.[10] Debates have swirled through the centuries over what constitutes a legitimate type and what merely reflects an interpreter's overactive imagination. Current research into literary methods and structures promises to aid our understanding of biblical typology, but where New Testament writers specifically cite how an Old Testament person or feature prefigures the person and the work of Christ—as with Adam, David, Melchizedek, the Passover, and the temple—the preacher may already safely use typological exposition.

Types allow the preacher to approach appropriate Old Testament passages with a biblically certified preunderstanding of their redemptive connotations. These connotations might not be apparent if the texts were examined without the New Testament information, but, on the basis of this inspired input, explanations of such passages remain

10. David L. Larsen, *The Anatomy of Preaching: Identifying the Issues in Preaching Today* (Grand Rapids: Baker, 1989), 166.

incomplete if the preacher does not take into consideration what the Bible itself indicates are the text's ultimate purposes. Of course, this does not mean that every time an Old Testament passage contains a type, the preacher must identify it as such. However, where typology exists, it may prove to be a profitable avenue for redemptive exposition particularly when other alternatives seem remote.

Context Disclosure

Texts that specifically mention Jesus or reveal him typologically remain few,[11] relative to the thousands of passages where there is no reference to Christ. How can the preacher remain Christ-centered and expository when dealing with these Christ-silent texts? Where neither text nor type discloses the Savior's work the preacher must rely on context to develop the redemptive focus of the message.

By identifying where a passage fits in the overall revelation of God's redemptive plan the preacher relates the text to Christ by performing the standard and necessary exegetical task of establishing its context. Preachers concerned for Christ-centeredness recognize that their exegetical method has necessary implications for their theological conclusions if they are to deal consistently with Scripture.[12] In its context, every passage possesses one or more of four redemptive foci. Every text is predictive of the work of Christ, preparatory for the work of Christ, reflective of the work of Christ, and/or resultant of the work of Christ.

Predictive. Some passages predict God's redemptive work in Christ by making specific mention of his coming person or work. Messianic psalms and passages from prophetic and apocalyptic literature provide many examples. A sermon from Isaiah 40 that offers comfort to God's people without mention of Christ plainly misses the future source of comfort the passage identifies in its context.

Other texts reveal what Christ will do or be without making specific reference to him. Examples include those passages relating to the Old Testament sacraments, the exodus, the purification codes, etc. The predictive nature of these passages may only become apparent in New Testament light, and the expositor assumes an unnecessary and inappro-

11. Of course the number will vary greatly depending on how one defines a type. Cf. the implication of Gerard Von Groningen's discussion of the wide and narrow notions of the messianic concept in *Messianic Revelation in the Old Testament* (Grand Rapids: Baker, 1990), 19–23.

12. Walter C. Kaiser, Jr., *Toward an Exegetical Theology: Biblical Exegesis for Preaching and Teaching* (Grand Rapids: Baker, 1981), 139–40.

priate blindness when attempting to handle such texts without this illumination.

Preparatory. The inspired intention of other texts is to prepare the people of God to understand aspects of the person and/or work of Christ. When Paul writes to the Galatians that the purpose of the Mosaic law was to lead the people of God to Christ, we not only learn why God provided the commands (3:24); we should understand why a sermon that only exhorts believers to not steal is incomplete. The eighth commandment like every other tenet of the law was more than a moral standard. It was also a theological lens picturing the frailty of the soul.

The Old Testament believers were to understand their need of faith in a redeemer based on their own inability to keep any divine imperative perfectly. Exposition on the law that fails to make this point misses the explanation the Bible itself offers for God's commands and advances an implicit legalism.[13] Our people, too, must understand that neither a sophisticated understanding of a commandment nor the most vigorous attempts to heed it will merit grace. Comprehensive explanation of what God requires falls short of adequate exposition if it fails to say why God set the standard.

Not only did God prepare for Christ's work by planting the perception of need in the hearts of the Old Testament saints, he also prepared them (and us) to understand how the need would be satisfied. Paul writes of Abraham, "Now it was not written for his sake alone that it [i.e., righteousness] was imputed to him; but for us also, to whom it shall be imputed, if we believe on him that raised up Jesus our Lord from the dead; who was delivered for our offences and was raised again for our justification" (Rom. 4:23–25, KJV). The apostle's statement alerts us that imbedded in *at least* some of the narratives and proclamations of the Old Testament is the theology of grace. For the sake of the original as well as the present readers, God prepared a Testament establishing what Christ would have to do and how his work would apply to us. Exposition fair to this grand purpose excavates the Old Testament texts to expose implicit spiritual, psychological, or theological preparations that enable us to embrace redemptive truths where no explicit statement about the Redeemer may exist.

Reflective. Our path to implicit aspects of the gospel of grace that are imbedded in every biblical passage does not require tortuous expeditions of logic or theological safaris to remote mountains of higher learning. Where the text neither plainly predicts nor prepares for the

13. Calvin, *Institutes*, 2.7. 1–3, 9.

Redeemer's work the expositor simply should explain how the text reflects key facets of the redemptive message. This is by far the most common tool for constructing Christ-centered messages where there is no direct reference to Jesus' person or work. The preacher who asks these basic questions takes no inappropriate liberties with the text: What does this text reflect of:

God's nature that provides the ministry of Christ;
and/or human nature that requires the ministry of Christ?

Without doing violence to the text these questions actually place every biblical text within a redemptive context.

By asking what the text reflects of God's nature that prompts the work of Christ, the expositor can examine any narrative, genealogy, commandment, proverb, proposition, or parable to see what it reveals of God's justice, holiness, goodness, lovingkindness, faithfulness, provision, or deliverance. These attributes of God's redemptive character emanate from texts that may make no mention of Christ but make sense of Paul's assessment that "[E]verything that was written in the past was written to teach us, so that through endurance and the encouragement of the Scriptures we might have hope" (Rom. 15:4). Because everything that was written is the self-revelation of the God whose mercy endures forever (Ps. 136) and in whom there is no shadow of turning (James 1:17), all Scripture possesses some aspect of our redemptive hope. All Scripture reveals God in either his words or doings. The redemptive truths made evident by these means may appear in seed or in mature form, but Scripture by its revelatory nature bares these divine features for those with eyes to see.

We need to be careful however that the theocentric nature of all Scripture does not lead us to slight the redemptive lessons that God may also be presenting through the human characters in the Bible.[14] The Creator may reveal himself in contradistinction to his creatures. We should not be surprised at the poverty of moral perfection and the absence of consistent heroics in the partriarchs, apostles, and persons who dominate the biblical accounts, because their weaknesses reveal the deep human need in even the most spiritually privileged saints. There are certainly commendable aspects of character in many biblical figures, but Scripture seems to take great care to demonstrate how deeply flawed the

14. Sidney Greidanus, "Redemptive History and Preaching," *Pro Rege* 19, 2 (December 1990): 14.

entire human race is so that all will acknowledge dependence on the Savior for salvation, sanctification, and spiritual victory.[15]

Preachers who ignore the human flaws in biblical characters out of deference for the reputation of past saints or out of a desire to hold a moral example before present believers unconsciously distract attention from the only hope of true faithfulness.[16] By demonstrating his love and his use of those who were shamefully human God, throughout Scripture, reveals himself to be a Savior of sinners (1 Tim. 1:15) and the Deliverer of those who cannot help themselves (Ps. 40:17).[17] Unquestionably God uses persons in Scripture as both positive and negative models of the behaviors and commitments he requires (cf. 1 Cor. 10:5–6), but he never implies that human actions alone can procure or secure our relationship with him.[18] Had God wished to communicate to us that our acceptance hinges on our goodness he would have chosen another sort of person than those he most typically uses in the Bible to reveal the basis for our faith; but then he would have revealed himself to be a different kind of God. Expository preaching faithful to the intent of Scripture neither shies from the flaws in biblical saints nor flaunts their strengths apart from the divine aid that makes God the ultimate champion of every passage.[19]

Aspects of his redemptive character, which God presents in Scripture through his own activity or through human contradistinctions, may be specifically stated in the text or may be implied by the place of the passage in the history of redemption. Yet, whether the preacher gleans these conclusions from the historical sweep of Scripture or from its direct statements, the redemptive themes must be harvested lest preaching sow mere moral commentary and reap pharisaism as its inevitable fruit.[20]

Resultant. Scripture includes many instructions that are often preached as conditions for divine approval. Such preaching errs not by detailing what God requires but by implying or directly stating that

15. Calvin, *Institutes*, 2.6.1.

16. Edmund Clowney, *Preaching and Biblical Theology* (1961; reprint, Grand Rapids: Eerdmans; Phillipsburg, N.J.: Presbyterian and Reformed, n.d.), 80.

17. Kenneth J. Howell, "How to Preach Christ from the Old Testament," *Presbyterian Journal*, 16 January 1985, 8.

18. Greidanus, "Redemptive History," 14.

19. Sidney Greidanus, *Sola Scriptura: Problems and Principles in Preaching Historical Texts* (Toronto: Wedge, 1970), 145; see similar comments by the same author in *The Modern Preacher and the Ancient Text*, 305–6.

20. Howell, "How to Preach Christ," 8–9.

God's favor is a consequence of our obedience rather than proclaiming that obedience itself is a blessing that results from the favor God purchased for us in Christ.[21] Divine love made conditional upon human obedience is mere legalism even if the actions commended have biblical precedent. The only obedience approved by God is that which he himself has sanctified through the work of Christ. For example, my prayers do not win God's blessing. With their mix of human motives and their reflection of my own frail wisdom and resolve, my prayers could never, by their own merit, activate a holy God's blessing. I pray not on the basis of the good intentions I can churn out, but as a result of the position of blessing Jesus provided for me by his death and resurrection. Thus, the writer of Hebrews enjoins, "Therefore, since we have a great high priest who has gone through the heavens, Jesus the Son of God, let us . . . then approach the throne of grace with confidence, so that we may receive mercy and find grace to help us in our time of need" (4:14–16). The blessings of prayer are a result of Christ's ministry, and to promise them without mentioning him is to consign Christian prayer to the hapless hope of prayer wheels and mindless incantations.

To preach matters of faith or practice without rooting their foundation or fruit in what God would do, has done, or will do through the ministry of Christ creates a human-centered (anthropocentric) faith without Christian distinctions. Truly Christian preaching must proclaim, "[T]here is now no condemnation for those who are in Christ Jesus, *because* through Christ Jesus the law of the Spirit of life set me free from the law of sin and death" (Rom. 8:1–2, emphasis added). His work releases us from the guilt and the power of our fallen condition. Now what we do in faith as ones whose pasts he sanctifies, whose resolves he strengthens, and whose futures he secures must be seen as a result of what he has done and is doing through us (Phil. 1:12–13; 1 Cor. 15:16–17, 58; 1 Pet. 4:10–11). Every aspect, action, and hope of the

21. To be sure, some passages *seem* to present a conditional character to God's love for his children. However, in such cases the interpreter almost always will gain a more biblically consistent and spiritually healthy perspective on the passage by properly identifying the subjects of the apparently conditional love as unregenerate persons whose acceptance depends entirely on their works rather than on the finished work of Christ (John 15:1–8; Matt. 12:31); understanding Scripture simply to be stating what is (or will be) the situation of those *characterized* by such behavior rather than by establishing a cause-and-effect relationship between a particular action and God's love — statement of fact v. statement of cause (Matt. 7:1–2; 18:35; Heb. 10:26); or determining the doctrinal idea a biblical writer wants to communicate through a hypothetical situation understood by the writer to be impossible (a common, though debated, approach to Heb. 6:4–6).

Christian life finds its motive, strength, and source in Christ or it is not of Christ. The truths of Scripture that do not anticipate or culminate in Christ's ministry must, at least, be preached as a consequence of his work or we rip them from the context that identifies them with the Christian message.[22]

In recognizing that all Scripture predicts, prepares for, reflects, or results from the ministry of Christ preachers unfold the road map that keeps them traveling to the heart of the Bible no matter where they journey in its pages. Such a road map makes this seemingly quaint advice of Spurgeon to a young preacher now ring with great spiritual wisdom:

> Don't you know, young man, that from every town and every village and every hamlet in England, wherever it may be, there is a road to London? . . . So from every text in Scripture there is a road towards the great metropolis, Christ. And my dear brother, your business is, when you get to a text, to say, now what is the road to Christ? . . . I have never found a text that had not got a road to Christ in it, and if ever I do find one . . . I will go over hedge and ditch but I would get at my Master, for the sermon cannot do any good unless there is a savour of Christ in it.[23]

By identifying the redemptive content, character, or context of the passage one can now heed Spurgeon's instruction so as to discern not merely the savor of Christ in every text but also his pervading presence.

RECOGNIZING NONREDEMPTIVE MESSAGES

Messages that are not Christ-centered (i.e., not redemptively focused) inevitably become human-centered even though the drift most frequently occurs unintentionally among evangelical preachers. These preachers do not willingly exclude Christ's ministry from their own, but by consistently preaching messages on the order of "Five Steps to a Better Marriage," "Improving Your Prayer Life," and "Achieving Holiness through the Power of Resolve," they present godliness as a product of human endeavor. Although they mean well, this focus on actuating divine blessing through human works carries the message, Doing these things will get you right with God and/or your neighbor. No message is

22. Jones, "Preaching the Cross of Christ," 1; Adams, Preaching with Purpose, 152.
23. Charles Haddon Spurgeon, "Christ Precious to Believers," in The New Park Street Pulpit, vol. 5 (London: Passmore and Alabaster, 1860), 140.

more damaging to true faith. By making our efforts the measure and the cause of godliness evangelicals fall victim to the twin assaults of legalism and liberalism, which make our relationship with God dependent on human goodness.

Preachers may protest, "But I assume my people understand they must base their efforts on faith and repentance." Why should we assume our listeners will understand what we rarely say, what the structure of our communication contradicts, and what their own nature denies? Can we not as preachers confess that even we feel more holy when our devotions last longer, when we parent well, when we pastor wisely, or when tears fall during our repentance? While there is certainly nothing wrong with any of these actions, we deny the basis of our own faith when we begin to believe or act as though our actions, by their own merit, win God's favor. Were this true, then instruction to "take hold of those bootstraps and pick yourself up so that God will love and bless you more," would not be wrong. But it is *very* wrong, and faithful preachers must not merely avoid this error the human heart so readily accepts, they must war against it.

THE DEADLY BE'S

Messages that strike at the heart of faith rather than support it often have an identifying theme. They exhort believers to "be" something in order to be blessed. Whether this equation is stated or implied, inadvertent or intentional, overt or subtle, the result is the same: an undermining of biblical faith. Such damage is usually inflicted by preachers striving to be biblical and unaware of the harm they are causing because they see their ideas supported in the narrow slice of Scripture they are expounding. They can point to the five steps for a better marriage in the text. They can support the standards of holiness they advocate with flawless exegesis. What they do not see is the erosion of hope they cause weekly by preaching messages biblical in origin but not biblically complete. We can recognize such messages by the be categories into which they frequently fall.

"Be Like" Messages

"Be like" messages focus the attention of listeners on a particular biblical character while the preacher exhorts them to be like that person or some aspect of his or her personality. In what is often called biographical preaching, pastors urge congregants to be like ... Moses, Gideon, David, Daniel, or Peter in the face of some trial, temptation, or challenge. [24] One difficulty with such preaching is that it typically fails to honor the care that the Bible takes to tarnish almost every patriarch or saint within its pages, so that we do not expect to find, within any fallen form, the model for divine approval. Were we to ask David who we should emulate can we imagine that his answer would be, "me"? If not even the biblical characters themselves would exhort us to model our entire lives after theirs, how can we remain faithful to their message by ignoring their own perception of their place in the biblical record? Neither do we greatly help others by encouraging them to be like Jesus if we do not commensurately remind them that his standards are always beyond them, apart from him.

Preachers today may quickly protest that in encouraging a person to be like some biblical character they are not really encouraging the listener to be entirely like any individual but to imitate the commendable aspects of persons the Bible itself praises. Some passages unquestionably encourage us to use persons in the Bible as examples (e.g., 1 Cor. 11:1; Heb. 11:39). Still, before we preach on such passages we must be sure to identify the source of the character quality that Scripture commends. Since the source of any holy trait we advocate is grace, then not only must we echo the biblical caution, "Where then is boasting?" We must also make it plain to our listeners that grace cannot be self-stimulated nor self-sustained and, since it is of God, it offers no personal merit (cf. Rom. 3:27; 1 Cor. 3:5–23). Simply telling people to imitate godliness in another without reminding them that anything more than outward conformity must come from God forces them either to despair of spiritual transformation or to deny its need.

"Be Good" Messages

Preachers may as readily preach nonredemptive messages when they focus on behaviors rather than biographies. Again, such preachers are unaware of the harm of devoting an entire sermon to telling people to be good or holy. God expects holiness. He commands it. He devotes innumerable passages in Scripture to telling us what to do and what not to do. So, what could possibly be wrong with exhorting people to be good? Again the problem lies not in what the preacher says, but in what the sermon may fail to present.

When the focus of a sermon becomes a moralistic—Don't smoke, or chew, or go with the girls (or guys) who do—then listeners will most

24. Greidanus, *Modern Preacher and the Ancient Text*, 162, and discussion of pp. 161–81.

likely assume that they can secure their relationship with God through proper behaviors. Even when the behaviors advocated are reasonable, biblical, and correct, a sermon that never moves from expounding standards of obedience to explaining the source, the motives, and the results of obedience, places people's hopes in their own actions. In such a situation each succeeding Sunday sermon carries the implicit message, "Since you weren't good enough for God last week, hunker down and try harder this week."

Preaching of this sort sounds biblical because the Bible can be quoted at length to support the exhortations. As it runs its course, however, such preaching destroys all Christian distinctives. Preachers caught in a purely moralistic mode of instruction end up speaking in tautologies: "Be good because it's good to be good, and it's bad to be bad. Boy Scouts are good, Girl Scouts are good, and Christians are good. So be good!"

Ringing clearly through such preaching is the implied promise, "Obey God because he will love you if you do, and get you if you don't." A following week's sermon may be an evangelistic appeal to come to the cross for grace freely offered, but what grace means in this context probably has little to do with biblical teaching. Evangelical preaching that implies we are saved by grace but held by our obedience not only undermines the work of God in sanctification but it ultimately casts doubt on the nature of God, making salvation itself suspect.

"Be Disciplined" Messages

Close kin to "be good" messages are those sermons that exhort believers to improve their relationship with God by more diligent use of the means of grace. Such messages are not merely advocating moral behavior, but are typically encouraging believers more regularly, sincerely, lengthily, or methodically to practice those disciplines that allegedly will lift them to higher planes of divine approval (or, if left undone, will reap divine displeasure). Such preachers intone, "Pray more, read the Bible more, go to church more, or have better quiet times with God." If pressed to explain these exhortations theologically, few would actually say that they believe the practice of these Christian disciplines earns the believer brownie points with God. However, few will argue with the parishioner who says, "I had a terrible day today. This always seems to happen when I get up too late for my quiet time."

The reason so few preachers will object to such a statement is that so many of us live as though our disciplines make us acceptable to God. Because our identity is so tied to observances of our own religious practices we too feel unworthy if we have neglected daily prayer or short-changed our Bible memorization. Something in us also believes that the day would have probably gone better if we had only been more diligent. There are, of course, real consequences of faithlessness. Short-changing sermon preparation tends to result in poorer sermons, and regular neglect of prayer tends to result in a perceived distancing of God's hand. The warping of our faith and our preaching occurs, however, when we believe that our disciplines ward off God's ire or warrant his favor. In such a case the problem is not the biblical discipline we practice but the type of God we perceive. He becomes the ogre in the sky who needs the daily satisfaction of our toil to dispense his favor or restrain his displeasure.

Few preachers intentionally paint this picture of a God so readily vexed, but when they present the Christian disciplines in isolation from the grace that motivates, sanctifies, and secures, such a portrait necessarily emerges. If devotion to our disciplines procures our position or privileges with God, then grace becomes meaningless. And, since no degree of human diligence can compensate our Lord for all we truly owe him, bare insistence on the disciplines only makes those most honest about their merits least sure of their standing. Brownie points count for little in an economy where absolute holiness remains the only acceptable currency.

The Bottom Line

"Be" messages full only of moral instruction imply that we are able to change our fallen condition in our own strength. Such sermons communicate (although usually unintentionally) that we clear the path to grace and that our works earn and/or secure our acceptance with God. However well intended, these sermons present a faith indistinguishable from that of morally conscientious Unitarians, Buddhists, or Hindus. Romper Room may fulfill a legitimate social purpose in teaching children the difference between being a "Do Bee" and a "Don't Bee," but the Bible has more important lessons to teach.

The fundamental biblical truth that differentiates the gospel from a morality lesson is the assertion that our works always remain tainted by our humanity. Of themselves our actions can never earn God's blessing or secure his favor (Isa. 64:6; Luke 17:10). Although there are blessed consequences to heeding divine commands designed for our good, mere conformity to biblical commands offers no heavenly merit.[25] If we had

25. Adams, *Preaching with Purpose*, 146.

to earn grace prior to, or after, our salvation it would not be grace that we gained.

There are many "be" messages in Scripture, but they always reside in a redemptive context. Since we cannot be anything that God would approve apart from his sanctifying power, the source of that grace must permeate any exhortation for biblical behavior. "Be" messages are not wrong in themselves; they are wrong messages by themselves. People cannot do or be what God requires without the work of Christ in, for, and through them. Simply railing at error and hammering at piety may convince others of their inadequacy or callous them into self-sufficiency, but these messages also keep true godliness remote. Thus, instruction in biblical behavior barren of redemptive truth only wounds, and though it is offered as an antidote to sin such preaching either promotes pharisaism or prompts despair. Christ-centered preachers accept neither alternative. They understand that if they wound, they are obligated to heal. The holy standards that pierce the heart whenever people recognize the depth of their divine obligations become salve to their souls when we preach their fulfillment in Christ and their enablement by his Spirit.

Christ-centered preaching does not fail to present the moral imperatives his lordship demands, but neither does it deny him the position of honor in all that his Word says or in all that his creatures do.[26] Challenges to holiness must be accompanied by a Christ-focus or they promote only human-centered, doomed-to-fail religion. When we exhort congregations to stand for God against the assaults of Satan we must never forget the balance of the Pauline imperative: "Finally, brethren, be strong in the Lord and in the power of his might" (Eph. 6:10, KJV). Amidst his most strident "be" message, the apostle remained Christ-focused. Today's preacher has no lesser task.

Faithful expository preaching unfolds every text in the context of its redemptive import. The success of this endeavor can be assessed by a bottom-line question every preacher should ask at the end of each sermon: When my listeners walk out the doors of this sanctuary to perform God's will, with whom do they walk? If they march to battle the world, the flesh, and the devil with only me, myself, and I, then each parades to despair. However, if the sermon has led all persons within

26. James A. De Jong offers an excellent discussion of this balanced approach in "Principled Paraenesis: Reading and Preaching the Ethical Material of New Testament Letters," *Pro Rege* 10, 4 (June 1982): 26–34.

sight of the Savior and they now walk into their world with his aid firmly in their grasp, then hope and victory brighten the horizon. Whether people depart alone or in the Savior's hand will mark the difference between futility and faith, legalism and true obedience, do-goodism and real godliness.

QUESTIONS FOR REVIEW AND DISCUSSION

1. How does clear identification of an FCF prepare the preacher to construct a redemptive message?

2. How can a message advocate biblical behavior and still remain sub-Christian?

3. How does biblical theology act as a fish-eye lens?

4. What are four possible redemptive foci that characterize biblical texts?

5. The most common method of identifying a redemptive message in a text that makes no specific mention of Christ requires the preacher to ask the questions: What does this text reflect of God's nature that _____; or human nature that _____?

6. What are the "deadly be's"? Explain why they are not wrong *in* themselves but become dangerous *by* themselves?

EXERCISES

1. Explain how you could present redemptive messages on three of the following passages:
   Judges 7   Ezra 2
   Proverbs 5   Colossians 3:18–4:1
   James 2:14–26

2. Discuss how the redemptive thrust of all Scripture should affect the way you instruct listeners about matters of Christian obedience.

CONTENTS OF CHAPTER 11

GOAL OF CHAPTER 11

To explain how to construct expository sermons that reflect the redemptive content of every biblical text

11

DEVELOPING REDEMPTIVE SERMONS

METHODS OF REDEMPTIVE EXPOSITION

Once preachers recognize the danger of preaching messages that imply a person is able to achieve self-justification or self-sanctification, they have a natural compulsion to preach Christ-centered messages. Such messages will not simply tell people to hunker down and try harder this week, but will lead them to understand that Christ's work rather than their own supplies the only basis of God's acceptance and that Christ's strength rather than their own provides the only hope of Christian obedience. Such messages are difficult to develop for two reasons: they go against the flow of so much that we are accustomed to hearing in the evangelical church, and they seem to stretch the bounds of precise expository preaching. Understanding how to overcome these difficulties is the next step in developing Christ-centered sermons.

CAPTURE THE REDEMPTIVE FLOW

A rather notorious book chapter entitled "The Menace of the Sunday School" captures the essence of much evangelical teaching. In an effort to promote moral behavior and deter sin the stereotypical Sunday school teacher implores each child to be a good little boy or girl so that Jesus will love them and take care of them. The stereotype is unkind and unfair, but it comes painfully close to characterizing much contemporary preaching, which paints God as the perpetual Santa Claus who is making a list and checking it twice to punish the naughty and reward the nice. I recognize that even as I write these words there are those readers who will wonder what is wrong with that characterization. The wrongness lies in the fact that such teaching becomes a menace to faith because it makes the ministry of Christ irrelevant.

Proper concerns to gain holiness and/or compel purity engender much improper teaching by making human activity the ground of divine favor. Almost every generation has to rediscover grace because our human nature's worldly perspective wars with the notion that we can do nothing to gain God's acceptance. "We cannot by our best works merit pardon for sin . . . nor satisfy for the debt of our former sins."[1] After we have done everything we have been told to do, we are still unworthy servants (Luke 17:10) because our works are mixed with so much weakness and imperfection of motive that they remain defiled before a holy God.[2] Our best works remain as "filthy rags" before God (Isa. 64:6).[3] They are acceptable to him only to the degree that their defilement is covered by Christ and to the extent that they proceed from his Spirit.[4]

While there are blessed consequences to moral behavior and God honors the homage we offer him in the name of his Son, our actions in themselves offer us no opportunity for boasting and no leverage against heaven. Since our ability to do good works is from God and our pardon for wrong is by him, our goodness alone neither merits our blessing nor secures God's acceptance.

As apparent as these truths may seem in theological discussion we too easily divorce them from our homiletical methods. We may regularly encourage people to improve their relationships, polish their ethics, and discipline their habits without mentioning the enabling power of the Spirit or the grace that keeps their best efforts from offending God. One reason for this failure is the fact that Babel is never far from any of us. In our humanity we consistently ignore Scripture and con-

---

1. *Westminster Confession of Faith*, 16.5.

2. Ibid. This classic statement of Christian orthodoxy reads: *We cannot by our best works merit pardon for sin*, or eternal life at the hand of God, by reason of the great disproportion that is between them and the glory to come; and the infinite distance that is between us and God, whom, *by them we can neither profit*, nor satisfy for the debt of our former sins, but *when we have done all we can we have done but our duty, and are unprofitable servants*; and because, *as they are good they proceed from His Spirit; and as they are wrought by us they are defiled*, and mixed with so much weakness and imperfection, that they cannot endure the severity of God's judgement [emphasis added].

3. Note that the words translated "filthy rags" are the Hebrew terms for menstrual cloths. Although our modern sensibilities may dislike the reference, the prophet calls to mind the imagery of even our righteous works being covered with blood — an apt foreshadowing of New Testament truths.

4. *WCF*, 16.3.6.

tinue to practice obedience as a ballistic assault to break down heaven's resistance against blessing us. In doing so we not only ignore the nature of our humanity but we also tar God's character. This is part of the reason why, when the message of grace goes underground in the history of the church, the worst abuses of faith occur. Without a proper perspective on the nature of God, man's efforts toward righteousness inevitably lead to intolerance, futility, and despair.

These historical patterns can repeat themselves in the lives of believers in a local church if the pastor tends to preach mere moral precepts from the Bible. But even preachers who see the fault in such preaching may question what else they can do if they are committed to expository preaching from the whole of Scripture. How, after all, can one preach a redemptive message from a passage of the Bible where there is no mention of Jesus, the cross, the resurrection, the atonement, or other central redemptive themes? In other words, it is not simply our humanity that causes some ministers to preach messages that contain no reference to Christ's work. Expository commitments to remain faithful to the truths of their texts motivate many pastors to neglect preaching grace. Such preachers rightly question, "How can we make a message Christ-centered when the passage contains no Christ-reference?" This legitimate exegetical concern deserves a biblical response.

LAY THE REDEMPTIVE FOUNDATIONS

Identify the Fallen Condition

A good place to begin the construction of a Christ-centered sermon is with a clear statement of a Fallen Condition Focus that the text addresses.[5] This is not simply to bring to the surface a need that will make listeners want to hear the message. Clear identification of a fallen condition automatically locks the preacher into a redemptive approach to the exposition of any biblical passage. Because each text was inspired to complete our hearers in some way, when we specify the text's purpose, the people appear before us with a void or a hole in their spiritual being that God alone can fill. Scripture's intent characterizes us all as beings made of Swiss cheese . . . full of holes human efforts cannot fill. If we turn our listeners to themselves as the source of removing these holes we will preach human-centered messages that have not fully taken into account the nature and degree of human fallenness.

---

5. See earlier discussions of the Fallen Condition Focus in chapters 2 and 10.

The simple step of making sure that we identify (at least in our own minds) the hole that our text addresses will keep us from offering solutions that merely call for human responses. Fallen creatures cannot remedy true fallenness by an act of the will. Legalistic, moralistic, self-help messages become self-evident and self-defeating when the preacher begins with a strong awareness of the full implications of the fallen state in which each hearer exists.

Real exegetical problems begin when the preacher recognizes that human effort will not alleviate a fallen condition and the text seems to offer no Christocentric solution. Many passages seem only to offer moral instruction (e.g., do not lie, do not steal), spiritual-discipline exhortation (e.g., pray more, show more concern for others, be more faithful) or character examples (e.g., the faith of Moses, the courage of Joshua; and, conversely, the deceitfulness of Saul, the rashness of Peter). How does the preacher proceed to redemptive truths when the text seems to present none?

SPECIFY THE CHRIST-FOCUS

Two answers need to be rejected at the outset. First is the denial of the continuing validity of all instructions, disciplines, or examples provided in passages that apparently offer no redemptive themes. Second is the attempt to make Jesus appear in every biblical account, forcing a reference to the incarnate Christ into the exegesis where no textual material justifies such (e.g., seeing aspects of Christ's triumphal entry in the account of Balaam's donkey because both "prophets" rode the same kind of animal). Both of these errors arise from an errant view of Scripture that does not recognize the organic nature of the entire biblical record.[6] Proper exposition does not discover its Christ-focus by disposing of any passage or by imposing Jesus on the text, but by discerning the place and role of the text in the entire revelation of God's redemptive plan.

Following the creation passages at the outset of Genesis, all of Scripture is a record of God's dealings with a corrupted world and its creatures. But the record does not merely recite historical facts. It reveals an ongoing drama whereby God systematically, personally, and progressively discloses the necessity and detail of his plan to use the Son

---

6. Sidney Greidanus, *Sola Scriptura: Problems and Principles in Preaching Historical Texts* (Toronto: Wedge, 1970), 135; Geerhardus Vos, "The Idea of Biblical Theology" from Vos's inaugural address upon assuming the new chair of biblical theology at Princeton Seminary (n.d., 1895 probable), 16.

to redeem and restore creation.[7] Sidney Greidanus states the implications this organic view of Scripture holds for proper exposition of any text:

> The unity of redemptive history implies the *Christocentric* nature of every historical text. Redemptive history is the history of Christ. He stands at its center, but no less at its beginning and end. . . . Scripture discloses the theme, the scopus of its historiography right at the beginning. "Gen. 3: 15," Van't Veer says, "places all subsequent events in the light of the tremendous battle between Christ coming into the world and Satan the ruler of this world, and it places all events in the light of the complete victory which the Seed of the woman shall attain. In view of this, it is imperative that not one single person be isolated from this history and set apart from this great battle. The place of both opponents and 'co-workers' can only be determined Christologically. Only in so far as they received their place and task in the development of *this* history do they appear in the historiography of Scripture. From this point of view the facts are selected and recorded."[8]

A passage retains its Christocentric focus, and a sermon becomes Christ-centered, not because the preacher finds a slick way of wedging a reference to Jesus' person or work into the message but because the sermon identifies a function this particular text legitimately serves in the great drama of the Son's crusade against the serpent.

This mature view of Christ-centered preaching warns preachers not to believe they have properly expounded a text simply because they have identified something in it that reminds them of an event in Jesus' life and ministry. When the preacher uses a geographical reference to a well in the Old Testament to introduce a discussion of Jesus' conversation with the woman at the well, no real explanation of the original passage's place and meaning in redemptive history has occurred. The preacher has only engaged in a bit of word play. The same is true when the preacher leapfrogs to the New Testament from some feature of Moses' law or some event in Israel's kingship simply because some detail in the account seems similar to something Christ did (see fig. 11.1).

When preachers interpret Rahab's red cloth, the wood on Isaac's back, the saddle on Rachel's camel, and the spices in Solomon's house (to name only a few possibilities) as representing some aspect of Christ's

---

7. Geerhardus Vos, *Biblical Theology* (1948; reprint, Grand Rapids: Eerdmans, 1975), 5–7.

8. Greidanus, *Sola Scriptura*, 135.

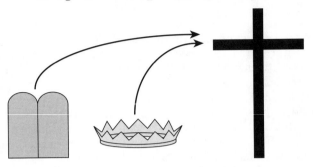

FIGURE 11.1

Imaginative Leapfrogging to Christ

The preacher says, "This passage *reminds* me of. . . ."

ministry, their conclusions may sound biblical. However, if Scripture does not confirm this interpretation such preachers actually only relate what their minds suggest rather than what the text means. To the extent that what is in the preacher's mind actually reflects a truth found elsewhere in Scripture no harm may occur, but the minister's imagination is a poor place to discern what a biblical passage means. After all, some preachers may say that Rahab's red cloth stands for the blood of Christ, but others may conclude that the scarlet represents sin. These nearly opposite interpretations may relate to biblical truths found elsewhere in Scripture, but neither interpretation relates a definite meaning of the immediate text.

Similar interpretive errors occur when pastors believe that they must find Christ hiding behind every bush on the plain of Old Testament history. Feeling the obligation to discern Jesus in such passages, these preachers search out the implications of tiny "messianic lights" in precrucifixion texts in order to make some reference to the atonement.[9] The water in a lake becomes the water that flowed from Christ's pierced side, the rocks in the desert translate into the solid hope we have in his solitary death, trees metamorphize into crosses, oil transubstantiates into blood, and mountains conform to the contours of Calvary.

The problem with each of these nonexpository explanations is not that they ignore Christ, but that they connote that he is adequately represented only when the preacher makes some direct reference to Jesus' incarnation or atoning work—regardless of the text's statements or pur-

9. Ibid., 143.

pose. Since Scripture as a whole is God's revelation of his redeeming activity in Jesus Christ,[10] the preacher needs only to demonstrate where and how a particular text functions in the overall redemptive plan in order to retain its Christocentric focus. The Word of Christ and the Word about Christ operate in every Scripture passage as God unfolds the mystery of his grand design.[11] Writes Greidanus,

> This conception of Christ as the eternal Logos actively at work throughout history removes the props from the traditional insistence that every sermon must somehow point to Christ Incarnate in order to be Christocentric. It bursts the confining mold which has caused so many aberrations throughout the history of preaching; it creates more room for the text itself to speak. The preacher is no longer required "to land with an acrobatic leap at Golgotha" in order to *make* the text and the sermon Christocentric, for Christ is already present at that point of redemptive history which the text relates.[12]

Expository preaching need not mention Golgotha, Bethlehem, or the Mount of Olives to remain Christ-centered. So long as the preacher uses a text's statements or context to expose the theological truths or historical facts that demonstrate the relation of the passage to the overall war between the Seed of the woman and Satan, Christ assumes his rightful place as the focus of the message.

Discern the Redemptive Purpose

As unlikely as it seems, this perspective on the overall purpose of Scripture means that preachers may not specifically mention Jesus in some sermons and yet these messages can remain Christ-centered. So long as the preacher explains ways in which God uses a text to reveal his own plan, purposes, and/or reasons for redemption, the sermon leads listeners away from human-centered religiosity. By concentrating on what God is accomplishing with the record of every event, the account of every character, and the principles in every instruction, the preacher keeps the message from degenerating into mere human hero worship. God is the hero of every text. This does not mean that biblical characters have no exemplary qualities for us to emulate (e.g., Rom. 15:4; Phil.

---

10. Vos, "Inaugural," 11, 14.
11. The words are from Edmund Clowney's *The Unfolding Mystery: Discovering Christ in the Old Testament* (Phillipsburg, N.J.: Presbyterian and Reformed, 1988).
12. Greidanus, *Sola Scriptura*, 145.

3:17), but we must understand that when these positive qualities appear—in their lives or ours—grace is the cause (Rom. 11:36).

> [T]he slighting of biblical characters cannot be justified. . . . The first thing to notice about biblical characters is that they are incorporated into the biblical text not for their own sake but to show what God is doing through, in and for them—to show how God advances his kingdom through the efforts of human beings and sometimes in spite of them.[13]

When preachers place the text within the context of what God is revealing about his own nature that provides redemption, or about the nature of man that requires redemption, self-reliance vanishes.

Theocentric preaching inevitably becomes Christocentric not because the sermon always cites the name of Jesus or draws to mind some event from his earthly ministry, but because it demonstrates the reality of the human predicament that requires divine solution.[14] Theocentric preaching is Christ-centered preaching. Focus on God's redemptive activity sets the stage for Christ's work, alerts the human heart to its necessity, and/or exposes the divine nature. When we see God at work, Christ's ministry inevitably comes into view (John 1:1–3; 14:7–10; Col. 1:15–20; Heb. 1:1–3).[15] A sermon remains expository and Christ-centered not because it leapfrogs to Golgotha, but because it locates the intent of the passage within the scope of God's redemptive work (see fig. 11.2). Thus, the sermon's purpose remains faithful to the text's original aim of preparing the people of God to understand his redemptive activity; predicting it, reflecting its need, and/or detailing the results of Christ's work in our lives.[16]

With this perspective of God's redemptive plan (and Scripture's organic presentation of it) each person, precept, and event in the biblical record assumes its proper role in faithful exposition.[17] Preachers will not present biblical patriarchs whose conduct was often far from exem-

---

13. Sidney Greidanus, "Redemptive History and Preaching," *Pro Rege* 19, 2 (December 1990): 14.

14. Ibid., 12–13; see also Greidanus, *Sola Scriptura*, 143–44.

15. John Calvin, *Institutes of the Christian Religion*, 2.6.4.

16. See further discussion of these four uses of biblical texts in chapter 10.

17. Jonathan Edwards in his remarkable "Letter to the Trustees of the College of New Jersey" proposes such an approach to all of Scripture "considering the affair of Christian Theology, as the whole of it, in each part, stands in reference to the great work of redemption by Jesus Christ" as the "summum and ultimum of all divine operations and decrees." See Clarence H. Faust and Thomas H. Johnson, eds., *Jonathan Edwards* (New York: American Book, 1935), 411–12.

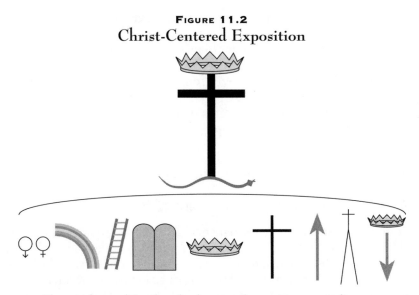

FIGURE 11.2

Christ-Centered Exposition

The preacher explains the role of any epoch, event, person, and passage within the divine crusade of redemption; i.e., the sovereign victory of the Seed of the woman over Satan.

plary as perfect models for listeners to emulate. The ancient saints will be presented as God intended—hopelessly fallen creatures whose faith and favor are entirely the product of God's mercy.[18]

Sermons on the law will not merely detail moral precepts, but will show the contemporary people of God what they were intended to teach: the necessity of divine dependence as well as holy conduct (Gal. 3:24).[19] We will not inadvertently teach that God's acceptance depends on our righteousness when we consistently demonstrate that the law itself pointed to the need of a greater Provision of righteousness than human accomplishment.

Messages on the times of the judges and kings will shed the veils we so often put over these giants of faith to shield their reputations from their too frequent flaws. We will then more freely herald all dimensions of the biblical leaders' characters because we understand that their weaknesses underscore a righteousness which was from God.

18. Edmund Clowney, *Preaching and Biblical Theology* (Grand Rapids: Eerdmans, 1961; Phillipsburg, N.J.: Presbyterian and Reformed, n.d.), 80. See also Clowney's "Preaching Christ from All the Scriptures" in *The Preacher and Preaching*, ed. Samuel T. Logan (Phillipsburg, N.J.: Presbyterian and Reformed, 1986), 163–91.

19. Calvin, *Institutes*, 2.7; 10.3–5.

Even New Testament instruction on marriage, stewardship, church relationships, and worship practices will cease to function as an aberrant reinstitution of Old Testament law qualifying God's people for his approval. All biblical standards (whether presented in the form of written precept or human example) will function as God intends—guiding God's people into the paths that reflect his glory and promoting their good as the natural outflow of gratitude for what he has done in their behalf and what he alone can further do.

MEASURES OF REDEMPTIVE EXPOSITION

A PROCEDURE FOR REDEMPTIVE EXPOSITION

From this broad perspective that encompasses the expanse of the biblical record the preacher needs more precise tools to assess faithfully the redemptive truths of particular passages preached on a weekly basis. The three-step expository procedure described below is one such tool.[20] It not only serves as a means of tracing how the redemptive truths that course through biblical texts should appear in our sermons, but also provides a measure of assurance that the preacher will disclose a text's ultimate purposes.

A Procedure for Christ-Centered Exposition

I. Identify the redemptive principles evident in the text.
   A. Revealed aspects of the divine nature that provides redemption
   B. Revealed aspects of human nature that requires redemption
II. Determine what application these redemptive principles were to have in the lives of believers in the biblical context.
III. In the light of common human characteristics or conditions contemporary believers share with the biblical believers, apply the redemptive principles to contemporary lives.

This procedure obviously echoes the process by which the preacher determines the FCF of a message with two substantive differences.

---

20. Cf. Kenneth J. Howell, "How to Preach Christ from the Old Testament," *Presbyterian Journal*, 16 January 1985, 10. Note this procedure moves beyond what is commonly called the redemptive-historical method to a redemptive-doctrinal approach that expounds in light of redemptive truth as well as redemptive context.

First, this procedure is not merely directed toward determining why our listeners need to hear the message. Rather it makes the aim of the message the determination of what God expects listeners to do, believe, or accept as a result of his dealing with this need. The second difference is a product of the first. As a result of this redemptive focus the aim or emphasis of the message shifts from a human orientation to a concentration on what God has done, is doing, or will do.[21]

Although the FCF reveals why people need to listen and why God chooses to act, the redemptive exposition keeps the solution divine and precludes human presumption. Such exposition returns preaching to its foundational function of transformation. Men and women are still called to devotion but preachers issue the summons on the basis of God's actions and by his power. We never inadvertently teach others to seek answers without his truth, perform his bidding without his strength, or reap his blessing without the acceptance he alone provides. Faithful preaching is the practice of pointing others to a Provision beyond self so that they are able to do what God requires and what the regenerate heart desires. The doxological focus of redemptive exposition keeps this process intact.

MODELS OF REDEMPTIVE EXPOSITION

What does redemptive exposition look like? How do these principles actually shape the structure of an expository message? Standard cues rather than a standard form tend to designate a sermon as Christ-centered. At times the preacher may begin the message by underscoring the redemptive truths that underlie the instruction in the passage. On other occasions the preacher may build the redemptive case as the instructions unfold, or alternatively provide all the instructions and then in the sermon's waning moments point out the redemptive truths that will enable, or properly motivate, faithful service. I am wary of the last alternative because it may simply be a human-centered message with a Christ-mentioned ending, but I recognize that an ironic twist in a message can make a powerful theocentric thrust—if the preacher does not practice this method too often.

Redemptive preaching does not require the preacher to make the Christ connection at some correct place in the message. If preachers expound messages with any arbitrary standard of where or how much

21. Jay Adams, *Preaching with Purpose* (Grand Rapids: Baker, 1982), 152. Cf. John Piper, *The Supremacy of God in Preaching* (Grand Rapids: Baker, 1990), 17–46.

FIGURE 11.3
"Three Points Plus" Problems

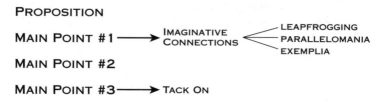

The Christ-centered aspects of the message do not arise from the natural exposition of the text when arbitrary stadards determine when to mention "the cross."

Christ needs mentioning, they will inevitably fall into the errors of making imaginative rather than expository references to Christ or of tacking on some mention of Calvary. An expository sermon based on redemptive truths is not "Three Points Plus the Cross," which only causes messianic leapfrogging, parallel word play, and similar event- or personal-example comparisons (fig. 11.3).

A truly expository Christ-centered sermon is not so concerned with the location of the cross in the message as with the necessity that each listener walk away from the sermon with a keen awareness of the personal import of God's redeeming work (see fig. 11.4). When the listeners depart do they focus on themselves or on their Redeemer? Do they look to their own works as their source of hope or to God's work in their behalf? Has the message as a whole directed people to a fuller under-

FIGURE 11.4
Grace-directed Preaching

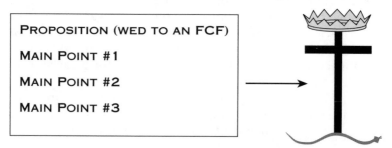

The message as a whole leads listeners to understand the place of the text and/or the role of its features in God's redemptive plan.

standing of grace? Answers to these questions rather than an imposed homiletical structure will determine whether the message has expounded the counsel of God in the light of his historical, theological, and personal purposes. Whether the preacher develops the redemptive theme in the first main point, the second main point, the conclusion, the introduction, or some combination of these the Christ-centeredness will be determined by the development of the text and the purpose of the message rather than by some artificial standard. Artificiality will be replaced by a genuine exposition of what the text means within the scope of the biblical record and according to the situation of a specific people.

MESSAGES OF REDEMPTIVE EXPOSITION

As our preaching efforts mature into explaining how a text functions as well as what it says—expounding its aim as well as its words—we naturally desire confirmation that our messages reflect Scripture's intent. Surely a method of exposition that centers on God's redemptive work will have characteristics that distinguish it from preaching that tends toward legalism or license, which arrogates works or cheapens grace. Such indicators emerge when we identify the types of messages that typify Christ-centered sermons. Because Christ-centered preachers consistently extract redemptive truths from all of Scripture, their messages highlight the central themes of the atonement as they relate to all the issues of faith and life. These themes, the messages they spawn, and the subjects they address typically fall into four categories.

Grace despite our sin. This theme of God's faithfulness despite human failure, weakness, and rebellion often arises when pastors must deal with passages that detail the waywardness or frailties of the covenant people. Messages on our adoption as children of God and the assurance this relationship brings despite our sin typically result. Topics preachers will consider in these messages include the privilege believers have of resting in God's love (the Sabbath principles of Scripture) and our confidence in God's love (the glory of human sonship).

Grace cancelling the guilt of sin. Messages on justification and forgiveness flow from the theme of cleansing grace. Topics of such messages quickly move to the need for confession, repentance, and confidence in the sufficiency of Christ's sacrifice.

Grace defeating the power of sin. Messages of sanctification and spiritual enablement reverberate from the Bible's proclamation of the spiritual efficacy of the ever-present Christ. With this message of overcoming grace preachers equip the saints to do battle with the world, the flesh, and the devil by concentrating on the victory available in the power of the Spirit and the truth of his Word.

Grace compelling holiness. When believers see that the whole of Scripture—the entire sweep of biblical revelation—is a stage for the portrayal of grace, their hearts respond in awe and humility. Such responses ground messages of worship and obedience in their proper motivations and make the application of all biblical truth the fruit of thanksgiving, praise, gratitude, and loving service. Christ-centered preaching does not abolish the normative standards of Christian conduct, but rather locates their source in the compelling power of grace. The rules of obedience do not change, the reasons do.

MARKS OF REDEMPTIVE EXPOSITION

How we motivate others to be holy (the chief concern of the last theme of the previous section) is often the telltale sign of Christ-centered preaching. Regard for the necessity of obedience has historically caused much criticism of grace-centered preaching because it is difficult to remove obedience as a qualification for divine favor without seeming to remove biblical standards of conduct as imperative for Christians.[22] Consistent preaching of the necessity and proper motivation for holiness is one of the most difficult tasks that preachers face in every generation.[23] Successful (i.e., biblical) Christ-centered preaching bears the marks of grace-motivated obedience—insisting on the contemporary application of biblical mandates while grounding the source of Christian behavior in appreciation of God's provision.

UNDERSTANDING THE EFFECTS OF GRACE

Historic Understanding

Historians tell us that one of the amazing features of the life of John Bunyan was his refusal to let prison deter him from his pursuit of ministry. The author of *Pilgrim's Progress* wrote many of his most influential words while incarcerated. In fact prison helped strengthen and galvanize much of his thought. Bunyan's theology took more concrete

---

22. Consider also the similarity of current "lordship salvation" debates with the Marrow Controversy in Reformation history. Cf. Greidanus, *Sola Scriptura*, 131–33.
23. Cf. Rom. 6:1; Gal. 3:21–22; 5:13–26.

form when, though facing death, he debated with fellow religious prisoners whether the assurance of God's love promoted holiness or license. Through his own experience, Bunyan recognized that love was a far more powerful motivator than fear.[24] He maintained his convictions and his testimony despite persecution, not so much because he feared greater harm from his God, but because he had such an overwhelming love for his Savior. Had intimidation alone motivated him, Bunyan would have quickly yielded to the more immediate threats of his persecutors with the intention of appeasing God later. Love for the Savior kept the suffering pilgrim faithful.

Bunyan's realization reflects the understanding that characterizes the applications of Christ-centered preaching. Since every instruction of Scripture functions within the frame of God's explanation and provision of his redemptive work, we must use grace to urge others to implement what we expound. Grace does not merely aid righteous conduct, it aids in the apprehension of the unerring love of God that makes human righteousness possible. If obedience is merely a defensive posture our listeners assume to avert divine wrath or to curry divine favor, then human holiness is but a euphemism for selfishness. Self-protection and self-promotion are sad substitutes for "glorifying God and enjoying him forever," but the former alternatives are the definite products of lives devoted to God out of servile dread and slavish fear.[25]

If logic and Scripture both make it apparent that selfish fear is a greater menace to holiness than assurance of love,[26] why does the

---

24. I use the word fear in this chapter not in the biblical sense of reverential awe but according to the more common usage of a response to intimidation or threat of personal harm.

25. *Westminster Shorter Catechism*, question 1; *Heidelberg Catechism*, question 1; cf. *WCF*, 20.1, 6, 7:

> The liberty which Christ hath purchased for believers under the Gospel consists in their freedom from the guilt of sin, the condemning wrath of God, the curse of the moral law; and in their being delivered from ... the dominion of sin; as also, in their free access to God and their yielding obedience to him, *not out of a slavish fear, but a child-like love and willing mind.*
>
> ... [A] man's doing good, and refraining from evil, because the law encourageth to the one and deterreth from the other, is no evidence of his being under the law; and not under grace.
>
> Neither are the forementioned uses of the law contrary to the grace of the Gospel, but do sweetly comply with it; the Spirit of Christ subduing *and enabling* the will of man to do that *freely, and cheerfully*, which the will of God, revealed in the law, requireth to be done (emphasis added).

26. Cf. Rom. 8:15; 2 Cor. 5:14; 1 John 4:18.

debate persist over whether threat of guilt or promise of grace better stimulates holiness? The simple answer is that preachers feel the need for a corrective. We wonder how we can compel others, or even ourselves, to pursue righteousness if we do not threaten rejection, promise retribution, or impose guilt. We recognize that each of these approaches is powerfully suasive, and in the secrecy of our hearts question, What reason will God's people have to obey if all we do is keep assuring them of his love?

Personal Understanding

Ultimately the issue all preachers must confront is what they believe to be the relationship between people's conduct and God's acceptance. Are we holy for God's acceptance, or are we holy because of God's acceptance? I did not understand the importance of that question until after several years of pastoring. Despite my good intentions, an honest assessment of my congregation revealed many who seemed far from the Lord. Their spiritual emptiness was all the more discouraging because the church was almost two centuries old. Many of the families had attended for generations. Some knew their Bibles far better than I knew mine and after being in church so long almost everyone knew well how Christians should act. Most conscientiously observed a community code of conduct—they were faithful to their spouses, did not rob banks, drink to excess, or swear in polite company. Outward Christian conduct ruled.

Attitudes, however, were not so exemplary. I could not understand how people who were so knowledgeable about God could be so bitter, so guilt-ridden, so often depressed, so cold to each other, and so intolerant of the faults of newer Christians. Their words and external behaviors professed loyalty to Christ, but love, joy, peace, patience, and long-suffering were in scant supply. I used to get so angry at those people for their lack of heart response to the Word they said they loved. Then, I began to realize that the problem was not so much them as it was me, and others like me.

I was using guilt and fear to motivate people to obey God. What I had to confess, however, was that though my messages often secured changed behavior my ministry seemed to produce little spiritual maturity. For instance, I addressed couples whose marriages were coming apart because they were not honoring the Word of God in their relationships with each other. I told them that if they changed their behaviors, God would bless them, but that as long as they continued in their disobedience they could not expect his love. I saw changed behavior, but few signs of real spiritual growth. Instead, a year or two later these same people were locked into depression, were pursuing other addictive behaviors, or had grown spiritually disinterested.

Finally the Lord opened my eyes to my error. I was telling people that the way to get rid of their guilt before God and to assure his blessing was by behaving differently. But, what did this imply? If people expect behavior change to rid them of their guilt, who are they trusting to take their guilt away? Themselves!

I was forcing people to question, "What action of mine will make me right with God?" No wonder their faith did not mature. Their faith was in what they could do to fix their own situations with God. I was encouraging people to look to themselves rather than to the cross as the place for erasing guilt and finding God's favor. Without my conscious intent—and contrary to theology in my head—I was driving the wedge of human works between my hearers and God. The people who listened to me, though they may have changed some aspect of their lives to get my approval and secure God's affection, were actually farther away from understanding God than when I had begun to minister to them.

Works righteousness had jumped into my preaching without my even knowing it. I was implying (if not directly stating) that we become acceptable to God by being good enough. No wonder the people were so hard and bitter and cold. I was teaching them that if they just offered God more filthy rags, he would favor them more, or smile more, or love them more.

What a cruel God I painted for them. What a merciful God I had denied them by teaching them that God's love was dependent on their goodness. I was the one who made them intolerant of less mature believers. Because they listened to me, they gauged their holiness by their works, and then what better way was there to confirm their own righteousness than by finding greater faults in others? The people in my church had bad attitudes and had lost interest in matters of faith, and I was as culpable as they.

Formula Understanding

If behavior change erases guilt or overcomes its effects by satisfying the holy requirements of God then the Pharisees were right (i.e., God loves and favors those who are more righteous than others). We can represent such an understanding of faith with this simple formula:

$$\text{Guilt} \neq> \text{cancelled by behavior change} = \text{legalism/moralism}$$

Evangelical preachers have no desire for this formula to represent their messages, but this is the message our hearers receive when believers are not assured that God's provision is the sole cause of divine acceptance and the proper impetus of human righteousness.

Only when believers act with a conscious awareness that God accepts them and their works solely as a result of the work of his Son does their righteousness have the potential to glorify God rather than to serve self. Such an awareness makes righteousness and its motive a thanksgiving and praise response to the work that God has done. Guilt drives us to the cross but gratitude propels us from it into lives of true obedience. Conformity to God's will thus becomes a form of praise rather than an attempted bribe. Selfish performance and grovelling ineffectiveness dissolve into the reality of the divine embrace that inspires confidence in God's love, instills desire to return to his ways, and empowers the sacrificial pursuit of his purposes. True repentance results. Without the perceived need to compensate God for our guilt, confession can be expressed with the godly sorrow that makes his glory, rather than personal gain, the focus of our words and actions.

Guilt $\neq>$ cancelled by $\dagger$ $\longrightarrow$ yields grateful behavior = repentance

This formula of faithfulness challenges preachers to recognize the danger of sermons that do not contextualize their instructions in redemptive truth. Where understanding of God's full provision and unfailing love does not precede right conduct, spiritual damage occurs.

EMPLOYING THE MEANS OF GRACE

Commanding people to do what is right without explaining why or how inevitably hurts them because they are left to consider their works and abilities as the cause of God's acceptance or affection. As a result, much well-intended instruction, dispensed with the motive of helping people, hurts them. If all they hear are the shoulds, believers either will face despair or feign self-righteousness. Healing of the soul begins with the message that God graciously accepts our works offered to him in gratitude for our salvation, but our acceptance and our sanctification are never a result of anything but grace.[27] Christians cannot gain or earn any more of God's love since grace has already granted and secured all the

---

27. Charles Hodge, *Systematic Theology*, vol. 3 (New York: Scribner, Armstrong and Co., 1875), 231–32; Louis Berkhof, *Systematic Theology*, rev. ed. (Grand Rapids: Eerdmans, 1953), 532, 535; cf. Anthony Hoekema, *Christian Spirituality: Five Views on Sanctification*, ed. Donald Alexander (Downers Grove, Ill.: InterVarsity, 1988).

love there is to have. We may experience more of God's blessings and sense more of his fellowship as a result of our obedience but do not risk God's rejection because of our failures.

Our weaknesses do not jeopardize God's love. This does not mean that sin has no consequence in the life of believers. We may experience divine discipline as a result of our sin or simply face the repercussions of ignoring standards that God gives for our good. Nevertheless, fatherly discipline, even when harsh, expresses love for a child and concern for his welfare (Heb. 12:5–11). As a child is healthier emotionally when there is never any question about his parent's unconditional love, God's children are spiritually healthier when they are taught there is no question about their heavenly Father's unconditional love.

> We are saved by grace alone.
> We are sanctified by grace alone.
> We are secured by grace alone.

Preaching that is faithful to these biblical truths never prods believers toward holiness with the threat of divine rejection, for to do so would be to make works rather than grace the foundation of our relationship with God. This does not deny preachers the right and the responsibility to challenge the impenitent with the necessity of change that will avert discipline and evidence true faith. We simply do not use the denial of love as leverage for holiness. The former cannot produce the latter.

The Motives of Change

Nowhere are the effects of Christ-centered exposition more apparent than when preachers apply biblical truths to everyday life.[28] Motives for obedience that allow grace to replace divine threat or personal gain include:

A response to the love shown us by Christ. Concentration on the love God lavished upon us makes righteousness a gift we offer God in grateful devotion for his full provision for our sin. Without this appreciative response, obedience cannot maintain its doxological intent or grant proper vent to the guilt we feel as a consequence of our sin.

When love motivates Christian obedience the guilt we feel in spiritual failure is the remorse that we have forsaken the One who loves us enough to sacrifice his own Son in our behalf. This "good guilt" is not

---

28. Recall that application in expository preaching must answer four questions: what, where, why, and how (see chapter 8).

the selfish shame of rejection nor the self-oriented payment of an emoted penance. It is a reaffirmation of our value and standing before God, which produces renewed zeal for his purposes, a deeper sense of the measure of his grace, and a greater longing to glorify him with our lives. These affirmations do not expose a sappy unwillingness to preach with authority but rather reverberate from the solid conviction that love—not fear, or hate, or self—is life's most powerful force. That is why the apostle Paul, who identified love as his greatest compulsion in ministry (2 Cor. 5:14), urges us to offer ourselves as living sacrifices "in view of God's mercy" (Rom. 12:1), and proclaims grace as the power that teaches us to deny ourselves and live for God (Titus 2:11).

An avoidance of the consequences of sin revealed by a loving God. If God did not love he would not warn. Preachers should not interpret the consequences of sin that Scripture reveals to be indications that God's love is conditional. This instruction does not mean that we should avoid mention of sin's biblical consequences. Instead we should present biblical identification of sin's consequences as the gracious revelation of a loving Father who wishes for us neither to experience the consequences of our own rebellion nor face the discipline he must dispense in order to turn us from even more serious harm. Such preaching never characterizes the wrath of God toward his people as punitive damage, but enables listeners to understand saving discipline.

A love for others loved by God. When an appreciation for God's love despite our sin, motivates our obedience to him, then the need to establish our righteous standing by comparisons with others dies. Love for God overflows into the desire to please him by caring for others he loves. Pride and judgmentalism vanish. Christians unite with the needy precisely because grace assures them they can "afford" to do so. Only Christ-centered preaching will produce such fruitful confidence.

Because many view their obedience as the dues that maintain their membership in the kingdom, preaching grace as the motive of Christian conduct has risks. We must realize that many preachers think the goal of good preaching is to bludgeon people with their guilt, just as many parishioners believe it is their duty to take it. Both parties are habituated to *feel* relief only after one has felt bad enough long enough to *gain* grace. For such people guilty feelings and laborious obedience are penance they do not wish to be denied. Even the shallowest apprehension of the true holiness of God and the real heinousness of sin will soon convince of the futility of such gestures and will either callous or break the one expressing them. True holiness flows not merely from an awareness of the malignancy of sin, but from a deep apprehension of the ability of grace alone to cure it.[29]

The Means of Change

Applications of biblical truth are not complete until the preacher explains how to plug in to the power that God provides.[30] Since Christ-centered preaching teaches people that they cannot be the instrument of their spiritual healing, preachers must also explain how to obey God. Just as the shoulds of Christian conduct can lead one astray if not practiced for the right reasons, right motives without the right means of obedience will profit little.[31]

Preachers object that many texts indicating what people should do make no reference to how. For example, the Ten Commandments seem only to list God's imperatives, but the basic rubrics of Christ-centered exposition come to the rescue in such situations. By virtue of their inclusion in the redemptive record, all texts participate in the message of God's adequacy and human inadequacy.[32] Thus, even if a passage makes no direct reference to the typical means by which believers seek God's enablement (e.g., prayer for his work, trusting in his providence, acting on his truths, and seeking his Spirit), aspects of the text or its context point us away from self-solutions and toward seeking God's provision.

By exposing a passage's perspective on human inadequacy, the preacher naturally leads listeners to confession of the need of God. This most basic of Christian postures is the essential path to divine power. In our humility is the how of obedience, for in whatever way we

29. Cf. Richard Lovelace, *Dynamics of Spiritual Life* (Downers Grove, Ill.: InterVarsity, 1979): "Only a fraction of the present body of professing Christians are solidly appropriating the justifying work of Christ in their lives. Many have so light an apprehension of God's holiness and of the extent and guilt for their sin that consciously they see little need for justification, although below the surface of their lives they are deeply guilt-ridden and insecure. Many others have a theoretical commitment of this doctrine, but in their day to day existence they rely on their sanctification for justification drawing their assurance of acceptance with God from their sincerity, their past experience of conversion, their recent religious performance or the relative infrequency of their conscious, willful disobedience. Few know enough to start each day with a thoroughgoing stand on Luther's platform: you are accepted, looking outward in faith and claiming the wholly alien righteousness of Christ as the only ground for acceptance, relaxing in the quality of trust which will produce increasing sanctification as faith is active in love and gratitude" (101).

30. Ian Pitt-Watson, *A Primer for Preachers* (Grand Rapids: Baker, 1986), 18–19.

31. C. John Miller, *Outgrowing the Ingrown Church* (Grand Rapids: Zondervan, 1986), 90.

32. Pitt-Watson, *A Primer for Preachers*, 22.

acknowledge our weakness, we become conduits for the strength God provides to perform his purposes (2 Cor. 12:9). By contrast, when our messages merely encourage human efforts, we do not merely deny personal inadequacy, we deprive God of the homage he deserves as the result of whatever good people do. Moses preceded the Ten Commandments with a recounting of God's deliverance so that Israel would not believe that their salvation had been in their hands.[33] God would not even allow the rocks of the altar that honored him to be fashioned by human hands, so that the people would understand the limitations of their work and the singular glory of his own (Exod. 20:25). Confidence in God's work and confession of our need is the consistent message of Scripture and the only basis of believers' hope that they can carry out God's commands.

No precise formula should instruct preachers how to maintain a Christ-centered perspective regarding the application of biblical truth. However, when people walk away from a message understanding that grace both motivates and enables them to serve God, futile human striving and vain self-vaunting vanish. Preachers, then, should make God's redemptive work the content, the motive, and the power behind all biblical exposition. Only when people look beyond themselves for spiritual health do they find their sole hope and source of power to do what God requires appear.

In a well-known image, Francis Schaeffer taught that we must approach God with hands empty of our own works in order to claim his salvation. Similarly Schaeffer taught that we must bow *twice* for sanctification.[34] We must bow before the truths of God *and* the moral obligations in his Word. Christ-centered preaching puts these acts of obedience in order. Homage to the truths of grace must precede service to moral obligation, or actions will be irrelevant and wrong. The hands of believers must remain empty of self both before and after conversion if we are to experience the fullness of grace.

---

33. Howell, "How to Preach Christ," 9.
34. Francis Schaeffer, "True Spirituality" in *The Complete Works of Francis Schaeffer*, vol. 3 (Wheaton, Ill.: Crossway, 1982), 200; and *The God Who Is There* (Downers Grove: InterVarsity, 1968), 134.

My Eternal King

My God, I love Thee;
Not because I hope for heaven thereby,
Nor yet because who love Thee not must die eternally.
Thou, O my Jesus, Thou didst me upon the cross embrace;
For me didst bear the nails and spear, and manifold disgrace.
Why, then why, O blessed Jesus Christ, should I not love
    Thee well?
Not for the hope of winning heaven, or of escaping hell;
Not with the hope of gaining aught; not seeking a reward;
But as thyself hast loved me, O ever-loving Lord!
E'en so I love Thee, and will love, and in Thy praise will sing;
Solely because Thou art my God, and my Eternal King.

Anonymous seventeenth-century Latin poem
Translated by Rev. Edward Caswall

QUESTIONS FOR REVIEW AND DISCUSSION

1. How does Genesis 3:15 relate to the Christocentricity of all Scripture?

2. What is the difference between allegorical leapfrogging to the New Testament Christ and true redemptive exposition?

3. In what way does theocentric preaching ensure a Christ-centered message even if there is no specific mention of Jesus?

4. What is the proper place for the Christ-centered focus in an expository sermon?

5. What themes typify Christ-centered preaching?

6. How does Christocentric preaching affect sermonic application?

EXERCISES

1. Explain why gratitude must be the motive behind Christian obedience if our deeds are to become truly holy.

2. Explain how the key to Christian power resides in humility.

3. Explain how Christ-centered preaching maintains the doxological focus of all Scripture and all life.

Appendix 1

DELIVERY, DRESS, AND STYLE

A Philosophy for Delivery

The elocution movement that taught speakers there was one correct way to gesture, stand, or sound died nearly a century ago. Natural delivery rules our day. Those preachers most respected are those most able to sound like themselves when they are deeply interested in a subject. Bombast and oratorical flourishes remind one of pulpit caricatures; they do not stimulate pastoral respect. At the same time staid, unenthusiastic solemnity communicates irrelevant tedium rather than sincere seriousness. Congregations ask no more and expect no less of a preacher than truth expressed in a manner consistent with the personality of the preacher and reflective of the import of the message. Today's pulpit excellence requires that you speak as you would talk, especially when fully convinced that God has charged you to deliver a life-changing, eternity-impacting message.

Delivery Hurdles

The great challenge for today's preachers is to maintain this natural expression of urgency that both pulpit mimicry and public timidity deny. Two hurdles contribute to the challenge. The first is the mistaken notion that our preaching will reach its zenith when we sound like our grandfathers or like pulpit idols. If God had wished for George Whitefield or Billy Graham to be in your pulpit he would have placed the great evangelists there. You should learn all you can about delivery from previous generations and contemporary greats, remembering that from a universe of possibilities God chose you with your personality, insights, manner, and gifts to preach in this place at this time. Do not undermine his wisdom by adopting a delivery not true to you.

The second great hurdle of naturalness is intimidation. We stop speaking in a manner true to ourselves when we get too concerned about a crowd of people watching our every move and listening to each syllable we utter. Speaking at our kitchen tables we move our hands when expressing something that excites us. When we do not concentrate on how we are saying particular words our voices move up and down to emphasize different thoughts; voice intensity varies to reflect different degrees of seriousness; and volume naturally rises to reach everyone while modulating so as to overpower no one. Were we secretly to videotape a meal in your home we would discover virtually everyone there possesses this natural facility of so-called kitchen-table expression. Thus, you already have excellent delivery skills.

But something happens when we move from kitchen tables to church pulpits. All those eyes staring at us somehow straightjacket our gestures and paralyze our expressions. We seem to lose the ability to speak naturally when standing in front of others. This means the real challenge of pulpit excellence is not to add something to our delivery that is atypical of us, but to reclaim the naturalness that is most true to us.

HEIGHTENED CONVERSATION

When you speak to others in the way most natural to you, your voice and gestures are conversational. If what you have to say is important and you wanted a number of people to pay attention you would intensify your expressions while still speaking in a manner characteristic of you and plain to others. This heightening (not changing) of your normal speech would be the most natural and effective way for you to communicate important matters. In such heightened conversation resides the key to truly powerful preaching.[1] Preachers who use this mode of expression recognize the oddity of speaking without enthusiasm about eternal matters, and the equal abnormality of adopting a peculiar manner to expound so vital a message. A speaking style that is most true to you when you are not intimidated offers your most effective delivery tools.

1. The heightened-conversation concept is common in contemporary homiletics, but not new. John Wesley advised the same (Woodrow Michael Kroll, *Prescription for Preaching* [Grand Rapids: Baker, 1980], 85), as did Spurgeon (John Stott, *Between Two Worlds: The Art of Preaching in the Twentieth Century* [Grand Rapids: Eerdmans, 1982], 273).

Even the most skilled preachers experience some intimidation when they face a congregation (if you have no concerns about preaching you have not fully comprehended the magnitude of the task). In fact, most preachers learn to appreciate the "butterflies" that energize their preparations and presentations. So, how can we speak naturally when we feel (and even value) the pressure of the occasion? Understanding what characterizes natural delivery helps. The delivery guidelines described in the next section keep preachers plugged into the power of natural expression. Although instructors sometimes teach these skills as rules others must heed, students of preaching will benefit when reminded that these standards simply reflect the natural expression of persons who feel confident and free to be themselves.

An important caution should precede these standards: When delivery techniques (skilled or unskilled) dominate a sermon's impressions listeners tend to reject the message.[2] Listeners remember the delivery of poor speakers, they remember the content of good speakers. We communicate messages best when our delivery is transparent. Neither showy oratory nor a staid presentation accomplishes this goal. Both draw attention to themselves. The technique of someone who stands like a statue and speaks in a monotone intrudes on the content of a message no less than the flimflam of the showman who dances across a stage.

Excellent delivery disappears from the awareness of the listener. Thus, the goal of the preacher is to get out of the way of the message . . . to deliver the sermon so aptly that its thought alone dominates the listener's thought. We achieve this goal by practicing[3] sound delivery skills until they become so natural to us that we use them as unconsciously as we would in conversation. When our manner of expression so readily conforms to the content of our words, we can make the crucial mental transition of concentrating on getting the message into others rather than out of ourselves. At that point our delivery becomes a vehicle for the message rather than a stage for our skills.

2. Ralph Lewis offers this list of delivery techniques that create listener distrust of speakers: obvious skills, artifice, or cleverness; labored didacticism; forthright sermonizing; loud haranguing—especially too much volume too early; constant hard driving; persistent aggressiveness; ornateness; too evident use of technical skills; high-flown language; glib tongues, in *Speech for Persuasive Preaching* (self-published, 1968), 95.

3. Let no one make you ashamed of practicing. Great communicators are made, not born. While it is possible to overpractice to the point that a message becomes mechanical, the far more likely result of conscientious preparation is excellence. The best speakers practice. Only poor speakers, and those who were once good, feel no need to hone their gifts. Practice in the early stages of ministry is especially crucial.

COMPONENTS OF DELIVERY

Voice and gesture are the primary tools of our delivery. Each can be subdivided into various features that are best employed when their use is *appropriate, varied, and purposeful*. The nature of the occasion, the congregation, the message, and the speaker contribute to determining appropriate delivery. Each delivery tool will also have a greater impact if the preacher varies the way that it is used. The purpose the preacher has for each delivery feature will determine which standards of delivery will best be employed—or are better broken. The study of these features may seem foreign to the preaching task (for we can too easily emphasize technique over the anointing of the Spirit, which truly makes preaching effective), but faithfulness in communicating God's truth requires us to pay attention to how we present his Word. Haddon Robinson explains:

> . . . [R]esearch and experience agree that if nonverbal messages contradict the verbal, listeners will more likely believe the silent language. It seems more difficult to lie with the whole body than with the lips alone. . . . A pastor's words may insist, "This is important," but if his voice sounds flat and expressionless and his body stands limp, the congregation will not believe him. If a preacher shakes his fist at his hearers while he says in scolding tones, "What this church needs is more love and deep concern for each other!" the people in the pew will wonder whether he knows what he is talking about. Since a vast amount of preaching involves attitudes that either reinforce or contradict what our words proclaim, a preacher dare not ignore delivery.[4]

When our manner conforms to our sermon's content it becomes obvious that our message has had an impact on us. Thus, delivery acts as a window to our sincerity, which ultimately carries the power of our words.

VOICE

The many aspects of professional vocal delivery can dizzy us with their intricacies, rules, and exceptions. Cut to the quick with this key: Fill the room but speak to individuals. Learning how volume, variety, and intensity of speech affect your speech will help you accomplish this goal.

4. Haddon Robinson, *Biblical Preaching: The Development and Delivery of Expository Messages* (Grand Rapids: Baker, 1980), 194.

Volume. The most natural way of determining the proper volume for your message is to speak so that those most distant from you can easily hear. As you begin your sermon, look at those in the back row and address them. Your voice will automatically rise to reach them and those in the front rows will unconsciously adjust to (and forgive) the increase in volume that they all know is needed. Understand that reaching everyone does not require blasting anyone. Save the explosions for the moments they are needed. Recognize, however, that beginning preachers unaccustomed to speaking with power consistently drop their volume at the end of sentences to express seriousness and fervor. Most of us have to be reminded to keep our volume up when we are learning to preach.

If you use a microphone, do not depend on electronics to carry your voice. Pulpit microphones work best (carrying the full dynamics of your voice) if you project over them rather than speak into them. Microphones in large auditoriums spare you from having to shout, but they do not allow you to drop your voice to a normal speaking register without serious damage to your delivery. Move your body in a wedge-shaped pattern when using a microphone so that your voice consistently pours over the microphone while you address different segments of the congregation (fig. A1.1).

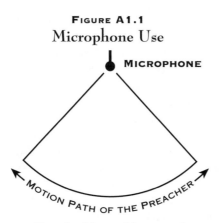

FIGURE A1.1

Microphone Use

MICROPHONE

MOTION PATH OF THE PREACHER

Keep shoulders and face toward microphone as body turns to address different segments of the congregation.

Variety. Volume, tone, and pace should vary to emphasize the many thoughts and feelings present in any sermon. Many types of monotone impair effective delivery, but three predominate: low and slow; high and fast; and rhythmic. Each results from different responses to pressure.

Some speakers respond to intimidation by becoming very deliberate. These persons speak in low tones at a slow pace. Others overreact to the silent audience pressure by filling every space with sound. They speak without pause, at a high pitch, and frequently at great speed. Such animated and energetic speaking hardly seems like a monotone until the speaker recognizes that the rapid-fire delivery gives equal emphasis to every word. Everything sounds the same and the constant barrage will ultimately make listeners glaze over. Rhythmic speakers find a comfortable pattern of speech (e.g., starting a sentence at low frequency and ending high, or vice versa) and return to that haven over and over again. The pattern itself contains some variety of expression but the constant repetition of the pattern homogenizes thought.

The best way to break all forms of monotones is to say things as though you mean them. If you say someone grieves, do not say the word as though their sorrow has no consequence for you. Say the word *grieves* as though you are grieved. Whether you are expressing joy, humor, seriousness, or contemplation, use the tone, pace, and volume that say what your words mean. Learn to use silence to emphasize your thought. The best speakers not only vary their expression from thundering to whispering[5] and their pace from crawling to racing, they also let their most telling statements echo in pauses that intensify impressions. Repetitive, vocalized pauses (e.g., "uh," "O.K.," "ya' know") fill the spaces skilled preachers prefer to use for powerful effects.

Intensity. We speak with intensity when love for our listeners, commitment to the Word of God, and conviction of the importance of our words dominate our manner. Even though intensity is difficult to quantify, others readily perceive it. The fervor of one who preaches with Richard Baxter's compulsion to speak "as a dying man to dying men" cannot be masked or feigned for long (cf. Rom 9:1–2; 1 Cor. 9:16). Remember, however, that if you say everything with maximum intensity, then nothing will make an exceptional impression. Whether we speak of the horrors of hell, the wonders of grace, or the necessity of repentance our voices should convey the import of our words.

We help maintain intensity of expression through both spiritual and physical preparation. Praying for the peace of the Holy Spirit can calm nerves and grant confidence that allows us to preach with power. Often you can expend some of the adrenalin affecting nervousness by walking around, taking a few deep breaths, talking to others, or animatedly read-

5. A whisper in the pulpit is not actually said so softly that no one can hear you. Keep volume up while sounding as though you are whispering by pouring breath over your voice.

ing your text aloud. Remember, a degree of nervousness serves you by fine-tuning your physical and mental faculties. You usually will preach best when well rested, physically fit, and not too recently well fed (milk products, carbonated drinks, heavy foods, and being quite full can negatively affect vocal delivery). Be aware some medications create dry mouths and may slow thought. Practical suggestions for maintaining fervor aside, however, remember, nothing will substitute for the unction the Spirit alone grants to the heart set afire by his work and set free for his purposes.

GESTURE

Our bodies combine with our voices in the communication process. Our eyes, faces, hands, and movements participate in what we say, or may carry a message all their own that we never intended to communicate. Some communication studies have actually concluded that we communicate more by what we gesture than by what we vocalize. The precise weight our gestures carry will always be debated, but no one denies that they heavily influence what others perceive. The following guidelines help keep our gestures saying what we intend:

Eye contact. The primary instrument of gesture is the eyes. A speaker who will not look people in the eyes is deemed aloof, afraid, and/or incompetent. One who looks at the ceiling while explaining how Jesus held little children appears distracted. One who looks at the floor while exhorting others to repent seem intimidated. One who looks over heads (or even at foreheads) instead of in the eyes of listeners, seems untrustworthy because "he won't meet my eyes." Preachers too tied to notes, especially when seeking to exhort, project a lack of preparation or preoccupation with their own thoughts.

You must look at people! The eyes can spit fire, pour out compassion, and preach Christ in you. When you deny people your eyes, you really deny them yourself. No one else talks to them without looking at them—unless to insult them. Everyone expects you to glance at your notes from time to time, and even to read an occasional quotation, an anecdote, or a carefully worded thought, but preachers greatly err when they think that by reading every word precisely as written they have better communicated. Far better to stumble over a phrase, smile confidently, and correct it, than to speak perfectly while displaying the top of your head as you read the bulk of the sermon.

Include everyone. Scan the entire congregation while pausing briefly on particular sets of eyes as you make special emphases. Take encouragement from those who look at you with appreciation. Take note of those who seem troubled or confused so that you can clarify or adjust your message in appropriate ways. Gifted preachers need eye contact in order to monitor this feedback that in turn allows them to improve and more precisely refine their messages even as they preach.

Facial animation. Smile. If you can smile in the pulpit you can convey every other needed expression. Too often students of preaching try to control the thumping in their chests by showing no expression. This feels all right because the message is serious, but the result is a dead-pan look that implies: I have no feeling about what I am saying. If our faces do not move, our voices get tied down. We have trouble expressing a variety of tones or emotions when our faces do not reflect what we want to communicate. Try this experiment. See if you can make your voice sound joyful when you say, "The love of God frees us from our sin" while not smiling. It is practically impossible. For your words to express what you want, you have to free your face from the deep freeze.

When you have managed to animate your expressions make sure others can see them. Keep your face toward the congregation. Push your notes high on the pulpit and stand a half step back from it so that even when you look at the notes you are facing forward and not down. This way, not only will your voice continue to project outward when you read, but also the congregation will still be able to read your face.

Hand gestures. Perhaps no aspect of pulpit speech seems as unnatural as keeping your hands in natural positions. Standard instruction advises students to let their hands hang at their sides when not gesturing. Unfortunately, when we are standing in front of people this natural position makes us feel exposed and we adopt any number of unnatural stances to cover our discomfort: clasping hands behind our backs; holding hands together at the waistline; plunging hands into pockets (jingling keys and coins unconsciously); dropping one arm while hanging the other in midair just below the rib cage; folding arms across the chest; twisting wedding rings; fiddling with fingernails; grabbing neckties; adjusting cuffs; stroking hair, lips, nose, or face; and a host of variations that make us look even more awkward than we feel. These unnatural hand positions not only telegraph our discomfort, but so preoccupy our hands that we cannot freely gesture what we need to communicate.

A compromise between the standard advice and these unnatural aberrations is to let your hands rest on the front of the pulpit.[6] This posi-

---

6. In settings without pulpits a Bible can help preoccupy one hand, while the other does most of the gesturing. This takes away some of the sense of exposure if you absolutely cannot let your hands rest at your sides when they are not gesturing.

tion will make you feel less exposed while keeping your hands free to gesture. Grasping the sides of the pulpit at the upper corners (the greater horns) or the lower corners (the lesser horns) is a very common but unnatural stance speakers adopt. Not only does this stance tend to lock hands into place so that the shoulders and head are forced to bob in the place of hand gestures, but grasping the horns of the pulpit also forces the preacher to hunch over. When the preacher wants to project an intense, an aggressive, or a domineering demeanor this is appropriate, but otherwise the preacher's body forms a "pulpit shell" that seems to exclude the listeners—which is precisely what our bodies are unconsciously doing when nervousness makes us grasp for the pulpit horns.

When our hands gesture, we need to make sure the motions appear natural. Natural gestures occur with the hands above the sternum and away (both frontally and laterally) from the body. When gestures stay within the plane of the body and drop to the breadbasket (i.e., below the ribs) the preacher appears constrained. When gestures do not rise above the waist the preacher projects disinterest or fear. In a lively conversation our hands naturally come up so that they are within the line of sight of the persons we address. When our hands do less in the pulpit we appear awkward and uncomfortable.

Gesture concepts and sentences, not words and syllables. While many public-speaking courses advise using two gestures per sentence in practice to get your hands moving, no one wants you to gesture so frequently throughout a message. Personality governs the degree of gesturing that is natural for you, but when preachers begin accentuating words and syllables rather than concepts and sentences, they tend to develop repetitive chopping and pointing motions that listeners find distracting and/or annoying. Let your hands indicate *the idea* you are developing rather than the cadence of your words. Remember also that no gesture at all is better than the half-hearted hand motions that expose distraction or intimidation.

The situation as well as the content of your message will determine the appropriateness of your gestures. In a small Sunday school classroom, fully extending your arms may seem pretentious. In a large auditorium, you may have to walk the length of the stage to communicate expansiveness. Gestures, like voices, should expand to fill the room but not press the space. When you put one hand in a pocket you communicate informality—putting both you and your listeners at ease. If this is what you want to communicate, fine. However, if you are trying to impress others with the nobility, importance, or urgency of an idea, the hand in your pocket will undermine your message. Almost any gesture (even those homiletics professors warn against) can be used for specific purposes by skilled speakers. Preachers tend to get into trouble when there is no obvious purpose behind their gestures, they seem too intimidated to gesture, or their gestures seem mechanical rather than natural. The cure for each of these ills is the freedom that experience *and* familiarity with your message provide. Prepare, prepare, prepare. Greater freedom will come the more you preach, but you can accelerate the process greatly with conscientious preparation.[7]

Posture. The most natural way to speak to others if you have something important to say is to level your chin, place your feet shoulder-distance apart, and stand erect with shoulders squared and body slightly inclined toward your listeners. Variations from this posture send other messages.

A preacher who leans on the pulpit initially conveys the desire for intimacy or informality. However, when the leaning continues beyond the expression of a thought or two the same posture implies fear or sloth—the pulpit seems to have become a shield or a crutch. A common stance for people of all ages experiencing nervousness involves crossing one leg in front of the other below the knee while leaning on the nearest solid object. Inexperienced speakers often unconsciously mimic this stance while placing one or both hands (or even their elbows and forearms) on the lesser horns of the pulpit. This posture automatically and immediately conveys great discomfort to the listeners.

When preachers' balance or posture (or lack of it) cause them to lean, rock, sway, bob, or bounce without apparent purpose listeners lose respect for the words that accompany these eccentricities. Conversely, when preachers lean back, put their chins in the air, and talk "down their noses" to congregations, people tend to feel that the preachers have no respect for those in the pew.

Do not let concerns for correct posture turn you into a statue. If you say something about great pain, joy, or sorrow, your whole body should express the thought. Most pulpits allow you some degree of movement and you should feel free to move your feet and body as long as you do not pace. Different congregations have varying degrees of tolerance for the amount of walking the pastor can do outside the pulpit, but, when such movements have obvious and definite purposes, few will object. If you do move about freely, keep your shoulders facing your listeners

7. My own practice is to go through the entire sermon two to four times out loud before presenting it. I know of no great preacher who did not develop similar habits, particularly in the early stages of their ministry.

even when you move in different directions. Also, beware of trying to express something strongly while taking steps backward. The retreating motion conveys fear of the congregation or lack of confidence in your words.

FINAL CAUTIONS FOR DELIVERY

Two cautions should conclude any modern discussion of effective delivery. First, an appeal for naturalness is not an excuse for slovenliness. While you must be yourself in the pulpit, the majesty of your task and the obligations of your office require you to be the best you can be. Bad grammar, slurred speech, and mannerisms detract from your sermon even if they are true of you. Correct what does not strengthen your message.

Second, no set of delivery dos and don'ts supersedes the power of caring deeply about what you say. Let earnestness be your eloquence. Preaching that is all polish and no fire shines reputations but does not melt hearts. Even if the words you say barely trip over the lip of the pulpit, if you speak with the sincerity of a burdened spirit, others will listen. You communicate this authenticity when your manner reflects your content. Let your heart show in your work. Showing genuine enthusiasm for what you deeply believe is the only unbreakable rule of great delivery.

A PHILOSOPHY OF DRESS

How we present ourselves affects our presentation of the gospel (2 Tim. 2:15). Expounding Scripture is a sacred task. Our dress is one of the cultural gestures we possess to communicate this. We damage the gospel if our presentation of the Word does not honor God's work (Mal. 1:6–12) or becomes a stumbling block for others' reception of it (Rom. 14:13; 1 Cor. 8:9).

We need to be careful that the exercise of our freedom does not indicate disregard for our calling or disrespect for our hearers. No Bible verse indicates what clothing we should wear in every situation, but prudent observation of biblical principles requires us to consider what apparel seems *appropriate* for particular situations, congregations, and cultures.

Formal preaching situations require you to dress in what that community considers formal attire. Usually this does not mean finery.

There is something fundamentally at odds with the gospel when preachers' garb seems designed to draw attention (Prov. 25:27; Mal. 2:2; Matt. 23:6). Our clothing should be so appropriate for the situation that it simply passes notice. This will not occur if we wear silk shirts in a rural church or frayed blue jeans beneath a suit coat. To the objection that these are but cultural preferences that are beneath the concern of serious expositors (who want fully to embrace their Christian liberties), we must reply that even the apostle Paul did not allow his spiritual privileges to impede the gospel (1 Cor. 9:19–25). As long as a community's standards did not require the apostle to forsake the gospel, he willingly bowed to them to promote it. If we object too strongly to others' expectations for our dress, we should also question whether we are more concerned for our rights than we are for the effective transmission of the Word (Rom 12:10; Phil. 2:4).

Where informal situations call for informal attire we will still find it difficult to communicate credibility if our clothes are ill-fitted, dirty, rumpled, immodest, out of style, or poorly matched. Poor hygiene and an unkempt appearance can also get in the way of a ready reception of our messages (1 Cor. 3:16, 17). Some communities will find certain lengths of hair, facial hair, or some clothing and jewelry styles difficult to accept (cf. 1 Cor. 11:14; 1 Tim. 2:9). Before crying that these standards are unfair and artificial, remember that identification with people is a key aspect of biblical persuasion (1 Cor. 9:22).[8] Those who minister to the poor and homeless know that this means dressing with the clothes a thrift shop provides may best speak of your biblical priorities in their communities. Pastors called to an urban financial district, however, cannot usually afford to dress so simply.

We should not conform to improper cultural standards or reinforce community prejudices, but we gain little for the gospel when we force our own preferences on others. The goal is not to dress for success or wear camel-hair tunics, but to have our clothes and personal appearance be nonissues in our ministries. We have more important matters for people to consider. Congregations will better focus on the more vital

8. Kenneth Burke is the chief twentieth-century figure articulating identification theory as it relates to communication. For a study of identification principles as they relate to preaching see the author's "Facing Two Ways: Preaching to Experiential and Doxological Priorities," *Presbyterion* 14, 2 (Fall 1988): 98–117; or these book-length treatments: Craig Loscalzo, *Preaching Sermons that Connect: Effective Communication through Identification* (Downers Grove, Ill.: InterVarsity, 1992); Hans Van Der Geest, *Presence in the Pulpit: The Impact of Personality in Preaching*, trans. Douglas W. Stott (1978; reprint, Atlanta: John Knox, 1981).

issues when we care enough about the people and the gospel to dress "transparently."

A PHILOSOPHY OF STYLE

The warm, humble dignity most conducive to effective preaching is usually best expressed by those who cultivate a natural and personal style.[9] Natural expression avoids all pretense that makes the gospel seem artificial, high blown, or complex. A personal style communicates care, transparency, and acceptance (of oneself and others), thus exhibiting the reality of the grace.

A PLAIN STYLE

In our conversational age, complex sentences, multiple syllables, and one-hundred-dollar words mark poor communicators. "Clarity increases as sentence length decreases." Communication improves as words simplify. This is not because people are dumber than they used to be. We all simply understand more when others address us plainly. This is why the Bible consistently admonishes preachers to develop a plain style of speaking (1 Cor. 2:4–5; 14:19; 2 Cor. 3:12; 4:2). The Bible does not hesitate to frame its greatest truths in simple words (e.g., Ps. 23; Zacchaeus; the Lord's Prayer; *koine* Greek). Where simple words can be used, we should not detour to more complex terms.

The great preachers of our day all speak in such a way that people can understand. These pulpit experts believe it is better to be understood than to be worshiped. They want to communicate more than to impress. Yet, for speaking in such plain terms, people come to think of these preachers most highly. People love to listen to what they can understand. They hate hearing someone talk over their heads even if they are wowed by the intellect that makes them feel so dumb. This does not mean that any minister should talk down to a congregation. Haddon Robinson wisely offers this balance: "Don't overestimate the people's vocabulary or underestimate their intelligence."[10]

Speak plainly and people will listen. These dynamics are not new in our day. Henry Ward Beecher decried the ornate pulpit speech of the

---

9. Traditional elements of rhetorical style include clarity, interest, evocation, energy, and emotion. See William H. Kooienga, *Elements of Style for Preaching*, The Craft of Preaching Series (Grand Rapids: Zondervan, 1989), 54.
10. Robinson, *Biblical Preaching*, 183.

established preachers in his age by advising, "A switch with leaves doesn't tingle." Richard Baxter and John Wesley both forbade their disciples to use "church tones" and "stained-glass speech." John Calvin said he constantly "studied to be simple."[11] We err greatly and actually abandon the principles of these faith fathers when we try to import their manner of speech (which was plain enough in their day to make them objects of ridicule) into our age on the pretext that this will make us *sound* like preachers. Such anachronistic, out-of-the-norm speech was the very type of language these preachers wanted out of their pulpits.[12]

At some point in your preaching career you must make a decision: Will you preach to people or will you preach for preachers? The latter may win you acclaim, but the former will far more likely win souls. Deep thought, plainly expressed, most clearly exposes a pastor's heart.

A Genuine Style

Your heart becomes most apparent to people when you are not afraid to share it. This personal transparency occurs not when you make yourself the focus of your sermons, but when you are willing to share your feelings, doubts, and fears with others *as well as* your faith. Some preaching gives the impression that the preacher has no personal contact with the ordinary concerns of life. Such remote commentary offers little comfort. Because it seems unrealistic, this style of preaching possesses little authority for persons of mature thought even though the preacher may attempt to sound authoritarian.

The pulpit is not a confessional, a cry room, or a sympathy bench, but neither should it become a sky box for addressing people *en masse,* as if removed from realms above regular existence. It was said of Spurgeon that he "addressed two thousand people as though he were speaking personally to one man."[13] This sort of heart-to-heart preaching demands that the preacher know enough of grace to have no need to hide behind pretenses of perfection. Learning to express your own struggles while heralding without compromise the gospel that gives you hope demands

11. As quoted in Stott, *Between Two Worlds,* 128. Cf. *Westminster Larger Catechism* question 159. See also J. C. Ryle's pastoral classic, "Simplicity in Preaching," in *The Upper Room* (1888; reprint, London: Banner of Truth, 1979), 35–55.

12. A hallmark of the Reformers and later Puritans was their commitment to preach in the vernacular of the people.

13. Woodrow Michael Kroll, *Prescription for Preaching* (Grand Rapids: Baker, 1980), 84.

deep soul-searching. Still, this type of vulnerability will provide more hope than a thousand exhortations to "be strong and courageous" from one who seems never to have faced a battle.

To be heard we must show that we can rejoice with those who rejoice and weep with those who weep (Rom. 12:15). In short, we must demonstrate that we are real persons whose warmth, convictions, compassion, commitments, encouragement, and hope have weathered enough storms of life to be genuine. As others have written, it should not appear from the storm-tossed pew that the preacher is the only one who cannot see that the waves are twenty feet high. The apostles told their congregations that the Word progressed so swiftly through the ancient world because "we were delighted to share with you not only the gospel of God but our lives as well" (1 Thess. 2:8). The modern world can be as powerfully impacted if today's preachers are as authentically inclined.

A CREATIVE STYLE

Genuine care for others can be expressed only with a realistic understanding of their situations and struggles. Despite the fondest wishes of the preacher, most parishioners struggle to pay attention to each word from the pulpit . . . just as most preachers do when they happen to sit in the pews. As listeners we tend to canoe through sermons. We float with the general thought of the message, but only dig our cognitive paddles deep into the stream of spiritual truths flowing by us when some turbulence, point of particular interest, or the need to progress makes us respond with greater vigor.

Rather than blame listeners for their canoeing tendencies, skilled preachers anticipate the ebb and flow of their listeners' concentration levels. Such pastors use their creative skills to produce delivery, structure, wording, and images that frame the sermon's ideas so as to capture and periodically recapture the thought of those in the pew.[14] Such creativity does not require artifice or entertainment, but it does demand a deep desire to be heard that is reflected in the preacher's evident enthusiasm for the message. Energy, imagination, innovation, intrigue, and insight keyed to the sermon's rhythm mark a preaching style sympathetic to the needs of listeners and serious about communicating the gospel.

14. J. Grant Howard, *Creativity in Preaching,* The Craft of Preaching Series (Grand Rapids: Zondervan, 1987), 26–29.

A COURAGEOUS STYLE

The willingness and ability to proclaim the Word of God authentically and authoritatively derives from the deep conviction that when we say what the Bible says, we speak what God desires. Confidence that our words carry a divine imprimatur spares us the need to shield ourselves behind an affected style, cover our feelings in coded pulpit speech, or hide from truths that may bring criticism (2 Tim. 4:1–2). When faithfulness to God becomes the primary motive of our preaching, we find ourselves freed from inordinate concern about personal acceptance, reputation, and offense (Acts 4:29). Self-serving anxieties and self-promoting mannerisms wither before a selfless love for the Word and the souls of those God commends to our care (2 Cor. 10:1–2). The results are boldness produced more by sincerity than calculation, and authority secured by evidence of an intimate familiarity with God rather than projected by a prescribed manner (2 Cor. 3:12).

Our convictions concerning the efficacy of Scripture are most evident not when we strive to make the Word effective by pumping our authority into it, but when we have the courage to let it speak for itself. The proper authority of spiritual leaders lies not in a peculiar style or an arrogated manner but solely in the validity of the Word they proclaim. Such authority matches expression to content—neither apologizing for what the Word of God makes plain, nor making remote what the Bible designs for intimacy. Thus, courageous preaching does not rely on a bombastic style or an authoritarian manner, but instead seeks to express the truth of God in a manner so appropriate for the truth, situation, and personalities involved that the mind, heart, and glory of God shine without hindrance, artifice, or shadow.[15]

15. For more study of preaching delivery, dress, and style see the dated yet excellent work by Dwight E. Stevenson and Charles F. Diehl, *Reaching People from the Pulpit: A Guide to Effective Sermon Delivery* (New York: Harper and Row, 1958); also Charles L. Bartow, *Effective Speech Communication in Leading Worship* (Nashville: Abingdon, 1988); and Calvin Miller, *Spirit, Word, and Story: A Philosophy of Preaching* (Dallas: Word, 1989), 107–225.

DIVISIONS AND PROPORTIONS

Conscious of the artistry of expression and freedom of style needed for the crafting of fine sermons, homiletics instructors hate establishing iron-clad rules for the proportions and lengths of sermon divisions.[1] However, students who have never prepared a sermon often want a general idea of how much time each feature should take. The tables below attempt to provide some general guidance without intending to impose these specifics on any particular sermon.

These tables assume the time allotted for a sermon will average thirty minutes, and project that if the sermon were typed entirely with standard spacing and margins, each page would take approximately three minutes to read aloud at an expressive, moderate pace.

TABLE A2.1
Sermon Proportions and Discussions
Average Page and Time Lengths for Material Surrounding the Body of a 30-Minute Message

Sermon Component	Average Time	Typed Pages
Text announcement, Scripture introduction	1 minute	1/3
Scripture reading	1–2 minutes	1
Prayer for illumination	1 minute	1/3
Sermon introduction	3 minutes	1
Sermon conclusion	2–3 minutes	1
Closing prayer	1 minute	1/3
Approximate totals:	10 minutes	4

1. George E. Sweazey, *Preaching the Good News* (Englewood Cliffs, N.J.: Prentice-Hall, 1976), 80.

Average Time and Page Lengths for the Body of a 30-Minute Message
(Note: 20 minutes remain for the sermon body)

Sermon Component	Average Time	Typed Pages
Each main point in a 3-point message (assuming equal proportions)	6 minutes	2
Each main point component (assuming 1/3, 1/3, 1/3 proportion)		
explanation	2 minutes	2/3 (2-3 paragraphs)
illustration	2 minutes	2/3 (" ")
application	2 minutes	2/3 (" ")
Each subpoint (assuming 2-3 subpoints per main point)	2/3–1 minute	1/3 (1 paragraph)
All extemporized comments	2 minutes	2/3

Conclusion: The written content of a thirty-minute sermon that includes only the Scripture introduction, sermon introduction, sermon body, and sermon conclusion will run 7.5–8.5 pages (this standard may lengthen somewhat with healthy spacing between components).

METHODS OF PREPARATION

The steps preachers take in preparing their messages vary according to the personality of the preacher, the time available, the nature of the occasion, the type of sermon, the prior knowledge one has of the text, and many other factors. Still, students of preaching often find it helpful to have some general guidance so that they know they are not far astray as they begin developing their own personal approach to developing sermons.[1]

Sometimes this guidance comes in colloquial terms: "I read myself full, think myself clear, pray myself hot, and then let myself go." Other times the guidance receives more academic treatment: "Read the text, research the material, then focus everything on a single idea."[2] The following preparation pyramid captures the essence of these formulas while emphasizing ideas central to expository preaching as defined in this book:

---

1. Woodrow Michael Kroll lists the personal preparation habits of a number of well known preachers in *Prescription for Preaching* (Grand Rapids: Baker, 1980), 138–41.

2. For excellent discussions of formal methods see Donald E. Demaray, *An Introduction to Homiletics* (Grand Rapids: Baker, 1978), 79–92; and, the eminently realistic Ian Pitt-Watson, *A Primer for Preachers* (Grand Rapids: Baker, 1986), 37–38.

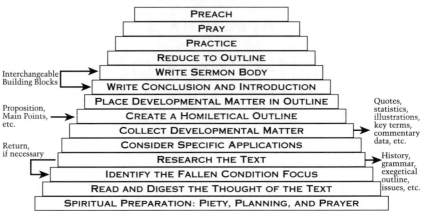

FIGURE A3.1

A Sermon Preparation Pyramid

PREACH

PRAY

PRACTICE

REDUCE TO OUTLINE

Interchangeable Building Blocks

WRITE SERMON BODY

WRITE CONCLUSION AND INTRODUCTION

PLACE DEVELOPMENTAL MATTER IN OUTLINE

Proposition, Main Points, etc.

CREATE A HOMILETICAL OUTLINE

COLLECT DEVELOPMENTAL MATTER

Return, if necessary

CONSIDER SPECIFIC APPLICATIONS

RESEARCH THE TEXT

IDENTIFY THE FALLEN CONDITION FOCUS

READ AND DIGEST THE THOUGHT OF THE TEXT

SPIRITUAL PREPARATION: PIETY, PLANNING, AND PRAYER

Quotes, statistics, illustrations, key terms, commentary data, etc.

History, grammar, exegetical outline, issues, etc.

METHODS OF PRESENTATION

These outlines present the options preachers have for preparing materials (notes, outlines, manuscripts) necessary to present sermons effectively.

I. Basic Options for Presenting Sermons
A. Reading
B. Reciting
C. Extemporizing
D. Combinations of the above

II. Options for Fully Written Sermons
A. Full manuscript carried into pulpit and read.

Chief Advantages:	Ensured preparation
	Precision of expression
Chief Disadvantages:	Damages eye contact
	Limits spontaneity and freedom of expression
	Tendency to speak in a "written" style
	Extensive preparation time

B. Full manuscript memorized and recited in pulpit.

Chief Advantages:	Precision of expression
	Promotes eye contact
Chief Disadvantages:	Difficulty (for most persons) of memorizing materials
	Woodenness of expression
	Extensive preparation time

C. Full manuscript studied, practiced, and converted to an outline[1] with the sermon preached from the written or memorized outline.[2]

Chief Advantages:	Ensures complete preparation of thought
	Maintains eye contact
	Maintains spontaneous style of expression
Chief Disadvantage:	Extensive preparation time

III. Options for Partially Written Sermons

A. Largely-written Manuscript: a manuscript with most of its key portions fully written, but with some portions outlined.

Chief Advantages and Disadvantages: Basically the same as II, C, with some reduced preparation time.

B. Types of Outlined Messages

1. Extended Outline: an outline with main point and subpoint statements, key features, connecting ideas, and key passages either entirely written out or significantly indicated.

   a. Options for Using Extended Outlines

      i. The extended outline is repeatedly extemporized in private, so that the message is ultimately memorized and then recited in public.

      ii. The extended outline is practiced for familiarity in private, then taken into the pulpit, and semi-extemporized there.[3]

      iii. The extended outline is practiced, then converted to a bare-bones outline (see below) that is taken into the pulpit, and semi-extemporized there.

   b. Chief Advantages and Disadvantages of Extended Outlines

      i. The more extensive the outline the more complete the preparation of thought.

1. The outline may be transferred to separate pages—or, for those who prefer to take the manuscript into the pulpit—highlighted within the manuscript, or placed in the margins of the manuscript (in this last option it helps to place the outline in a widened left-hand margin so that the eyes naturally scan it first rather than being forced to read past the manuscript).

2. A. A. Bonar attributes this method to Robert Murray McCheyne, writing in the preacher's biography, "From the beginning of his ministry he reprobated the custom of reading sermons, believing that to do so exceedingly weakens the freedom and natural fervor of the messenger in delivering his message. Neither did he recite what he had written. But his custom was to impress on his memory the substance of what he had beforehand carefully written and then to speak as he found liberty." *Robert Murray McCheyne: A Biography* (1844; reprint, Grand Rapids: Zondervan, 1983), p. 42.

3. Used by most preachers most of the time.

        ii. The more practiced the outline the more precise the expression of thought.

       iii. The more dependent the preacher is on an extensive outline the more wooden will be the expression of the sermon, and the more limited will be the eye contact.

2. Bare-bones Outline: an outline containing only key points, words, phrases, or thoughts—usually compressed onto notecards, scrap(s) of paper, or impressed on memory alone.

    a. Options for Using Bare-bones Outlines:

       i. Bare-bones outlines may be used in all the ways that extended outlines are used. (Note: Bare-bones outlines are most easily committed to memory for those wanting to preach without notes.)

       ii. Bare-bones outlines are often used to organize thought when there is no time (or need) for more formal preparation of a message.

    b. Chief Advantages and Disadvantages of Bare-bones Outlines:

       i. Spontaneous expression.

       ii. Enforced eye contact

       iii. Rapid preparation

       iv. Likely imprecise expression

       v. May encourage ill-prepared thought

       vi. May cause extreme brevity or length (depending on personality)

C. Hints for Preparing Partially Written and Outlined Messages

1. Use variations in margins, print size, and boldfacing to indicate differences between major, subordinate, and supporting ideas.

2. Use highlighters (but do not use so many colors that you need a color key to chart your way through the outline).

3. Make it "seeable." Use large enough print and sufficient spacing so that your eyes can quickly see what you have written from an appropriate pulpit distance.

4. Keep main points separate. (E.g., in an extended outline start new main points at the top of a page rather than having them "bleed" from the end of another point at the bottom of a preceding page. This way your eye never has to guess where to look when you begin each new idea.)

5. Use consistent marking (asterisks, colors, circles, underlining, indentations, boldfacing, number symbolization, etc.). Develop a system for indicating main points, illustrations, applications, etc., so that you train your eye to recognize at a glance the portion of

the outline you need. (E.g., for years I have circled illustrations in my outlines while putting stars by applications so that my eye can almost instantly navigate through the outline with these visual cues that keep me from having to read through the material to find my place in it.).

6. If you will have no pulpit (or yours is small) put your notes on pieces of paper that will easily fit inside your Bible.

7. Remove from view what can confuse. Try to keep before your eyes only the notes that you presently need. When notes that you have finished lie alongside notes you are using or plan to use your eyes can easily get lost. To avoid this problem (if you are using more than one page of notes) keep your notes stacked and, then, as you finish with the material on each page unobtrusively slide it beneath your Bible or to a shelf beneath the pulpit face.

IV. Options for Unwritten Sermons[4]

A. Mental Outline: basic ideas mentally organized (usually in bare-bones outline form) that only take full form in the pulpit.

B. Impromptu Presentation: unprepared messages delivered on the spur of the moment due to press of circumstances (hopefully not due to irresponsibility).

V. Hints on Preaching from Memory

A. Use consistent parallelism and brevity in the wording of main points and subpoints so that memorization of "key words" alone puts the entire outline before the mind.

B. Use the illustration of a traditionally developed main point to trigger the memory. Since the summary of the explanation acts as the introduction to the illustration and the summary of the illustration acts as the introduction to the application, then remembering the illustration will help remind you of the contents of the entire main point.

C. Use consistent "eye-catchers" when developing the written outline in order to imprint the outline in memory.

---

4. These presentation options carry the advantages and disadvantages of bare-bones outlines only to greater degrees.

Appendix 5

READING SCRIPTURE

The first exposition of the text is the reading of Scripture. The way the preacher emphasizes words, characterizes dialogue, and even holds the Bible communicates meaning. One preacher's inflection can extol a biblical character's actions while another preacher's tone when reading the identical words can mock those actions. Oral reading requires and expresses interpretation. Thus, the expositor who sets the text before the congregation needs to prepare and present the Scripture reading as responsibly as any other portion of the sermon. The following guidelines will help make your Scripture reading responsible and reliable:[1]

Read meaningfully. Let your voice express the meaning the author intended to convey. This means your vocal expression, inflection, and intonation should vary to express the actions, emotions, and truths of the text. You do not convey the meaning of the words *Jesus wept* if your voice makes it sound as though he did not care.

Read expectantly. You believe that "the word of God is living and active; sharper than any double-edged sword" and that it "penetrates even to dividing soul and spirit" (Heb. 4:12). Read it that way. The preacher who reads the text in a monotone communicates that the Word has no power over him. A preacher who reads the Word rapidly implies, "Let's get through this stuff, so we can get to the really important things in my sermon." Read the text with the belief that every word carries the power that comes from the mouth of God.

---

1. For a more thorough discussion of this subject see the author's "The Incarnate Voice: An Exhortation for Excellence in the Oral Reading of Scripture," *Presbyterion* 15, 1 (Spring 1989); "A Brief History of Scripture Reading," in *Resources for Music and the Arts,* vol. 4 of *The Topical Encyclopedia of Christian Worship* (Nashville: Abbott-Martyn, 1993); and Thomas Edward McComiskey, *Reading Scripture in Public: A Guide for Preachers and Lay Readers* (Grand Rapids: Baker, 1991).

Read naturally. Conveying the import of the Word does not mean that you should read theatrically or in "stained-glass" tones. A dramatic reading draws attention to the preacher rather than to the text. The preacher who tries to make every reading sound as though Moses were speaking from Sinai's heights removes Scripture from the real world of the average person. If the text contains a conversation speak conversationally. If the text contains a narrative let your voice tell the story as realistically as the author would have first expressed it. Bring the text into the world of the listeners with such "natural, appropriate, and controlled"[2] speech that the Bible seems readily accessible rather than terribly remote.

Highlight emphatic elements. The best way to make your voice and the text come alive is to emphasize the words and phrases that carry the author's emphases. Typically authors place their emphases in verbs and modifiers. Your voice should highlight these terms. Sometimes authors will express their intentions by contrasts, comparisons, repetitions, parallel wording, etc. Where you spot these techniques emphasize them. The introduction of new characters, plot turns, new concepts, or unexpected actions or reactions, all require vocal underlining.

Maintain thought units. Sentences, phrases, and combinations of them express thought units. The concepts of the author come unglued when the reader runs one sentence into another, expresses a question as though it were a statement, or cuts a thought short by taking a breath in the middle of a phrase. Observe the punctuation that signals when to pause; breathe so as to keep thought units whole; and use your voice to manage the flow of the author's thought rather than mangle it.

Prepare. Unusual thought turns, unfamiliar terms, and words needing emphasis will elude, confuse, and escape the reader who does not prepare. Nothing so quickly damages a preacher's credibility as stumbling, skipping phrases, and mispronouncing words during the sermon's opening moments. Practice reading your Scripture portion aloud several times so that your tongue, ear, and mind grow familiar with the passage's thoughts, twists, and tones. Train by reading to children. If you can read Scripture naturally and expressively enough to hold the interest of a child you are well prepared to read meaningfully to a congregation.

Maintain eye contact. Know the text well enough so that when you read it to the congregation you can look up at frequent intervals. In even the most literate congregations 25 to 50 percent of your listeners will be watching you during the Scripture reading rather than following along

---

2. McComiskey, *Reading Scripture in Public*, 62.

in their Bibles. Keep minds focused on the Word by maintaining a good deal of eye contact as you read. The most natural way of reading with eye contact is what I call "ladling"—look down at the text to scoop the wording of a sentence into your mind and then look up to ladle it out to your listeners. Do not break the flow of your reading as you ladle it. Simply recognize that your words will appear lifeless and removed if people see only the top of your head while you read.

Preach from an open Bible. When the preacher bases the message on Scripture, the message's authority comes from God. While keeping the Bible open during the message does not assure the preacher's faithfulness, the preacher who closes (or keeps closed) the Scripture after reading the text inadvertently implies, "Now that we're done with that ritual, let's get to my message." Although no Bible verse commands us to preach from an open Bible, sound communication and theological principles make this the most natural expository stance.

Appendix 6

WEDDING MESSAGES

I. A Common Order for the Wedding Service

(Note: Books of common worship and denominational directories of worship offer very dependable orders and forms for the readings and prayers below; as well as many variations in the order of the wedding service.)

Prelude

*

Seating of the Families (if uncertain of order consult a marriage etiquette book)
Entrance of Groomsmen, Groom, and Pastor
Bridal Procession

*

Words of Institution
Prayer

*

Presentation of Bride

*

Marriage Vows (Note: In some church traditions the Scripture reading and wedding message occur before the marriage vows.)
Exchange of Rings (with ring vows, if desired)

*

Unity Candle Lighting
(Such ceremony options vary widely by region and era.)

*

Scripture Reading
Wedding Message

*

Prayer of Commitment

*

Benediction

Declaration of Marriage (". . . I now declare you husband and wife.")
Wedding Kiss ("You may kiss the bride. . . .")
Presentation of the Couple ("I present to you Mr. and Mrs. . . .")

* There are opportunities for special music or a hymn at these points in the service. Of course, you would not use all these opportunities in any single ceremony.

II. Message Guidelines
A. Preach from an Appropriate Text (examples below).

Genesis 2	Philippians 2:3ff.
Proverbs 31:10ff.	Colossians 3:18–19
1 Corinthians 13	1 John 4:16
Ephesians 5:21–33	1 Peter 3:1–7

B. Be Brief. (The average wedding message lasts seven to ten minutes—fifteen minutes is too long unless the couple has requested a formal message. Remember how many people are standing and how nervous they are. Show sensitivity to the nature of the occasion. An entire wedding service, apart from the music, averages only twenty minutes in length.)

C. Be Personal.
- Address the couple, not the crowd (but speak with sufficient projection for the congregation to hear).
- Mentioning something personal about the couple and tying it to a gospel truth bearing on marriage is a good way to begin.
- Do not idealize the couple or the institution of marriage.
- Do not reveal matters related to you in confidence, but make the message applicable to the couple personally.

D. Develop a Theme (based on a key idea or two in your text) rather than preach verse-by-verse exposition.
- No one will bring a Bible to read.
- Exceptions may be made if *the couple* requests a full, formal sermon.
- Messages based on two or three "key" concepts in your text with concise explanation, illustration, and application serve well.

E. Be Encouraging (most marriage instruction specifics should have been handled in premarital counseling; this is not the time for a course on budgeting, lovemaking, fair fighting, etc.).
- Present the joys of marriage in Christ, rather than lecture on marriage pitfalls and problems; remember how special the occasion is.
- This is the time to speak *for* Christian marriage, not *against* society's marital ills.
- Do not focus on this couple's failure to follow specifics of the pastor's premarital advice.

F. Be Redemptive.

- Present Christ as the Marriage-Bonder (explain our dependence on his strength for building our relationships).
- Proclaim God's forgiveness as the model for ours, and selfless service to him as the true cement of our relationships.
- Make clear the implications of the cross for marriage (e.g., acceptance and acknowledgment of imperfection; necessity of repentance, forgiveness, and reconciliation; value and humility of each person before God; obligations and beauty of holy union; etc.). This emphasis is absolutely crucial if the wedding message is to avoid simply being romantic advice and/or patronizing marriage instruction.

FUNERAL MESSAGES

I. A Common Order for the Funeral Service

(Note: Books of common worship and denominational directories of worship offer very dependable orders and forms for the readings and prayers below; as well as many variations for the traditional funeral service).

* *Prelude*

Words of Institution (Often called "Opening Lines" or "Processional Verses" in the books of common worship, these are the verses that open the service. Traditionally these verses were read as the casket was borne to the front of the church. Now they function much the same as a brief call to worship to begin the funeral service.)

*Prayer of Consolation (Discern appropriate content from the forms even if you extemporize your own prayer here; the pastor's prayer often leads into a congregational recitation of the Lord's Prayer.)

*Old Testament Readings (Typically a short selection or two from the forms.)

*New Testament Readings (Typically a short selection or two from the forms. Often these readings conclude with the selection that will be used as the text for the message.)

Personal Biography (Often called the "obituary" but not like a newspaper obituary notice. Rather, an optional minute or two recounting the person's life endeavors and family. Often preachers weave this biography into the funeral message introduction. This makes the funeral personal without *overeulogizing*. If a eulogy is to be given this is usually the place for it.)

*Funeral Message (Typically brief—five to ten minutes—unless otherwise requested by the family).

*Closing Prayer (Discern appropriate content from the forms and your message.)

Benediction (The pastor may choose for there not to be a benediction if a committal service will follow the funeral service.)

* Special music or a hymn often occurs after this component of the funeral service if the funeral is in a church. Few services would include music at all these points. Funerals in a funeral home (where most funerals are conducted in this era) will only have a prelude and postlude unless arrangements are made for special music.

II. Principles for Funeral Messages

   A. **Comfort and Reach with Gospel Hope.** Do not berate or lecture.
   B. **Be Brief.** This is a very difficult time for people. More than five to ten minutes for the sermon itself indicates insensitivity in the preacher unless the family requests a longer, traditional sermon. In some settings the stature of the deceased and/or particularly tragic circumstances may also require a more lengthy address. Messages typically are a logical development of a basic idea (or two) in a text, *not* verse-by-verse expositions—no one will have their Bibles with them to follow along.
   C. **Praise God,** more than the person. Acknowledge God's grace more than laud human accomplishment. Although it is certainly appropriate to give thanks for the good God has worked through this individual's life, care must be taken not to imply that divine acceptance is based on human goodness—the message the world almost inevitably hears.
   D. **Hold the Cross High.** This is *not* an evangelistic sermon. However, most pastors will address more nonbelievers at funerals and weddings than at any other time. The truths of the gospel need to be plainly stated because they bear upon every person's ultimate condition.
   E. **Do Not Damn to Hell Nor Preach into Heaven**. If persons "be not known as believers" take care that you neither judge their hearts nor give false hope. State the blessing of the gospel that those who profess Jesus Christ share without saying such apply to this person. Preachers in older times said that when preaching a funeral for one who was not known as a believer they would "Read the man's facts, then preach the Lord's gospel"; i.e., let people know whose funeral it is by some personal reference, but then move on to preach the gospel without judging whether the one applied to the other. This is still good advice.
   F. **Simple Truths Sincerely Spoken are Required.** This is not the time for theological treatises or exegetical insights. The simple truths of our resurrection and reunion based upon God's grace alone are the most compelling, meaningful, and comforting things you can say. The gospel has real power in these moments. Do not be afraid to let the Word do its work.

III. **Contents of Funeral Messages (Key concept: Begin personally, then move higher.)**
   A. Begin with something personal related to the deceased or their family. Let the family know you care for them and their loved one. Address the family directly and let others listen in by projecting so all can hear.
   B. Tie the personal reference to a gospel truth evident in the text(s) you read prior to the message.
   C. Logically develop the hope Christians have in the face of death based on the theme you have introduced and the passage(s) you have read. Funeral messages typically contain references to the joys of heaven, the believer's release from suffering, the ultimate reunion with loved ones, etc. All funeral sermons must include explanations of Christ's victory over sin and death, believers' resurrection hope, and the need of all the living to claim this gospel by faith alone.
   D. Make sure all know that this person's hope is in Christ's work, not the person's work.
   E. Genuinely rejoice in the joy deceased believers now know, but at the same time affirm the right for loved ones to grieve for the separation they now experience.
   F. End with hope, the assurance of Christ's victory.

IV. **Cautions for Funeral Messages**
   A. Be cautious about references such as "We are gathering here to *celebrate* the passing of Joan Smith into glory." Yes, there are truths in which believers can rejoice, but there is much pain present, too. Jesus wept in the face of death. We should not treat the horror of a fallen world's ultimate consequence without hope *or* without regard for the real pain it causes. Do not forbid grief.
   B. Provide the comfort of your sympathy to the families of those that were not known as believers. If you do not know what else to say, you can at least say that you are sorry for the family's loss and that you grieve for their hurt. Your sorrow is no more an endorsement of faithlessness than your callousness would be an affirmation of the gospel. Remember, ultimately you do not know others' hearts. If you have questions about the spiritual state of the deceased, simply preach the gospel treasures of those who *do* have faith without saying this person does, or does not, share in them.
   C. Avoid exaggeration of anyone's good life. But at believers' funerals certainly let the glory of their life and hope in Jesus fill your message. It is not at all inappropriate to cite the goodness that God has accomplished through a believer's life or to rejoice in the service and testimony such a person has provided the kingdom.
   D. Do not use the funeral as a time to "guilt-trip" friends and relatives into heaven. Although it is certainly legitimate to invite others to share in the gospel hope, and even to express the concern the deceased

may have had for others' salvation, these appeals should be made with compassion, not futile, manipulative condemnation.

E. Remember your *primary* task is to comfort, not to evangelize. Even though evangelistic truths are presented, this is a funeral sermon. The *main* purpose is to bring the hope of the gospel to loved ones facing the pain of death.

IV. Common Texts for Funeral Messages:

Deuteronomy 33:14	Isaiah 40:11	2 Corinthians 1:3–5
Job 19:25	John 11:25–26	2 Corinthians 4:17–5:1
Psalm 23	John 14:1–4	Philippians 1:21
Psalm 46:1–7	Romans 14:8	1 Thessalonians 4:13–18
Psalm 121	1 Corinthians 15	Revelation 20:11–21:4
Psalm 139	(selected)	

EVANGELISTIC MESSAGES

In an evangelistic sermon we are not preaching merely to convey facts. Listeners should understand that the Bible says they are in peril if they shrug off the message with: Let us move to receive this sermon as information (cf. Acts 17:32). We are pleading a case—the Lord's—and calling for a verdict. Martin Luther told Philipp Melanchthon, "Preach so that if the people don't hate their sin, they will hate you." This does not mean that we should make our manner offensive, but that we must courageously proclaim the eternal consequences and immediate requirements of the gospel.[1]

I. Presuppositions of Evangelistic Preaching
   A. We are speaking so that people will respond.
   B. We must indicate (and construct the sermon to prompt) a specific response.
   C. We need the following to be truly effective:
      1. Genuine fervor; and,
      2. Prayer for the work of the Holy Spirit.

II. General Principles of Evangelistic Preaching
   A. The Evangelistic Sermon Should Be Biblical.
      Alhough the sermon need not (and when addressed to the uninformed probably will not) be a verse-by-verse exposition, the message must identify the biblical basis for its claims, appeals, and authority. Every evangelistic sermon must explain the seriousness of sin; the significance of the cross; and the nature of faith.

1. Cf. Lloyd M. Perry and John Strubhar, *Evangelistic Preaching* (Chicago: Moody, 1979).

B. The Evangelistic Sermon Should Be Positive.

The gospel is not based upon what people should not do, nor on what they should do. The gospel is the *Good News* about what God has done, is doing, and will do for those who place their hope in the work of Jesus Christ.[2]

C. The Evangelistic Sermon Should Be Clear.

Today's mass-media experts have determined that they cannot exceed sixth-grade comprehension levels even on broadcast news shows without losing large segments of their audience. General literacy rates and still lower biblical literacy rates in our age demand that evangelistic preaching eliminate theological intricacies and pulpit jargon from messages designed to reach the unchurched. In our day the "language of Zion" creates caricatures not avenues of communication. The gospel must be expressed in simple terms. *Sin, salvation,* and *repentance* may be familiar concepts to the preacher, but we must define each simply (or substitute more familiar, and less culturally twisted, terms) in the evangelistic message. If this approach seems too unsophisticated, remember an understanding of the gospel not the wisdom of the preacher is the power of salvation. I know of no greater barrier to effective evangelistic preaching than preachers' own deep-seated doubt that the simple truths of the gospel are not capable of turning modern minds from their idols to the true and living God.

D. The Evangelistic Sermon Should Be Relatively Brief.

No iron-clad rules can be enforced on the appropriate length of the evangelistic sermon. The skills of the preacher, the nature of the message, and the occasion can all influence the attention spans of modern listeners. Still, reason dictates that those unaccustomed to a long church sit are likely to have little tolerance for unrestrained exposition. The Holy Spirit can change all human dynamics but those who regularly preach evangelistic messages rarely exceed twenty minutes.

E. The Evangelistic Sermon Should Communicate Urgency.

An evangelistic sermon without fervor and authentic emotion can hardly communicate the significance of the message. Although "sobbing evangelists" may soil the reputation of all those who feel deeply about the gospel, we err if we try to eliminate expressions of concern from preaching designed to reach hearts and save souls. Be sincere when you relate the urgent demands of the gospel and trust God to use what you truly feel along with the truth of his Word to melt skepticism. For you and the Lord to know that you have shared your heart is more important than dodging the accusation that your fervor is insincere.

---

2. I borrow heavily from the excellent work by V. L. Stanfield, *Effective Evangelistic Preaching* (Grand Rapids: Baker, 1965), 20–21.

III. Summary Principles for Evangelistic Preaching
A. Be Biblical (Providing an authority for the *solution* you present).
B. Be Simple (No jargon or theological intricacies for the uninformed).
C. Make sure the following are clearly articulated:
1. Christ's work
2. Man's need
3. Personal response required —> faith < repentance / reliance on cross
D. Be Passionate.
"Prepare as though it all depends on you; pray as though it all depends on God."

IV. Distinctives of Evangelistic Preaching
A. Practice Different Approaches for Informed and Uninformed.
1. Challenge *uninformed* with biblical truths for persuasion using "felt needs" to indicate relevance and initiate points of contact. Quickly move from these issues to more biblical concerns.
2. Challenge *informed* with personal inconsistencies, "nondependables" (e.g., unbiblical matters they are trusting for salvation that are sure to fail such as baptism, family background, etc.), or untrustworthiness of other hopes (e.g., "I'm basically a good person.").

Note: The uninformed must be informed as well as challenged and called to repentance (e.g., Acts 17). The informed must be touched with inconsistencies or nondependables and called to repentance (e.g., the woman at the well). Beginning with a Fallen Condition Focus[3] gives every sermon opportunity to be evangelistic because an FCF requires a Christ-dependent response.

B. Frame the Message to Lead to a Specific Response.
1. Indicate in the message precisely what commitment or action you will require at the sermon's conclusion *and* what this will involve for the listeners. Surprising or manipulating people is inherently unethical and unbiblical.[4] Say precisely what prayer should be prayed. Explain exactly what signing a commitment card, etc. means. Tell plainly what one can expect during an invitation, or later private commitment.
2. Make clear the obligations of true repentance.
3. Do not ask people to respond in ways beyond their level of spiritual maturity or biblical understanding, but offer them some concrete

---

3. For definition of Fallen Condition Focus (FCF) see chapters 2, 10, and 11.
4. Leighton Ford, "How to Give an Honest Invitation," in *Preaching to Convince*, ed. James D. Berkley, The Leadership Library, vol. 8 (Carol Stream, Ill.: Christianity Today, Inc., and Waco: Word, 1986), 135–46.

way of expressing a commitment (e.g., offering a silent prayer in words the preacher supplies, pledging to learn more, telling a loved one of their decision, meeting with a church leader after the service, coming to the front of the meeting to receive prayer, raising a hand to affirm a decision, praying on knees at their bedside that night, etc.). The converted heart longs to affirm its faith.

STUDY RESOURCES

Study Bibles

Name	Editor/Author	Status*	Nature	Stance	Publisher(s)
Cambridge Annotated Study Bible (NRSV)		CS	NT	HC	Cambridge
Geneva Study Bible (NKJV)		CS	NT	R	Nelson
The New International Version Study Bible		CS	NT	E	Zondervan
New Open Bible (KJV, NKJV, NAS)		CS	NT	E	Nelson
The Ryrie Study Bible (NIV, KJV, NAS)	Charles Ryrie	CS	NT	Dsp	Zondervan Nelson
The Thompson Chain-Reference Bible (KJV, NIV)	Frank Charles Thompson	C	NT	E	Zondervan Kirkbride

Status: C=Classic
CS=Current Standard
D=Dated (still a common reference but not current and, in some cases, out of print)

Nature: T=Technical
NT=Not Technical
HT=Highly Technical

Stance: C=Conservative (generally)
Dsp=Dispensational
E=Evangelical
HC=Historical Critical
R=Reformed
RC=Roman Catholic
J=Jewish

Note: Many works take no specific stance, and these designations indicate emphases that are not necessarily mutually exclusive (e.g., Reformed and evangelical).

TABLE A9.2
Lexical Aids

Type/Name	Editor/Author	Status*	Nature	Stance	Publisher(s)
Lexicons					
A Hebrew and English Lexicon of the Old Testament (Revised)	William Gesenius, Francis Brown, S. R. Driver, and Charles Briggs	C	HT	HC	Hendrickson Oxford
Index to Brown, Driver, and Briggs Lexicon	Bruce Einspahr	CS	T		Moody
A Greek-English Lexicon of the New Testament and Other Early Christian Literature (Revised)	Walter Bauer, William F. Arndt, F. Wilbur Gingrich, with Frederick W. Danker	C	HT	HC	University of Chicago Press
Index to The Revised Bauer, Arndt, Gingrich Greek Lexicon	John R. Alsop	CS	T		Zondervan
Greek-English Lexicon of the New Testament Based on Semantic Domains (2 vols.)	Johannes P. Louw and Eugene A. Nida	CS	T	HC	United Bible Societies
Word Study Books					
Expository Dictionary of Old and New Testament Words	W. E. Vine	CS	NT	E	Revell Nelson
Theological Dictionary of the Old Testament (20 vol. projected)	G. Johannes Botterweck and Helmer Ringgren	CS	HT	HC	Eerdmans
A Theological Wordbook of the Old Testament (2 vols.)	Gleason Archer, R. Laird Harris, and Bruce Waltke	CS	T	E	Moody
Exegetical Dictionary of the New Testament (3 vols.)	Horst Balz and Gerhard Schneider	CS	T-HT	HC	Eerdmans
A Greek-English Lexicon (broader Greek context from classical era to A.D. 600.)	Henry George Liddell and Robert Scott	C	HT	HC	Oxford
The New International Dictionary of New Testament Theology	Colin Brown	CS	T	HC orig.; w/ E rev.	Zondervan

pe/Name	Editor/Author	Status*	Nature	Stance	Publisher(s)
heological Dictionary of e New Testament (10 ols.)	Gerhard Kittel and Gerhard Friedrich	C	HT	HC	Eerdmans
heological Dictionary of e New Testament; the Little Kittel"	Geoffrey W. Bromiley	C	T	HC	Eerdmans
he Vocabulary of the reek Testament Illus- ated from the Papyri and ther Non-Literary Sources	James Hope Moulton and George Milligan	C	HT		Eerdmans
ord Pictures in the New estament	A. T. Robertson	C-D	NT	C	Baker

xegetical Analysis

pe/Name	Editor/Author	Status*	Nature	Stance	Publisher(s)
nalytical Key to the Old estament (4 vol.)	John Joseph Owens	CS	T		Baker
ld Testament Parsing uide (2 vols.) keyed to rown, Driver, and Briggs ebrew Lexicon	Todd Bell, William Banks, and Colin Smith	CS	T		Moody
Grammatical Analysis of e Greek New Testament eyed to Zerwick's gram- ar, see table 3)	M. Zerwick (translated by M. Zerwick and M. Grosvenor)	CS	T	RC	Biblical Insti- tute
nalytical Greek New estament	Barbara and Timo- thy Friberg	CS	T		Baker
inguistic Key to the Greek Jew Testament	Fritz Reinecker and Cleon Rodgers	CS	T	E	Zondervan
he New Analytical Greek exicon	Wesley Perschbacher	CS	T		Hendrickson
nalytical Lexicon to the reek New Testament	William D. Mounce	CS	T		Zondervan
Parsing Guide to the reek New Testament	Nathan E. Han	CS	T		Herald

*Symbol key appears after table A9.1.

Lexical Aid Guides

Type/Name	Editor/Author	Status*	Nature	Stance	Publisher(s)
An Introductory Bibliography for the Study of Scripture	Joseph A. Fitzmyer	CS	T-HT		Biblical Institute
Multi-Purpose Tools for Biblical Study (use most recent edition)	Frederick W. Danker	CS-D	NT-T	E	Concordia
Old Testament Books for Pastor and Teacher	Brevard S. Childs	CS-D	NT	HC	Westminster
Old Testament Commentary Survey (pp. 37–44)	Tremper Longman III	CS	NT-T	R, E	Baker
Basic Bibliographic Guide for New Testament Exegesis	David M. Scholer	CS-D	T	E	Eerdmans
New Testament Exegesis: A Handbook for Students and Pastors (pp. 137ff.)	Gordon Fee	CS	NT-T	E	Westminster

*Symbol key appears after table A9.1.

TABLE A9.4
Original Language Grammars

ype/Name	Editor/Author	Status*	Nature	Stance	Publisher(s)
n Introduction to Biblical ebrew Syntax	Bruce Waltke and M. O'Connor	CS	T	E	Eerdmans - InterVarsity
ebrew Grammar	William Gesenius; trans. A. E. Cowley and E. Kautzsch	C	HT	HC	Oxford
Practical Grammar for lassical Hebrew	J. Weingreen	CS	T		Oxford
asics of Biblical Greek	William D. Mounce	CS	T		Zondervan
iblical Greek	M. Zerwick	CS	T		Biblical Institute
Grammar of the New Testament (4 vols.)	J. H. Moulton, F. W. Howard, and Nigel Turner	CS	HT		T & T Clark
Greek Grammar of the New Testament	F. W. Blass, A. Debrunner, and R. W. Funk	CS	HT	HC	University of Chicago Press
Manual Grammar of the Greek New Testament	H. E. Dana and Julius R. Mantey	D	T		Macmillan
yntax of New Testament Greek	James A. Brooks and Carlton Winbery	CS	T		University Press of America

*Symbol key appears after table A9.1.

TABLE A9.5
Concordances

Type/Name	Editor/Author	Status*	Nature	Stance	Publisher(s)
Print Concordances					
Analytical Concordance to the Bible (KJV); English keyed to original Hebrew and Greek terms.	Robert Young	C	NT		Hendrickson
Exhaustive Concordance of the Bible (KJV) with numerical system keyed to other aids	James Strong	C	NT		Nelson Hendrickson
NAS Exhaustive Concordance		CS	NT		Holman
The NIV Exhaustive Concordance with numerical system keyed to Strong's	John R. Kohlenberger III and Edward Goodrick	CS	NT		Zondervan
The NRSV Exhaustive Concordance	Bruce M. Metzger	CS	NT		Nelson
The Englishman's Hebrew and Chaldee Concordance of the Old Testament	George V. Wigram	C	NT		Hendrickson
A New Concordance of the Bible (Hebrew, OT only)	Abraham Even-Shoshan	CS	HT	J	Baker
Analytical Concordance of the Greek New Testament	Philip S. Clapp	CS	HT		Baker
Computer-Konkordanz zum Novum Testamentum graece von Nestle-Aland	H. Bachmann and W. A. Slaby	CS	HT		de Gruyter
A Concordance to the Greek Testament	W. F. Moulton and A. S. Geden	CS	HT		T & T Clark
The Englishman's Greek Concordance of the New Testament	George V. Wigram	C	NT		Hendrickson
The Greek-English Concordance of the New Testament	John R. Kohlenberger III	CS	NT		Zondervan

*Symbol key appears after table A9.1.

pe/Name	Editor/Author	Status*	Nature	Stance	Publisher(s)
omputer Concordances					
nyText (multiple English xts with research tools, id original language helps)		CS	NT-T		Linguist's Software
bleSource (based on NIV xhaustive Concordance; ses numbering system for ferencing other tools)		CS	NT-T		Zondervan
ble Windows (RSV w/ origi- al language study tools; icludes LXX)		CS	T-HT		Silver Mountain Software
D WordLibrary (variety : English text versions; iterrelated concordance, riginal language helps w/ iultiple reference works udy system)	Currently coordi- nates efforts of Dallas and West- minster Theologi- cal Seminaries, and Logos Research Systems	CS	T-HT		CD Word Software Inc.
ramCord (an interrelated rammar and concordance) the whole Bible in the riginal languages with exe- etical and parsing aids vailable)	Trinity Evangelical Divinity School	CS	T-HT		GramCord Institute
iacBible (multiple English ersions and original inguages concordance) or Macintosh users.		CS	NT-T		Zondervan
nLine Bible (NIV and RSV nglish versions w/ original inguages and reference elps)		CS	NT-T		OnLine Bible
C Study Bible (multiple inglish versions with inglish reference tools)		CS	NT		BibleSoft
Vordsearch (coordinated iultiple study tools)	Dallas Theological Seminary	CS	NT-T		NavPress

Note: Any listing of computer resources will quickly become dated. Rapid advances in computer technology and the proliferation of computer tools require preachers to consult the most current sources before making computer resource purchases.

*Symbol key appears after table A9.1.

TABLE A9.6

Bible Dictionaries and Encyclopedias

Name	Editor/Author	Status*	Nature	Stance	Publisher(s)
The New International Dictionary of the Bible	J. D. Douglas and Merrill C. Tenney	CS	NT	E	Zondervan
The New Unger's Bible Dictionary	Merrill F. Unger	CS	NT	E	Moody
Baker Encyclopedia of the Bible (2 vols.)	Walter A. Elwell	CS	NT	E	Baker
The Illustrated Bible Dictionary (3 vols.)	J. D. Douglas	CS	NT	E	InterVarsity and Tyndale House
The International Standard Bible Encyclopedia (revised; 4 vols.)	Geoffrey W. Bromiley	CS	T	C	Eerdmans
Zondervan Pictorial Bible Encyclopedia (5 vols.)	Merrill C. Tenney	CS	NT	E	Zondervan
Anchor Bible Dictionary (6 vols.)	David Noel Freedman	CS	T	HC	Doubleday

*Symbol key appears after table A9.1.

SAMPLE SERMON EVALUATION FORM

Speaker:_____ Evaluator:_____ Date:_____

OUTLINE AND COMMENT

Scripture Intro and Reading:

Sermon Introduction:

Proposition (Specific Wording):

Body: (Note main points and significant features of each.)

General Comments:

Content____, Stucture____, Delivery____
(S=Superior, E=Excellent, G=Good, N=Needs Work)

Delivery Concerns (circle or comment):

Volume	Eye Contact
Vocal Variation	Swaying or Pacing
Distracting	Use of Bible
Mannerisms	or Notes
Gestures	Other_____
Pulpit Use	

	DEFINITELY	
Introduction	YES	NO
Introduces a F.C.F. derived from *this* text.	1 2 3 4 5	
Arouses attention (usually with a human-interest account)	1 2 3 4 5	
Proposition		
Weds Principle and Application	1 2 3 4 5	
Establishes *this* sermon's Main Theme	1 2 3 4 5	
Summarizes Introduction in concept and terminology	1 2 3 4 5	
Main Points		
Are clear	1 2 3 4 5	

Are universal truths in hortatory statements	1 2 3 4 5
Are proportional and not co-extensive	1 2 3 4 5
Contain adequate and appropriate:	
Exposition (1/3)	1 2 3 4 5
Illustration (1/3)	1 2 3 4 5
Application (1/3)	1 2 3 4 5

Exegetical Support

This sermon is what *this* text is about	1 2 3 4 5
Problems and overall passage content are sufficiently handled	1 2 3 4 5
Proofs are accurate, understandable, and support the points made	1 2 3 4 5
The context and genre of the passage are adequately considered	1 2 3 4 5
The exegesis is not belabored once the points are sufficiently proven	1 2 3 4 5
The exegesis seems designed to aid rather than impress	1 2 3 4 5

Application

Is clear, helpful, and practical	1 2 3 4 5
Is redemptive not legalistic in focus and motivation	1 2 3 4 5
Accurately distinguishes a scriptural mandate from a good idea	1 2 3 4 5
Supported with sufficient biblical proof from *this* passage	1 2 3 4 5

Illustrations

Contain sufficient "lived-body" detail	1 2 3 4 5
Truly clarify or strengthen the arguments or overall sermon impact	1 2 3 4 5
Are in appropriate proportion (number and length) to the sermon whole	1 2 3 4 5

Conclusion Contains

Summary	1 2 3 4 5
"What-do-you-want-me-to-do"	1 2 3 4 5
Climax	1 2 3 4 5
A definite, purposed, pointed end	1 2 3 4 5

SELECT BIBLIOGRAPHY

Adams, Jay E. *Preaching with Purpose: A Comprehensive Textbook on Biblical Preaching.* Grand Rapids: Baker, 1982.

———. *Truth Applied: Application in Preaching.* Grand Rapids: Zondervan, 1990.

Allen, Ronald J., and Thomas J. Herrin. "Moving from the Story to Our Story." In *Preaching the Story,* edited by E. Steimle, M. Niedenthal, and C. Rice. Philadelphia: Fortress, 1980.

Barber, Cyril J. *The Minister's Library.* Grand Rapids: Baker, 1974, with later supplements.

Bartow, Charles L. *Effective Speech Communication in Leading Worship.* Nashville: Abingdon, 1988.

Baumann, J. Daniel. *An Introduction to Contemporary Preaching.* Grand Rapids: Baker, 1972.

Berkhof, Louis. *Systematic Theology.* Rev. ed. Grand Rapids, Eerdmans, 1953.

Bettler, John F. "Application." In *The Preacher and Preaching.* Edited by Samuel T. Logan. Phillipsburg, N.J.: Presbyterian and Reformed, 1986.

Blackwood, Andrew. *Expository Preaching for Today.* Nashville: Abingdon, 1953.

———. *The Fine Art of Preaching.* 1937. Reprint. New York: Macmillan, 1943.

Broadus, John A. *On the Preparation and Delivery of Sermons.* Edited by J. B. Weatherspoon. New York: Harper and Row, 1944.

Bryan, Dawson C. *The Art of Illustrating Sermons.* Nashville: Cokesbury, 1938.

Buttrick, David. *Homiletic: Moves and Structures.* Philadelphia: Fortress, 1987.

Chapell, Bryan. "Alternative Models: Old Friends in New Clothes." In *Handbook of Contemporary Preaching,* edited by Michael Duduit. Nashville: Broadman, 1992.

———. *In the Grip of Grace.* Grand Rapids: Baker, 1992.

———. *Using Illustrations to Preach with Power.* Grand Rapids: Zondervan, 1992.

Clowney, Edmund. *Preaching and Biblical Theology.* Grand Rapids: Eerdmans, 1961; Phillipsburg, N.J.: Presbyterian and Reformed, n.d.

———. "Preaching Christ from All the Scriptures." In *The Preacher and Preaching,* edited by Samuel T. Logan. Phillipsburg, N.J.: Presbyterian and Reformed, 1986.

361

———. *The Unfolding Mystery: Discovering Christ in the Old Testament.* Phillipsburg, N.J.: Presbyterian and Reformed, 1988.

Cotterell, Peter, and Max Turner. *Linguistics and Biblical Interpretation.* Downers Grove, Ill.: InterVarsity, 1989.

Craddock, Fred B. *As One Without Authority.* Nashville: Abingdon, 1971.

———. *Preaching.* Nashville: Abingdon, 1985.

Dabney, Robert L. *Lectures on Sacred Rhetoric.* 1870. Reprint. Carlisle, Penn.: Banner of Truth, 1979.

Davis, Henry Grady. *Design for Preaching.* Philadelphia: Fortress, 1958.

De Jong, James A. "Principled Paraenesis: Reading and Preaching the Ethical Material of New Testament Letters." *Pro Rege* 10, 4 (June 1982): 26–34.

Demaray, Donald E. *An Introduction to Homiletics.* 1974. Reprint. Grand Rapids: Baker, 1978.

Duduit, Michael, ed. *Handbook of Contemporary Preaching.* Nashville: Broadman, 1992.

Eggold, Henry J. *Preaching Is Dialogue: A Concise Introduction to Homiletics.* Grand Rapids: Baker, 1990.

Eslinger, Richard L. *A New Hearing: Living Options in Homiletic Method.* Nashville: Abingdon, 1987.

Farmer, Herbert H. *The Servant of the Word.* New York: Scribner's, 1942.

Fee, Gordon D. *New Testament Exegesis: A Handbook for Students and Pastors.* Philadelphia: Westminster, 1983.

Fee, Gordon D., and Douglas Stuart. *How to Read the Bible for All Its Worth.* Grand Rapids: Zondervan, 1982.

Fisher, Walter R. "Narration as Human Communication Paradigm: The Case of Public Moral Argument." *Communication Monographs* 51 (1984): 1–22; and the subsequent article "The Narrative Paradigm: An Elaboration." *Communication Monographs* 52 (1985): 347–67.

Flynn, Leslie B. *Come Alive with Illustrations: How to Find, Use, and File Good Stories for Sermons and Speeches.* Grand Rapids: Baker, 1987.

Ford, D. W. Cleverley. *The Ministry of the Word.* Grand Rapids: Eerdmans, 1979.

Frame, John. *Doctrine of the Knowledge of God.* Phillipsburg, N.J.: Presbyterian and Reformed, 1987.

Garrison, Webb B. *Creative Imagination in Preaching.* Nashville: Abingdon, 1960.

Giorgi, Amadeo. "The Body: Focal Point of 20th Century Cultural Contradictions." *South Africa Journal of Psychology* 13, 2 (1983): 129–69.

Golden, James L., Goodwin F. Berquist and William Coleman. *The Rhetoric of Western Thought.* 3d ed. Dubuque: Kendall-Hunt, 1978.

Greidanus, Sidney. "Redemptive History and Preaching," *Pro Rege* 19, 2 (December 1990): 9–18.

———. *Sola Scriptura: Problems and Principles in Preaching Historical Texts.* Toronto: Wedge, 1970.

————. *The Modern Preacher and the Ancient Text: Interpreting and Preaching Biblical Literature*. Grand Rapids: Eerdmans, 1988.

Halvorson, Arndt. *Authentic Preaching*. Minneapolis: Augsburg, 1982.

Hodge, Charles. *Systematic Theology*. 3 vols. New York: Scribner, Armstrong and Co., 1875.

Hoekema, Anthony. *Christian Spirituality: Five Views on Sanctification*. Edited by Donald Alexander. Downers Grove, Ill.: InterVarsity, 1988.

Hogan, William L. "It Is My Pleasure to Introduce..." *The Expositor* 1, 3 (August 1987).

————. "Sermons Have Structures." *The Expositor* 2, 1 (April, 1988).

Hostetler, Michael J. *Illustrating the Sermon*. The Craft of Preaching Series. Grand Rapids: Zondervan, 1989.

————. *Introducing the Sermon: The Art of Compelling Beginnings*. The Craft of Preaching Series. Grand Rapids: Zondervan, 1986.

Howard, J. Grant. *Creativity in Preaching*. The Craft of Preaching Series. Grand Rapids: Zondervan, 1987.

Howell, Kenneth J. "How to Preach Christ from the Old Testament." *Presbyterian Journal* (16 January 1985), 8–10.

Hunter, Barbara, and Brenda Buckley Hunter. *Introductory Speech Communication: Overcoming Obstacles, Reaching Goals*. Dubuque: Kendall-Hunt, 1988.

Johnson, Byron Val. "A Media Selection Model for Use With a Homiletical Taxonomy." Ph.D. diss., Southern Illinois University at Carbondale, 1982.

Jones, Ilion T. *Principles and Practice of Preaching*. Nashville: Abingdon, 1956.

Jones, Thomas F. "Preaching the Cross of Christ." Unpublished essay presented in 1976–77 homiletics lectures at Covenant Theological Seminary.

————. "Truth Has Consequences: or, Balancing the Proposition." In *The Preparation and Delivery of Sermons*, edited by Bryan Chapell. 1976. St. Louis: Multi-media Publications, reprint, 1992.

Kaiser, Walter C., Jr. *Toward an Exegetical Theology: Biblical Exegesis for Preaching and Teaching*. Grand Rapids: Baker, 1981.

Kemper, Deane A. *Effective Preaching*. Philadelphia: Westminster, 1985.

Killinger, John. *Fundamentals of Preaching*. Philadelphia: Fortress, 1985.

Knox, John. *The Integrity of Preaching*. New York: Abingdon, 1957.

Koller, Charles W. *Expository Preaching without Notes*. Grand Rapids: Baker, 1961.

Kooienga, William H. *Elements of Style for Preaching*. The Craft of Preaching Series. Grand Rapids: Zondervan, 1989.

Kraft, Charles H. *Communicating the Gospel God's Way*. Pasadena: William Carey Library, 1979.

Lane, Beldon C. Rabbinical Stories: A Primer on Theological Method." *The Christian Century* 98 (December 1981): 1306–10.

Larkin, William J. *Culture and Biblical Hermeneutics: Interpreting and Applying the Authoritative Word in a Relativistic Age*. Grand Rapids: Baker, 1988.

Larsen, David L. *The Anatomy of Preaching: Identifying the Issues in Preaching Today.* Grand Rapids: Baker, 1989.

Lehman, Louis Paul. *Put a Door on It.* Grand Rapids: Kregel, 1975.

Lenski, R. C. H. *The Sermon: Its Homiletical Construction.* 1927. Reprint. Grand Rapids: Baker, 1968.

Lewis, Ralph L. with Gregg Lewis. *Inductive Preaching: Helping People Listen.* Westchester, Ill.: Crossway, 1983.

Lewis, Ralph. *Speech for Persuasive Preaching.* Wilmore, Ken.: Asbury Theological Seminary, 1968.

———. "The Triple Brain Test of a Sermon." *Preaching* 1, 2 (1985).

Liefeld, Walter L. *New Testament Exposition: From Text to Sermon.* Grand Rapids: Zondervan, 1984.

Lloyd-Jones, D. Martyn. *Darkness and Light: An Exposition of Ephesians 4:17–5:17.* Grand Rapids: Baker, 1982.

———. *Preaching and Preachers.* Grand Rapids: Baker, 1971.

Longman, Tremper, III. *Old Testament Commentary Survey.* Grand Rapids: Baker, 1991.

Lovelace, Richard. *Dynamics of Spiritual Life.* Downers Grove, Ill.: InterVarsity, 1979.

Lowry, Eugene L. *Doing Time in the Pulpit: The Relationship Between Narrative and Preaching.* Nashville: Abingdon, 1985.

———. *How to Preach a Parable.* Nashville: Abingdon, 1989.

———. *The Homiletical Plot: The Sermon as Narrative Art Form.* Atlanta: John Knox, 1980.

MacArthur, John Jr., et al. *Rediscovering Expository Preaching.* Dallas: Word, 1992.

MacPherson, Ian. *The Art of Illustrating Sermons.* Nashville: Abingdon, 1964.

Markquart, Edward F. *Quest for Better Preaching.* Minneapolis: Augsburg, 1985.

McComisky, Thomas Edward. *Reading Scripture in Public: A Guide for Preachers and Lay Readers.* Grand Rapids: Baker, 1991.

McGrath, Alister E. "The Biography of God" *Christianity Today* 35 (22 July 1991): 23–24.

McQuilkin, J. Robertson. *Understanding and Applying the Bible.* Chicago: Moody, 1983.

Merleau-Ponty, Maurice. *The Phenomenology of Perception.* Translated by Colin Smith with revisions by Forrest Williams. 1962. Reprint. Atlantic Highlands, N.J.: Humanitas, 1981.

Miller, Calvin. *Spirit, Word, and Story: A Philosophy of Preaching.* Dallas: Word, 1989.

Miller, C. John. *Outgrowing the Ingrown Church.* Grand Rapids: Zondervan, 1986.

Morgan, G. Campbell. *Preaching.* 1937. Reprint. Grand Rapids: Baker, 1974.

Muck, Terry. "The Danger of Preaching to Needs." Jackson, Miss.: Reformed Theological Seminary, 1986. Sound cassette.

Murphy, James J. *Medieval Rhetoric: A Select Bibliography.* Toronto: University of Toronto Press, 1971.

————. *Rhetoric in the Middle Ages: A History of Rhetorical Theory from Saint Augustine to the Renaissance.* Berkeley: University of California Press, 1974.

Packer, J. I. *God Speaks to Man: Revelation and the Bible.* Philadelphia: Westminster, 1965.

Perry, Lloyd M. *A Manual for Biblical Preaching.* 1965. Reprint. Grand Rapids: Baker, 1983.

————. *Biblical Sermon Guide.* Grand Rapids: Baker, 1970.

Perry, Lloyd M., and Charles M. Sell. *Speaking to Life's Problems.* Chicago: Moody, 1983.

Peterson, Eugene, et al. *Weddings, Funerals, and Special Events.* Vol. 10 in The Leadership Library. Waco: Word, 1987.

Piper, John. *The Supremacy of God in Preaching.* Grand Rapids: Baker, 1990.

Pitt-Watson, Ian. *A Primer for Preachers.* Grand Rapids: Baker, 1986.

Postman, Neil. *Amusing Ourselves to Death: Public Discourse in the Age of Show Business.* New York: Viking, 1985.

Ramm, Bernard. *Protestant Biblical Interpretation.* 3d rev. ed. Grand Rapids: Baker, 1970.

Ramsey, Arthur Michael, and Leon-Joseph Suenens. *The Future of the Christian Church.* SCM: London, 1971.

Robinson, Haddon. *Biblical Preaching: The Development and Delivery of Expository Messages.* Grand Rapids: Baker, 1980.

Robinson, Wayne Bradley, ed. *Journeys Toward Narrative Preaching.* New York: Pilgrim, 1990.

Rogness, Michael. "The Eyes and Ears of the Congregation." *Academy Accents* 8, 1 (Spring 1992): 1–2.

Runia, Klaas. "Experience in the Reformed Tradition." *Theological Forum of the Reformed Ecumenical Synod* 15, 2 & 3 (April 1987): 7–13.

Ryken, Leland. *Words of Life.* Grand Rapids: Baker, 1987.

Ryle, J. C. "Simplicity in Preaching," from *The Upper Room.* 1888. Reprint. London: Banner of Truth, 1979.

Sangster, W. E. *The Craft of Sermon Construction.* 1951. Reprint. Grand Rapids: Baker, 1972.

————. *The Craft of Sermon Illustration.* 1946. Reprint. London: Epworth, 1948.

Schaeffer, Francis. *The God Who Is There.* Downers Grove, Ill. : InterVarsity, 1968.

————. "True Spirituality." In *The Complete Works of Francis Schaeffer,* vol. 3. Wheaton, Ill.: Crossway, 1982.

Shaw, John. "The Character of a Pastor According to God's Heart." Ligonier, Penn.: Soli Deo Gloria Publications, 1992. Sermon reprint.

Silva, Moisés. *Has the Church Misread the Bible: The History of Interpretation in the Light of Current Issues*. Foundations of Contemporary Interpretation, vol. 1. Grand Rapids: Zondervan, 1987.

Smedes, Louis B. "Preaching to Ordinary People." *Leadership* 4, 4 (Fall 1983): 116.

Spurgeon, Charles Haddon. *All Round Ministry* 1933. Reprint. Banner of Truth, 1960.

————. "Christ Precious to Believers." In *The New Park Street Pulpit*. Vol. 5. London: Passmore and Alabaster, 1860.

————. *Lectures to My Students*. 3d series. 1894. Reprint. Grand Rapids: Zondervan, 1980.

————. *The Art of Illustration*. 3d series. Lectures to My Students. London: Marshall Brothers, 1922.

Steimle, Edmund A., Morris J. Niedenthal, and Charles Rice, eds. *Preaching the Story*. Philadelphia: Fortress, 1980.

Stendahl, Krister. "Preaching from the Pauline Epistles." In *Biblical Preaching: An Expositor's Treasury*. Edited by James W. Cox. Philadelphia: Westminster, 1983.

Stevenson, Dwight E., and Charles F. Diehl. *Reaching People from the Pulpit: A Guide to Effective Sermon Delivery*. New York: Harper and Row, 1958.

Stott, John R. W. *The Preacher's Portrait: Some New Testament Word Studies*. Grand Rapids: Eerdmans, 1961.

————. *Between Two Worlds: The Art of Preaching in the Twentieth Century*. 1982. Reprint. Grand Rapids: Eerdmans, 1988.

Stuart, Douglas. *A Guide to Selecting and Using Bible Commentaries*. Dallas: Word, 1990.

————. *Old Testament Exegesis: A Primer for Students and Pastors*. 2d ed. Philadelphia: Westminster, 1984.

Sweazey, George E. *Preaching the Good News*. Englewood Cliffs, N.J.: Prentice-Hall, 1976.

"The Controlling Image: One Key to Sermon Unity." *Academy Accents* 7, 3 (Winter 1991): 1-2.

Thielicke, Helmut. *Encounter with Spurgeon*. Grand Rapids: Baker, 1977.

Trimp, C. "The Relevance of Preaching." *Westminster Theological Journal* 36 (1973): 1–30.

Van Der Geest, Hans. *Presence in the Pulpit: The Impact of Personality in Preaching*. Translated by Douglas W. Stott. Atlanta: John Knox, 1981.

Van Groningen, Gerard. *Messianic Revelation in the Old Testament*. Grand Rapids: Baker, 1990.

Veerman, David. "Sermons: Apply Within." *Leadership* (Spring 1990): 120–25.

Vines, Jerry. *A Practical Guide to Sermon Preparation*. Chicago: Moody, 1985.

von Eckartsberg, Rolf. "The Eco-Psychology of Personal Culture Building: An Existential Hermeneutic Approach." In *Duquesne Studies in Phenomenological Psychology*. Edited by Amadeo Giorgi, Richard Knowles, David L.

Smith, III. Atlantic Highlands, N.J.: Humanitas/Duquesne University Press, 1979.

Vos, Geerhardus. *Biblical Theology*. 1948. Reprint. Grand Rapids: Eerdmans, 1975.

———. "The Idea of Biblical Theology" from Vos' Inaugural Address upon assuming the new Chair of Biblical Theology at Princeton Seminary. N.d., 1895 probable.

White, R. E. O. *A Guide to Preachers*. Grand Rapids: Eerdmans, 1973.

Whitesell, Farris D. *Power in Expository Preaching*. Old Tappan, N.J.: Revell, 1963.

Wilson, Joseph Ruggles. "In What Sense Are Preachers to Preach Themselves." *Southern Presbyterian Review* 25 (1874).

Yohn, David Waite. *The Contemporary Preacher and His Task*. Grand Rapids: Eerdmans, 1969.

INDEX